Goldwin Smith

The United Kingdom

A political History - Vol. II

Goldwin Smith

The United Kingdom
A political History - Vol. II

ISBN/EAN: 9783337171285

Printed in Europe, USA, Canada, Australia, Japan

Cover: Foto ©ninafisch / pixelio.de

More available books at **www.hansebooks.com**

THE UNITED KINGDOM

A POLITICAL HISTORY

BY

GOLDWIN SMITH, D.C.L.

AUTHOR OF "THE UNITED STATES," ETC., ETC.

The best form of government is that which doth actuate and inspire every part and member of a state to the common good. — PYM.

VOLUME II

New York
THE MACMILLAN COMPANY
LONDON: MACMILLAN & CO., LTD.
1899

All rights reserved

CONTENTS

CHAPTER I
CHARLES II. . . . . PAGES 1–52

CHAPTER II
JAMES II. — THE REVOLUTION AND ITS RESULTS 53–99

CHAPTER III
WILLIAM III. 100–127

CHAPTER IV
ANNE 128–153

CHAPTER V
GEORGE I. AND GEORGE II. — THE MINISTRIES OF WALPOLE AND CHATHAM 154–194

CHAPTER VI
GEORGE III. 195–312

CHAPTER VII
GEORGE IV. AND WILLIAM IV. 313–340

CHAPTER VIII

PARLIAMENTARY REFORM 341–357

CHAPTER IX

THE FRUITS OF PARLIAMENTARY REFORM . . . 358–383

CHAPTER X

THE EMPIRE 384–431

INDEX 433–482

CHAPTER I

CHARLES II

BORN 1630; RESTORED 1660; DIED 1685

THE poet of Puritanism, at the beginning of the third book of "Paradise Lost," rejoices in his re-ascent from the obscure sojourn of the Stygian pool to the realms of heavenly light. From a realm comparatively of light we descend to the Stygian pool in passing from the Revolution to the Restoration. In the Revolutionary period, with all its violence, havoc, and suffering, we have at least been among great men, lofty aspirations, and heroic actions. In the succeeding period we are in the midst of all that is the reverse of great, lofty, or heroic. Such is the nemesis of revolution. Over-tension is followed by collapse; over-excitement by prostration of spirit; the wreck of chimerical hopes by loss of faith in rational effort.

Puritanism, aiming at an unattainable standard, had denied the multitude pleasure, not only evil pleasure, such as that of bear-baiting, cock-fighting, and tippling, but the innocent pleasures of the drama, the may-pole, the Sunday dance or archery, the Christmas feast of family love, such pleasure as is a moral necessity of human nature. The consequences, when the Puritan yoke was cast off and the recoil ensued, were the manners, the literature, and the drama of the Restoration.

Religion, associated with a gloomy repression, could not fail to become odious; associated with political power and pelf, it could not fail to become hypocritical; associated with crazy fanaticism and spiritual mania, it could not fail to incur contempt. The inevitable sequel to a tyranny of godliness was an outburst of ungodliness; the hypocrisy of piety was followed by an ostentation of profanity; and vice became not only a propensity but a fashion.

The political philosopher of this age, and the guide of some of its most active spirits, is Hobbes, who had once been Charles's tutor. Revolution and civil war had bred in Hobbes the belief that man is the natural enemy of man, every man by nature desiring to take everything for himself; and that nothing can limit desire and keep the peace in the human herd but absolute government, that of the great Leviathan, submission to which must be unbounded. Religion, which has been the cause of all the confusion and anarchy, must be regulated by the government, thought alone being left free. He who made religion a matter of state, not of conviction, must have been a practical atheist, whether he was a theoretical atheist or not. Hobbes's own conversation was profane. He was, however, a great intelligence as well as a writer of uncommon vigour, and he had a clear conception of a government.

The spirit of the triumphant party, with its hatred of high aspiration and austere morality, was embodied, to the delight of a merry monarch and his court, in the rhyme of "Hudibras," a clever, coarse, and dirty imitation of "Don Quixote"; while over the grave of Puritanism rose "Paradise Lost."

There could not have been a fitter king of his epoch than Charles II. He was a thorough man of pleasure, good-natured, affable, and witty, but careless, selfish, cynical, and heartless. He openly kept concubines, and owned a troop of bastards. "Your Majesty," said a flatterer to him, "is the father of your people." "Of a good many of them," was his reply, "I believe I am." When treating with him was suggested, Cromwell replied, "He is so damnably debauched that he would ruin us all." No mean section of British aristocracy owed its origin to Charles's seraglio. Perhaps he and the other royal libertines of these times, as it was their doom to marry ugly princesses for the purpose of begetting heirs, might be partly excused if they kept pretty mistresses for love. Charles had to marry a Portuguese princess who, he said, was like a bat; yet, if he had been a gentleman, as some pretend, he would not have forced his mistress on the society of his wife. He painted his own character as a king well when, being worried by the inquiries of parliament into his scandalous finance, he said that he did not wish to sit like the grand Turk bowstringing people, but that he objected to have a set of fellows prying into his affairs. The Tory Johnson pronounced him a very good king. In a certain sense he was; for had a respectable bigot and absolutist, attentive to business and loyal to the Anglican church, been in Charles's place, with the tide of loyalty running so high, he might have extinguished the liberties of England.

At his side Charles had his brother James, Duke of York, an active and aggressive, while Charles was a lazy, absolutist; an avowed, while Charles was a secret, convert to catholicism; a bigot, while Charles, if not at heart a sceptic, was indifferent about religion. The chief minister of the crown during the first years of the reign was Hyde, Charles's political tutor, and made at his coronation Earl of Clarendon, the author of that picturesque and stately narrative classed by Hallam among histories to be read for the delight which they afford us by their literary beauty without reference to their truth. Clarendon has veiled the fact that he was a reformer in the first days of the Long Parliament, when he almost certainly voted for the attainder of Strafford. He was in the highest degree respectable, though not incapable of countenancing a plot for the assassination of a regicide Protector. His ideal was the rule of a monarch with a loyal and obedient parliament, as a necessary support of which he was bent on restoring the Anglican church and hierarchy to the plenitude of their wealth and privilege. Nor did he err in thinking that a clergy, richly endowed and dependent on the state, would, with ritualism and orthodoxy, be the bulwark of monarchical power. Hyde had a colleague in Southampton, a thoroughly upright and honourable gentleman, the most moderate of loyalists and a staunch upholder of indemnity. Ormonde, the Lord Lieutenant of Ireland, was another man of the same school. All three were men of a bygone, serious, religious, and, in the eyes of Restoration rakes and courtiers, antiquated generation. Southampton's influence was not enough felt. He seems to have been wanting in force, perhaps from the weakness of his health.

The time was propitious to absolutist designs. The monarchy of Louis XIV. was rising like the sun in its power and magnificence, and was holding forth to all kings an example of unrestricted rule, awakening within them a sense of their divinity, and giving new life to the monarchical as well as to the catholic cause. The Stuart brothers, having long lived in France, and as refugees from a republic, were thoroughly imbued with the idea of French monarchy and prepared to look up to the French monarch as their cynosure and the patron of their interest.

The Convention Parliament, in restoring the king, had stipulated for a general indemnity, from which, however, the regicides were excepted. Ten of these at once, and three more, caught afterwards in Holland, suffered the penalties of treason in their most barbarous form, while a number of others were imprisoned for life or deprived of civil rights. These men had no doubt taken their lives in their hands. They had no warrant but their conviction and their cause. Confident in the goodness of those warrants, such as were put to death met their fate like martyrs. "Take notice," said Harrison, the valiant soldier and visionary of the Fifth Monarchy, "that for being instrumental in that cause and interest of the Son of God which hath been pleaded amongst us and which God hath witnessed to by appeals and wonderful victories, I am brought to this place to suffer death this day. And if I had ten thousand lives, I would freely and cheerfully lay down them all to witness to this matter. Again, I do not lay down my life by constraint, but willingly; for if I had been minded to have run away, I might have had many opportunities. But being so clear in the thing, I durst not turn my back nor step a foot out of the way, by reason I have been in the service of so glorious and great a God." His last words were characteristic of the Fifth Monarchy man militant: " He hath covered my head many times in the day of battle. By God I have leaped over a wall; by God I have run through a troop; and by my God I will go through this death, and He will make it easy to me. Now into Thy hands, O Lord Jesus, I commit my spirit." So, not ignobly, passed away the dream of dominion founded on grace, which had been dreamed by Wycliffe three centuries before.

The gentle Evelyn missed the execution of some of the regicides, but "met their quarters mangled, and cut and reeking, as they were brought from the gallows in baskets on the hurdle." He piously ejaculates, "Oh, the stupendous and inscrutable judgments of God!" "The judgment of God was upon them, sir," said a Tory fop, speaking of the regicides to Quin, "the judgment of heaven was upon them; almost all of them came to violent ends." "So, my lord," replied Quin, "did almost all the apostles." The king was present at some of the executions.

1661 The bodies of Cromwell, Bradshaw, Ireton, and Pride were torn out of their graves, dragged to Tyburn, there hanged, and afterwards buried under the gallows, while their heads were set on the top of Westminster Hall. Ladies, we learn from Pepys, enjoyed the sight.

Much of this was the work of Presbyterians who predominated in the Convention Parliament, and had the king's assurance of favour to their sect. Prynne, with a cowl covering his head to hide the stumps of ears cropped by Stuart tyranny, was disgustingly forward in the hunt of vengeance. It is difficult to defend the participation of Manchester and others who, though they were not regicides, had met the king in battle. Axtell, who had commanded the guard at the king's execution, might well say that he was no more guilty than Essex, than Fairfax, who had remained in command of the army, than Manchester, Monck, or any soldier who had fought against the king's person under the orders of the parliament.

The Convention Parliament, from which Cavaliers were still, by the Ordinances, excluded, and in which Presbyterians predominated, was succeeded by a parliament full of Cavaliers thirsting for unlimited vengeance. The country gentlemen, many of whom had once been Puritans, had, since the reign of the sectaries, passed almost in a body to the royalist side, and were full not only of political and religious, but of social exasperation. This assembly would have made bloody work had not Clarendon and Southampton, to their honour, strenuously upheld indemnity. Clarendon tells us that an attempt was made in vain to find the body of Charles I. This story, as Hallam says, cannot be true, since it was known both to the attendants at the funeral and to workmen where the body had been laid. Perhaps Clarendon did not wish the body to be found, because its production and a performance of solemn obsequies might have excited beyond control the passions of the Cavaliers. Cromwell's soldiers, though disbanded, were still there. Vengeance, however, was further satiated by outrages on the dead. Upwards of twenty persons who had been buried in Westminster Abbey were dug up and thrown into St. Mary's churchyard; among them were the bodies of Pym, Admiral Blake, his gallant colleague Admiral Deane, May the poet and historian, Dr. Twisse the prolocutor of the Westminster Assembly, Cromwell's mother, his sister, and two other women. To this

1661

1662 period also belongs the judicial murder of Vane. Vane was not a regicide. Nor was there anything except superior ability and loftiness of spirit to distinguish his case from that of his fellows in the Council of State. His great crime in Cavalier eyes probably was his production of fatal evidence against Strafford. His execution was a dastardly murder. His lofty bearing at his trial had excited the craven fears of Charles, who was personally responsible for the execution after having pledged his word that Vane's life should be spared. The judicial 1661 murder of Argyle in Scotland was, if possible, still more 1661 infamous, as was also that of Guthrie, who seems to have been put to death simply as the most prominent Presbyterian, to strike terror into his sect. Charles had leaned on Argyle's support when he set up his banner in Scotland as a Covenanting king, and in subsequently accepting the Protectorate Argyle had done no more than Monck and many others who enjoyed impunity or were even taken into favour. Monck had the baseness, when evidence was wanting against Argyle, to produce private letters showing that the marquis had been hearty and zealous on the side of the usurpation of which Monck himself had been the vicegerent. The marquis showed in his death the difference between physical and moral courage. He looked calmly on the axe, though he had never been able to look upon the sword. How Milton, the great defender, if not the instigator, of regicide, escaped is a mystery. He must have had powerful and adroit friends. Well he might say that he was "with darkness and with dangers compassed round." The Solemn League and Covenant, the symbol of Presbyterian rebellion, was burned by the public hangman.

The Commonwealth perished, but with it by no means perished all the political fruits of the Revolution. The engines of the first Charles's arbitrary government which the Long Parliament had swept away, the star chamber, the court of high commission, the council of the north, the stannaries court, were not restored. The privy council no more dared to usurp the legislative powers of parliament. Ship money was not revived. There were to be no more benevolences or forced loans; nor were taxes to be imposed without a vote of the representatives of the nation. What the government hereafter did in the way of irregular exaction it had to do by fraud or sufferance, not by an exertion of the prerogative.

The personal government of Charles I. had been supported partly by exaction of feudal dues of the crown, its wardships, and its compositions for knighthood. In the war with Scotland it had called out its military tenants in feudal array. All this, suspended by the Revolution, was now formally abolished. The lands before held in military tenure were henceforth to be held in free soccage. The vexatious court of wards was never to vex more. The not less vexatious privilege of purveyance was resigned. Thus the nation finally took leave of feudalism and the middle age, while the king lost, with his feudal over-lordship, something of his dignity and power. To indemnify him for the surrender of his feudal revenues and perquisites he received an hereditary excise. A landlord parliament thus made the nation pay for a boon which was confined to a class. The Act which did away with the service of the lord of the manor to the crown confirmed the services of the copy-holder to the lord of the manor. Nearly at the same time the old feudal system of subsidies, which had been imperfectly and unfairly levied, was changed for that of regular assessments, the fiscal system of the Commonwealth.

The Triennial Act requiring the crown to call a parliament not less than once in three years, and providing remedies against the crown in case of its default, was 1664 repealed as being, what it unquestionably was, an infringement of the constitutional right of the king to call and dissolve parliaments. But in the repealing Act words were inserted affirming the principle of triennial parliaments which showed that the House of Commons, however, in its Cavalier mood, it might be disposed extravagantly to exalt the crown, was not disposed to part with its own power. In truth, after a few years, when the factitious haze of Restoration sentiment had been cleared away, it appeared that, instead of having been effaced, parliament had really been the winner in the long struggle, and that in it had vested the sovereign power. Henceforth, if the crown forms sinister designs, instead of setting the representatives of the nation at defiance, it will have to resort to packing and corruption; nor, pack and corrupt as it may, will it induce parliament, however devoid of public principle, by parting with power, to ruin the market for votes; opposition is necessary to extort the bribe. There was, however, no limit to the duration of parliaments, so that the king could keep a subservient parliament sitting as long as he pleased. The Cavalier parliament of Charles sat for eighteen years.

1661 The command of the military force was given back to the king, to whom both constitutionally and as a necessary adjunct of the executive it belonged, dangerous to freedom in his hands as it might be and as, in the next reign, it proved. Charles and his more absolutist brother had marked the support which was given to despotism by a standing army in France and had laid that lesson to heart. When the Commonwealth army was disbanded, three regiments, under the name of guards, were kept on foot, and the number was afterwards raised to about five thousand. The national safeguard was the necessity of parliamentary supplies to maintain the army. But by one stroke of the sword in the king's hand that safeguard might be annulled for ever.

A dangerous step was taken towards making the king independent of parliament by granting him a revenue for life of one million two hundred thousand pounds, made up of the port duties added to his hereditary excise. His extravagance proved an antidote to the unguarded liberality of the Commons. The mistresses and sycophants wrought for constitutional liberty in their way. 1660

The fangs of the treason law were sharpened, and it was made not only capital to conspire for the king's death or deposition, but punishable to affirm him to be a papist or a heretic, to write or speak against the established government, to maintain the legality of the Long Parliament, or to assert a legislative power in either or both houses of parliament without the king. 1661

The doctrine of non-resistance, pronouncing it treason to take up arms against the king on any pretence whatever, was ominously embodied in a statute. But to make the doctrine, thus affirmed in the abstract, practically effective, it would have been necessary to change the spirit of the nation. 1661

At the gorgeous coronation of Charles the religion of

etiquette was fully revived, though with innovation derived from the customs of the court of France, "whereof," says Clarendon, "the king and the duke had too much the image in their heads and than which there could not be a copy more universally ingrateful and odious to the English nation."

With the highest of all liberties, and that which is the salt of all, it fared for a time worst. But few, except the author of "Areopagitica," clearly saw the value of liberty of opinion. The press laws of the Commonwealth had been only occasional; they were the defensive measures of a government struggling for its life. The press law of the Cavalier parliament was an application of the paternal policy. The censorship of the press was appropriately conferred on L'Estrange, a royalist spy and conspirator, who had signalized his loyalty by an attack on Milton. This man was made inquisitor-general, not only for publications, but for the whole trade. His paper, published twice a week, was henceforth the whole newspaper press. Not only with freedom of the pen, but at a later period with freedom of the tongue, government sought to interfere. Coffee, now introduced, began to play a part in politics. Coffee-houses became resorts and centres of political gossip. These the government closed by proclamation; but, like other arbitrary governments, it found that it was more dangerous to aggress on the social pleasures of the people than on their rights, and the proclamation was withdrawn. In all our judgments on the conduct of the people at this time we must make allowance for the absence of a newspaper press, for the want of political information, and for the restraints upon liberty of discussion. Of this caution we shall soon have need. The want of a free press in England was to some extent compensated by the freedom of the press in Holland and the printing of English works there. As the reign went on, and political parties were developed, each party wanting to use the polemical pen, the press practically shook itself free.

The final triumph of the French Revolution over the old régime was assured by the new landed interest which it had called into being, and whose tenure was bound up with its cause. In England a good deal of the land of the ruined Malignants had found its way by purchase into new hands, in which, under the Indemnity Act, it remained, while its former owners, who had hoped to recover it, loudly accused the ingratitude of the Restoration, and complained that the Act of Indemnity and Oblivion was an Act of Indemnity for the king's enemies and of Oblivion for his friends. But the amount was not enough to anchor the Revolution. Confiscated estates reverted at once to the owners. On the broad lands of the church, which the Commonwealth had sold, and for which buyers had given fifteen years' purchase, showing thereby their trust in the stability of republican government, the bishops and chapters were enabled, by Hyde's policy, to re-enter without compensating the new owners. The leases having run out, the restored incumbents came in for a windfall of wealth in the shape of fines, to which Burnet partly ascribes the reign of clerical corruption which ensued. To the purchasers of crown lands some mercy appears to have been shown by the crown.

On the whole, therefore, much was left of the political gains of the Revolution; while nothing could expel from the veins of the nation the new life which had been

1660

infused into them by the struggle for civil and religious liberty, the grandeur of the united Commonwealth and the glories of the Protectorate.

So much as regarded the state. The consequences of a union of church and state, and of making religion a matter of government, were to be exemplified in the Restoration on the largest scale. The nation had perhaps not been ripe for the exodus from monarchy and aristocracy. For an exodus from prelacy it was ripe. It was, at all events, prepared for an ecclesiastical polity which would have reduced the bishop from the position of a lord to that of an officer in the church, associating with him a council of Presbyters in each diocese. Such was, in effect, Bishop Usher's scheme, and with it the English Presbyterians would at this time have been generally content. Cromwell's scheme of Comprehension seems also to have met with national acceptance. When the bishops in their pontificals first assembled in Westminster Abbey, the entry in Pepys's "Diary" is, "Lord, at their going out, how people did most of them look upon them as strange creatures, and few with any kind of love or respect!" For a scheme of limited episcopacy, with an inclusion of the Presbyterians, the Covenanted king had distinctly declared, no doubt with the approval of his mentor Hyde, when he was wooing the Presbyterian Convention; and as an earnest of his sincerity he had made Presbyterians his chaplains and offered bishoprics to Baxter, Calamy, and Reynolds. When he had won, his declaration was given to the winds, and legislation on its lines was defeated evidently by his own underhand influence and that of Hyde. About belief he cared little, but Presbyterianism, he was wont to say, was not a religion for a gentleman. The great fact had also dawned upon his mind that episcopacy was the religion for a king. At a conference between the bishops and the leading Presbyterians, held at the Savoy Palace, 1661 it plainly appeared that the bishops, with the king at their back, were resolved against any concession. Clarendon, who on this question was all-powerful, was bent on restoring the entire Anglican system, and reinstating the bishops as much as possible in their former power. He was seconded by the Cavaliers of the parliament, who with reason identified the religion of the Puritan with his politics, and with the source of their own sufferings and humiliations. The Act of Uniformity gave a death-blow 1662 at once to Presbyterianism, to Comprehension, and to protestant connection. It enacted that every parson, vicar, or other minister whosoever, should, upon some Lord's Day before the feast of St. Bartholomew, read the service according to the Book of Common Prayer, and afterwards declare his unfeigned assent and consent to all and everything contained and prescribed in that book. It further enacted that all clergymen, all heads and fellows of colleges, all university professors and lecturers, all schoolmasters and private tutors in families should, before the same feast, subscribe the doctrine of passive obedience and take oaths of conformity to the liturgy and of renunciation of the Covenant. On the black day of St. Bartholomew a number of clergymen, reckoned at two thousand, among whom were probably the most 1662 zealous ministers of the Gospel in England, and the most acceptable to the people, rather than comply with the Act went forth out of their homes, many of them to penury, for in their case no indemnity beyond a few months' stipend was given. The royalist clergy, ejected by the Puritans, had met with more mercy, and harsh as their treatment still was, in their case it might be truly alleged, while it could not be truly alleged in this case, that there was political danger to the government. Had not Charles I. said that if he could save the Anglican church, that church would give him back the sword? In face of the resignation of the two thousand, who shall say that Puritanism was mercenary or hollow? By the Act of Uniformity the line was finally drawn between the state church of England and the free churches. English Christianity was divided into two sections, the privileged and the excluded, the relations of which were those of legalized jealousy and hatred. Over the fall of the Presbyterians, considering the intolerance which they had shown, their blasphemy and heresy laws, and the general part which they had played, it is not easy to shed a tear.

Episcopal ordination had not hitherto been required. Foreigners ordained after the manner of the protestant churches of the continent had been admitted, however rarely, to benefices in the English church, and the communion of the church of England with the protestant churches of the continent, which carried with it a political connection, had been preserved. The Act of Uniformity, by requiring episcopal ordination, put an end to the connection, and consigned the church of England to the strange position of isolation between catholicism and protestantism, from which the high church party has in vain striven to extricate her by courting re-union, now with the Eastern church, now with the church of Rome. The Eastern church is hide-bound; Rome is infallible and can listen to nothing but submission.

Of Puritanism we hear no more. That mould nature breaks, as she had broken the mould of the Roman Stoic, of the Crusader, of the Huguenot, not without working something of each character into the abiding fibre of humanity. In its place came political Nonconformity, having its seat chiefly in the middle or lower middle classes; sober-hued, staid, and comparatively unaspiring; lacking culture, since it was excluded from the universities, lacking social refinement, since it was out of the pale of high society; uncongenial, therefore, to apostles of sweetness and light; yet keeping the tradition of a sound morality, as we still acknowledge in speaking of the nonconformist conscience; not rebellious or revolutionary, but struggling from age to age by purely constitutional effort for the removal of its disabilities, and as an oppressed body fighting always on the side of freedom. Its annals are not poetic or picturesque; but England might have been an Anglican Spain, less the Inquisition, if the nonconformists had not been there.

The efforts of Hyde, his bishops, and his Cavalier parliament to re-instate the true church in power did not stop with the Act of Uniformity. The Corporation Act 1661 required all holders of municipal offices to renounce the Covenant, to take the oath of non-resistance, and to receive the sacrament according to the Anglican form; thus once more degrading the holiest rite of the church of England into a political test. The Conventicle Act forbade the meeting of more than five persons in addition to the members of a family for any religious service not in conformity with the church of England, under the penalty of a small fine and a short imprisonment for the first offence, a longer imprisonment and a heavier fine for the second offence, and a fine of a hundred pounds, equivalent to several times the amount in money of our day, or transportation for seven years, on conviction of the third offence. The Act was to be construed in the sense most unfavourable to the conventicles, and magistrates, that is, Cavalier squires, were empowered to convict without a jury. The Five Mile Act enacted that no nonconformist ex-minister or teacher who had not taken the oath of passive obedience should come within five miles of any city or town corporate, or of any parish where he had formerly preached, under a penalty of forty pounds. It also enacted that no one who had not taken the oath of passive obedience and conformed, should teach any school or take pupils in his house. The objects of this Act were to cut off nonconformist ministers from the centres of population in which they would find friends, and from the calling of a teacher, on which almost alone they could fall back. This completes the "Clarendon code."

The Five Mile Act followed close upon the great plague of London, in which a hundred thousand persons died. During the plague, some of the state clergy having fled from their cures, the pulpits were occupied by nonconformists. If this was in the minds of the framers of the Act, the infamy of the measure is enhanced.

The Acts were administered with cruel zeal by the local authorities; the squires, who were justices of the peace, having since the Revolution and the reign of the saints become bitter foes of nonconformity. Spies and informers of course were bred and actively plied their trade. The state church of England had no holocausts of heresy such as were celebrated on the Quemadero of Seville. But she had under Charles II. a mild and decent substitute for those "holy severities" in the imprisonment of a multitude of nonconformists, not a few of whom met their death in the filthy and noisome dungeons of that day. Among the sufferers under the general persecution, though he was committed before the Acts, was the author of the "Pilgrim's Progress." The Quakers averred in a petition that four hundred of their number were in the prisons of London and a thousand in those of the country. That sect had multiplied exceedingly, sweeping into itself most of the extreme and enthusiastic sects which had sprung up in the revolutionary era, while the meek and indomitable tenacity of the Quaker was in the highest degree provoking to the squire upon the bench. The refusal of the Quakers to take oaths had been the object of a special penal law, and their meetings for worship to the number of five or more were prohibited on 1662 pain of imprisonment with hard labour, and on the third conviction, of banishment to the plantations.

No pretext had been afforded for persecuting legislation beyond a petty insurrection in London headed by Venner, a fanatical cooper, which was put down with the 1661 greatest ease, and a disturbance still more petty in Yorkshire, which seems to have been nursed for a sinister purpose by the government. There was, therefore, no valid excuse for the violation of Charles's promise, in his declaration from Breda, that there should be liberty to tender consciences and that no man should be disquieted or called in question for differences of opinion in matters of religion which did not disturb the peace of the kingdom. The Cromwellian soldiery had become quiet and industrious citizens noted only for their good character in their trades.

The ecclesiastical leader of the persecution and the opponent in council of indulgence for the nonconformists was Gilbert Sheldon, Archbishop of Canterbury, who, if we may trust the evidence adduced by Pepys, himself represented not only the religious opinions but the social tastes of the time. Pepys gives an account of a parody on a Puritan sermon performed at Lambeth for his Grace's amusement. Sheldon had once been a member of the liberal circle of Falkland.

The motive of the persecutions was, however, not so much religious bigotry as political revenge or fear, at least so far as parliament and the politicians were concerned. The libertine king was too careless about religion, too careless about anything, as well as too good-natured, to take an active part in persecution. Among men of the world scepticism, sometimes after the fashion of Hobbes, was making way. Temple, the model man, thought religion "fit only for the mob." In this reign 1677 the writ *De Hæretico Comburendo* was abolished. It is a redeeming feature of the period that men were ceasing to waste their intellectual powers on theological questions at once insoluble and barren, and were turning their thoughts to political studies, moral and mental philosophy, or natural science. The Royal Society now took a regular form, though its origin was earlier. Science and mathematics were the fashion. We see this in the "Diary" of Pepys. The king dabbled in chemistry. Prince Rupert found time amidst his sea fights and his debaucheries to study the same science and introduce Rupert's Drops. The age, if it was not more tolerant than that which preceded, was less theological, more secular, and in that respect a period of progress. In theology itself there was a liberal movement, of which Cudworth and the Cambridge Platonists were the chiefs. These men drank liberalism at the fountain of Greek philosophy.

Nor, with the desire of re-instating the church whose safety henceforth became the watchword of the royalist party, was there combined a desire of exalting the clergy. It was at this time that the privilege of taxing itself in Convocation was definitely taken from the clerical order and settled in the House of Commons, in which clergymen were not allowed to sit, though the order was represented by the bishops in the House of Lords. The clergy, once a powerful estate of the realm, being thus fiscally and politically merged in the general community, ceased to be an estate of the realm at all. The church had her bright stars of learning, but the clergy as a body were low and in low esteem. 1662

Of all the achievements of the Council of State and the Protectorate the grandest had been the union of Scotland and Ireland with England. What a train of calamity was ended for Ireland by that union, what a vista of calamity to come would it have closed! The heir of the Protector, by omitting to call Scotch and Irish members to his parliament, had slighted his father's work. But that work was utterly and formally undone by the ignoble policy of the Restoration.

In Ireland, the great garrison of Cromwellian landowners was too strong and too firmly seated to be dispossessed. Had it been threatened with ejectment it would have drawn the Cromwellian sword. It had in its favour the tremendous force of the English prejudice against the catholic natives, and the memory, ever fresh, of the great massacre, to which and to the advantage of possession it

added the influence of bribery. Ejected catholics, some of whom had fought on the king's side, in vain besieged the throne with their clamorous demands for restitution. Something was conceded to them, at least to the more powerful of them, but in the main the Cromwellians kept the land. The unequal compromise was embodied in the
1662 Act of Settlement, to the Saxon and protestant proprietor a grand assurance of title, to the dispossessed Celt a sentence of disinheritance, which he passionately desired, and at the first opportunity madly strove to reverse. The
1661 parliament of Ireland met once more at Dublin. The protestants having kept their lands, it was necessarily a parliament of protestant ascendancy. The Cromwellian settlement remained, but without Cromwell, and without the broad ægis of the united Commonwealth to cover and gradually reconcile two races and religions. To fill the caldron of future discord and misery to the brim came
1661 back the Anglican episcopacy under Bramhall, an old ecclesiastical myrmidon of the government of Charles I., with a religion alien and odious alike to the catholic and Presbyterian, with a church which was no church, but an intrusive establishment as oppressive as the yoke of a foreign invader. The Celts of Ireland were catholic by accident. A fervent and preaching protestantism might have succeeded as well with them as it did with the Celts of Wales or with those of the Scotch Highlands. That door of hope was shut by the intrusion of the state church of England.

In Scotland absolutism felt that it had a privy realm where it would not be curbed by the parliamentary institutions and the force of national sentiment by which it was still curbed in England. A long succession of civil conflicts, devouring party after party, English invasion, repeated defeats, and the military dictatorship which ensued, had levelled the political ramparts and broken the high spirit of the Scottish nation. The aristocracy, by which the nation had been led in the early days of the Covenant, had been decimated or estranged from the people. The religious enthusiasm of many had been worn out or chilled, and power had departed from those assemblies of the Kirk which for a time had been the real parliament of the Covenanting nation. The parliament was turned into a mere tool of the government by the revival of the Lords of Articles, a committee which controlled all legislation and was nominated by the crown. Absolutism, civil and ecclesiastical, was now openly installed. Scotland relapsed into a satrapy; its administration fell by turns to Middleton and Lauderdale, scoundrels both; the first coarse and overbearing, the second crafty and intriguing. Lauderdale, once a Presbyterian, and still at heart no friend to bishops, did not scruple to bear his part in the intrusion of episcopacy into Scotland and the destruction of the Kirk. The reactionary fury of the Council was constantly inflamed by drink. "It was a mad, roaring time," says Burnet, "full of extravagance; and no wonder it was so when the men of affairs were almost perpetually drunk." Legislation was not reckless only, but mad. By the Act Rescissory a clean sweep was made at once of the whole Scotch statute book for the period of twenty-eight years during which the Presbyterian establishment had been on foot. Episcopacy was again forced upon the nation by which it was passionately hated. Presbyterians were excluded from parliament. The Covenanters who abounded most in the wild west

1661

1661

were hunted down among their hills where they met by stealth to worship. But Covenanters were not Quakers; they were intractable and fierce; not less intractable or fierce than their persecutors. If compromise was offered, they spurned the Black Indulgence. Sometimes they turned to bay. Once they gained a victory over the forces of the king. Dalziel and Turner, rude and ruthless soldiers of fortune, carried on the reign of terror. At last, to break the spirit of the people, the wild Highlander was let loose upon their homes, where he lived at free quarters as dragoons did on the Huguenots of France. Opponents of the government were judicially murdered on the most frivolous pretences after trials which were a mockery of justice, and torture in the shape of the thumbikins and the boot, abhorred by English law, was used in the satrapy to extort confessions. Tortured Covenanters died in religious ecstasy. Confiscation went hand in hand with persecution, and, as Burnet tells us, on Valentine's day members of the council, instead of drawing mistresses, drew estates. The most rampant doctrines of absolutism were made law, and for merely demurring to them Argyle was accused of treason and condemned to death.

The ecclesiastical head of reaction and persecution in Scotland was Archbishop Sharp, a renegade from the faith and the counterpart of Sheldon. It is well known how on Magus Moor the cruel apostate met at the hands of James Balfour of Burleigh and a band of wild and fanatical Covenanters his well-deserved though lawlessly inflicted doom. The angelic Leighton accepted a Scotch bishopric in the hope of mediating between the extremes, both of which, by shrinking from them, he condemned.

But he gave up the idea as hopeless, and with him moderation and charity quitted the scene.

The free trade with England given to Scotland and Ireland by union was cut off, to the impoverishment and general back-setting of Scotland, to the ruin of Ireland, whose cattle-breeders and wool-growers lost their one good market. A bill to prohibit the importation of Irish cattle was driven through both Houses by the landowning interest in England, as Clarendon says, with incredible passion, in spite of the remonstrances of the Irish government and of a strong opposition from the better sense of England. This may perhaps be regarded as the first pitched battle between protectionism and free trade. 1666

The course of Clarendon, the restorer of monarchy and episcopacy, had for some years been smooth and triumphant. His daughter, Anne, was married, though not without scandal, to the Duke of York, and he was building himself a sumptuous mansion on a site near St. James's Palace, given him by a grateful master. But his barque ran upon a sunken rock, of the existence of which he can hardly have helped having a suspicion, though he was bound to dissemble. It was treason to assert that the king was a papist. A papist, nevertheless, at heart he was, and had been for some time before his restoration. Catholicism, debased and in low hands, was the religion of kings, to whom it promised absolute rule over an unreasoning people, and of voluptuaries, to whom it held out salvation through magical rites and death-bed absolution. Charles was a secret and careless papist; his brother James was a papist avowed, and by no means careless, but most serious and aggressive; not the less so because his 1660 own life was vicious. They conceived the scheme, afterwards tried again by James as king, of an Indulgence which, intended nominally for the benefit of all nonconformists and alluring them all alike, should in the end inure to the benefit of the true and royal religion. It was by thwarting this policy, as a stiff and devout liegeman of the church of England, that Clarendon lost the king's favour and fell. But he had also fretted his royal master's character on its other side. The solemnity of his antiquated virtue was oppressive to Charles and to the new morality of the court and harem. Having been Charles's tutor in exile, he had not doffed the tutor. Killigrew, the court jester, set the circle in a roar by mimicking the chancellor's gait with a bellows held like the seals before him. By hot Cavaliers, Clarendon was hated as the upholder, to his honour, of the Indemnity Act; by selfish land-owners as the opponent of the Irish Cattle Act. To the people he became odious by mismanagement in war, by his part in the sale of Dunkirk, an acquisition to which national pride attached a fictitious value, by his suspected wealth, and, what was most cruel, by the notion that he furthered the papistical designs of the king. He was accused of marrying the king to a barren wife that his own daughter, the Duchess of York, might be queen. Even the great plague and the fire of London were laid to the charge of his government. His fashions, formed before the political deluge, were old; long an exile, he was somewhat of an alien in a changed England, and to win hearts he neither knew how nor cared. Amidst the jubilation of the harlots and the buffoons he was deprived of his great office. Our mild method of getting rid of a prime minister by a vote of want of confidence was still unknown. Impeachment was the only mode. On pretences, of which that of arbitrary imprisonments alone was not hollow, Clarendon was impeached. By the evil, 1667 perhaps treacherous, advice of the king, he withdrew himself from trial and was banished for life. He had been the restorer of an intolerant prelacy, and if the bishops originated, he fathered, the code of persecution. But he had been comparatively inclined to moderation and the upholder of indemnity, as well as by his character and manners a living rebuke to court vice and corruption. He had refused a bribe from France which his royal master advised him to accept. His friend Ormonde, who had been governing Ireland honourably and as well as evil conditions would permit, was presently ejected from 1669 office by the same faction. About this time his colleague, the lord treasurer Southampton, perhaps the worthiest of all the men of that time, died. With these three sur- 1667 vivors of a nobler generation, integrity and even decency left the councils of the king. The spirit of the Restoration broke loose and henceforth reigns.

Power passed by this intrigue into the hands of the 1667 Cabal, a ministry so called because the initial letters of the names of its five members, Clifford, Arlington, Buckingham, Ashley, and Lauderdale, made up that word. It was an embryo cabinet though without a regular parliamentary basis, and to the cabinet the old constitutional privy council is gradually giving way. The privy council, consisting of fifty members, was too large for business, and an inner council became a necessity, especially for foreign affairs. Parliament had to be managed, and it could not be managed through a large body without union in itself. An inner and very confidential council, moreover, was required for the special designs of the king and his brother.

Revolutions, strewing their course with wrecked hopes and broken oaths of allegiance, breed and bequeath political infidels, who, at the same time, are restlessly ambitious, of daring temper, and sagacious after their kind. Such products of the French Revolution were Fouché, Talleyrand, and the men of the Directory; and such a product of the English Revolution was Ashley Cooper, presently made Earl of Shaftesbury, the Achitophel of Dryden's glorious satire. Shaftesbury was a born leader of opposition. At college he led the opposition of the freshmen to the tyranny of the seniors, and of all the students to the authorities when they reduced the strength of the beer. At the outbreak of the Revolution he had joined the royalist camp. Thence, receiving some disgust, he had passed to that of the parliament, in which his zeal and ferocity were distinguished. He sat in the republican, then in the Cromwellian, Council of State; was a member of the Barebones Parliament; was probably one of those who urged Cromwell to accept the crown; then headed the opposition, first to Cromwell, and afterwards to his son. He struggled to re-instate the Rump; went over to Monck; took part in the Restoration; flew to meet the king at Canterbury; won not only his forgiveness, but his favour, and was taken into the privy council. Having solemnly declared that if the king should be brought back not a hair of anyone's head should be touched, he sat on the commission for the trial of the regicides. His scepticism and moral cynicism probably combined with his wit and his charm of manner to recommend him to the friendship of Charles, whom he treated with the utmost familiarity.

"Shaftesbury," said the king, "you are the greatest rogue in my dominion." "Of a subject, your Majesty," replied Shaftesbury, "I believe I am." A salient feature of Shaftesbury's character was his restlessness. He was

> A fiery soul, which, eating out its way,
> Fretted the pigmy body to decay,
> And o'er informed the tenement of clay.

Religious belief he had none. If he believed in anything it was astrology, one of those superstitions which fascinate in an eclipse of faith.

Buckingham was a brilliant, versatile, and witty rake, who touched Charles's character partly on the same side as Shaftesbury,

> And in the course of one revolving moon
> Was poet, fiddler, statesman, and buffoon.

He had been Charles's tutor in morals, and his cynical companion and fellow-sufferer under Covenanting sermons and zealotry in Scotland. He seduced the Countess of Shrewsbury and killed the earl in a duel, the countess in the disguise of a page holding her lover's horse while the duel was being fought. Lauderdale, with his ungainly figure, his shock of red hair, and his tongue too large for his mouth, was a shrewd Scotch jobber also of the cynical tribe. He had been a zealous Covenanter, he had represented the Kirk in the treaty of Uxbridge; he was now its Holophernes, trampling it out with dragoons and wild Highlanders, or torturing its confessors with the boot and the thumbscrew. These three men were the libertines and the free-thinkers of the cabinet. Clifford was a thorough-going Roman Catholic, violent and over-bearing, but comparatively honest.

1667

Arlington seems also to have been a Roman Catholic at heart; he certainly died one; in politics he was an unscrupulous intriguer. In the two Roman Catholics who shared the king's inmost designs the Cabal had a cabal within itself.

Charles and James launched their measure of catholic propagandism in the disguise of toleration, having first, by a turn of the persecuting screw, prepared nonconformists to hail the proffered relief. A royal Declaration of 1672 Indulgence was put forth suspending the penal laws. But the brothers found, as did James when he tried it again, that they had demanded the one thing which a royalist parliament would not grant, and done the one thing which would make a Cavalier disloyal. Considering how weak the Roman Catholics were in England, to understand the intense fear and hatred of them we must take in the whole European situation, especially the menacing power of the propagandist bigot on the throne of France, as well as the indelible memories of Smithfield, the Armada, and the Gunpowder Plot. The House of Commons met the Declaration with a resolution denying the prerogative and 1673 affirming that the laws could be suspended only by Act of Parliament. Wisely and nobly on this, as on a later occasion, the nonconformists, ground down as they were by the Conventicle Act and the Five Miles Act, refused to embrace the Declaration of Indulgence, seeing that it put the king above the law, and divining that though general liberty of conscience might be the beginning, Roman Catholic ascendancy would be the end. Only the Quakers, as political quietists, regardless of everything but their souls, were ready on this as on the later occasion to accept the sinister boon. A glance at Scotland might have told nonconformists what towards them were the real intentions of the crown. After some sparring between the king and the Commons, the Declaration was withdrawn, and the prerogative of dispensation was renounced. But the honeymoon of the Restoration was over, and an uneasy wedlock of king and parliament ensued. Not content with its constitutional victory, parliament proceeded to strike a fell blow against the Duke of York and the Roman Catholic church by passing the Test Act, disqualifying for office, civil or military, anyone who had not taken the oaths of Allegiance and Supremacy, received the sacrament according to the usage of the church of England, and renounced the doctrine of transubstantiation. To this no subtlety of interpretation could reconcile the conscience of a Roman Catholic. James resigned the office of high admiral, and Clifford left the government. The protestant nonconformists seem to have acquiesced in the Act; rather than that popery should escape they were willing to see the sword thrust through themselves. With a Roman Catholic king in power unfettered by the laws, the fate of the Huguenots would assuredly in the end have been theirs. 1673 1673

Parliament might suspect, but it did not know, as we do, that Charles had sold himself and his country to the arch-enemy of protestantism and freedom. By the secret Treaty of Dover he had engaged, on payment of a large sum of money to him by the king of France, to join Louis in making war upon the Dutch, to furnish a contingent of English troops for the invasion of Holland, and to assist Louis in his designs upon the inheritance of the kingdom of Spain. He had further engaged, in consideration of an annual pension, at the first convenient opportunity, to 1670 declare himself a Roman Catholic, and in case of resistance on the part of the English people had covenanted for the assistance of French troops, which were to be conveyed in his own vessels for the invasion of England. The first part of the treaty had been made known to the whole Cabal; the second part to the Roman Catholic section only. Much apparently overstrained mistrust of the court, much apparently misplaced fear and hatred of popery, must be forgiven to a people who were thus betrayed. To bind Charles by his lusts as well as by his interests, a French harlot, Madame De Kéroualle, was sent by Louis into Charles's harem.

1670

Already England had been again drawn into war with the Dutch by commercial rivalry, collisions of trading companies in the far east, and the preposterous claim of England for the supremacy of her flag in the narrow seas, combined with the hatred of the court for the Dutch republicans and with the insidious machinations of the French king. A series of battles, fought with the same stubborn valour on both sides, had once more wasted in mutual destruction the forces of the two free and protestant nations, while the common enemy looked on with joy. Victories had been won by England under Montague, the old admiral of the Commonwealth, Monck, and Prince Rupert, who, according to the usage of the times, commanded by sea as well as by land. But the war was mismanaged, the admiralty like everything else was corrupt, and England saw a Dutch admiral sweep the Channel, come up the Thames, bombard Sheerness, and burn men-of-war in the Medway. It was believed that on that day of national disgrace the king supped with the ladies of the harem and the party amused

1667

themselves by chasing a moth about the room. The thoughts of the people, Pepys tells us, turned to Cromwell.

For a moment the English government was reclaimed from its evil way and drawn to the right course by Temple, a patriotic diplomatist, who induced it to enter into what was called the Triple Alliance, a league of England and Holland with Sweden, which from the victories of Gustavus and his military heirs retained a high position in Europe, for the purpose of checking French aggrandizement. That this was the personal work of Temple, feeling himself seconded by national opinion, in concert with the Dutch statesman and patriot De Witt, soon appeared by the coldness with which its author was treated by his own government. Once more, in pursuance of the Treaty of Dover, the waters were dyed with protestant blood and strewn with the wreck of two navies which ought to have been united in defence of the same imperilled cause; while six thousand soldiers, led by the king's bastard son, the young Duke of Monmouth, under the French standard invaded Holland, which despair saved from conquest by cutting the dykes. English valour and seamanship were again suicidally displayed. They were displayed in spite of maladministration, corruption, abuse of patronage, sale of appointments, which reigned in the navy as in every other department of the state. War was commenced on the part of England, before the declaration, by a piratical attack on the Dutch Smyrna fleet. To provide funds the government, closing the exchequer and suspending payment, laid its hands upon the money of its creditors to the amount of one million three hundred thousand pounds. Ruin of

1668

1672

1672

1672

1672

goldsmiths who acted as bankers, distress of depositors and wreck of public credit ensued.

Rottenness was everywhere. An Irish desperado named Blood, who had been outlawed for an attempt to surprise the castle at Dublin, set, with a gang of banditti, upon the Duke of Ormonde in the streets of London, and nearly succeeded in hanging him. The same brigand attempted to carry off the regalia from the Tower, after wounding the keeper, but was overtaken and secured. Charles attended the examination of the prisoner, forgave his crime, obtained for him a pardon from Ormonde, kept him as a gentleman at court, and gave him an estate of five hundred pounds a year in Ireland to compensate him for one he had forfeited when outlawed there. Vice reigned at Whitehall and, for an allusion to it in parliament, Sir John Coventry's nose was slit by the bravoes of the court.

Shaftesbury, being an enemy to catholicism, if he was not a believer in protestantism, and seeing that the wind now sat in the protestant quarter, had opposed the ecclesiastical policy of the royal brothers, supported the Test Act, and advised the banishment of the Duke of York. His attitude, with the proscription of Clifford by the Test Act, broke up the Cabal, and, with the levity of intriguers of that day, of whom he was the paragon, he at once passed into violent opposition.

To the Cabal succeeded the ministry of Danby, whose general policy seems to have been much the same as that of Clarendon, a strong monarchy supported by a strong state church. He appealed to the old cavalier spirit, and restored the statue of Charles I. at Charing Cross. He was unscrupulous enough to be a party to his master's acceptance of another bribe from the French king. Yet he had an English heart, and was opposed to the aggrandizement of France. He made peace with Holland, employing Temple as his plenipotentiary for that purpose. He did more. He married Mary, daughter of the Duke of York, and in the succession to the crown, to William, the young Prince of Orange, rendering thereby, as it turned out, an immense service to the country. The king might approve the match as a sop to protestantism; the duke, hated and in jeopardy as he was, might fear to oppose it. The Orange connection, however, was the policy of the Stuarts in opposition to the connection with the republican or Louvestein party dominant at Amsterdam, which was the policy of Cromwell. In his combination of royalism and anglicanism with high protestantism and nationality, Danby foreshadows the Tory of a much later day. He was a master of parliamentary management, and, what was the same thing in that posture of affairs, of parliamentary corruption. The parliament having sat for sixteen years without re-election, members had lost their sense of responsibility to their constituents; they were tainted by the general depravity of the times, and were commonly open to bribery. Danby may claim the honour of having first organized the system. Andrew Marvell has the credit of having, though poor, resisted all temptation. There is a story of a visit paid him by Danby, who found him at his desk up two pairs of stairs in a little court in the Strand, and offered him preferment in the king's service, but in vain. One version of the story makes Marvell, in Danby's presence, call for his servant, and say to him, "What had I for dinner yesterday?" "A shoulder of mutton." "And what have you for me to-day?" "The remainder hashed." Then Marvell turns to Danby and adds, "To-morrow I shall have the sweet blade-bone broiled." Danby, hopeless of corrupting virtue so impracticable, retires. Marvell was a relic of the Commonwealth and the author of the magnificent Ode on its chief.

An opposition called the country party had been formed with Shaftesbury, Holles, and Essex for leaders in the Lords, with Russell, Algernon Sidney, Hampden, Capel, and Coventry for leaders in the Commons, and animated by the reviving spirit of the Commonwealth. This opposition attacked the government at all points, especially wherever it could play on the public feeling against popery. It carried an Act disabling for the first time catholic peers for sitting in the House of Lords, from the operation of which the Duke of York was exempted only by a majority of two. It assailed Buckingham; it assailed Lauderdale, who was suspected of forming an army for sinister purposes in Scotland as Strafford had done in Ireland. It overthrew Danby's government and impeached him for privity as a minister to the corrupt intrigue of the court with France, though while privy to the intrigue he had been strongly opposed to French connection, had checked its influence by the Orange marriage, and was, in fact, betrayed for his patriotism by the French. It protested against financial extravagance, against parliamentary corruption, against standing armies, against Monmouth's auxiliary force. It demanded a dissolution of the parliament, which, having now sat for seventeen years, could no longer, it contended, be said truly to represent the nation. It did not fail to ply the usual arts and wield the usual weapons of faction, embarrassing as much as it could the administration which it denounced, and pandering to passion by reckless imputation. It clamoured for war with France yet withheld the requisite means. Some of its members were even misguided enough to intrigue with the French king, and, it appears, actually to accept money from Barillon, the ambassador of Louis, and the agent of his master's villainous game. The French king hated republicans and protestants, but his paramount object was to keep England weak and subservient. For this he was ready to intrigue and bribe all round. It is charitable to presume that if money was taken by opposition leaders it was for the purposes of their party, not for their own. But public morality on this subject was very lax.

In dealing with the question of war with France the parliamentary leaders were distracted between their fear of the French king's ambition and their fear of a standing army such as that by which his despotism was supported. The king and the Duke of York, on the other hand, looking to the same example, were always for keeping a standing army on foot. The duke's design in this policy was unveiled when he came to reign.

In the House of Lords, where the government was still sure of a majority, Danby had brought in a Bill imposing upon all members of parliament, privy councillors, magistrates, and others holding office under the crown, a test oath of non-resistance. The Bill required all who came under it not only to declare that it was unlawful under any pretence whatever to take up arms against the king, and that it was traitorous to take up arms, as the Roundheads had professed to do, by his authority against his person, but to swear that they would not endeavour the alteration of the government either in church or state. The Bill was evidently a blow aimed by Danby at the reviving spirit of republicanism in the Commons; while it appealed to the national fear of a renewal of the civil war. A fierce debate ensued. Charles, in accordance, as he said, with ancient custom, came in person to the House of Lords, hung about the fireplace, and in his winning way talked members into voting for the Bill. By the Lords the Bill was passed, though with its stringency reduced; and with the aid of Danby's arts and appliances it might have made its way through the Commons had not a quarrel between the two Houses brought on a prorogation. It appeared, however, that the doctrine of non-resistance had lost ground.

1675

The period of storm and confusion was not unfruitful of constitutional improvement. The principle of appropriating supplies was affirmed in the case of supplies granted for war. In Danby's case it was asserted that a royal pardon could not be pleaded in bar of impeachment, and that an impeachment did not determine with the sitting of the parliament. By the impeachment or arraignment of ministers, though sometimes factious, the control of parliament over the executive was confirmed. Better than all was the Habeas Corpus Act, passed after a stubborn opposition by the Lords, which secured personal liberty against illegal imprisonment by sweeping away all impediments hitherto raised by judicial or official trickery to the issue of the writ, and rendering its operation sure. Of this the credit belongs to Shaftesbury, whatever his motive may have been. Superior in importance to any legislation was the lapse, by the expiration

1679

of its term, of the Licensing Act, which, as the temper of the new parliament forbade re-enactment, tacitly put an end for a time to the censorship and gave freedom to the press. But that freedom was curtailed by the power of the government to prosecute for libel.

After sitting eighteen years the parliament was dissolved. Its successor, elected in a crisis of national discontent, could not fail to be hostile to the court. The boroughs and the small free-holders prevailed. In Danby's place came Sunderland and Halifax. Sunderland was a first-rate courtier and intriguer. Halifax was a man of a very different stamp, a philosophic statesman, an excellent political writer, broad in his views, with a mind only too well balanced, since it could never incline to decisive action. Courage was wanting to him, while from passion and prejudice he was free. Of revealed religion he "believed as much as he could." Government, however, was in convulsions. Sir William Temple, the Solon of the age, the author of the Triple Alliance, was called in to prescribe for the sick state. His prescription was a return from the unconstitutional Cabal to the constitutional privy council. He proposed to substitute for a privy council of fifty members, one of thirty, without an inner ring, made up half of ministers of the crown, half of popular members of parliament selected by the crown, with a proviso that the aggregate income of the councillors should not be less than three hundred thousand pounds, about three-fourths of the computed income of the Commons. This body, its projector probably thought, would not be too unwieldy for administration, would exclude cabal, would stand between the crown and the raging parliament, would absorb oppo-

1679

sition by giving a share in the government to its leaders, and perhaps would relieve the popular assembly, the tempestuous character of which must have been little congenial to a diplomatist, of the initiative of legislation. But diplomacy seldom makes parliamentary statesmen. 1679 The experiment at once failed. Not only was the council still too large for business, but the elements of which it was made up were too alien to each other for common action. The oil of office would not mingle with the vinegar of opposition. Charles, who hated no enemy so much as trouble, had made Shaftesbury president of the council to keep him quiet. The great agitator was now at liberty to ride the storm once more.

The storm which he did ride and which was chiefly of his own raising forms one of the blackest episodes in English history. The air was full of a panic fear of catholic plots, for which the intrigues of Louis XIV., suspected probably by the nation, and more than suspected by Shaftesbury, together with the restless activity of the Jesuits, afforded at least some ground; though fear must have been highly intensified by hatred when it could be believed, and inscribed on a public monument, that the great fire which had ravaged London was the work of the papists. The Duke of York had now publicly avowed his conversion; Coleman, his secretary, was indiscreet, writing of "a mighty work in hand, no less than the conversion of three kingdoms and thereby the utter subduing of a pestilent heresy which had long domineered over the northern world." By the opposition in parliament the feeling against the duke and against the catholics had been worked up for a political purpose. A mine of protestant suspicion was fully charged when upon it fell as a spark the mysterious murder, for murder it assuredly was, of Sir Edmund Berry Godfrey, a London magistrate who had taken depositions against the catholics, though in general he had rather been their friend. Of all vile informers in the pillory of history, the highest stand Titus Oates and Bedloe, men of infamous character and lives, who, with stories of catholic plots for the assassination of the king, the invasion of the kingdom, and the massacre of all protestants, monstrous as a maniac's dream, swore away the lives of a long train of Roman Catholics ending with the aged Lord Stafford and the blameless Archbishop Plunket. For a time mere frenzy reigned; its phantoms took the place of judicial evidence; while terrorism silenced all witnesses to the truth. No sane man would have believed such tales told by such wretches. But sanity is lost in multitude. Credulity was not startled even when an informer deposed that he had been in the palace and heard the queen assent to the assassination of the king. People lashed themselves into the belief that the capital, and the lives of all the protestants in it, were in imminent peril; took arms against the creations of their own disordered fancy; went about with small flails loaded with lead and called "Protestant Flails," for their protection against the catholic assassin. The Popish Plot ranks with the terrible illusions bred at Athens by the mutilation of the Hermæ, and in New England by the alarm of witchcraft. In all such cases probably the frenzy would be allayed by a free and active press. Whatever blame attaches to the English people for this murderous panic attaches in a higher degree to the judges, such as Scroggs and North, who turned the courts of justice

1678

1680

into dens of judicial murder, and to members of parliament, Shaftesbury above all, who for a political purpose fanned the raging flame. From political cowardice probably, rather than from fanaticism, the Lords countenanced the frenzy of the deluded people. Their House brought upon its records an indelible stain by allowing itself to be made the judicial instrument for the piteous immolation of Lord Stafford. It appears to have been actuated by selfish fear of the unpopularity which it was in danger of incurring by its rejection of a Bill for the exclusion of the Duke of York from succession to the crown. Not the least odious, however, was the conduct of Charles, who, too cool-headed and sensible to believe in the plots, signed the death-warrants because he did not want to go again upon his travels. Nor must Louis XIV. and the Jesuits escape their share of responsibility. That they were actively plotting for the extermination of protestantism was no fiction of Oates or Dangerfield, but a most certain and deadly fact. By his intrigues the Jesuit had presented Roman Catholicism as capable of anything, and by his casuistry he had destroyed confidence in a catholic's oath.

Of the catholic conspiracy denounced by Oates and Dangerfield the Duke of York was guiltless. Of the catholic conspiracy against protestantism and freedom, of which Louis XIV. was the head, the Duke of York was unquestionably a limb; and to put a free and protestant nation into his hands might well seem and was proved by the event to be national suicide. For one part of the royal office, the headship of the church of England, he was plainly disqualified. His conduct as satrap in Scotland, where he looked on unpityingly at torture, showed that he was a cruel tyrant as well as a bigot. But he was heir presumptive to the crown, and there was no longer any hope that Charles would have legitimate offspring. James had no son. His heiress was his daughter by his first wife, brought up, by the king's order, as a protestant, and married to William of Orange; after whom came her sister Anne, also brought up as a protestant. But he had taken as his second wife Mary of Modena, a Roman Catholic, and by her he might have a son who would cut out his two protestant daughters and perpetuate a Roman Catholic dynasty. That parliament had a right to deal with the succession to the crown there could be no doubt, since it had done this in the case of Henry IV., and still more signally by the Act which enabled Henry VIII. to dispose of the crown by will and exclude the Scottish line. To this extreme remedy it was now determined by the patriots to resort, at the evident risk of civil war, since there could be no doubt that James would fight for the crown or that he would have a large legitimist party on his side. A Bill excluding the Duke of York from the succession passed with ease through the Commons, now intensely anti-catholic and thoroughly opposed to the court. It would have passed through the House of Lords but for the influence of Halifax, the great Trimmer, in whose eyes the boldness of the measure would be its sufficient condemnation. The Bill was supported by ministers of the crown, Sunderland and Godolphin, as well as by the reigning mistress; but thanks to the oratory of Halifax it was thrown out by a majority of sixty-three to thirty. The patriots had compromised their cause and given a handle to the opponents of the Bill, of which Halifax took advantage in debate, by countenancing the pretensions

1680

of the Duke of Monmouth, Charles's bastard son, a beautiful and brave but brainless youth, his father's darling and a protestant idol. A story was set afloat of a secret marriage between Charles and Lucy Walters, Monmouth's mother, evidence of which was said to be preserved in a mysterious black box. On the faith of this Monmouth gave himself royal airs and even assumed the royal arms without the bend sinister. The king solemnly, and no doubt truly, declared that he had never been married to anyone but the queen. The Exclusion Bill seems to have been needlessly invidious and aggressive in form. Instead of indicting and proscribing the Duke of York personally, might it not simply have extended the principle of the Test Act to the crown?

Halifax, ever the friend of middle courses, advocated, in place of an Exclusion Act, an Act of Limitation, to which, or something like which, it seems the king would have assented, though he refused to deprive his brother of the birthright. A Bill was drafted under the guidance of Halifax depriving James of his negative voice in Bills passed by the two houses, transferring from him to the parliament the right of treating with foreign states and that of appointing to offices, and banishing him to a distance of five hundred miles from England during the king's life. James, as might have been foreseen, rejected with scorn a plan which would have left him the mere name of king. From engagements the Jesuit would have released him. He would as certainly have taken arms against limitation as he would against exclusion; there would have been civil war in either case; and limitation would have had no name wherewith to conjure, no sentimental rallying cry upon its side. It would seem that there was nothing for it but to take the bold course, bring forward the effective measure and try the sinew of the nation. If for the present the sinew failed, the tyrant, having full swing, might brace it, as in the sequel he did.

Charles again dissolved parliament. An agitation was then organized by the patriots in the form of petitions for its re-assembling. But now the royalist and legitimist feeling of the country was aroused, and with it the fear of a renewal of the civil war. The frenzy of the Popish Plot had abated; remorse had begun to take its place. The execution of Lord Stafford excited the pity even of the fanatical mob of London, which responded with sympathy to his protests of innocence on the scaffold. In opposition to petitioners for the meeting of parliament swarmed out Abhorrers of those petitions and of interference with the rights of the crown. Restoration sentiment showed its renewed force in a shower of loyal addresses. It began to be seen, Burnet says, how little dependence could be placed on the hot fits of popular fever or the flowings of the popular tide. The dominant party in the Commons, not contented with asserting the right of the subject to petition for a parliament, launched out into disgraceful excesses in the impeachment of the leading opponents of exclusion and in the denunciation and arbitrary punishment of Abhorrers, and a reaction against that tyrannical violence ensued.

Now were heard for the first time the two party names, famous in American as well as English history, and borne by the two great British parties almost down to the present day. In themselves the names have little meaning, Tory being a designation of Irish banditti, Whig that of wild fanatics in western Scotland; and perhaps they were not on that account less adapted for the service of party, since a man may change his mind about a principle, while he cannot change his mind about a name. The Tory, however, was the friend of government by prerogative and of church privilege; the Whig was the friend of constitutional liberty and toleration; in effect, the Tory was a supporter of monarchical, the Whig of parliamentary supremacy. To be the friend of monarchical supremacy was to be the friend of the house of Stuart; to be the friend of parliamentary supremacy was to be an adherent of the house by which, under an Act of Parliament, the house of Stuart was to be supplanted. In the Whig the Puritan opponent of the personal government of Charles I. may be said to have risen again, so far as the political part of the character was concerned, though the religious part of the character had dropped off. The Tory was an unromantic Cavalier. In later times, when the question between royal and parliamentary government had been finally settled, and the dynastic question connected with it was no more, the Tory party became that of political and ecclesiastical reaction, the Whig party that of general progress, till the Tory was softened into the Conservative, while the Whig blossomed into the Liberal.

1681 Charles showed his wisdom by holding his last parliament, not at Westminster, under the influence of the great city of London with its protestantism, its liberalism, and its inflammable populace, but in quiet and loyal Oxford. Had Louis XVI. taken the hint and held his States-General at some provincial city instead of holding them at Versailles, he might have had less trouble. Not having London to back them, and fearing or affecting to

fear violence, the Whig leaders came to Oxford with
armed trains as the patriot barons had come to the same
meeting place in the reign of Henry III. Now the abyss
of civil war seemed to open under the feet of the nation.
A violent recoil ensued. The king felt himself strong
enough in national opinion to take the aggressive and
turn the tables on the Whigs. He suddenly dissolved 1681
parliament, the liability of which to dissolution at the
will of the king was always its weak point in the struggle
for power. His appeal to the people was well received;
yet to avoid the fatal suspicion of popery he signed the
death-warrant of Archbishop Plunket, the last victim of 1681
the Popish Plot, a prelate of the church to which he
himself in heart belonged, and innocent, as he knew.

Judges who held their places at the king's pleasure
were his creatures, and such men as Scroggs and North
would be not less ready to serve power by murdering
Whigs than they had been to serve it by murdering catholics. But there had now come on the stage a figure
which more hideously profaned the judgment-seat than
even those of Scroggs and North. To any defence which
political superstition may attempt to set up for James
as king, it is a sufficient reply that he patronized, advanced to the highest office of the law, and employed
as his trusted counsellor and instrument, such a scoundrel, ruffian, and assassin as George Jeffreys. A judicial
reign of terror now commenced. The first blow struck
was the execution of College, the protestant joiner as he 1681
was called, the inventor of the Protestant Flail. Shaftesbury was indicted, but the venue was in London, where 1681
his name was still mighty, and a Whig grand jury ignored
the Bill. After a vain attempt to make his peace with

1683 the court, the arch-agitator fled to the continent, and there ended his restless days.

At the head of the Whig party were Lord Russell, son of the Earl of Bedford, Lord Essex, and Algernon Sidney. Russell was a scion of one of those houses which originally had been attached to the protestant Reformation and the political principles connected with it by large grants of church lands. But he was also a sincere Whig and a genuine patriot, deservedly honoured, though, like other Whigs, he had disgraced himself by countenancing the Popish Plot. Algernon Sidney was an old soldier of the New Model, a regicide in sentiment though not in act, a member of the Council of State under the Commonwealth, a thorough-going republican of the old Roman type, and a political writer of that school. It is a strange stain on the character of this Whig saint and martyr that he should have taken money from the king of France, for however patriotic a purpose he may have meant to use it. Lord Essex was a politician of moderate sentiments and no great force. These men feared, and with good reason, that the cause of law and liberty was now going by the board. There is little doubt that they contemplated armed resistance in case of extremity, and took counsel with each other as to the means of organization. It does not appear that they went further or did anything which could be legally designated as treason. But there was a knot of men of a lower grade, fanatical republicans and heirs of the regicidal Independents, who entered into a
1683 plot called, from the intended scene of its execution, the Rye House Plot, for an attempt upon the person of the king. By the artifice of the court lawyers the counsels of the Whig leaders were confounded with the Rye House

Plot, and with the help of the patrician treachery of Lord Howard, who betrayed his friends Russell and Sidney, the patriots were brought to the block. Tyranny has never laid their ghosts; the picture of Russell at the judgment bar, with his wife acting as his secretary at his side, is familiar to English eyes, and his powerful house has constantly appealed to the people in his name. Essex committed suicide in the Tower, probably to save his heirs from the consequences of his attainder for treason. Party whispered that he had been murdered. The king was quite incapable of any but judicial murder. In laying the wreath on the graves of these patriots we must remember that their party was responsible for the Popish Plot and that Russell had voted for the death of Lord Stafford. 1683

1683

It was now seen what a king with subservient judges might do without overstepping the strict limits of the law. On pretence of a technical breach of the charter of London on the part of the citizens, the charter was, at the instance of the crown, declared forfeit by the courts. Thus the defeat of the crown in the case of Shaftesbury was avenged, and the liberties of the great Whig city were laid at the feet of the king. From London the process was extended to other boroughs which were the strongholds of the Whig party. Charter after charter was declared forfeit by a servile judiciary. The king remodelled the corporations at his pleasure, filled them with his creatures, and became master of the urban representation. The landed gentry, who commanded the rural constituencies, having now for the most part turned Tories, he was master of the parliament. 1683

1684–1688

By the Act repealing the Triennial Act it had been laid

down as a principle that a parliament should be held at least every three years, but no provision was made in it for enforcement. During the last four years of his reign Charles, following his father's example of personal government, held no parliament. In no other way can he be said to have broken the law. All the other acts of his tyranny, the confiscation of the charters and the judicial murders, were technically legal. It is a lesson to those who rely too much on the forms of institutions.

The political atmosphere was now dark with the most slavish doctrines of prerogative. At this time was put
1680 forth, amid the general applause of the Tories, above all of the Tory clergy, Filmer's theory of the divine right of kings, the patriarchal origin of government, and the indefeasible claim of the first-born. With this fancy solid interests, monarchical, aristocratic, and clerical, were closely bound up, otherwise its author and his disciples would have had little right to deride the hallucinations of any fanatic. From Oxford, the heart of ecclesiastical
1683 Toryism, came a decree, afterwards burned by the hangman, against a string of damnable doctrines, such as that civil authority is derived originally from the people, and that there is a compact, express or tacit, between the king and his subjects. The decree did not, as did Filmer, condemn limited monarchy, but it affirmed primogenitary right, which is truly said to come practically to the same thing. On the University of Oxford the reproach is cast, but the voice was in truth not that of a university; it was that of the clergy who filled the headships and fellowships and had banished from the place all studies, all interests, and all sentiments but their own. By the clergy throughout the country, who had probably been

the soul of the political reaction, Filmer's doctrine was zealously preached.

In opposition to the religious absolutism of Filmer and the unreligious absolutism of Hobbes will come Locke with his original compact and pervading spirit of Liberal Christianity. Oxford, at the bidding of the Stuarts, has expelled him. He is in exile in Holland. But he and his political philosophy will return. Light lingers on the horizon and will broaden into day. 1684

Circumstances favoured political reaction. In spite of misgovernment and perversion of justice, the country seems to have been prosperous. Trade increased; the price of land was high. London, after the Great Fire which followed the Great Plague and perhaps purified its filthy and infected scene, had risen with surprising rapidity from its ruins. There was anguish among patriotic politicians, but among the people probably little discontent. The army had been increased to an amount fully sufficient for the purpose of repression. 1666 1665

Charles was good-natured and too lazy actively to play the tyrant. Having at last got rid of the parcel of fellows who pried into his affairs, he might have been contented with the quiet enjoyment of his concubines, in the midst of whom, with a French boy singing love-songs and the courtiers at a gambling-table, Evelyn and two other grave gentlemen were scandalized by seeing him one memorable Sunday afternoon. But his pleasures were cut short by a somewhat sudden death, which contemporaries paid the usual compliment to the morality of their times by attributing to poison. On his death-bed he declared himself a Roman Catholic, was admitted by a priest, furtively brought to his bedside, into the church, 1685 and after a confession which, if at all complete, must have been highly condensed, received absolution and the sacrament. To the courtiers who, according to the hideous custom of that day, thronged the chamber of death, he apologized for being so unconscionably long in dying. Exile, which obliged him to be gracious, had taught him, if nothing else, the urbanity which was his saving grace as a king.

The prince whom the Exclusion Bill would have proscribed ascends the throne.

CHAPTER II

JAMES II. — THE REVOLUTION AND ITS RESULTS

BORN 1633; SUCCEEDED 1685; LEAVES THE KINGDOM 1688

A REVOLUTION proper is a violent change of the form of government. Such was the French Revolution. Such have been the revolutions and counter-revolutions by a series of which it has been followed. Such were the revolutions which often occurred in the states of antiquity and in the city republics of the middle ages. Such had been the English Revolution in the time of Charles I., commonly known as the Great Rebellion. Such was the revolution which separated the American Republic from the British crown. The Revolution of 1688, though glorified by that name, was not in fact a revolution at all; it was a change of dynasty, not of the form of government. The form of government it preserved from the change attempted by a king who strove to turn a limited monarchy into a despotism, and at the same time to impose an alien religion on the nation. It was in fact the defeat of revolution attempted in the interest of reaction. It was attended by no revolutionary violence, went through none of the phases of revolutions, produced no Girondists or Jacobins. Nor was it propagandist, though its results inspired Montesquieu and Voltaire.

In the next reign a trial of a great political cause gave the Whig leaders the opportunity for an exposition of the principles on which the party had acted in 1688. Nothing can be less revolutionary than their speeches. Their creed is that no part of the constitution was altered or suffered the least damage; but that the whole received new life and vigour. They studiously minimize resistance. Still, 1688 is a landmark. It closed the long conflict of which the first great crisis was the struggle for the Petition of Right. It established the supremacy of parliament. From the point of view of constitutional liberalism, it was not unworthy of the admiration with which it was regarded by Burke.

Not only was this a British, it was a European event of the first order. It redressed the balance of power in Europe. Under the Stuarts England had become the subsidized and subservient ally of the French king's rapacious ambition, and of the popery, cognate to despotism, of which he, more than the pope himself, was the head. The Revolution of 1688 transferred her to the side of William of Orange and of the liberties of Europe.

When James, as Duke of York, fearing for his brother's life, offered him his own guard, Charles, as the story went, replied, "Don't be afraid, brother; nobody will kill me to make you king." Charles was not by nature a tyrant. He was not malignant or cruel. His only personal murder was that of Vane. His desire was not absolute rule, but freedom from inspection and control. James was a tyrant by nature. He was malignant and cruel in a high degree. His heart was as hard as flint. We have no reason for rejecting the positive statement of Burnet that James, while acting as viceroy in Scotland, used to sit out the applications of the boot and thumbscrew when other members of the council left the room.

That as king he beheaded one aged woman and burned another alive for showing womanly kindness to a hunted fugitive, are certain facts. It is not less certain that he presided over a cruel persecution of peasants in Scotland and rewarded the perpetrator of a most savage and dastardly butchery of peasants in England. Nor can it be doubted that he aimed at absolute power. Louis XIV. and French monarchy were always in his mind. He was almost more than absolutist. He fancied himself the vicegerent of God. To his council at his accession he had proclaimed his resolution of reigning according to law; yet the first thing that he did on ascending the throne was to show his contempt for the law of parliamentary taxation by ordering the customs to be collected before they had been voted by parliament. He addressed his first parliament in the menacing language of a master. A still more ominous sign of his intentions was his immediate increase of the standing army. That if he had not been prevented he would have used that army to crush constitutional liberty, to introduce French despotism, and afterwards to force popery on the nation, cannot reasonably be doubted. Fortunately for the nation, while Charles had been an unprincipled man of sense, James was an obstinate fool.

Of loose life, like his brother, and scandalously given not only to concubinage but to adultery, James, unlike his brother, was devout and under the dominion of priests, to whose influence he, like Louis XIV., would be exposed by an old sinner's cravings for specifics to save his soul, as well as by the general tendency of kings. Especially was he under the dominion of the Jesuits, who in directing his perverted conscience for their own objects showed their usual unscrupulousness, their usual cunning, and their usual lack of wisdom. The intrigue of the sons of Loyola is often a web woven with infinite skill and labour, but in the moment of accomplishment swept away. Even the failures, however, have cost humanity dear. In England the Jesuits brought ruin upon themselves and upon their dupe. In France their influence, exercised through a priest-ridden woman and a royal confessor over the conscience of the French king, enabled them to obtain the revocation of the Edict of Nantes and cruelly to persecute or expatriate the best and most industrious part of the French people. The house of Bourbon in the end paid for its submission to Jesuit guidance even more dearly than the house of Stuart.

The disgraceful vassalage to France commenced by Charles II. was continued by his successor. With abject expressions of gratitude James received the dole sent him on his accession by his French patron. It was his pride, not his patriotism, that afterwards rebelled, and led him at a decisive moment peevishly to reject his patron's advice and aid.

The twin objects of James's policy, absolute monarchy and the conversion of England from protestantism to popery, were thoroughly akin, as the history of Europe has shown; yet, happily for the nation, one of them crossed and wrecked the other. Had he aimed at absolute monarchy alone there is no saying what the event might have been. In the end, probably, national spirit and the love of liberty innate in the race would have gained the day. But there might have been an evil time. When James came to the throne everything was propitious to his design. The tide was running in favour of royalty almost as high as on the morrow of the Restoration. The clergy were preaching the doctrines of Filmer, in support of the power to which they were beholden for their restoration to wealth and privilege, and which set their feet on the necks of their nonconformist enemies. James was a Roman Catholic, but he had pledged his word to uphold the church of England, and the clergy believed him, as they reasonably might, knowing that they were at least as good friends to absolutism as any Roman Catholic priesthood; better friends, in fact, since their dependence was solely on the crown. It was passed round among them that they had for their security the word of a king who never was worse than his word. From the University of Oxford, their mouthpiece, came professions of unlimited obedience. James's bluntness was taken for honesty by those who did not know that his hand was held out behind his back for French gold. The attempt to deprive him of his birthright, having failed, had increased his popularity. After the defeat of the Exclusion Bill and the discovery of the Rye House Plot, the Whig party, which was that of liberty and the constitution, lay prostrate. Its electoral strongholds, the boroughs, had, by the remodelling of the corporations after the wholesale confiscation of their charters, passed completely into the hands of the crown, which already had the support of most of the squires, and of the county constituencies which were under their control. Where there was still any room for doubt about the election, official influence and intimidation were unscrupulously used. The electorate of Cornwall, which had forty-four petty boroughs, was openly packed with guardsmen. Here was plain treason to the constitution.

1685   When the House of Commons met, the king said that it contained not more than forty members whom he would not himself have chosen. In the Lords, though not Tory principles, the conservatism of wealth, rank, and privilege would prevail. Thus the parliament was the king's own, and he might keep it, as the law then was, if he pleased, to the end of his reign. In fact, the parliament was too much the king's own. His majority was too overwhelming. He had left not enough of an opposition to stimulate and keep in exercise the loyalty of his friends. For want of Whigs to combat there was a danger that the assembly, as no assembly likes to efface itself, would in time be led to combat the crown. Scarcely, in fact, had parliament met when the voice of Seymour, a Tory magnate, was heard denouncing the interference of the government with the purity of election. In the second session something like an opposition was formed, and it took the turn, ominous for James, of praying that the law might be put in force against papists. Here the danger-signal appeared.

1685   In its first session, however, the House carried loyalty to the verge of suicide. It almost repeated the great self-betrayal of the parliament of Richard II. It condoned the illegal collection by James of the customs voted only for his predecessor's life. It gave him for his own life the whole revenue of Charles II. with the addition of a tax on sugar and tobacco, the means, in fact, if he was frugal, not only of carrying on the government but of paying troops independently of the vote of parliament. This would have made him eventually absolute, provided he only advanced with caution and refrained from doing what would drive the nation to rebellion.

James would fain have repealed the Habeas Corpus Act, which he justly deemed fatal to absolute monarchy. He was baffled for the time in an attempt to extend the treason law so as to make it treason in any member of either House of Parliament to move for a change in the succession to the crown. He succeeded in obtaining the re-enactment of the law against the liberty of the press. 1685 As soon as parliament showed the slightest independence it was prorogued and met no more. That James was marching to despotism as well as to the establishment of his own religion there can be no shadow of doubt.

The king's temper was soon shown by inflicting on 1685 Oates and Dangerfield, the inventors of the Popish Plot, a punishment which amounted to scourging to death, though Oates, by a miracle, escaped with life. His real feeling towards the nonconformists, whom he afterwards hypocritically courted, was shown by the fining and imprisonment, after a trial brutally conducted by Jeffreys, 1685 of Richard Baxter, that excellent and blameless minister of Christ, to whom, as a Presbyterian loyal to the crown, a bishopric had been offered at the Restoration.

Still further to strengthen James's government and 1685 thus to increase the peril of the constitution, came Monmouth's rebellion, an enterprise doomed from the outset to failure, since it was premature, managed by wild enthusiasts without national influence, and raised in the name of a pretender in whose legitimacy none but peasants could believe. What is wonderful is that the insurrection should have shown such a front as it did in the west of England, and struck such a blow as it did at Sedgemoor. Where, now, are the English peasants or mechanics who would sally forth with scythes and pitchforks to fight against regular troops in a great cause or for a beloved name, and who would come as near as those west country peasants did to defeating a royal army? Argyle, whose accession lent character to the undertaking in the north, redeemed the madness of the attempt by the heroic calmness with which he met his end. When James bade one of his victims remember that it was in his power to show mercy, the man replied that it might be in his power but that it was not in his nature. So Monmouth found when he grovelled at the feet of his pitiless uncle praying for life in vain. On the scaffold Monmouth bore himself better; he at least went out of the world unshriven by the bishops who would have had him profess the doctrine of non-resistance as one of the conditions of his absolution. The church of England had marked her political character by allowing her sacrament to be used as a political test. She here marked it by making a political doctrine a condition of her membership. In truth Royalism has always been a part, not to say a vital part, of her creed. She accepted Eikon Basiliké almost as an addition to her canon, and her preachers put the royal martyr only a little, some of them not at all, below the Saviour. Her offsets in the colonies, though not established, have preserved her political character. They preserve something of it, even in the United States, at the present day.

In the west there followed a hideous slaughter of peasants who had been merely misguided, who, since their defeat, were harmless, and to whom true policy as well as generosity would have shown mercy. First came a murderous raid of Colonel Kirke with his regiment of "Lambs," so called from the emblem of Christ which they

bore on their banners as a Tangier regiment destined
to fight against Mahometans. Then came the Bloody 1685
Assize, conducted by Jeffreys, whose name is enough,
and who butchered on his circuit three hundred peasants,
besides inflicting wholesale deportations, scourgings, and
fines. The chief justice and the king afterwards cast
the blame of these cruelties upon each other. Which of
the two lied we cannot say. What is certain is that
James polluted the highest office in the realm by paying
Jeffreys for his massacre with the chancellorship. The
beheading of Alice Lisle, and the burning alive of 1685
Elizabeth Gaunt, for obeying the commonest impulses of
humanity in sheltering fugitives, as well as the judicial
murder of Cornish, an eminent London citizen, for opposing court influence in city elections, combined with
the Bloody Assize to show all men what there was upon
the throne.

The rebellion having been crushed and followed by a 1686
reign of terror, with an army, which by this time had
been made strong, with Churchill to take the command,
and Louis to help in time of need, James and his
Jesuit guide, Father Petre, might well think that the
time had come for the opening of their attack upon the
church. Resistance on her part they could hardly fear.
Had she not preached unlimited submission? She had;
but they failed to see that what she meant was unlimited
submission to a king who would subdue her enemies before
her, and secure her wealth and power.

In another quarter James had prepared support for his
policy. His father had intrigued with the catholic Celts
of Ireland, irresolutely and to his own ruin, because he
was not a catholic himself. James, being catholic him-

self, could without hesitation enlist their aid, so far at least as the religious question was concerned. Rochester, the Lord Deputy of Ireland, though brother-in-law of the king and a thorough-going Tory, was driven from his office to make way for the catholic Tyrconnel, a reckless and profane ruffian, whose nickname was Lying Dick, and who had once served James's lusts. By this man all the powers of government and all the offices of the army, the civil service, and the judiciary were transferred from the protestants to the catholic Celts, who were organized for an onslaught on the protestants and the recovery of the forfeited land. Outrage, pillage, and terrorism reigned. The days of the Ulster massacre seemed about to return. A panic exodus of protestants began. At the same time, to the disgust of England, Irish catholics were imported into the English army of coercion.

The king's game was the same which had been played in the last reign. It was probably played in both cases by the same hand. The nonconformists were first to be made, as before, by a fresh turn of the screw, to feel the need of relief. Then was to be put forth a Declaration of Indulgence suspending all the penal laws, which, it was hoped, would unite the nonconformists with the Roman Catholics against the church of England. In the end, Roman Catholics having been put in command of the army and into the offices of state, and their religion having thus been made dominant, the nonconformists, it cannot be doubted, were to share the fate of the Covenanters in Scotland and the Huguenots in France. Then in England, as in France, the true church and the church of kings would reign alone. To the ambassador of Louis James frankly avowed his aim.

Wise Roman Catholics abroad, and notably the Italian statesman who wore the triple crown, having some insight into the English temper, advised caution. But to the king and to his chief adviser, the Jesuit Father Petre, apparently triumphant as they were over all opposing forces, caution seemed mistrust of God. They went forward at a pace which soon left the staunchest Tories behind, and threw off the most devoted and servile ministers of the crown. Halifax, who had been Charles's last adviser, and to whom was due the defeat of the Exclusion Bill, was thrown off early in the race. Danby, a thorough-going Tory, but also a strong protestant and churchman, did not hold on long. The king's two brothers-in-law, Rochester and Clarendon, desperately clinging to power and pelf, were at last compelled to resign. In the midst of all appears Catherine Sedley, the king's protestant mistress, comically crossing by her unholy influence the threads of priestly intrigue. Otherwise none but apostates kept their places. By apostasy Sunderland kept his. With apostates such as Sunderland, who presently proved a traitor, with Jeffreys, who apparently was beneath apostasy, with Jesuits like Father Petre, and some Roman Catholics of the better sort, who, as they had been excluded from public life, could not be statesmen, for his advisers, the king rushed onwards to his doom. Public sentiment, instead of being spared, was recklessly provoked. The popery of the court was proclaimed and paraded in the manner most offensive to the nation. Priests and friars in the garb of their order stalked the streets of London. An embassy was sent with scandalous ostentation to Rome, and a papal nuncio was with ostentation equally

1685

1687

1687

scandalous received in England. In recent times, papal aggression, though impotent and harmless, has set England in a flame; and those were the days of the expulsion of the Huguenots, the days in which the fires of the Inquisition were still burning at Madrid.

1850

Under colour of a decision in a collusive suit the laws excluding Roman Catholics from office, civil and military, were set aside by an exercise of the prerogative of dispensation, and the king proceeded to fill the services with Roman Catholics. It was certain that if this went on, other offices, civil and military, would in the end be filled by men of the king's religion. Above all things menacing were the enlistment of Roman Catholics, especially the Irish, in the army, and the evident determination of the king to place a force, which the nation had no means of resisting, in Roman Catholic hands. The struggle was not against Roman Catholic equality, which, coming in a lawful way, might have been welcomed by wise and good men, but against Roman Catholic ascendancy. English protestantism was fighting for its life.

1686

Dispensation of particular persons from particular laws and for special reasons is allowed to have been always a part of the prerogative. But what James asserted was a power of general dispensation which would have set prerogative above all law.

To give a legal colour to royal encroachment, a bench of subservient judges was necessary. So much of respect for the constitution still remained. It was by means of such a judiciary that Charles II. had been able, without technical usurpation or breach of law, to deprive the corporations of their chartered rights and commit political murders. The crown had the power of appointing and dismissing judges at pleasure. This power was used by James to weed the bench of independence, learning, and eminence, and to fill it with court tools, for whom, to the credit of the bar, he had to look in the lowest grades of the profession. Here again he treasonably assailed the foundations of the constitution.

An ecclesiastical court of high commission had been instituted by Elizabeth for the protection of the church of England. It was revived by James for her destruc- 1686 tion. Three bishops, Cartwright, Crewe, and Sprat, were found servile enough to sit in it beside the debauched and polluted Jeffreys for that purpose. A course of aggression was commenced on the universities, the high offices of which were then clerical, evidently to pave the way for ulterior designs upon the church. Massey, a dis- 1686 credited apostate to Romanism, was thrust into the deanery of Christ Church; Obadiah Walker, another apostate, 1686 was allowed to hold the headship of University College; law being set aside by prerogative in their favour. A Roman Catholic head was forced by royal mandate upon Magdalen College; Hough, who had been duly elected, with his Fellows, was expelled, and the college was turned into a popish seminary. Cambridge also was dragooned to force her to admit a Benedictine friar, 1688 clearly against the law, as a Master of Arts. Parker, a political tool of the king's designs against the church, was made Bishop of Oxford. The violent ejection of Hough and the Fellows of Magdalen from their freeholds, striking at all free-holders, created general alarm and disaffection.

At his accession James had promised to uphold the

church as by law established, calling her a good friend to monarchy, and delighted pulpits had re-echoed his words as those of one whose plighted word was his bond. The University of Oxford had promised him submission without limits. But when the king proceeded to lay his hand on Oxford headships and fellowships, a limit to submission was found.

Finally James, advised no doubt by the purblind cunning of his Jesuits that the time for the grand stroke had arrived, put forth his Declaration of Indulgence, suspending, in favour of catholics and nonconformists, the penal code in matters of religion. He here openly set his foot upon all law. If by his fiat he could suspend one statute, he could suspend all. He had hoped to cozen the nonconformists; though on this point he might have been warned by his experience under the late reign. The nonconformists once more were better advised. As before they saw the snare, and discerned to whose advantage the triumph of Jesuitism and despotism over law would in the end enure. They were warned by the treatment of Baxter, whom Jeffreys, James's second self, had proposed to whip at the cart's tail. If they looked to Scotland they there saw their Presbyterian brethren harried and slaughtered by dragoons, such as Claverhouse, Dalziel, and Turner, hung up at their own doors, or tortured with the boot and the thumb-screw; while a woman for her religion was tied to a stake on the seashore and left to be slowly drowned by the tide. If they looked around them they saw Huguenot refugees who had fled from the persecuting sword of James's patron Louis and of the Jesuits who were masters of his counsels. They saw the bread which protestant charity gave to the

1687 and 1688

Huguenot refugee in England snatched from his mouth by James's hand. Could they believe that a most bigoted son of a church avowedly intolerant, and wherever it had power persecuting, was a genuine friend and patron of toleration? Still, the pressure of the penal laws upon them had been cruel. Relief must have been sweet, and a tribute is due to the constancy as well as to the prudence which rejected the unhallowed and insidious boon. A few of the nonconformists only went astray. Of these the most notable was William Penn, whose admirers must perforce digest the fact that a really eminent philanthropist may at the same time be a courtier and an intriguer, to use no harder term. Beyond doubt Penn both cringed to James himself and tried as a go-between to seduce Anglican clergymen and other protestants from their duty. Such are the perils of spiritual ecstasy untempered by the common moral rule. In the demeanour of the Anglican clergy towards dissenters there was wrought a wonderful change. All at once they found out that the nonconformist was their brother. There were among them some on whose part these demonstrations of amity were consistent and sincere. The circle of Tillotson and Stillingfleet, heirs of the Cambridge Platonists, and, from the breadth of their views and sympathies nicknamed Latitudinarians, were genuine liberals, desirous of the widest comprehension, and precursors of the Broad Churchmen of the present day. But in the mass of the order, sympathy with nonconformists was new-born and proved short-lived.

The Jesuit Father Petre had boasted that he would make the Anglican clergy eat dung. It would seem to have been in fulfilment of this boast, it was at all events in the mad insolence of tyranny, that he and James resolved to force all the clergy of the church of England to read the Declaration of Indulgence from their pulpits. After much searching of heart and an agonizing struggle between loyalty and professional duty, the great body of the clergy refused, while the few who complied found that they had forfeited the respect of their congregations. Seven bishops, with the Archbishop of Canterbury at their head, drew up a remonstrance in the shape of a petition couched in the most respectful terms, which they presented to the king. The petition, presented in private audience, became public, and Jeffreys, with the shallow craft of a pettifogger, suggested the prosecution of the seven bishops for a seditious libel. The bishops at once became the idols of the people, who followed them on their way to prison with prayers and blessings. The court might think that it could count upon a bench which it had packed with tools. But even to that bench and into the box of a packed jury the tidal wave of national sentiment found its way. After a trial, equal in political importance to that of ship-money and full of critical and changeful interest, the verdict was acquittal. The court made its defeat more shameful by putting into the box its secretary of state, the recreant Sunderland, to prove at the expense of the king's personal honour the publication of the alleged libel. A roar of national exultation greeted the verdict, and was taken up by the camp which James, to coerce London, had placed at Hounslow; unadvisedly, for troops quartered in or near a disaffected city are likely to catch the disaffection, as the French Guards did when they were quartered in revolutionary Paris.

James saw the public men, the church, the army, the

country, falling away from him. Even the servile Sprat, discerning the gathering storm, fled from his seat in the high commission. The king's only hope was in a parliament subservient enough to support his system. To get such a parliament elected, corruption, fraud, and violence of every kind were tried, and tried in vain. Test questions for candidates, circulated by the court, were parried by concerted answers. Local officers of the crown resigned rather than do the infamous work which was imposed upon them. Corporations, bedevilled by regulators to secure the return of court candidates, had to be bedevilled over again, and even then the court candidates were not returned. Some, elected in the court interest, ratted after the election. These open aggressions upon electoral rights, assailing the foundations of the constitution, have been truly called James's capital delinquency. No hope was left the subject but rebellion.

1688

The king found himself confronting a nation which, saving the catholics, the Quakers, and a few other nonconformists, was unanimously hostile to his designs, and felt the ground beneath his feet heave with revolt. Still, he had his army, numbering now forty thousand men, faithful, as the event showed, for the most part to its paymaster, notwithstanding the shout at Hounslow, and with Churchill in command. That the levies of rebellion, undisciplined and scattered, would be unable to cope with such a force, the fate of Monmouth's brave peasantry had shown. The memory of civil war and its horrors had not died out. There was still a fund of blind loyalty to which the king, if he would renounce his evil courses, might appeal, and which in the sequel gave him a party, and a strong party, after his forfeiture of the throne. The conduct of Halifax is not a bad criterion of the sentiments of all but the most thorough-going enemies of tyranny, and Halifax declines to take part in any strong measure of resistance. The king had no son. His heiress was his daughter Mary, married to the great European champion of protestantism and freedom. After her came his second daughter, Anne, also a steadfast protestant. His system would come to an end with his life, and that thought filled him and his Jesuits with such despair that they had conceived desperate projects of altering the succession. Most patriots, therefore, were probably inclined to content themselves with keeping up the fight in elections and law-courts, with the certain assurance that in the course of nature the tyranny must come to an end.

But an event took place which crowned the wishes of the king and the Jesuits, filled them with ecstatic gratitude to heaven, and precipitated their ruin. A son was born to the king. All now admit that the child was really his son, though so little care was taken at the time of the birth to establish that fact, and so much suspicion of foul play had been created beforehand by the silly prayers and prophecies of the Jesuits, that few even of the cool-headed and well-informed believed in the legitimacy of the Prince of Wales. James and the Jesuits had now an heir of their policy, and the door of future deliverance was closed to the nation. On the day on which the bishops were acquitted, Admiral Herbert, disguised as a common sailor, carried over to Holland a letter setting forth the discontent of the people of England, and inviting the armed intervention of William of Orange. The letter was signed by Henry Sidney, brother of the republican martyr; the Earl of Devonshire, who was the leader of the Whigs; Lord Shrewsbury; Danby, the Tory and protestant minister of Charles II.; Compton, Bishop of London, who had been a soldier before he was a clergyman; Lord Lumley; and Edward Russell. The names of the seven men who thus faced the penalty of treason to save the country and its religion are written in light, though two afterwards sadly fell from grace.

Of the Seven, four were peers, while the families of the other three were noble. This was largely an aristocratic movement. It was led by members of the aristocracy and it left the aristocracy in power. From the days of the Great Charter onwards nobility in England had been far less of a caste and more popular, than on the continent. But the Reformation had given birth to a group of houses bound to protestantism and liberalism by their traditions and by possession, with a title not even yet absolutely assured, of the Church lands. The nobles, moreover, were the immediate competitors of the court for power, and they looked on the great offices of state, into which Jesuits and sycophants were being intruded, as of right their own. Even the standing army was a special offence to their class, which commanded the national militia.

The arrival, in response to the address carried by Herbert, of William of Orange with his Dutch army of deliverance saved England at once from the tyranny and from civil war, binding her by a debt of eternal gratitude to the Dutch nation.

The portrait of William of Orange has somewhat lost by oratorical painting. He was a man of his century, in character a thorough-bred diplomatist and politician. He is thought to have shown no extreme anxiety to prevent, no excess of moral delicacy in turning to his account, the murder of the brothers De Witt, the two leaders of the opposite party in Holland. He had fought a battle with a treaty of peace in his pocket, though not to give him a safe lesson in his trade, but to save an important fortress. Nor had he any scruple when he came to the English throne in taking into employment such men as Kirke and Sunderland. The massacre of Glencoe, cast in his teeth by the scribes of a king who had bombarded Genoa, ravaged the Palatinate, and expelled the Huguenots, leaves no very dark stain on his memory; on the advice of his minister he sanctioned a proposal for the extirpation of a robber clan, having no means of knowing what the passions of a Highland feud would do. His only serious fault in that case was failure adequately to punish a powerful man when it was perhaps beyond his power. His Calvinism, painted as peculiar and sublime, was the creed of his party in Holland. Whatever he might say about predestination, his faith probably did not much affect his action, nor did it wholly save him from the lax morality of his time. His religion was hatred of French aggrandizement and devotion to the independence of Europe. He was the worthy heir of William the Silent, whom in character he resembled. So fitted was he by his temper and by his diplomatic genius for the part he had to play as the organizer and leader of a motley confederacy of nations against their common enemy and oppressor, that destiny might seem to have framed the great drama of the century and to have cast the part for the express purpose of bringing on her stage this man. Rarely has there been such a union of the qualities of the soldier with those of the negotiator and statesman. Rarely have such courage, such con-

1602

stancy, such fortitude, self-control so serene in adversity and amidst trials of every kind, been seen in any man, as were seen in this man with his feeble frame always under the depressing influence of disease. Of all William's qualities, the most admirable perhaps was a magnanimity which no waywardness, no folly, no ingratitude, no treachery on the part of those with whom and through whom he had to act for the attainment of public objects, could overcome. Ambitious he no doubt was; but his ambition was identical with the interest of his country and of Europe. On his pensive and careworn face, pensive and careworn from his very boyhood, which had been passed under the jealous eyes of the political enemies of his house, England, Holland, and every friend of the independence of nations will always look with peculiar interest and gratitude. The youthful heir of a house, idolized by the people, but excluded from its ancestral power by the burgher aristocracy of Amsterdam, he had been irresistibly called by the popular voice to command in an agony of national peril. Nobly he had answered the call, and by the spirit which he infused he had saved the nation. His political character, thus formed, would be monarchical, but popular at the same time.

The Prince of Orange had, of course, watched events in England with an anxious eye, not only as the husband of Mary, the heiress presumptive to the throne, but still more as the head of the European coalition. On the question whether England should be a vassal of France, or a member of the confederacy of nations against France, he must have felt that the fate of Europe hung. With Monmouth's enterprise he could have no sympathy. Insane in itself, it would, had it succeeded, have cut his wife out of the inheritance. He had kept on friendly, though on distant, terms with James, had given him none but sound advice, had listened to the growing complaints against him, but had not intrigued. While James had no son, wisdom bade William wait. But now that James had a son William could wait no more. A secret proffer of support from the renegade Sunderland, while it must have curled his lip with scorn, would show him that James was falling, and that the hour was come. He accepted the invitation of the Seven. Fortune at the critical moment played into his hands. Louis, in his reckless arrogance, had estranged the Dutch by blows struck at their commerce, and disposed the cautious traders to hearty sympathy with the daring enterprise of their Prince; while James in his fatuous pride had mutinied against his patron, disregarded the advice of Louis, and for the time forfeited his aid. The French arms, instead of being directed against Holland, were turned against the Empire, and William was left at liberty to form his army, collect his fleet, and sail for England. In the storm which, when he first put to sea, scattered and drove back his fleet, his serene fortitude did not forsake him. Running down the Channel he was carried by the wind past Torbay, his destined landing-place, and for a moment all seemed lost. A change of wind saved the expedition. An invasion of England by steam would be liable to no such accident.

William had landed on the shore which had been the scene of Monmouth's hapless enterprise and had been scourged by the Bloody Assize. There people came in to him slowly. But they came in from the whole country presently under leaders of mark. He put forth

a declaration skilfully framed by the Dutch statesman
Fagel, enumerating the grievances which, at the invitation of leading Englishmen, he came to redress, disclaiming any design of conquest, and submitting all to the
decision of an English parliament. At the doubt respecting the birth of James's son he cautiously and
decorously glanced. Sensible at last of his peril, James
fell into an ignoble agony of fear. He solemnly promised
to protect the church and to maintain the Act of Uniformity. He said that he would no longer insist upon
the admission of Roman Catholics to the House of Commons. He notified his intention of replacing all magistrates and deputy-lieutenants who had been displaced for
refusing to further his policy in the elections. He abolished the court of high commission. He restored to the
city of London the charter which had been forfeited six
years before, and sent his chancellor to carry it back in
state to Guildhall. He re-instated Bishop Compton, whom
he had deprived of his episcopal functions for refusing to
suspend Dr. Sharp, the preacher of a sermon against
popery. He charged the visitor of Magdalen College to
re-instate the ejected president and Fellows. To his
dispensing power he still clung; nor would he remove
Roman Catholics from civil or military office.

Even now there was the army, strong enough to resist
the invader and apparently not inclined to desert the
king; at least the first attempt to carry over a part of
it to William failed, and Cornbury, the commander who
had made that attempt, had to ride into the Dutch camp
without his men. A battle, even supposing that William
had gained the victory, would have deprived his enterprise of its character as a deliverance and fatally stamped

it as a conquest. But of the army the master was Churchill, afterwards Duke of Marlborough, and Churchill had sent William a message worth a good deal more than the tendered support of Sunderland. On this man's decision the fate of the undertaking hung. Churchill's character has been painted in violent colours. He was a scion of the court of Charles II., had won the heart of the Castlemaine by his beauty and his surpassing grace, had intrigued with her, had jumped out of her window, had received a large present of money from her, though to say that he was kept by her is harsh. When to be the mistress of a prince was deemed an honour, he had been well pleased to see his sister in the arms of James. His morality was thoroughly loose, his aims were utterly selfish, he was ignobly covetous, and he was presently to be guilty of villainy, the dark memory of which can scarcely be lost even in the blaze of his after glory. In any other age his unscrupulousness would have been portentous. His course, now as always, was determined by his interest, and his interest was bound up with that of the Princess Anne, heiress presumptive to the crown after Mary, who had no child, and under the influence of his domineering wife. For liberty or the principles of the constitution he probably cared nothing. He was a soldier and a courtier, and would perhaps have liked best to serve a king such as the king of France. But to his personal aspirations the birth of a Prince of Wales, as it shut out Anne, was a fatal blow. His strong sense, moreover, must have shown him that the king was rushing upon his own ruin or that of the realm. He saw that, like all who served James, he would in the end have to choose between a loss of his office and a change of his religion. Fear of having to change his religion was the justification which he pleaded for his desertion in his highly decorous and sanctimonious letter of farewell to James. Nor need we assume that this was mere hypocrisy. Marlborough had long before told Burnet that nothing would induce him to apostatize. That with all his unscrupulousness he was not wholly devoid of religious sentiment, his habit of having prayers read and receiving the sacrament before battle, seems to show. Nor can popery as a system, with its Jesuits and its thaumaturgy, have failed to repel his powerful mind. To tax him with military desertion would be absurd. At such a crisis the duty of the soldier was lost in that of the citizen. Neither can much be said about personal ingratitude to James, for whom Churchill had done at Sedgemoor as much as ever James had done for him. That he should conceal his intention of passing over to William was inevitable; had he betrayed it he would have been arrested; and the concealment involved deception which those who were deceived would brand as treachery. Churchill inflicted another and a heavy blow on James by carrying over with him Anne and her husband, Prince George of Denmark.

James now resolved on flight. He sent his queen with the Prince of Wales over to France, and himself set out in disguise to follow them. That he might leave anarchy behind him he threw the great seal into the Thames, burned the writs for the new parliament, and issued an order for the disbandment of the army. A night of anarchy and terror in London, in fact, ensued. Then such of the peers as were at hand met and formed themselves into a provisional government, which restored order

1688

and issued injunctions to the commanders of the forces not to resist the Prince of Orange. James was unluckily detained, as he was embarking, by some fishermen, who, not recognizing him, ruffled by their treatment the divinity of the Lord's anointed; an impiety for which they were never forgiven by James, who afterwards excepted them from his promises of pardon. He was thus thrown back on the hands of William, to William's extreme embarrassment. There was nothing for it but to frighten him into a second flight. This time care was taken that he should not be detained. Sacred majesty, dethroned by the profane hands of rebels and heretics, was received with open arms by Louis, treated with generosity the most profuse and delicate, installed in the royal residence of St. Germains, and provided with a magnificent income, wrung, like the rest of the grand monarch's magnificence, from the starving peasantry of France. St. Germains was thenceforth the Mecca of Jacobite pilgrimage and intrigue.

Now came the task of settling the kingdom. William had declared that he would leave all to parliament. Legal parliament there was none, James having destroyed the writs. But a substitute morally sufficient was found in a Convention formed by the House of Lords with a House of Commons comprising all who had sat in the House during the previous reign, that is, before the House had been packed by James. William, faithful to his engagement and his character, stood apart in silence. So far Tories and Whigs, united by common grievances and perils, had acted together. The divergence of their principles now appeared. The Whigs, holding the doctrine of the original contract between king and people, and

1688

deeming that James had broken that contract, would have deposed him and elected a successor. The Tories clung to their doctrine of hereditary succession and divine right. Some would have had James restored under conditions and with pledges, as though he had not ascended the throne under conditions which he had shamelessly broken, and as though any pledge could be more binding than the coronation oath. Archbishop Sancroft proposed a regency, which would have severed the allegiance of the subject from his obedience, his allegiance being due to the legitimate king in exile, while his obedience would have been due to the regent at home, and the result of which might have been a succession of regents on one side of the water maintaining themselves by arms against a succession of legitimate kings on the other. To such absurdities could political superstition lead. The high Tory Danby maintained that the throne of England could never be vacant, and would have had Mary proclaimed sole sovereign. From a measure which would have deprived England and the coalition of their indispensable head, the good sense of Mary herself saved the nation, and lasting gratitude is due to her for what she did and for the sweet forgetfulness of self with which she did it. The Whigs and Tories mixed, though they could not fuse, their principles in the famous resolution "that king James II., having endeavoured to subvert the constitution of the kingdom by breaking the original contract between king and people, and having, by the advice of Jesuits and other wicked persons, violated the fundamental laws and withdrawn himself out of the kingdom, has abdicated the government, and that the throne is thereby vacant." The spirit of Locke triumphs over

Filmer in the reference to the original contract between king and people. The reference to "the fundamental laws" shows that the idea of a constitution had been fully formed, the whole discussion shows the growing influence of political philosophy in the practical counsels of statesmen. The crown was given jointly to William and Mary; the executive authority was given to William alone, who was thus sole king, though everything was done in the joint name.

James had fled the kingdom, carried off his son with him, and abandoned the nation to anarchy by making away with the great seal, burning the writs for the election of parliament, and disbanding the army. It might have been sufficient, without raising any theoretic or debatable question, to recite these facts and declare that James had ceased to reign, letting Mary take the vacant throne, and at once, by Act of Parliament, associating William with her in joint sovereignty and giving him the sole administration. But this would not have laid the ghost of hereditary right divine and indefeasible, or for ever precluded attempts on the part of the monarch to bring the practice into conformity with the right. It was better that James should be deposed for violation of the constitution and breach of the original contract between king and people, the sanctity of the constitution and the existence of the contract being thereby affirmed. Deposed he was; that he had abdicated was a politic fiction, as his actions speedily proved.

To settle the principle on which James was to be deposed amid conflicting theories had been difficult. It was not so difficult to enumerate the reasons for deposing him. This it was wisely resolved to do without delay.

that the crown might pass under no doubtful conditions
to the new dynasty. The Declaration of Right framed
by the Convention, and afterwards ratified by a regular
parliament in the Bill of Rights, ranks with the Great
Charter and the Petition of Right among the muniments
of constitutional liberty. It sets forth and asserts all the
principles of the law and the constitution which had been
violated by the tyranny. It denies the pretended power
of suspending the laws or dispensing with them assumed
in the Declaration of Indulgence. It condemns the erection of such courts as the ecclesiastical commission; levying money by prerogative without parliamentary grant, as
the customs had been levied by James in the beginning
of his reign, or for longer time or in other manner than
the same had been granted; and maintenance of a standing
army in time of peace unless with the consent of parliament. It asserts the right of protestant citizens to have
arms for their defence, of which James's emissary had
deprived them in Ireland. It asserts the right of subjects
to petition the king, infringed in the case of the seven
bishops. It proclaims that the election of members of
parliament, with which James had arbitrarily interfered,
shall be free, and that speech in parliament shall be free
also. It prohibits excessive bail, excessive fines, and
such extraordinary punishments as had been inflicted
upon Oates and Dangerfield. To prevent the packing of
juries, especially in cases of high treason, as they had
been packed by sycophant sheriffs like Dudley North,
under James and Jeffreys, it provides that jurors shall
be duly empanelled, and that in cases of treason they shall
be free-holders. For the redress of grievances and for
the amendment and preservation of the law it ordains

1688–1689

that parliaments shall be frequently held. By the Bill of Rights, papists, and any who, like James, should marry a papist, are declared incapable of wearing the crown. In such a case the people are absolved from all allegiance, and the crown is to pass to the next heir; a near approach to the principle of election. Thus the Exclusion Bill was accepted by the nation after all. Papists being what they then were, and what James and Mary of Modena had shown themselves to be, this last article, which might now be one of religious intolerance, was, as well as the rest, one of political self-defence. Upon these terms William and Mary ascended the throne. Their title was, and the title of the Princes of the house of Hanover, whom the Act of Settlement made their heirs, is still, an Act of Parliament, subject to repeal or amendment by the same authority by which it was made.

1696 To the safeguard for the composition of juries in cases of treason secured by the Bill of Rights was added after some delay the abrogation of the barbarous rule which, treating a man accused of treason as guilty before he had been tried, had denied him counsel, denied him an inspection of the indictment, denied him the benefit of sworn evidence in his favour, and made a treason court, with a Stuart judge on the bench, an instrument of legal murder. At the time it was against a king who was the soul of the Whig cause that the dagger of the assassin was turned, and from Tories came the support of the reform, from Whigs came such opposition as there was to its immediate adoption. In the debate, by a happy artifice of rhetoric, for such it probably was, a speaker in support of the measure affected to break down, and then, apparently recovering himself, bade the House consider, if his nerve thus failed him when there was so little to shake it, what must be the case of a poor prisoner unskilled in the law, and without power of expression, when he was set to plead for his life against the skilled advocates of the crown. The character of the courts, however, was changed, and a treason trial before Holt was far different from a treason trial before Jeffreys.

One vital security for personal liberty was still lacking. It was added towards the end of the new king's reign by a statute which established the independence of the judges by providing that they should receive fixed salaries, and hold their offices, not at the pleasure of the crown, but during good behaviour, and be removable only on the address of both Houses of parliament. The office of the lord chancellor, the highest judge in Equity, is still political and its holder goes out of office with his party. Otherwise no judge since the time of William III. has been deprived for a political reason. The appointments to the bench long continued to be political, though within a circle traced by professional eminence. But of late even the appointments have become more professional. Since the independence of the English judiciary was secured, the purity of the ermine has been preserved. To this great principle America has been less faithful than England, for if the judge holds the office not during good conduct but at pleasure, as he does when he has to look for re-election, it signifies little whether the pleasure is that of a king or that of a political party styling itself the people. At the same time the coercion or intimidation of juries, practised hitherto, as in the case of Alice Lisle, ceased, and their independence, as well as that of the judges, was secured.

1701

Whatever principles might be laid down, there was no safety for liberty, as recent experience had shown, if the crown could maintain a standing army without the leave or control of parliament. Against this the Declaration of Right and the Bill of Rights provided by denunciation of the abuse, and, more effectually, by prohibiting the raising of the money necessary for the maintenance of the army without a parliamentary grant. Hitherto there had been no military laws to enforce discipline and prevent desertion, other than the ordinances which the crown assumed the power of putting forth for the regulation of the forces when called into the field. An abuse of this power by Charles I. had been the subject of a remedial article in the Petition of Right. But the question having been raised by the mutiny of one of the regiments against the new government, parliament took the matter into its own jurisdiction and passed a Mutiny Act. The Mutiny Act ultimately being made annual, parliament has the power from year to year of terminating the control of the crown over the soldier, and practically breaking up the army. No one will confound the martial law which regulates the army, with the martial law which is a supersession of ordinary law by court-martial in time of great public danger, applying to the whole community alike and forming a counterpart to the French State of Siege. Martial law in the second sense is still unrecognized by the constitution and unregulated, as abuse of it has shown. From the passing of the Mutiny Act may be said to date the existence of the standing army as a British institution. The fears of which it then was, and long continued to be, the real or pretended object proved unfounded. An army, recruited from an

1689

obedient peasantry and commanded by gentlemen belonging to a thoroughly constitutional class, never menaced British liberties. Public order, when the police fails, is best restored by the regular soldier, who, unaffected by political passion and obedient to discipline, fires when the word of command is given and not before. The people respect and fear him, so that riot is generally quelled without bloodshed by his appearance on the scene.

The Bill of Rights, with the annual Mutiny Act, makes monarchy constitutional. It ends the long struggle for supremacy between king and parliament. If this did not fully appear during William's reign, it was partly because his position as head of a European confederacy, together with his sole mastery of foreign affairs, made him necessarily supreme in that department; partly because the House of Commons could not at once organize itself for the exercise of its powers and the virtual control of the executive. But if after William's reign personal government was renewed, it was for the time only, and in the way of influence, rather than by prerogative or in avowed exercise of an authority recognized by the constitution. The ministers of state are still appointed by the king, whose influence for some time to come will be largely felt in the appointments, but his choice is gradually limited to the leaders of the party which has the majority in the Commons, until at last it has become little more than a formal recognition.

Not only was the raising of money by the king without parliamentary grant condemned, but the king was docked of a part of the fixed revenue which the reckless royalists of the last parliament had granted James for his life.

William felt hurt by what he deemed want of confidence, but the change was a corollary of the Revolution.

By the poor, to whom bread is more than politics, the Revolution made itself felt as a power of good in the abolition of the grinding and inquisitorial hearth tax, which had been imposed by the Restoration.

For the settlement of the church question two policies presented themselves; that of comprehension, and that of toleration. The best policy of all, perfect liberty of conscience, had even now found access only to a few prophetic and a few erratic minds. Comprehension had been the policy of the Protectorate. It was the cherished policy of William. It was the policy of the excellent Archbishop Tillotson, the adviser of William and Mary in religious matters, of Stillingfleet and the Latitudinarians. But the Latitudinarians were strong only in London and other centres of intelligence. The clergy generally, the danger to the church from James's aggression being overpast, had soon recovered from their fit of charitable feeling towards nonconformists. They were by this time resolved to abate not a jot of their pretensions and firmly set against any change in Anglican ritual or polity. Their intolerance had found an excuse in the treatment of the episcopal clergy by victorious Presbyterians in Scotland, yet their conduct was odious and reprobated by the best men of their own order. Those sects which no comprehension could comprehend, because they objected to state connection altogether, such as the Baptists and Quakers, would, of course, be opposed to a measure by which they could not benefit. Comprehension would have practically strengthened the establishment; it was, in fact, supported by the Tory Nottingham and by Bishop Compton with that view. There seems to be truth in the surmise that the leading nonconformist ministers themselves cared little to exchange the lucrative and influential preacherships of rich city congregations for the position of parochial clergy in the state church. A Bill which would have brought within the pale of the national church Presbyterians and other Trinitarians who did not object to state connection was framed and ardently pressed. The king, more Liberal than Calvinist, was all for comprehension. But as discussion went on support flagged, and in the end the Bill was allowed to drop. Formally relegated to convocation, in the lower house of which the rural and high-church clergy prevailed, though the upper house, where sat the Liberal bishops, was in its favour, it speedily found its grave. 1689 1689

The policy adopted was that of toleration. Narrow enough to us the measure of toleration seems, though it was regarded as a great charter of religious liberty in its day. Compulsory attendance at the services of the state church was abolished. But of the penal statutes of conformity none were struck off the statute book; the Act only provided that they should not extend to anyone who had proved his loyalty by taking the oaths of allegiance and supremacy, and his protestantism by making his declaration against transubstantiation. The Act of Uniformity and the Conventicle Act were not repealed; they were only relaxed. Dissenting ministers, before they could preach, were to be required to sign all the Articles of the church of England, saving those which affirmed that the church had power to regulate ceremonies, that the doctrines of the book of homilies were sound, and that there was nothing superstitious or idolatrous in the 1689 ordination service. Baptists were to be excused from assenting to infant baptism. For Quakers, who would take no oath, a declaration against transubstantiation, a promise of loyalty, and a confession of Christian belief, were to be the test. Nonconformists acquired legal security for their chapels and funds, with something approaching a clerical status for their ministers. The Test Act and the Corporation Act remained in force, and it was specially declared that no indulgence was intended for any papist or for anyone who denied the doctrine of the Trinity. The Toleration Act has been lauded as forming, by the practical wisdom which shines through its manifest imperfections and inconsistencies, an ideal specimen of English legislation. It may readily be conceded that the utmost which could be done at the time was the best thing to do. But it should also be remarked that by this policy was perpetuated, it might be inevitably, the division of the nation into the two hostile, or at least mutually estranged, bodies of churchmen and dissenters. The division was social, political, and intellectual, as well as religious. The dissenters, being excluded by tests from the universities, were denied culture, and contemned for their lack of it. They were trained apart from their fellow-citizens of the state church, with different ideas and sympathies. They always felt themselves, and had reason to feel themselves, in every way disrated; always looked on churchmen not only as a privileged set, but as a dominant class; were always more or less disaffected towards the whole polity of which Anglican supremacy formed a part.

Niggardly, however, as the Toleration Act was, it at least recognized dissent and shook the belief, held, be it remembered, by Presbyterians as well as by Anglicans, that the state was bound to provide all its members with religion and to force it on their acceptance. The recognition of Presbyterianism in Scotland, and the connection of the crown with it, would have the same effect. Nor could the religious headship of the king, and the national respect for him as a sacred personage, fail to be impaired when the king was a Calvinist, an avowed Latitudinarian, and out of the line of divine succession. Charles II., his harem notwithstanding, had been "our most religious and gracious king," and had touched tens of thousands for the King's Evil. No one was touched for the King's Evil by William III.

Most of the bishops and clergy took the oath of allegiance to William and Mary, the high churchmen blinking their doctrine of divine right with more or less of effort and more or less of sophistical explanation. But the primate, Sancroft, and seven other bishops, of whom five, besides Sancroft, had been among the famous Seven, with some minor dignitaries and about four hundred other clergymen or graduates, refused the oath and incurred the penalty of deprivation. The recusants, under the name of Nonjurors, seceded and founded a little church of their own, to which, if it was made ridiculous by crazy pedants like Hickes and Dodwell, dignity was lent by the character of Ken. That saintly prelate, having required of Monmouth, on the scaffold, a profession of non-resistance as the condition of absolution, could hardly himself have taken the oath to a government of resistance. Yet his secession was avowedly reluctant, nor did he seek to draw others with him. The clergy of the little church of nonjurors furnished chaplains and tutors to Jacobite

1689

squires. Having few laity to engage their pastoral care, they took to political, and, it was said, sometimes to domestic intrigue. Without substantial basis or real spiritual life their church lingered, ever dwindling, on the verge of existence, for nearly a century, when it expired in the person of a bishop, who had been constrained to earn his bread as a surgeon. It would be difficult to find another instance of religious secession on a purely political ground, as it would to find a church which avowedly treated a political dogma as a vital article of its faith. Lake, Bishop of Chichester, said on his deathbed that he looked on the great doctrine of passive obedience as the distinguishing character of the Church of England and as a doctrine for which he would lay down his life.

1805

The Revolution in England was bloodless, saving one or two petty skirmishes between the soldiers of James and those of William. It was peaceful, saving the few hours of riot in London. Against any outpouring of vengeance William's character was a guarantee; even Jeffreys, instead of being torn in pieces or hanged by a lamp-chain, was allowed to die in prison, and to bequeath his ill-gotten wealth and title to his son, who took his seat in the House of Lords. Crewe and Sprat remained in possession of their bishoprics; Kirke kept his regiment; the statue of the fallen tyrant stood unmolested over the gate of University College at Oxford, though the apostate Master of the College was removed. There were wrongs to be righted, and reparations to be made. The attainders of the Whig martyrs Russell and Sidney were reversed, that of Russell amid general emotion. The wretched Oates was released and pensioned. Liberal

1689

philosophy in the person of Locke returned from its exile in Holland. The charters of cities and boroughs, forfeited under Charles, were restored. The Whigs would have disfranchised for several years all who had taken part in the surrender. They would have imposed an abjuration of king James upon all office-holders and all to whom a magistrate might tender it. They would have made a number of exceptions from indemnity. But William came down with an Act of Grace extending indemnity to all with a few exceptions, and those mostly of a nominal kind.

1690

At the head of the exceptions from grace stood the judges of Charles I. One of them, the Republican Ludlow, inspired by the Revolution with hopes for the good old cause, came over from his Swiss asylum to England. But he found that for the good old cause there was no hope, and that the name of the regicide was as much abhorred as ever. He represented one of the forces of which 1688 was the resultant; but the resultant did not recognize the force. Yet William was in great measure taking up the work of Cromwell.

Even the enforcement of oaths of allegiance to the new government was a policy of the times from which true policy perhaps would have departed. It awakened scruples which might have slept; it made secret enemies of many who complied, but whose self-respect was wounded by compliance. It drove the non-jurors to secession. Wisdom would have been content with submission.

In Scotland the tyranny had been worse than in England, and the reaction had been proportionately strong. There, instead of declaring the throne vacant, in language balanced between the theories of hereditary right and original contract, James was summarily deposed for his misdeeds. If this was unavoidable in a case where, royalty being always absent, the throne was never full, and, so could hardly be said to have been vacated, it was at the same time the hearty act of the people. Nor was the Revolution in Scotland free from violence. The episcopalian clergy, especially in the west, were rabbled, that is, mobbed and turned out of their manses, by the peasantry who had been hunted down and whose kinsmen had been hanged over their doors by episcopalian troopers. The prelatical establishment was swept away, and the Presbyterian establishment was restored, with its democratic organization, with its general assembly, with its simplicity of worship, and with its intolerance. William would have preferred a moderate episcopacy, both as in itself more congenial to monarchy, and because he, like Edward I., Bacon, and Cromwell, desired the union of Scotland with England, to which the severance of the churches was a bar. The Kirk was not restored entirely in its pristine beauty. Something of royal influence, such as a high-flying Covenanter would deem Erastian, over the assembly of the Kirk was reserved to the king or his commissioner, and an element of lay patronage in the appointment of ministers was retained. Besides, William was not a Covenanting king. On these grounds the extreme Covenanters seceded and formed a separate sect. On the other hand, the staunch episcopalians founded an independent church in Scotland, naturally indemnifying themselves for disestablishment by indulgence in doctrine or sentiment somewhat higher than that of the state church in England. Thus Scotland had two sets of nonjurors, episcopal and Covenanting. The sect of Cove-

haunting nonjurors, slender as was its thread of life, long clung with Scotch tenacity to existence, but at last died. The episcopalian church of Scotland still lives, and it was enabled by its independence to transmit apostolical succession to the Episcopal Church of the United States, rent from the state church of England by the American Revolution, which the church of England was precluded from doing by the closeness of its connection with the state.

There was more than rabbling in Scotland; there was civil war, not, however, among the Lowland Scotch, nor properly speaking as an incident of the Revolution. This was a Highland war of clan against clan, none of the clans knowing or caring much about English politics or parties, though a section of them was brought into the field in the name of king James. The Earl of Argyle, by Highlanders called McCallum More, head of the powerful and domineering clan Campbell, was a Whig, and had carried with him his clansmen to that party. This was enough to make the rival clans Tory, while all the clans alike were ready for a raid, no matter in what cause, on the lands of the Saxon. Thus James's lieutenant and emissary, Claverhouse, now Viscount Dundee, the romantic and ruthless leader of the persecuting bands, was able to raise a Highland army in his master's name. At the pass of Killiecrankie he encountered a body of the regular troops under William's general, Mackay, and, thanks to the impetuous charge of his Highlanders with their claymores, gained a brilliant victory. But Dundee himself fell. The Highland host melted away as it had gathered, like a snow wreath, and there was soon an end of the war. Two effects, however, remained. One was

1689

the extension of the system commenced under Cromwell by Monck of bridling the wild Highlanders with forts. The other was an improvement of the bayonet, to the clumsiness of which Mackay owed his defeat at Killiecrankie. In place of a bayonet fixed in the muzzle of the gun, which prevented firing, Mackay invented one which could be fixed without plugging the gun. The missile weapon and the steel, that of the pikeman and that of the musketeer, long separated, were thus brought together again, as they had partly been in the hands of the Roman soldier, who threw the javelin before closing with the sword. This would give the foot soldier an advantage over the horseman; and no military change is without its political effect.

The chief scene of calamity and bloodshed once more was hapless Ireland. There the struggle was still not one of political principle, but one between races and for the land, embittered by difference of religion. Little recked the catholic Celt of questions between Whig and Tory, or of disputes about hereditary right and the original contract. Nor cared he much for king James, though king James was, like himself, a Roman Catholic, except so far as James was an enemy to the English government and lent his countenance to Irish revolt. What the Celt wanted was to expel the Saxon from the island and to win back the land for the Celt. Towards that mark Tyrconnel and his crew madly drove. They assembled at Dublin a parliament of Celts and catholics, the action of which was a presage of what the bent of such a parliament if again assembled might be. It repealed Charles II.'s Act of Settlement, which secured to protestants their lands. It thus gave the word for a sweeping

1689

reconfiscation which, had it kept its power, would certainly have ensued. It did not stop here. In its frenzy of hatred it passed a great Act of Attainder embracing between two and three thousand names, and including, with half the peerage of Ireland, baronets, clergymen, squires, merchants, yeomen, artisans, women, and children. Days were fixed before which those whose names were on the list were to surrender themselves to the mercy of their raging enemies at Dublin. Anyone failing to appear was doomed to death and confiscation without trial. To make sure work, the power of pardoning was taken from the king. The worst part of the Act may have been merely ferocious menace; but the Celt was not in a merciful mood. A fitting concomitant of such legislation was a boundless issue of base coin, if pieces of old brass could be dignified with the name of coin at all. This also to the protestant merchant and creditor was a measure of confiscation. The protestants were excluded from the jury box, that is, from any chance of justice; were disarmed, and thus marked out as sheep for the slaughter. Over the island meanwhile reigned misrule, havoc, and rapine. Protestants were everywhere flying panic-stricken from their homes. Massacre like that of 1641 impended. There was a design of severing Ireland from Great Britian and making it a dependency of France; as, if ever it were severed from Great Britain, it would probably become. Louis, having now taken up arms against England in the cause of catholicism and kings, sent James to Ireland with subsidies and French commanders. The Celts, flocking to his standard, formed an army large but ill-armed, ragged, predatory, and tumultuous. At Dublin he found himself harassed by factions

1689

1689

among the patriots like those of the Parnellites and anti-Parnellites in after days. A catholic and the enemy of a usurping king of England, he was still himself an English king, and it was with reluctance that he assented to the dispossession and proscription of his race, coupled with the suspension of his own prerogative. Nor was his the character, nor were his the manners, to win the Irish heart.

In Ulster, its chief seat, the ruling race gathered in places of refuge, turned to bay, and gave memorable proof of its superiority in moral force. Sallying forth from Enniskillen, one of its last strongholds, it utterly overthrew a Celtic army at Newton Butler. But its most famous exploit was the defence of Londonderry, where it heroically held a weak and mouldering wall against a great Celtic host under French command, and still more heroically bore the utmost extremities of famine, while Kirke, coward or traitor as well as butcher, lay with the relieving squadron inactive in sight of the city. Irish protestantism has never ceased to draw proud confidence in its power from the story of the siege of Derry, or to glory in the memory of Walker, the protestant clergyman, who was the religious soul of the defence. The most vivid of narrators in our day has given immortal splendour to the story.

It was some time before the force of England, troubled and divided in herself, could be brought effectually to bear on Ireland. Schomberg, William's marshal, and the first of European strategists, came over with an army. But under Stuart government the public service and notably the commissariat had become utterly corrupt and rotten. Contracts, as well as honours, commands, offices, and pardons, had been sold in open market at Whitehall. Schomberg's army was paralyzed and wasted away by want owing to the frauds of contractors combined with the disease bred by the dampness of the climate and aggravated by the helplessness of the raw levies, though the veteran managed with his famishing and dwindling battalions to show a front which commanded the respect of the foe. At last William himself came over, and at 1690 the Battle of the Boyne, a name ever dear to Orangemen, and repeated in their songs of triumph, overthrew the army of James and entered Dublin. James, who had shown no courage or conduct in the field, fled to France to return no more. The war, however, did not end here. Again the Celts, under the French General, St. Ruth, encountered the army of William under Ginkell, and at Aghrim were again overthrown. But they redeemed their 1691 reputation as soldiers by the stand which they made at Limerick under Sarsfield, a gallant partisan leader. By 1691 a bold move of Sarsfield, William's battering train was cut off, and he was compelled to raise the siege. Whatever may have been the cause, whether he was inclined to temporize or not, he did not show the decisive vigour of Cromwell in putting an end to the war. He seems hardly to have understood the Irish question, or to have seen that it was not merely a religious quarrel which his liberal policy of toleration might allay, but an internecine struggle between the two races and religions for the possession of the land. In the end Limerick surrendered to 1691 Ginkell, while Marlborough's resistless genius completed the work. The flower of the Celtic soldiery with Sarsfield left their native land to take service in the catholic armies of the continent, in which some of them rose high. In arms, though not in industry or political intelligence, they were an off-set for the Huguenots, whom the head of the catholic cause had driven as exiles to protestant lands.

Now came the day of retribution for all that the protestants had suffered, for the repeal of the Act of Settlement, and for the passing of the Act of Attainder. William was always tolerant, always disposed to amnesty, and would have restrained vengeance if he could. But to restrain it in this case was beyond his power. The weary and hateful story of transfer of the land by confiscation for an insurrection of race was repeated. The victorious race which had barely escaped with property and life proceeded to bind down the vanquished with iron fetters of penal law. Cruel and hateful as the penal code was, it was penned not so much by bigotry as by political and social fear. It assumed a religious form because religion was identified with race. To deprive a hostile race of all means of rising again and renewing the conflict rather than to repress a rival religion was its aim. To prevent combination among the catholics, it confined all native priests to their own parishes, while to deprive conspiracy of encouragement from abroad it banished foreign priests on pain of death. It contained provisions framed with ruthless ingenuity for breaking up the landed estates of catholics, and preventing them from acquiring free-hold property in land. It enabled and tempted, against natural affection, the protestant son to dispossess his catholic father. It forbade catholics, as the catholics in their hour of ascendancy had forbidden protestants, to have arms. It forbade them to have a horse of above five pounds' value. It prohibited them from keeping schools. To deprive them of political power, they were excluded from parliament and from all public offices. To deprive them of social influence they were excluded from the university and from the bar. The victorious protestant reduced the catholic to a political and social pariah. The catholic, had he been victorious, would have exterminated or expelled the protestant. When he had been completely crushed, and the fears of the protestants had abated, evasion of the code began and at last the most cruel of its enactments fell into practical desuetude. The enactments against the catholic priesthood took not full effect. The priest-hunter was odious, and the priest, disestablished and poor, but preserved by his poverty from corruption, remained the guide and comforter of the vanquished Celt through the night of penal serfdom; while the people clung to the religion of their race, the efforts to convert them from which, if a corrupt and plethoric establishment made any, proved vain. The property clauses of the penal code, however, had their effect, and at last only one-tenth part of the land of Ireland remained in catholic hands. To fill the cup of bitterness to overflowing, came back the intrusive Anglican establishment with its bloated hierarchy, devouring by its imposts the substance of peasants to whom it was alien and hateful, while it could render them no sort of service; making protestantism doubly odious to the catholics; and at the same time persecuting free protestant churches, by which it was possible that something in the way of conversion might have been done. In the history of political folly and iniquity few things will be found to match the Anglican establishment in Ireland.

CHAPTER III

WILLIAM III

BORN 1650; DECLARED KING 1689; DIED 1702

WILLIAM III., though at first he reigned in the name of his gentle partner, as well as in his own, was sole king.

William was cold in manner, though not in heart; grave, as one whose life was divided between the council chamber and the battlefield well might be; silent as his illustrious ancestor had been, and the more silent in England because he could not speak English well. As the head at once of a realm still troubled and of a European coalition, he had little time for small talk with men or dalliance with women. He had to be much abroad, and when he was at home his asthma made him a valetudinarian and a recluse, and prevented him from living in London. He withdrew to Hampton Court or Kensington, and at Westminster there was a court no more. His wife, though helpful, as well as sensible and virtuous, could scarcely make up for his social defects. A foreigner he could not help being; a foreigner among islanders: islanders, too, who had borne his fellow-countrymen, the Dutch, as rivals in commerce, little good will. He may have made a mistake in keeping his Dutch Guards. The feeling of Englishmen against the Dutch in general was an ungrateful prejudice. But with prejudice and ingratitude statesmanship has to deal. William made a serious mistake in his largesses to his Dutch favourites. Nor was he always well advised either in his choice of ministers or in his attempts to retain the remnants of the royal prerogative. Still, the treatment of the deliverer by the Tory party in England, and by the vulgar generally, while he was toiling and facing the shot for the great cause, is a dark blot on the annals of the nation. Its blackness is seen by contrast with the loyalty which glows in Defoe.

Scarcely had William rid the country of the tyranny when a Jacobite party for the recall of the tyrant was formed. Its busiest agents and preachers were nonjuring clergy, who, being without congregations, had all their time for politics. The country clergy generally leant to the same side, and, if not Jacobites, were Tories and enemies to the Revolution government. Addison twitted these parsons with their wisdom in holding that the church of England could never be safe until she had a popish defender. He did not see that absolutism rather than protestantism was the vital article of their creed. With the parsons went many of the squires, each of them a little autocrat in his own sphere, and, therefore, a friend of autocracy, while their jealousy was excited by the growing influence of the commercial and moneyed class, which adhered to the Revolution government and throve by its financial operations. As war went on and war taxation increased, the squire was further estranged by the reduction of his income and the increase in the price of his wine for objects little dear to his heart. The army was sore under the sense of having played rather a sorry part, and jealous of the Dutch Guard. One regiment broke out into mutiny. The mob hated the foreigner, and it is

1689

1689

naturally on the side of opposition. Disappointments, national and personal, follow every revolution. The scramble for place left many malcontents. Nor could William cure in an instant the deep-seated maladies of the Stuart administration. The military and naval departments, like the rest, were rotten and full of corruption. Schomberg's army in Ireland had been ruined by the roguery of the commissary-general Shales.

1689-1690

The tyrant, deposed and exiled, became an object of pity. So rapid and so strong was the reaction, that self-seeking and unscrupulous politicians deemed it for their interest to open communications with the exiled court, less, probably, with the intention of themselves restoring James, whose unforgiving temper they must have known too well, than with a view of hedging against a possible restoration. The perfidy of these men was unspeakable, and opened a revolting scene of treason, at the same time throwing back a lurid light on the public life of the preceding reign, in which they had been bred. Some of them, such as Godolphin, Shrewsbury, and Marlborough, were holding high office or command under William and enjoying his confidence while they betrayed him and the nation. Shrewsbury had signed the invitation to the Prince of Orange; so had Russell, who was also among the plotters, though it was pique probably rather than interest that led him astray. Mere pique, where there was such moral levity, would probably account for much, and had invasion been imminent, those who dallied with the fallen tyrant would very likely have ranged themselves on the national side. Sunderland, the most profligate of all the politicians, was not among the plotters. Either he deemed a restoration really impossible, or, having been a pretended convert to Roman Catholicism and afterwards relapsed, he despaired of reconciliation with such a bigot as James. Of all the traitors, the worst was Marlborough, who, to buy a pardon from James, betrayed to him the expedition against Brest, causing thereby the failure of the expedition and the death of the gallant Talmash, its commander. No other British soldier has been guilty of a crime so foul. Excuses are vain. It is said that other traitors had given the information before Marlborough. Unless he knew it, this makes no difference; and if he did know it, he was bound to warn the government. He well deserved to be shot, or rather to be hanged. His apologists had better leave his case alone, and let his political infamy be lost, as far as it may, in his military glory. He was a man, like Napoleon, devoid of moral sense. If he ever had any, he must have left it in the ante-chambers of Charles II. But it does not follow because a man has no conscience that his heart is cold. Alexander VI. was a very loving father. Marlborough passionately loved his wife, termagant as she was. Once, to vex him, she cut off her hair, the beauty of which was his pride, and threw it in his way. He picked it up, and when he died it was found among the cherished treasures of the victor of Blenheim. The depth of Marlborough's treason William never knew; but he knew that he was treacherous, and for a time disgraced him. The king either knew or strongly suspected that there was treason all around him. Yet he shut his eyes and made use of the men, trusting that their present interest would lead them to serve him and the country well, as it notably did in the case of the prince of administrators, Godolphin. To resent conspiracy against himself William was too

1694

magnanimous, provided he could prevent it from hurting the state. In the case of Shrewsbury, to whom he singularly and almost mysteriously clung, his magnanimity was justified by a bitter repentance.

There is no saying what might have happened had James been a man open to the teaching of adversity, and capable of stooping to discretion. But he was in his own eyes, as his priests and courtiers had taught him, a divinity, and his hallucination was confirmed by his contact with the solar autocracy of France. He made the cause of his friends in England desperate by his manifestoes, which, instead of promises of amendment on his own part, and of constitutional government, breathed nothing but the wrath of injured majesty. The idea that the impiety of men could actually prevail against the Lord's anointed, or that a nation could live without its legitimate king, seems never to have entered his mind. His party in England being damped and broken by his folly, his only hope lay in French assistance, and against French invasion the spirit of the whole English nation, saving the most fanatical Jacobites, took arms. Russell had intrigued with St. Germains; but when he met the fleet which was to convoy James with a French army to England, he became once more an English seaman, and gained the great victory of La Hogue. The Stuart scheme of establishing absolute government and catholicism in England by the help of France would always have been defeated, when it came to the point of intervention, by the spirit of the English nation.

1692

The first part of the reign was a period of distraction in the king's councils and confusion in parliament attendant on the final transition from the old system of the privy council, which included men of different principles and was not connected with a party in parliament, to that of the cabinet, formed of men united in principle with an organized party in parliament as its base. William at first refused to recognize party, and made up his government of Whigs and Tories combined; like Washington, who, treating party not as a permanent force but as a transient malady, combined Hamilton with Jefferson in the administration. He had even, as king, some leaning towards the Tories as the more decided monarchists, and the better friends to prerogative. while he was harassed by the unreasonable expectations and demands of the Whigs. The consequence was discord and jarring in every department, except that of foreign affairs, which, as not being national, but European, the chief of coalized Europe kept in his own hands. Sunderland, not less shrewd than unscrupulous, having stolen back to politics and the king's ear, taught William that to give unity and efficiency to his government he must call to his councils men of one party alone. To choose between the parties was after all not difficult, since it was upon Whig principles that William had been raised to the throne, and the Whigs, however some of them might have swerved from their fidelity, were enemies of the house of Stuart. A Whig ministry, accordingly, was formed, and the Whig party in parliament was organized as its base under a junto of powerful leaders. The Tory party formed an opposition, though organized apparently with less strictness than the Whig, the agreement between the pronounced Jacobites and the general body of Tories not being complete. At the head of the more moderate section was Daniel Finch, Earl of Nottingham, an honest man, devoted above all things to the interests of the church, who had all but joined the appeal to William, but had afterwards proposed a regency, kept clear of intrigue, and, by a distinction between a king *de facto* and a king *de jure*, enabled himself faithfully to support the new government.

Here we have the historical origin, not of party, which, besides tearing the Greek, Roman, and Italian republics, had raged in England under Charles I. and Charles II., but of party government, which has now been accepted as the regular system, not only of Great Britain and her colonies, but of other parliamentary countries, and whether legally recognized, as in America, or not, is, wherever it prevails, practically the constitution. Though from the beginning party showed itself to be only an exalted kind of faction, the system had in its origin, at least, an intelligible foundation. Between the party of the Stuarts and the party which had driven out the Stuarts, between the party of government by prerogative and the party of parliamentary government, there was a fundamental division such as might warrant a good citizen in submitting his convictions on minor points, and everything but his moral conscience, to the discipline of party till the object of the combination was secured. Burke's definition of party as "a body of men united for promoting by their joint endeavours the national interest upon some particular principle in which they are all agreed," though panegyrical, might then have had place. Deliverance from the Stuarts and their tyranny was a principle "particular" enough. But in the absence of a fundamental division party is nothing but faction, as in the sequel plainly appeared. Then the only bond is either blind adherence to a name which sometimes remains the same while principles change, or corruption in some form. All attempts to find for the party system a permanent and universal basis in human nature fail. Human nature cannot be bisected; it varies through countless shades, and the same man who is conservative on some questions is liberal or even radical on others. As a rule, age is conservative, youth loves change; yet the spirit of reaction is nowhere so strong as in the young men of a privileged class. Burke's system requires that the members of a government should be united among themselves and divided from their opponents on some organic question. Suppose no organic question is before the country, on what would Burke's party be based? But even suppose that such a question is before the country, ought the nation to lose the services of its best financier or its best war minister because he does not agree with the home secretary or the lord chancellor about the suffrage or the church establishment? Godolphin, as an administrator, was invaluable; but on organic questions he can scarcely be said to have had any principles at all; his paramount principle was self-interest; his only other principle was loyalty to his department. A party government is the government of only half the nation. It can appeal to the loyalty of only half the nation. The function, it may almost be said, of the other half is to oppose, traduce, thwart, and embarrass the government. In foreign policy this is particularly fatal. A perpetual strife of passion, a civil war of hatred, intrigue, and calumny, with their effects on national character and the dignity of government, are the necessary accompaniments of the system. Legislation is regulated by party tactics, not by a calm view of public good, and the party which is out of power and struggling to get back to it makes reckless promises of change. All this will presently appear. In the absence of organic questions the only valid plea for the perpetuation of the system is the necessity of an organizing force to define the issues, nominate the candidates, and concentrate the votes at elections, as well as to prevent the House from becoming a chaos. The machine of elective government must have a motor, and the motor hitherto in England has been party, in the absence of which there has been a reign of cabal. What the Instrument of Government would have done, fate forbade us to know.

The weakness of the system was seen at once by a keen eye and exposed in immortal satire. The parties of the Tramecksan and Slamecksan in Swift's Lilliput, distinguished only by the high and low heels on their shoes, yet in their struggle for place too bitter to eat, drink, or talk with each other, are the Tories and Whigs, the high churchmen and the low churchmen, of this and the succeeding reigns. To give full piquancy to the satire we have only to remember that the satirist himself was a partisan, political as well as religious, and that his bitterness was by no means diminished when he had changed his party.

In its natal hour English party produced its typical man in the person of Wharton, the manager of the Whigs, of whom Swift said that he was the most universal villain that he ever knew. Wharton, as he is described to us, was in private life a shameless profligate, a seducer, a duellist, a scoffer; in public life he was unscrupulous and without conscience in corrupting others, though, himself loving victory more than money, he lavished his own fortune in the game. His one black virtue was intense devotion to his party. He was an unrivalled master of all the arts of political management and electioneering, full of evil energy and daring, and, in spite of his vices, personally popular to a wonderful degree. In him at once appeared the consummate "boss," and the herald of all "bosses" to come.

Wharton was one of a junto of four who managed the Whigs. The other three were Somers, Russell, and Montagu. That Wharton and Somers should be political partners was strange, as strange as it would have been if Aristides had entered into political partnership with Themistocles. For Somers is presented to us as the perfection, not only of wisdom, unfailing and serene, combined with the highest culture, both political and general, but of spotless purity and of every public virtue, so that we feel it almost a relief to the strain on our powers of admiration when we are told that in private he was liable to amorous weakness. Russell, the victor of La Hogue, had little besides that victory to exalt him. He was turbulent, wayward, and treacherous; he had been implicated in intrigues with St. Germains. Montagu, with a high university training, destined originally for the church, and happily diverted from it into public life, was the great master of finance, in which he had few peers. As a statesman he kept up his university tastes and studies, patronized men of letters, and himself wrote verse. The union of statesmanship with literary tastes and the cultivation of the friendship and support of literary men by statesmen are features of this age. Statesmanship might gain breadth and liberality from the union.

The struggle between political parties brought with it an

1697

aftermath of the Revolution. There had hitherto been no fixed limit to the life of parliaments; they had sat as long as pleased the king. Charles II.'s first parliament had sat for eighteen years. The representation was thus divorced from the constituencies, divested of the sense of responsibility, and exposed to court corruption. Tenure during the pleasure of the court was corruption in itself. But even Tories might think with bitterness of the Long Parliament. A fixed and limited term was essential to representative government. A Triennial Act was passed providing for the election of a fresh parliament every three years. Radicalism looked back to it with wistful eyes when by a subsequent Act the three years had been made seven. There was no rectification of the constituency itself such as had been embodied in the Instrument of Government. But it is truly said that the abolition of the petty boroughs would have inclined the balance to the Tory side, inasmuch as it was in those boroughs that the leaders of commerce and finance, who were Whigs, as well as the nominees of the government, found seats.

1694

1716

The Triennial Bill was traditionally a Whig measure. From the side of the Tories, as the opposition, came a Place Bill, excluding from the House of Commons all who held places of any kind under the government. The effect of this sweeping measure upon parliamentary government in England would have been like that which has been produced in the American Republic by the exclusion of the members of the cabinet from Congress. There would have been nobody to lead for the government or to shape and control legislation. In the case of England the leadership and the centre of parliamentary power would probably have been transferred to the House of Lords.

1694

Of a reform excluding the minor placemen who swarmed in the House of Commons there was great need. In time it came. But unmeasured purism would have purged the House, not of corruption only, but of organizing force and life. The Lords introduced an amendment allowing a man who had accepted a place to be re-elected, thereby breaking the force of the Bill. The king nevertheless vetoed. He was bitterly convinced that the government could not afford to lose power.

Another bill, manifestly of Tory origin, as framed in 1696 the interest of the squires against their hated rivals, the leaders of commerce, was that which required the possession of land to a certain value as a qualification for membership of the House of Commons. This, after passing the House of Commons, where the squires predominated, found for the time its grave in the House of Lords. To exclude all but landowners from the borough seats might suit the small neighbouring landowner, but did not suit the territorial magnate who wished to nominate his kinsmen or dependents.

The Lords, however, were as a House at this time Liberal in their political and religious tendencies compared with the squires of the lower House. They lived in the great world, conversed with statesmen, and had access to political information which could find its way to the manor house only in the shape of the weekly news-letter. Some of them also were still bound to the protestant reformation and the political party associated with it by hereditary ties. Peerages and promotion in the peerage were still in the gift of the Revolutionary crown. The bishops too, appointed by a king and queen who sat at the feet of the Latitudinarian Tillotson, were more

Liberal at this than at any other time, and their Liberalism could not fail to be confirmed by the slanderous abuse with which they were assailed by the coarse bigotry of the Jacobite parsons. That the upper House of convocation was more Liberal than the lower House, had appeared in the debates on Comprehension. Addison's Tory and high-church innkeeper, who has not time to go to church, but has headed a mob for the pulling down of two or three meeting-houses, thinks his county happy in having scarce a Presbyterian in it except the bishop.

The Commons, becoming intoxicated by their increase of power, more than once tried a trick which if it had succeeded would have almost extinguished the controlling authority of the upper House. They tacked a Bill which they wished to force upon the Lords to a money Bill, so that the Lords should be forced to pass both or stop the supplies. But the trick was too shameless; after a few attempts it was laid aside and the House of Lords remained on general questions a real branch of the legislature, though necessarily weaker than the House which held the purse.

1701 The temper of the House of Commons was shown again in the case of the Kentish Petition. The House, at that time Tory, was delaying supplies and crippling the government in preparation for war. A petition was presented to it, signed by the justices, grand jurors, and a number of free-holders of Kent, praying it to turn its loyal addresses into Bills of supply. The petition was not less constitutional than that of the seven bishops to the king. But the many-headed autocrat, transported with despotic ire, voted it scandalous, insolent, and seditious, and committed to the Gate House the gentlemen by whom it had been presented. Public opinion revolted, the Lords passed a strong resolution, and the Commons had to beat a retreat.

On the Triennial Bill, as well as on the Place Bill, the king put his veto, though in regard to the Triennial Bill he at last gave way. He clung to what remained of the royal prerogative, not so much from personal love of power as because he wished to wield the full force of England in the mortal struggle with France. Neither he, however, nor those with whom he contended had as yet distinctly realized the fact that the sovereign power, executive as well as legislative, had passed, the legislative power directly, the executive power indirectly and imperceptibly, from the crown to the House of Commons.

Swayed to and fro between the parties, William found himself for a time in the hands of Danby, now Marquis of Carmarthen, who set about managing parliament in his own way, William sadly yielding to the necessities of a corrupt generation. Trevor, an old parasite of Jeffreys, being made Speaker of the House of Commons, kept open a regular office for bribery of members. This is rightly set down as an incident of the transfer of power to the Commons. In Tudor times, the crown being absolute, there was no occasion for bribery; opposition was not bribed but coerced; the member of the House who attacked the government was sent to the Tower. Corruption, however, has no fixed seat and is protean in its forms. Much depends upon the morality of the age. But under the party system, when there is no great question of principle to bind men to a political standard, other means of attaching them will be found; if they are poor, money or a place; if they are rich, a title, a ribbon, or an invitation to a court ball. In time, the demagogue who wants to get himself a following will learn to corrupt whole classes by legislative bribes. The publication of debates and division lists may, as is said, have abated the evil in parliament, but failed to prevent its existence elsewhere.

About this time came, noiselessly and almost in disguise, a momentous and auspicious change. Owing to a blunder made by a ridiculous censor, the censorship of the press lapsed and was not renewed. The reasons given for deciding against its renewal and thus setting the press free were not those of the "Areopagitica." They were of an administrative kind, touching only on the futility of the Act and the difficulty connected with its operation. It may be surmised that each of the parties, now definitely arrayed against each other, longed for perfect freedom to assail its adversary in the press. Whatever the motive, the effect was not less great. It has been remarked by one who had carefully studied the political literature of the time, that the violence and scurrility of political writing, instead of increasing, were diminished when the curb was removed. He justly observes that what was illicit was sure to fall into the worst hands. Nothing worse, assuredly, than the Jacobite libels against William and Mary in the earlier part of their reign could have been produced under any state of the law. A free press, however, was still exposed to the onslaughts of party vengeance, which could expel Steele from the House of Commons for a fair party pamphlet, order a pastoral of Burnet to be burned by the public hangman, and put Defoe in the pillory for what would now be deemed a harmless squib.

There yet remained a rule of the common law restricting the publication of news. But this was allowed to sleep, the general appetite for news being too strong to be restrained; and amidst the storm of a party conflict the newspaper press, born once before to a short life, was born anew. In its cradle it was feeble and insignificant, its editorials being slight and occasional; and, unlike its future self, it was timorously anxious to be on the government side. But the germ and assurance of its coming power lay in the union of editorial comment with the political news of the day. Everybody must have the news, and with it everybody reads the comment, which, published apart from the news, few or none would read. The combination is natural, yet the power derived from it is partly factitious, though of that power the world is full.

For some time, however, the party war outside parliament will be a war not of journals but of pamphlets. On one side we shall have Addison, with his "Tatler," his "Spectator," and his "Freeholder," polished, playful, and courteous; Steele whom some think the peer of Addison; and the homely vigour of Defoe. On the other side we shall have Swift, strangely combining some of the highest gifts of human genius with the malice as well as the filthiness of the ancestral ape. Swift's dominant passion was clerical hatred of dissenters. When the text of his sermon is brotherly love, hatred of dissenters is still the theme. He preached, and, as the writer of "The Day of Judgment" was evidently an unbeliever himself, practised political conformity to the state religion.

The ascendancy of the Whigs, with the support of the commercial and moneyed classes, during the middle part of the reign, is marked by the great achievements of their financial minister, Montagu, who restored the currency, funded the debt, founded the Bank of England, and reorganized the East India Company. Financiers, who still tamper with inconvertible paper and bimetallism, may profit by the study of his example. The coin hitherto had been unmilled, and the trick of clipping it had been practised till much of it was far, some of it fifty per cent., under due weight. Of course, the good coin took flight, and all the operations of commerce and wage-paying were disturbed. Montagu, with Newton at his side, undertook the perilous work of restoration, and, as he adhered steadily to public honesty and sound principle, he carried the nation with him, and his operation, after a fearfully anxious crisis, was crowned with complete success.

In funding the debt which war expenditure had created Montagu only followed the example of Holland. Here again he was perfectly successful. Nations, like men, must borrow in emergencies; nor is it unfair to throw upon posterity a share of so extraordinary a burden as the defence of Europe against Louis XIV. But facility for running into debt is not, as optimism seems to fancy, an unmixed blessing. It brings with it, as before long appeared, recklessness of expenditure, and especially of expenditure in war. It absorbs capital which would otherwise feed productive enterprise. If the debt were what the optimist pictures it, we should gain by increasing it without limit. Some have actually taken it for so much wealth and have proposed to base a paper currency upon it. That it called into existence gambling speculation, as the Tories alleged, has been disproved by the evidence of gambling speculation before the establishment of the Funds. Yet it must be attended by stock-jobbing, and stock-jobbing is an evil. It has had an incidental use as a weather-glass of national prosperity, notwithstanding the saying of one who was vexed by its fluctuations that the Funds were the greatest fools in Europe. Montagu deserves, at all events, the credit of adherence to principle. He issued no greenbacks; if he had he would have been taking up a forced loan, for which he must have paid dearly by loss of credit at once and by the rate of redemption in the end. His only lapse was the admission into his first funding scheme of the spirit of gambling under the form of a tontine. His other financial measure, the foundation of the Bank of England, was not less success- 1694 ful than the first two, and all the apprehensions of a great and unconstitutional power felt or affected by the opposition proved groundless and passed away. They recurred with disastrous effects in the United States when Jackson proclaimed political war against the Bank.

The last of Montagu's triumphs was the foundation of 1698 a new East India Company, which he consolidated with the old company on a better footing. A part of the aftermath of the Revolution was the withdrawal from the crown of the power to grant monopolies of trade, of which the usefulness ceased when, commercial enterprise becoming less dangerous and having no longer to go forth armed for its own protection in unfriendly waters, the stimulus of privilege was no longer required. Foreign trade was henceforth free to all. The old East India Company, a dark, exclusive, and unregulated power, had sustained its privileges by corruption, of which the president, Sir Joshua Child, had been the consummate master; and it had played no small part in the pollution of public life.

Old Danby, by this time created Duke of Leeds, ended
a chequered career of patriotism and corruption by being
found guilty of the acceptance of an East Indian bribe.
The new company was organized by Montagu under
parliamentary auspices and regulations in connection
with the government.

From the loans, the funded debt, the military and naval
contracts, the creation of the Bank of England, and the
foundation of the new East India Company, sprang a
money power which of necessity allied itself closely with
the Revolution government, since a restoration would have
stopped financial operations and contracts, ruined the
Bank, and probably passed a sponge over the debt. Addison's allegory depicted the fainting of Credit and the
shrinking of her money bags in the Bank hall on the entrance of the Pretender. The government thus gained a
strong support, while a new political force came on the
scene. But the moneyed men had to make their way into
parliament by buying the constituencies of the small
boroughs; and thus the money power, while it saved the
Revolution government, propagated parliamentary corruption. By ousting the influence of the neighbouring squire
from the small borough it of course incurred the jealousy
of his class and made him the more a Jacobite.

The hero meanwhile was facing death on fields of
battle for the independence of England and of all nations,
a noble contrast to his antagonist, the enshrined grand
monarch of Versailles. William's main object had been
not to make himself king of England, but to bring
England into line as a member of the great European
confederation against French aggression. Of that confederation under his leadership England and Holland

were now the soul. As a diplomatist, the chief of a motley coalition full of jealousy, self-seeking, and fractiousness, including the cumbrous majesty of the empire and the imbecile pride of Spain, William was superb. As a general he was not first-rate, and for some time he had to contend against first-rate generalship, as well as against armies better trained and not of motley nationality, on the French side. At Steinkirk he suffered defeat, and 1692 a worse defeat on the terrible day of Landen. But from 1693 each overthrow he rose indomitable, repaired his losses with wonderful rapidity, and upon the whole held the ground which a greater commander coming after him was to turn into the field of victory. At last, the despotism of Louis blasted by its withering influence in the military as in other spheres the genius which it had inherited. The balance began to turn and William took that great prize of strategy, the fortress of Namur. Earlier in the strug- 1695 gle the English seaman had shown his quality, and, though at Beachy Head disgraced through the fault of his superiors, he won at La Hogue a victory splendid in itself 1692 and hailed by the nation as the first great triumph over France since the day of Agincourt. The royal navy, as a regular profession, a great national institution profoundly affecting the national character, and the trident of maritime empire, might almost date its history from that day.

Though parliament sometimes had tried William's patience to such an extent that he more than once meditated returning to Holland, the nation on the whole had shown that its heart was in the war, and, like the kindred republic, its partner, had presented the energy, resolution, and resource of a free commonwealth in admirable

contrast to the bearing of the great monarchies with which the commonwealths were allied. The nation had good reason for its zeal. This war was a struggle for the independence of nations against a power of rapine, despotism, and bigotry combined, which, though sublimely gilded, was hardly less hostile to the best interests of civilization than that Mahometan power which, by its inroads seven centuries before, had united Christendom in the crusades. The French aggressor, indeed, notwithstanding his persecuting catholicism, had Islam for his ally in his attacks on the rest of Christendom. The
1697 treaty of Ryswick, following the taking of Namur, was on the whole, thanks to William's diplomatic force and wisdom, a treaty of peace with honour.

The hour of victory and of public joy was to William personally the hour of mourning. A few months before, he had been carried in convulsions from the death-bed
1694 of his wife. Mary, as regent in her husband's absence, had played her part well, and her tender and graceful manners had throughout been a great support to her husband on his weakest side. She had influence in the appointment of bishops, and Tillotson was the primate of her choice. Her position on the throne of a deposed father was painful; most painful when that father and her husband met in arms. She was called a parricide and "Tullia" by Jacobites, of whose obscene ravings against her character and that of her husband history takes little account. Greenwich Hospital bespeaks her sympathy for
1696 English seamen, and is a superb monument of her virtues as well as of the valour which won La Hogue. William can hardly be blamed if, after her death, his heart turned more than ever to the Dutch friends in whose attachment

alone, to the discredit of Englishmen, he could perfectly confide.

It might have been thought that a good peace would strengthen the Whig government; but the next general election showed the tendency of the party system to violent and incalculable oscillation; it went against the Whigs. The danger from abroad being over, home discontents and dissensions could be indulged with freedom. Taxation had been severe, the debt was heavy, and the squires had been angered by the failure of their Land Bank, a chimerical scheme devised for their special benefit in opposition to the Bank of England, as well as by taxation and the political encroachments of the money power. Harvests had been bad, and the blame as usual was laid on the government. Tories, and not Tories alone, attacked the standing army, which had been the dread of the country gentlemen since the days of Cromwell, and of the whole nation since the camp at Hounslow. The case was entirely altered since the army had been placed under the control of parliament, both as paymaster and as arbiter of the Mutiny Act. But this the common intellect failed at once to perceive. In vain Somers strove by skilful pamphleteering to convince the people that in face of the continental armies the nation could not be safe without regular troops, and that the militia on which patriots relied, whatever might be its native valour, would not stand against trained soldiers. In vain he cited history and showed how the best of all militias, that of ancient Rome, had gone down before the trained mercenaries of Hannibal. In vain William, touched in his tenderest point, exerted all his influence to preserve his army. The most that could be done was to preserve it

on a greatly reduced scale. All the men were to be
1699 natives. William was compelled to dismiss his cherished
Dutch Guards, who departed with the dignity of veterans,
amid some late expressions of compunction from the nation
which they had come to save. Marlborough, for his own
purposes, had joined in the agitation.

Nobody yet clearly understood the new machine. The
ministers, not being conscious that they held their offices no longer of the crown but of parliament, stuck
to place in spite of an adverse majority in the House of
Commons. The majority, instead of passing a vote of
want of confidence or, in the last extremity, withholding
the supplies, attacked the characters of the ministers with
the slanderous malignity of faction. Montagu, by greedi-
ness and by upstart show and arrogance, had given his
enemies a handle. Somers had given none. Yet an
attempt was made to blacken the character of this illustrious and incorruptible man, and to drive him from office
by accusing him of sharing the gains of a pirate. A viler
attack still was made by the Tories on Spencer Cowper,
a Whig, rising at the Bar, and a destined judge. He
was accused of having seduced and murdered a young
Quakeress, who had drowned herself for love of him. At
the trial sailors were brought by the prosecution as experts
to prove that the bodies of suicides never floated. Science, following them in the witness-box, rejoined that
it was the general belief of these nautical experts that
whistling would raise the wind. Toryism narrowly escaped, by the acquittal of Cowper, the guilt of judicial
murder.

A subject on which the opposition had unfortunately
a much better case was that of the enormous though over-

stated grants of forfeited lands in Ireland by the king to his Dutch favourites, and not only to those who had merit, such as Portland and Ginkel, but to the Countess of Orkney, who had less than none. The legal right of the crown to grant away the lands could hardly be disputed; the moral right could not be maintained. William was unable to prevent the appointment of a commission of inquiry and resumption, which in its report was hurried, as might have been expected, by party violence, beyond the mark of justice.

The early death of the Duke of Gloucester, Anne Stuart's son by her husband Prince George of Denmark and heir after his mother to the crown, rendered necessary a resettlement of the succession. By the Act of Settlement the crown was given after Anne to the protestant Sophia, Electress of Hanover, granddaughter of James I., and her line, being Protestants, to the exclusion not only of the house of Stuart, but of the Roman Catholic house of Savoy, which came before the house of Hanover in blood, and has some fantastic adherents even at the present day. This Act, perpetuating the Revolution monarchy and once more setting aside legitimacy and divine right, was passed under the pressure of necessity by the Tories, then in the ascendant in parliament, some of whom must have looked askance at their own work. They indemnified themselves by the addition of articles expressed as legally taking effect only with the new limitation of the crown, but morally glancing at Dutch William. The king is to join in communion with the church of England. The nation is not to be bound to go to war for any of his foreign dominions. He is not to go out of the realm, as William had been doing, without the consent of parliament. He is to act always with the advice of his responsible privy council, not, as William had been acting, with the advice of an irresponsible cabinet, or, in making treaties, by himself. No foreigner, though naturalized, is, like William's Dutch friends Bentinck, Earl of Portland, and Keppel, Earl of Albemarle, to be a member of parliament, hold office, civil or military, or receive grants of land from the crown. No holder of place under the crown or pensioner is to be capable of sitting in the House of Commons. This prohibition revives the defeated Place Bill. The article calling again into life the old privy council was speedily repealed, while that excluding place-men from the House of Commons was watered down to the requirement of re-election on acceptance of place. There are two other articles, one already noticed, enacting that the commission of the judges shall be during good behaviour, the other forbidding a royal pardon to be pleaded in bar of impeachment, which, though dictated perhaps by the same jealous opposition to the Revolutionary crown, may be numbered among the good fruits of the Revolution.

The king's popularity was revived by a plot against his life which put all that was manly or moral in the nation on his side. There seems to be no doubt that James was privy to the plot or that it had his approval, conveyed, of course, in language vague and guarded. Nor is there any doubt that Louis connived and was preparing to take advantage of success. Neither of them was the first religious king or the first eminent champion of the church who employed assassins. Philip II. had done the same.

It was in connection with this plot against William's

life that the ordinary course of justice was for the last time superseded by an Act of Attainder. Two witnesses were required by the treason law. In the case of Sir John Fenwick, one of the two had been spirited away, and the Act of Attainder was passed in effect to cure the flaw. Neither of the evidence which the witness would have given, nor of the guilt of Sir John Fenwick, was there any doubt; but justice must rejoice that this super-session of jury trial by an Act of Attainder was the last. That in a country heaving with conspiracy, full of traitors who were inviting foreign invasion and hatching plots against the life of the king, there should be suspensions of the Habeas Corpus could shock no friend of liberty, though it might enrage friends of treason and murder. An association for the protection of the king's life, like that which had been formed for the protection of the life of Elizabeth, was signed by all the members of the House of Commons.

1696

At the close of the reign the war cloud, which had lifted after the treaty of Ryswick, again settled down heavily upon Europe. The male line of the kings of Spain had ended in a childless cretin. The Spanish monarchy comprising in Europe, besides Spain, the Kingdom of Naples and Sicily, the Duchy of Milan, and Sardinia; in Asia the Philippines; in the New World all Central America and all Southern America except Brazil and Guiana, with Cuba and other West Indian islands, was about to be left without an heir. The succession was thrown for settlement on the councils of Europe. A case for European settlement it was, there being among the members of that motley and scattered empire no national unity to be respected, while the danger to the community of nations from leaving the question to be decided by a general scramble or by French ambition was manifestly great. Especially great was, or naturally seemed, the danger of the union of the French and Spanish monarchies in the rapacious and domineering house of Bourbon, to which, by the marriage of Louis XIV. with a Spanish princess, the vast heritage would have gone had the claim not been barred by her renunciation. Experience, it might be said, showed that family connection by no means entailed political union. But in this case the weakness of Spain would be too likely to make her a vassal of France. The cretin being morally incapable of making a will, to leave the decision to him would have been to leave it to intriguing priests and women. Therefore when his death was near, William leading the way, a partition treaty had been made, dividing the Spanish heritage among the powers and assigning Spain itself, with the Indies, to the young Electoral Prince of Bavaria, who stood in the line of succession. This arrangement would perhaps have been allowed to take effect, and the peace of Europe might have been secured. But unfortunately the Electoral Prince died. A second partition treaty was then made, giving Spain, the Spanish Netherlands, and the colonies to the Austrian Archduke Charles. Soon the flickering ray of life in the Spanish king expired, and it was then found that a will had been made by those who had him in their hands, and who were under French influence, naming Philip, Duke of Anjou, grandson of Louis, his heir. Louis had promised on his honour, on the word and faith of a king, and had sworn upon the cross, the Holy Gospels, and the Mass-book, faithfully to observe the renunciation. But on receiving news of the bequest, he gave his plighted honour and his oath to the winds, and presented his grandson to his court as king of Spain.

The English people, weary of war and laden with debt, might not have been willing to take arms again for the maintenance of the balance of power. They were more nearly touched by the aggressions of Louis in the Netherlands, where he was seizing Barrier fortresses and expelling Dutch garrisons in the name of his grandson, threatening thereby the commercial interests as well as the one sure ally of England. But Louis took another step which made war inevitable, and put his great enemy once more at the head of a united and enthusiastic nation. James II. died at St. Germains. The wisest counsellors of the French king dissuaded him from recognizing the son of James as king of England. Louis's own judgment agreed with theirs. But at his side was a priest-ridden woman. At her instigation, it seems, Louis recognized James's son, the pretended Prince of Wales, as king of England, offering to England an intolerable insult and virtually declaring war. Against the attempt to impose a king upon it the spirit of the nation once more rose, and an election gave a great majority to the Whigs, who were the party of war. An Abjuration oath renouncing the Pretender was imposed on the whole governing class. But William's ear could no longer hear the trumpet call. He was already sinking beneath disease and toil, when his horse, putting its foot into a mole-hole, hastened his end, and the conduct of the French war passed, with the leadership of Europe, into other hands. The Jacobites might show what they were by drinking to the mole. But the work of the hero had been done. England and Europe were free.

1701

1701

1702

1702

CHAPTER IV

ANNE

BORN 1665; SUCCEEDED 1702; DIED 1714

THE reign of Anne has been called the Augustan Age of England. There is a likeness. Both were ages of calm, self-complacency, and jubilant literature, after civil storms. War there was during the reign of Anne, but it was far away, glorious, seen only in processions of thanksgiving for victory, felt at worst in the increase of taxation. Besides its literature in the persons of Pope, Addison, Swift, Steele, Defoe, the reign had its science in the person of Newton, its philosophy in that of Locke, its scholarship in that of Bentley. It had its architect in the builder of Blenheim, a palace in majesty whatever may be said of the style. Its statesmen were literary and patronized letters. It was an age stately, refined, picturesque in a formal way, so far as the higher class was concerned. But beneath the rather artificial brilliancy of the surface lay much that was far from brilliant: coarse excesses, savage duelling, nightly outrage of young rakes styled Mohocks on the streets, and among the common people barbarous habits, brutal sports, crime prevalent, ill-repressed by the police, and savagely punished.

Queen Anne was virtuous, good-natured, well-meaning, dull, and weak, though obstinate when the fit was on her. As a Stuart, though not the heiress by divine right, she was accepted as half legitimate by the Jacobites. She touched for the evil; among others the boy Samuel Johnson, in whose case the miracle did not take place. She was at heart a Tory, or rather a high church-woman, her strongest sentiment being attachment to the Church of England, to whose clergy her accession was a new summer after the winter of Whig Revolution. Her piety restored to the church the First Fruits which Henry VIII. and afterwards Elizabeth had seized for the crown. There was joy in the cathedral closes. Anti-puritan maypoles went up by scores. Clarendon's "History of the Rebellion" was brought out, with its preface telling the queen, whose heart was open to such teaching, that the church was the great support of the throne, and that to hurt the church was next door to treason. Anne's husband, Prince George of Denmark, was a toper and a cypher. Their children did not live, and Jacobitism might suspend its conspiracies till her demise all the more willingly, as she was likely from family feeling to favour the succession of her Stuart brother. For the present, however, the high church queen was completely in thraldom to Marlborough's imperious wife, who called herself a Whig, but was simply for herself and Marlborough. They corresponded under the familiar names of "Mrs. Morley" and "Mrs. Freeman," but their friendship was the submission of the weak. 1703

Marlborough now finds the field of his ambition. As the head and the general of the Grand European Alliance against France he takes the place of William. He for the present is king. His prime minister is Godolphin, whose financial ability provides the sinews of war and the subsidies for hungry allies.

The House of Commons is still Tory and High Church, while in the House of Lords a Whig majority is led by Somers and Wharton, a Tory minority by Nottingham. Toryism in the House of Commons falls upon the nonconformists with an Occasional Conformity Bill. Nonconformists were in the habit of eluding the Corporation and Test Acts by taking the sacrament in an Anglican church as a qualification for office and then going back to the meeting house. High Church Tories did not object to the profanation of the sacrament, but they did object to letting the non-conformist thus slip his neck out of the yoke. The House of Commons passed a Bill punishing with deprivation and fine whoever after taking the sacrament for office should again attend a meeting house. The Lords threw out the Bill, Liberal bishops distinguishing themselves in opposition. The Commons then tried to force it through the Lords by tacking it to the land tax, but again for the time they were foiled.

1702-1704

Tories, the Jacobite wing of the party especially, were at this time ready enough to loosen the fangs of the treason law. The prisoner had been allowed counsel; an Act was now passed allowing his witnesses to be sworn. Hitherto the witnesses for the crown only had been sworn, so that the evidence for the prisoner was disrated; an iniquitous absurdity for which only the legal casuist and idolater of the common law could find a reason.

1708

The overbearing temper of the newly enthroned Commons was shown in the case of the men of Aylesbury, which brought the House into sharp collision with the Lords. The returning officer at Aylesbury had arbitrarily refused the votes of some electors, one of whom

1703

brought an action against him at common law. The case went up by writ of error to the Lords. The Commons took fire, denied the common law right, and declared that they alone were judges of elections and of the suffrage. The Houses were falling foul of each other when prorogation put an end to the strife. Substantially the Lords were justified. An elector had a legal right which could not be abrogated by the vote of a single House.

To extend their privileges, personal as well as political and judicial, was the strong tendency of the Commons at this time. They would have exempted not only themselves, but their servants and their property to a great extent from the jurisdiction of the common law. What had once been the protection of tribunes was becoming the prerogative of tyrants. Who can be trusted with power?

Marlborough, if he had any political principles, was a Tory. He would probably rather have served, and he could more fitly have served, a despot than the commonwealth. Of Tories he first formed his ministry, with Nottingham as secretary of state; the queen also strongly inclining to that side. But his theatre was the field of the French war. The Tories were against the war and inclined to the side of France, whence they hoped to receive the heir of divine right. The Whigs were against France and in favour of the war. Hence Marlborough, like William, was forced to drop the Tories and take in Whigs. This he did by degrees, dropping first strong Tories like Nottingham, afterwards moderate Tories, such as Harley and St. John then were. At last of the Tories the indispensable Godolphin alone remained.

From the party strife all eyes were turned to the field on which the battle between French domination and the independence of Europe was to be fought. Marlborough had then taken the place of William as the head of a Grand Alliance, comprising the Empire, Prussia, Hanover soon to be linked with England, the Palatine, and Holland, to which presently went over Savoy. The strength of the alliance, its financial strength especially, lay in the English and Dutch commonwealths. The Empire was a sprawling giant harassed in rear by Hungarian revolt and Turkish inroad. Default was made in contingents; there was always craving for subsidies; jarring interests and pretensions were always giving trouble; while on the side of the enemy was perfect unity of counsels and forces. In Holland, the Orange supremacy having ended with William's death, the government had passed into the hands of leaders who thought more of their own security than of the common cause, and sent field deputies to control and hamper the general, thereby robbing him of more than one victory. Marlborough's serenity was sorely tried, but never failed. In diplomatic address he was William's equal, while he was far superior as a general; and he had one resource which William had not: he could flatter, and his flattery was superb. The new-made and barely authentic king of Prussia he won by handing his Majesty the napkin. The erratic Charles XII. of Sweden, who seemed at one time to mean mischief, was propitiated by assuring him that Marlborough would gladly serve in a campaign under so great a captain to perfect himself in the art of war.

The army, of which Marlborough took the command, was as motley as the alliance. His English troops were a fraction of it, and England must not claim all the laurels. Tory jealousy had reduced the standing army by statute to seven thousand, really perhaps to ten thousand, at the end of the last reign. The condition of the English people was such that volunteer recruits were dear. Conscription was suggested, but on this parliament could not venture. Recourse was had to enlistment from the gaols and impressment of tramps. The gaol-birds and tramps under a great commander seem not to have made bad soldiers; Marlborough could depend on them for difficult manœuvres as well as for bravery in action. After all, the tramp, and perhaps even the petty criminal, may be a man out of whom the nomad has not been thoroughly worked and who finds his wandering home in the camp.

The French king struck at Vienna, the road to which was opened to him by Bavaria, whose past treasons to the father-land it took all her loyalty in the late war with France to redeem. The Empire was in extreme danger. Marlborough, a part of whose difficulties was the necessity of concealing his plans from his own employers, managed to give the trembling Dutch the slip, traversed Germany, was joined by his true brother in arms, Eugene, with an imperial army, and at Blenheim confronted the French and Bavarians under Tallard, Marsin, and the Elector. Early in the morning of the 13th of August, 1704, Tallard wrote to his king that the army of the allies was before him, predicting the direction of its further march. It would march no further that day; and in the evening Tallard found himself with two other French generals sitting as prisoners in Marlborough's coach, while of his army thousands strewed the field of battle, fourteen thousand of his infantry, whom he had jammed into the village of Blenheim, having been there surrounded, were prisoners, and of his cavalry a great number were in the Danube. The victory was complete. Its effect was decisive. Europe was set free from French domination, and was no more to be the pedestal of the Grand Monarch. Alone Marlborough did it, and nothing in military history is more striking than the confidence with which, at the head of a motley army used to defeat, he attacked in their chosen position the victorious veterans of France. To compare generals is difficult. The force to be overcome must be considered as well as the overcoming force. Hannibal beat militia with mercenaries inured to war. Napoleon beat Austrian and Prussian armies, then spiritless machines, with soldiers full of the fire of the Revolution. Marlborough beat the victorious veterans and renowned marshals of France with an army to which he alone could have given unity and spirit. Of what other general, in modern history at least, can it be said that he never fought a battle which he did not win, or besieged a place which he did not take? Nor did he ever fail in an operation unless it was through the fault of the timorous traders or the intractable potentates with whom he had to act. No commander ever more completely clipped the wings of victory. Addison's lines, describing his calmness and serenity amidst the rage of the doubtful battle, tell no more than truth. With all his meanness of character Marlborough is one of the most superb figures, if not the most superb, in the annals of war.

1707   Soon after Blenheim, and partly in consequence of it, the ministers at home gained a victory still more glorious, more fruitful, and more lasting. They effected the union of England with Scotland. How beneficent the work of the Commonwealth and the Protector had been appeared by what followed from its reversal. Scotland had been the scene of all that was worst in the tyranny of the Restoration. She had been a satrapy governed by a council of tyrannical and persecuting jobbers with thumb-screws and dragonades. Courts of justice had relapsed into corruption. The heritable jurisdictions had been restored. The national religion had been driven to the hills and the wilds. Anglicanism, hateful to Scotland in itself and because it was English, had been forced upon her. Her martyr peasants had been shot down by the troopers of Graham of Claverhouse, Turner, and Dalziel; her martyr women had been tied to stakes on the seashore to be drowned by the tide. When the Revolution came, theocratic Presbyterianism had resumed its sway, narrowed and embittered by persecution. The Episcopal clergy had been rabbled and Episcopacy had been persecuted in its turn. The dark theocracy had put to death a boy of eighteen for having spoken against the doctrine of the Trinity, refusing even a respite to his penitent prayer. The loss of free trade with England and her colonies had ruined Scotch commerce, and in place of the prosperity which had marked the reign of the great usurper, penury, with its attendant barbarism, prevailed. The habitations of the people were poor, their manners coarse and unclean. Vagabonds swarmed, and the great Scotch patriot, Fletcher of Saltoun, could see no remedy for the pest but slavery. The Highlands, Cromwell's fortresses having been dismantled and his arm withdrawn, had relapsed into lawlessness and heathenism. They were again the lair of predatory clans which raided on Lowland fields and herds. The clans had been brought down by the persecuting government as a scourge upon the covenanting Lowlands. William had earnestly desired a union, and with that view had done his best to prevent the continuance and deepening of the religious chasm which divided the two nations from each other. But instead of union the relations between the two kingdoms had been growing more strained than ever. The attempt of the Stuarts to force Episcopacy on Scotland had inflamed the antagonism of the churches. The terrible tragedy of Glencoe, though not only a purely Scotch but a purely Highland affair, and at the time unnoticed, had now, because the unlucky warrant had been signed by an English king, become a crime of England against Scotland. To give Scotland back her commerce and relieve her of her penury, Paterson, a clever but hair-brained adventurer, had devised the Darien Company, which was to bring to her wealth untold, irrespectively of her natural resources or industry, by occupying the Isthmus of Darien and there handling the trade of the golden east. Under the influence of the dazzling vision, Scotland went wild. Spanish hostility combined with the pestilential air of Darien and the inherent folly of the enterprise to produce a miserable failure. But enough jealousy had been shown by commercial England to breed in the Scotch a fancy that to English influence the failure was due. A paroxysm of bitterness and a dangerous crisis followed. Scotland assumed an attitude most hostile and offensive to England. The Scotch parliament passed an Act of Security separating the succession to the crown of Scotland from the succession to the crown of England.

At last the captain and crew of an English vessel were murdered under form of law at Edinburgh with the brutal fury of an Edinburgh mob. England, of course, met the hostile demonstrations of Scotland by similar demonstrations on her part. 1704

It was chiefly owing to the grievous need which Scotland felt of the English market that diplomacy at length prevailed over the rising storm of passion, and commissioners were appointed on both sides to treat for a union. Inflamed as Scotch nationality had been in the recent affray, its agonies were acute. It found champions in Lord Belhaven, a brilliant orator, and Fletcher of Saltoun, that Spartan republican who had proposed to restore economical prosperity to Scotland by making helots of the needy. The Scotch were told that the promised participation in English commerce was a delusion and a snare, that every seat at that board was already filled, that all the benefit would be to the devouring Southerner, that the Scotch workman would get English prices without English wages, and that English excise would snatch the jug of ale from his hand. The English were told by the opponents of union on their side that their substance would be devoured by hungry Scotch. To the Scottish parliament Lord Belhaven, in a speech which had immense vogue, unfolded a dire apocalypse of woe. He saw the peers of Scotland, after all their glorious achievements, walking in the Court of Requests like so many English attorneys, and laying aside their swords when in company with the English peers, lest their self-defence should be termed murder. He saw the Royal State of Boroughs walking their desolate streets, hanging down their heads, wormed out of all the branches of their 1706 old trade; Caledonia, like Julius Cæsar, ruefully looking round about her, covering herself with her royal garment and awaiting the fatal blow. He saw the Scotch artisan drinking water instead of ale and eating his saltless porridge; the ploughman, his grain rotting upon his land, cursing the day of his birth, dreading the expense of his burial. Lord Marchmont's answer was, "He dreamed, but lo! when he awoke behold it was a dream."

In the frame of mind in which the two nations were, to get a joint commission appointed, to get the English and Scotch commissioners to agree, to get the two parliaments, full of national jealousy recently excited, and with the hostile churches behind them, to accept the terms settled by the commission, was a task by which the most skilful of diplomatists might have been appalled. Yet, by the tact and temper of Godolphin, Somers, and Montagu, aided by that of the friendly statesmen of Scotland, the task was performed. Blenheim had deprived the Scotch Jacobites, deadly enemies to the union, of the hope of aid from France.

Passed by the parliament of Scotland, to which in the first instance it was wisely submitted, the Act of Union was afterwards passed by the parliament of England. With infinite skill and temper all questions were solved and all claims were adjusted. In pecuniary and fiscal arrangements England could afford to be, and was, liberal. The title of the United Kingdom was to be " Great Britain," which, however, its want of simplicity combined with the force of tradition has prevented from effectually displacing that of " England " in the language of the world. Scotland received a representation, fully proportioned to her share of taxation, in the House of Commons,

1707

with sixteen peers, elected from the body of her peerage, to represent her in the House of Lords, the principle of election being thus introduced, though in the mildest form possible, into the hereditary House. The Presbyterian establishment of Scotland was preserved and continued to form a strong line of demarcation. Scotland also retained her own law and her own judicial procedure, though the House of Lords became the ultimate court of appeal for the whole of the united nation.

Scarcely would the union have threaded the opposition of the high churchmen and Tories in the English parliament if they had been allowed to debate the articles in detail. The Bill might have been in committee till the day of doom. But that danger was eluded by the ingenuity of Harcourt, afterwards chancellor, who framed a Bill with the treaty recited in the preamble and a single enacting clause. To make all fast, in addition to the Acts imposing the abjuration oath, an Act was passed declaring it treason to impugn the settlement of the crown under the Act of Union or the right of parliament to limit the succession. This was aimed against the Jacobite enemies of the union and the succession in Scotland. It stamped the monarchy as parliamentary.

There was friction afterwards, as might have been expected, about questions political, fiscal, judicial, and religious. Scotland was surprised and somewhat shocked at finding that the British House of Lords had become the high court of appeal. Anglicanism and Presbyterianism did not easily fraternize in parliament. When the English Tories came into power, they showed their temper against the Scotch church. Jacobites made as much mischief as they could, and were aided by the venom of

1707

Swift. A motion for the dissolution of the union was all but carried in the House of Lords; but the argument that what had been done could not be undone happily prevailed. France made a last effort in conjunction with the Scotch Jacobites to restore the disunion which had served her malignant policy well. She sent an expedition. but it failed.

Scotch disunionists have fondly cherished the tradition that the independence of their country was sold by her leading men for the sum of £20,540 17s. 7d., of which sum Lord Banff received £11 2s. 0d. as the bribe to which his integrity and patriotism gave way. The money was payment for arrears of salary and other debts which, the Scotch treasury being empty, the English treasury defrayed.

Thus after long centuries of miserable enmity, mutual devastation, and progress retarded on both sides, nature had her way, and union came at last. The line of religious division which the Act of Union left is being softened if not effaced by the intellectual forces which are everywhere sapping dogmatic organizations. The line of legal division will probably in time be effaced by the progress of scientific jurisprudence. Yet the evil which the Norman Conquest did in severing Scotland and Wales from England is not yet wholly undone. Antiquarian whim or demagogic malice can still appeal to separatist sentiment in Scotland and Wales as well as in Ireland.

Lord Belhaven's dream was ruin; the reality was to be the warehouses of Glasgow, the ship-building yards of Clyde, and in time the farms of the Lothians. The shipping trade of Scotland had been ruined by the Navigation Act; but after the union Glasgow chartered ships and opened a growing trade with the American colonies. In 1716 or 1718 the first trading vessel that crossed the Atlantic was launched upon the Clyde. In 1735 Glasgow had sixty-seven vessels and had become a rival of England in the American trade. Greenock made herself a harbour; Paisley grew into a manufacturing town. The merchant marine of Scotland rapidly advanced, and the younger sons of the gentry, hitherto in want of occupation, took to commercial enterprise. The linen trade and the woollen trade kept pace with the mercantile marine. Products which before had been valueless or of little value, such as black cattle or kelp, became sources of wealth. Agriculture, retarded by a bad system of holdings, as well as by the want of good markets, followed the advance of commerce with a somewhat slower step. Improved habitations, comfort, cleanliness, civilized habits spread among the people.

Union with England gave Scotland unity in herself. The force which she had lacked for the incorporation of the Highlands was henceforth supplied. After the next rising of the clans military roads were made through the Highlands, hereditary jurisdictions were abolished, law took the place of the chieftain's lawless will, Christianity and in time the southern language, the indispensable instrument of education and culture, made its way. The mountain lair of the marauding cateran became a reserve of beauty and romance in a land of factories and forges, while the plaid, the sight of which had long been dreaded by the Lowlander, was by the genius of a military tailor improved into the picturesque costume which kings as well as warriors and sportsmen have delighted to wear.

Increase of material prosperity, however great, might

not have made up to the patriot for political degradation; but Scotland could not lose political dignity by exchanging the state of a satrapy, which under the union of the crowns had been and must always have been hers, for partnership in the illustrious destinies of a great nation. Nor can Scotch character have suffered if the present Scotch estimate of it is true. It is eminently commercial, and in that aspect must have been formed after the union, since before the union there was little trade. Lack of trade, in fact, it was that made the union. The heart of Sir Walter Scott was thoroughly Scotch and at the same time thoroughly British.

Unhappily, while to the statesmen of Anne undying gratitude is due for the achievement of union with Scotland, on their memory rests the heavy charge of rejecting union with Ireland. To span that fatal arm of the sea was harder than to overleap the Cheviots. But monopoly was even more estranging than the sea. Here we behold the dark side of commerce, of commerce at least as it was in those days when everybody was in the gall of protection. If the trader linked nations together by interchange and intercourse, too often he bred war among them by his spirit of monopoly and his malignant fancy that the gain of others must be his loss.

The sword of William and the penal code had thoroughly quelled for a time the hapless Celt of Ireland, who, for a full century, does not rise in rebellion again, not even when the Jacobite flag is unfurled in England. But to fear of Celtic insurrection had succeeded, on the part of those who swayed the commercial councils of England, a wretched jealousy of Irish trade, particularly of trade in wool, which Ireland produced of the best, and in cattle. Ireland is a grazing country, for the most part too wet for grain, as well as almost destitute of coal, and nature has thus marked her destiny in relation to the sister island, the swarming population of which it is her natural function to supply with dairy produce and meat. English greed dreaded the growth of rival industries in Ireland, which, depressed as the Irish people were, there was only too little need to fear. Small holdings, spade tillage, the potato, and the periodical famines which attended the treacherous tuber, and life in hovels shared with the swine, were the result. The Saxons of Ireland, seeing how their island as a dependency languished under monopoly, and sighing for a share of English trade, stretched out their hands for union. Their overture was coldly repelled. English commerce, possessed by the demon of jealousy not less irrational than sordid, protested against Irish competition; and commerce was the great support of the Whigs, who were then in power. Had Ireland been then allowed to become a commercial and industrial country in equal partnership with Great Britain, what calamities would both islands have been spared! She was forced, instead, to become a smuggling country, a recruiting ground for the armies of catholic Europe, and a seed-plot of disaffection destined to bear a hideous harvest at a later day.

Marlborough meanwhile pursued his career of victory. After Blenheim came Ramillies and Oudenarde, while the fortresses fell as usual to the conqueror in the field. France was exhausted and her king sued for peace, offering to abandon his grandson's claim on Spain. The allies insisted that he should turn his grandson out. This was a moral blunder; it gave Louis a strong ground for

1706;
1708

appeal to his people, and enabled the party opposed to the war in England to say that it was being protracted in the interest of Marlborough and others who gained by its continuance. In Spain the allies had not prospered. Spanish sentiment was strongly against them. Castilian pride revolted at the thought of partition. The Austrian Archduke, whose claim the allies supported, was a Serene Highness too dull and stiff to make way with the people, too slow to follow fortune when she beckoned him to Madrid. Peterborough, a knight-errant out of date, ran a meteoric course of victory; but he could only perform impossibilities, and, his career over, the fortune of war went against the allies in Spain almost as much as it had gone for them in other fields. The insulting demand of the allies raised a fresh army in France with an access of national spirit, and Malplaquet, the last of Marlborough's battles, though a victory, had been a fearful and sickening day of blood. After it he prayed that he might never be in battle more. It does not seem that he really wished to prolong the war. He seems to have been weary and to have longed to get back to his Sarah; though he saw that as Louis had set out to dictate peace to Europe at Vienna the right course was to dictate peace to him at Paris, whither victory had opened the way. Commercial England had borne much more than her share of the cost. Debt was being piled up and taxation was growing oppressive. Merchants might fancy that they gained by the destruction of French trade; but for the land owner and the people in general there was no compensation. In spite of trophies and processions to St. Paul's the nation was growing somewhat weary of the war. Marlborough's towering greatness and known ambition created a fear of military dictatorship, which was enhanced by his own imprudence in seeking the office of captain-general for life.

The murmurs of Jacobite disaffection and of Tory opposition had been drowned in the *Te Deum*. In vain the Tories had striven to set up the naval glory of Rooke, a Tory, against the military glory of Marlborough. Union with Scotland had come to crown the triumphs of their opponents. Still, the Tory party was strong in parliament, and in the country stronger still. It had on its side a solid phalanx of landed gentry, of whom was presently formed the October Club, so called from the strong ale by which its political spirit was fed, jealous of the commercial interest, and little favourable to the war by which it was supposed to be gaining at their expense. It had the lower clergy, especially in the rural districts. Personally the clergy were never less respected or less deserving of respect than at this time. Yet as an order they never were more powerful. They had their pulpits, which they used without scruple for political purposes, and of which the influence in rural parishes was far greater than that of the press. They had the ear of the squire who looked on their church as the bulwark against Puritanism and with whom their subserviency would be a merit. They hated the Revolution, were Tory, and often tinged with Jacobite sentiment if not Jacobite. Their political preaching was dangerous, since in the opinion of good judges the Stuart might have come back if he could have changed his Roman Catholicism for the Anglican religion, which, to his honour, as well as happily for the country, he steadfastly refused to do. The universities, which were entirely clerical and centres of clerical bigotry, were Tory. Oxford was Jacobite, having buried the memory of the attacks made on her by James.

The Whig leaders seem to have felt that there was a growing prevalence of anti-Revolution sentiment which, with the demise of the crown in view, might be dangerous, and to have looked for an opportunity of taking Jacobitism by the throat and binding the nation fast to Revolution principle and the Hanover succession. Sache-
1709 verell, a clerical demagogue, in a sermon preached on the anniversary of the gunpowder plot, impugned the Revolution doctrine of resistance. Upon this the Whigs
1709- pounced as a subject for their grand demonstration.
1710 They could not have chosen worse; for, in attacking an ecclesiastic they brought the order about their ears, at the same time offending the high-church queen. This the wisest members of the party saw; but it is said that he who generally was the wisest of all, Godolphin, allowed himself to be stung to imprudence by a personal allusion.
1710 The petty agitator was impeached. There was a grand state trial, in which the Whig leaders, as managers of the impeachment, expounded their political creed, asserting, while they strictly defined and limited, the principle of resistance, with benefit to political philosophy, perhaps in the end to the party, though to themselves the consequences were disastrous. The clergy were at once in a ferment. Their fury was seconded by the street mob, always on the side of violence. The terrible cry of "church in danger" was raised. The populace shouted for "high church and Sacheverell" round the carriage
1710 of the queen, whose heart responded. Sacheverell was condemned by an ineffective majority to a nominal sentence. He at once became the martyred hero of the hour.

and made a triumphal tour of agitation through the country. A tidal wave of fanaticism swelled and roared against the Whig administration.

At the same time a blow was dealt by an even more despicable hand. "It seems," says Hallam, "rather a humiliating proof of the sway which the feeblest prince enjoys, even in a limited monarchy, that the fortunes of Europe should have been changed by nothing more than the insolence of one waiting-woman and the cunning of another." There was a good deal more at work, but bed-chamber intrigue played a shameful part. Anne was at last growing tired of the insolence of Marlborough's wife. An opening was thus given to the wiles of Abigail Hill, whom the duchess in an evil hour for herself and her friends had introduced to the queen's toilet, and who became the tool of the Tory leaders. Under the influence of Abigail, combined with her own Tory and high-church leanings, the queen broke with the duchess, dismissed the Whigs, and called the Tories to power. 1710 Parliament was dissolved, and the new election gave the Tories a great majority. Thus partly by its own fault, partly through intrigue, the current of popular feeling at the time setting against it, fell the great Whig ministry of Anne.

The Tory leaders were Harley, presently created Earl of Oxford, and St. John, presently created Viscount Bolingbroke, both of whom had sat as moderate Tories in Marlborough's first ministry and been the last of that section to be dropped. Harley was given to mystifying his contemporaries about himself, and he has in some measure mystified posterity. He seems, however, to have been a man of second-rate ability, owing his position mainly to his parliamentary experience, irresolute in character and infirm of purpose. He gained a reputation for wisdom by holding his tongue. Nobody could speak of him with more intense contempt than did afterwards his partner in power. For his patronage of letters, if it was not political, he deserves to be remembered. Bolingbroke was a brilliant and daring knave. A scoundrel he is called by Johnson, who was on his side in politics though not in religion. The epithet is surely deserved by the man who, without being a Jacobite, conspired for the restoration of the Stuarts, who being a free-thinker at heart and loose in life led a mob of bigots in a persecution of nonconformists. Bolingbroke in his writings scoffs at divine right as a figment of kings and priests playing into each other's hands. "The characters of king and priest have been sometimes blended together; and when they have been divided, as kings have found the great effects wrought in government by the empire which priests obtain over the consciences of mankind, so priests have been taught by experience that the best method to preserve their own rank, dignity, wealth, and power, all raised upon a supposed divine right, is to communicate the same pretension to kings, and by a fallacy common to both impose their usurpations on a silly world. This they have done; and, in the state as in the church, these pretensions to a divine right have been generally carried highest by those who have had the least pretension to the divine favour." Such were the real opinions, afterwards disclosed, of the head of the Jacobite and Anglican party.

Bolingbroke's professed ideal of a government was embodied in his "Patriot King," which had some influence in later times, and has had some even in our own day. The "patriot king" was to be raised above all party and to rule for the general good. But Bolingbroke himself was a party leader in the narrowest sense of the term, affecting Jacobitism and Anglicanism merely for a party purpose. He compared himself to a huntsman cheering on his pack of hounds and showing them game. He avowed that the principal spring of his actions and of those of his friends was to have the government of the state in their hands, and that their principal views were the conservation of this power, great employments to themselves, and great opportunities of rewarding those who had helped to raise them and of hurting those who had stood in opposition. The aims of faction could not be more frankly described. The loss of Bolingbroke's speeches has been much deplored. They were no doubt brilliant, like his writings, in form, and effective with his party pack of hounds; but if the substance was no better than that of his writings, we may resign ourselves to the loss. The orations of a charlatan, pandering to the passions of boors and bigots soaked with October ale, can hardly have been in the noblest style of eloquence.

The Tory ministers at once dismissed Marlborough 1711 from his command; disgraced him; brought against him charges of malversation, of which, though greedy of money, he was not guilty, while he had refused an enormous bribe offered by France; put the Jacobite and traitor Ormonde in his place; and at once flung themselves into the arms of their friend and patron, the French king, to whom, in his desperate condition, their ascendancy was salvation. In the negotiations which they opened they were almost more ready to give than Louis was to ask.

1713 The Treaty of Utrecht, Bolingbroke afterwards owned, was less answerable to the success of the war than it might and ought to have been, though he lays the blame, of course, on everything but his own treason. Perfidy to allies, behind whose back negotiations with France were carried on; treacherous desertion of them in the field, 1712 which caused Eugene to lose the battle of Denain, and made Marlborough's victorious veterans hang their heads with shame; betrayal of the Catalans who had been induced to rise in favour of the candidate of the allies for the Spanish throne — not even defenders of the treaty can defend. Nor can it be questioned that England was lowered in the eyes of Europe. Louis entered into an engagement against the union of the French and Spanish crowns, out of which, had the case occurred, his French jurists and his Jesuits would have found him a way. England kept Gibraltar, to which she had scarcely a claim, since it had fallen into her hands, not in a war against Spain, but in a war waged ostensibly in support of the rightful candidate to the Spanish throne.

The redeeming part of the treaty was free trade with France; but this commercial prejudice, combined with jealousy of French connection, was strong enough in the British parliament to reject. Commerce was in bondage to monopoly, though politically it was on the Liberal side. The Tories were for free trade with France, not because they were economically more enlightened, but because they wanted French connection and French wines. All parties rejoiced in the hideous acquisition of the Assiento, that is, the privilege of carrying on the slave trade with the American colonies of Spain.

In the House of Lords the Whigs, aided by the Liberal

bishops, were still strong, and to carry the treaty the Tory leaders found it necessary to resort to a swamping creation of twelve peers. This was deemed at the time, and in fact was, an act of unscrupulous violence. Yet there is no other way, apart from physical force, of compelling the Lords to bow to the national will as declared by the representative House. One man had the spirit to decline the ignominious honour. 1711

The Tory squires and the high church parsons now had their carnival of reaction. The Act against Occasional Conformity, which had been more than once thrown out by the Lords, passed both Houses, helped in the Lords by an unholy compact of some of the Whigs with Tories, who were willing on that condition to vote against the Treaty of Utrecht. To the Occasional Conformity Act was added the Schism Act, prohibiting dissenters from educating their children. Bishop Butler, the one great theologian whom the Church of England produced in the eighteenth century, was educated at a non-conformist school; so was Burke, the great lay champion of the Establishment; so had been Harley himself. Striking, yet not unnatural nor perhaps unique, is this picture of persecuting priests headed in an attack on liberty by an unbeliever and a debauchee. Church interests in everything prevailed. A tax was put on coal to build fifty churches in London. The *Regium Donum*, the dole hitherto given to the Irish Presbyterians, was stopped; a blow was struck at the Presbyterian conscience in Scotland by the restoration of the rights of patronage; and protection was extended to the persecuted Episcopalians, not, assuredly, from love of toleration, but from enmity to their Presbyterian foes. 1711 1714 1710 1712

To strengthen the landed and depress the commercial element, the Bill vetoed by the king and rejected by the Lords in the last reign was now passed, requiring property in land as a qualification for all members of parliament. The Tory theory was that land was the only true basis of political power.

1710

Nor did the huntsman fail to show his hounds more personal game. Steele, for having written a telling Whig pamphlet, was accused of seditious libel and expelled the House. Robert Walpole, one of the managers of the Sacheverell impeachment and a rising speaker and financier, was falsely accused of embezzlement and sent to the Tower. Of Walpole the Tories had not heard the last.

A stamp duty was laid on newspapers and the cheap press, nominally for the purpose of raising revenue and repressing libel; really, it cannot be doubted, in the same spirit of hostility to a cheap press which led the same political party to oppose the repeal of the stamp duty at an after day. Press persecutions also were rife. But pamphleteering could not be suppressed. Both sides had become too fond of literary war.

1712

Bolingbroke has declared that there was no formal design of bringing in the Pretender. Formal or not, there was a design for bringing in the Pretender of which Bolingbroke was the soul. Correspondence was going on with St. Germains. A perilous crisis in the history of the nation and of liberty had arrived. Harley's nerve failed him when he approached the brink. He wavered, faltered, and at last, after a fierce altercation in the presence of the queen, was overthrown by his more daring partner and turned out of office. Bolingbroke was now sole master of the ship; but before he had time to lay his plans, fortune,

1714

to use his own phrase, bantered him. Harley was turned out on Tuesday; on Sunday the queen died. The Jacobites, dispersed all over the country, were not ready; the Whigs were gathered in the cities. A bold stroke made in the council by Whig Lords favourable to the Hanoverian succession, when the queen was dying, put the headship of the government with the staff of Treasurer, into the hands of Shrewsbury, thus setting Bolingbroke aside. Bolingbroke was taken by surprise; he was not ready, and his plot collapsed. Atterbury, the clerical leader of the Jacobites, a turbulent and designing priest, offered, as was believed, desperate counsels, but in vain. In a nonconformist chapel in the city, a handkerchief dropped from the gallery, which was the preconcerted signal, told the preacher that the queen was dead. He and his congregation at once broke forth into a jubilant hymn. Fortune had bantered Bolingbroke.

1714

1714

CHAPTER V

GEORGE I. AND GEORGE II. — THE MINISTRIES OF WALPOLE AND CHATHAM

GEORGE I. — BORN 1660; SUCCEEDED 1714; DIED 1727
GEORGE II. — BORN 1683; SUCCEEDED 1727; DIED 1760

IN whose hands after these political vicissitudes was the country left? Mainly in those of the landed aristocracy and gentry. Those yeomen freeholders who had once been numerous and of whom Cromwell had formed his Ironsides, were going out of existence; rising, if they were opulent, into the class of squires, falling, if they were needy, into the class of tenant farmers. Land, with the social rank and political influence attached to it, became the object of a competition in which wealth prevailed. A rise in the scale of living would draw the yeoman into expenses which led to embarrassment and enforced sale, while the great landowner of the neighbourhood, the rich East Indian or the successful trader, was always ready to buy. Great estates became the rule. Their lords designated the members of parliament for the county, nominated members for pocket or petty boroughs, exercised political influence everywhere, and as Lords-Lieutenant, Sheriffs, or Justices of the Peace, had the local administration in their hands. At the head of the landed interest were the peers, hereditary owners collectively of a vast amount of land. The order of baronets with hereditary titles, but without seats in parliament, formed a link between the peers and the squires. The estates were entailed. The eldest son took the family mansion and the acres. The younger sons were quartered on the family livings, on the army, or on the public services, appointments to which were patronage, to be obtained through the political interest possessed by the head of the house.

The landed gentry formed a social as well as a political aristocracy, distinct though not close. To propitiate the Duke of Wellington, who had been affronted, the Count d'Artois complimented him on the great things which he had done and the confidence reposed in him by the crowned heads. "More than that," replied the Duke, "I am an English gentleman, and no one shall insult me with impunity." "You would degrade a gentleman to the level of a king or a grocer," says a character in a novel to one who proposes to him an act of vulgar publicity. Only a gentleman could assume armorial bearings, be called "esquire," or fight a duel. Trade was against caste, and those who had made fortunes by it were with difficulty admitted into county society, though the squire, or even the peer, might not disdain to repair a dilapidated estate by marriage with the trader's daughter. All professions were derogatory except the church, the upper grade of the law, and the army. Even the navy was for some time barely within the pale; Smollett's Commodore Trunnion is its representative in fiction. There was a commercial as well as a landed interest; but the man who had made his fortune by trade laid it out in land as his passport to high society, and connected his family by marriage, if he could, with the landed gentry. Even East Indian and

West Indian wealth found its way through the same gate after a social quarantine, during which it was apt to be in political opposition. Manufactures were still in their infancy, and their influence in politics, destined in time to be so powerful, was as yet hardly felt. Thus the ascendancy of the landed gentry was paramount. The tenant farmers who held under them were, of course, their dependents; the labourers were almost their serfs. Social caste seems to have grown with the century.

That government should be parliamentary, not by prerogative, the Revolution had decided. But parliament, though it might roughly represent great interests, was far from representing the people. In the counties freeholders alone, the number of whom was decreasing, had votes; leaseholders, copyholders, tenants-at-will, and cottagers had none. In earlier days the crown had assigned representation to boroughs at its discretion, choosing originally those which were most taxable; afterwards, as political influence became an object, places where it could best control the representation, including a number of villages in Cornwall. But in the reign of Charles II. an attempt to exercise this power had been checked, and the borough representation was stereotyped thenceforth. The borough franchise was a medley of accidents. In a few towns household or even manhood suffrage was the rule; but most of them had fallen into the hands of local oligarchies, which themselves fell into the hands of the great proprietors or of purchasers of their venal votes. In sum, only London, Westminster, Bristol, and a few other great boroughs retained electoral freedom. A miserable village in Cornwall had as many members as a great county. Members were returned from an old mound or an old wall from which population had fled. Seats in parliament came to be regarded as property which was bought and sold without disguise, the price having reference to the political market of the day and the period for which parliament had still to run; though when the city of Oxford openly advertised its seats for sale, the House of Commons thought it decent to feign a transport of indignation. There were shameless bribery and treating at elections, and when the pride of rival county families was excited, enormous sums were spent in these contests. East Indian nabobs and West Indian planters when they came upon the scene were great buyers of seats in parliament and propagators of political corruption. Election petitions were decided at Westminster, as they still are at Washington, by a party vote, a minister telling his supporters, when the struggle was close, that no quarter must be given in elections; so that men held seats to which they had no elective right. Parliament sat in secrecy; to report the debates was forbidden, though meagre and inaccurate, sometimes imaginary, summaries of the speeches were published under fictitious names.

Still, the British constitution was free by comparison with all other countries except Holland and Switzerland. There was a public opinion, which, though not directly represented in parliament, at a crisis had its influence. It found organs in the great borough constituencies, especially that of London, the effect of whose free verdicts was enhanced by the general want of freedom. It found organs in the press, now liberated from the censorship, though subject to an illiberal libel law, and liable to censorial onslaughts by the dominant party in parliament. It found an organ sometimes in the mob of

London and other great cities, which was political, and in the absence of a strong police or army could make itself feared by the government. • Quarrels and struggles for place among the aristocracy would give leaders to the outside public at the expense of the ruling class. The politician, however aristocratic, stands in awe of the voter, and there is an amusing picture drawn by a French visitor of a nobleman cringing to an innkeeper who had influence in the local elections. The spirit of the Revolution of 1688, and even of that in the reign of Charles I., still lingered; that of the revolution in the time of Charles I., of course, very faintly. Nor was fear for the church lands in the event of a Jacobite or papal restoration even yet quite extinct in the Whig houses. The classics, which were the staple of education, kept up the ideas of Greek and Roman liberty. Brutus and Cassius were names wherewith to conjure. Examples of Greek and Roman history were cited against standing armies. A statesman of antique mould called the age of the Scipios the apostolic age of patriotism. Party, while it degenerated into faction, sustained a political life and an interest in public characters and affairs. Paley thought he could not spend his money as a taxpayer better than in buying for himself the amusement of the political arena; and this was an amusement higher, to say the least, than any which he could have enjoyed under the shadow of the Bastille.

In matter of taxation parliament does not seem to have been immoderately partial to its own class. Nothing in England resembled the fiscal exemptions of the aristocracy in France. Yet legislation by a class could not fail to be class legislation. The landed interest was first considered; after it commerce, which drew its share of the political fund in a protective tariff and commercial wars. For the mass of the people nothing in the way of legislation was done. The farm labourers especially were left under a Poor Law which was a code of degradation and a Law of Settlement which bound them like serfs to the soil. The farm labourer was as destitute of the power of making himself heard through any organ of opinion as he was of the power of the vote. That the squire was an autocrat, cruel game laws proved. Local institutions, the shire and the borough, organs of progress and liberty in early days, had lost their importance. The counties were now in the hands of the great landowners who, as Justices of the Peace, legislated for them at Quarter Sessions. The boroughs had, for the most part, lost their liberties to close corporations, sometimes self-elected and corrupt as well as close, which engrossed the offices, often abused the fund, and sold the parliamentary representation.

Guarantees of personal liberty, in Habeas Corpus and jury trial the British citizen still had, and jury trial extended to political cases. But an aristocratic legislature was prodigal of the blood of the poor. Blackstone counts one hundred and sixty capital offences; and in spite of the humane perjury of the juries and the merciful subterfuge of judges, the butchery was immense, while the executions were revolting, and Tyburn was at once a shambles and a brutalizing show. The death-warrant of a man who had altered the date of a small bill to postpone payment was signed by a king who had himself made away with his father's will. A woman whose husband had been pressed as a seaman, having stolen a trifle from a shop to feed her starving children, was borne to the gallows with an infant at her breast. Liberty could hardly be truly sacred in a nation which was carrying on the slave trade, in spite of the judgment, which perhaps has been glorified as much as it deserves, that on touching British soil the slave became free. Thousands languished through life in prison for petty debts. The prisons were found, on parliamentary investigation, to be most horrible and heart-rending scenes of cruelty and extortion. The judiciary was incorrupt as well as independent, for though Lord Chancellor Macclesfield was impeached and deprived, it was for the sale of appointments, not of justice. But justice, though not sold, was delayed and defeated by antiquated technicalities and barbarous chicane, the leavings of the Middle Ages, which Mansfield, as Chief Justice, though he did something, could not do much to reform. This, however, was better than *lettres de cachet*, judicial torture, and the Bastille.

Squires of course varied in character. There was a Roger de Coverley or an Allworthy, the benign patriarch of the parish, as well as a Squire Western who spent his mornings in fox-hunting and his afternoons in getting drunk. When the squire was good, the manorial system might not be bad, and the parish might not be unhappy. But idleness and autocracy are bad trainers, and duties which are not binding are seldom performed. The annals of the rural poor were sad as well as short and simple. The squire had little education. The universities, Oxford especially, buried in richly endowed torpor, barely retained the form of teaching, and the young man was lucky if he left them no worse in character than he came. The deep and dull potations of Heads and Fellows, as Gibbon said, excused the brisk intemperance of youth. The great public schools, Winchester, Westminster, and

Eton, were in a better state; their teaching was only a modicum of classics, but the character which they formed was manly and free. Little democracies in themselves, they did much to keep the character of the gentry in touch with that of the people. When squires began to frequent watering-places, they probably gained more varnish than culture. "My Lord" made the grand tour and acquired the polish of the court and of London society. Sometimes he became Parisian, as did Chesterfield; more to the advantage of his manners than of his morals. The English aristocracy, however, was rural, not a court aristocracy like that of Versailles. It was not, like the French nobility, utterly estranged from the people. Its pleasures were healthy and did something to preserve its virtue. Some of the great landowners became agricultural improvers, and by their experiments did a service which peasant proprietors or freehold yeomen could not have done. One of them, the Duke of Bridgewater, as the patron of Brindley, gave the country its canals.

The church, safely established, slept and rotted in peace. Many of the livings, being in the gift of the landowners, were used as pensions for younger sons. Pluralism and sinecurism prevailed to a scandalous extent, and the bishops, who deplored the abuse in the clergy, were samples of it themselves. Rectors drew the tithes, sometimes of more than one parish, while starveling curates did the work. Of spiritual life, of pastoral visitation, there was little. The reading of the service and the delivery of a sermon, of which the chief object was to shun enthusiasm as the badge of the nonconforming fanatic, satisfied a parson's sense of duty. The common people were left in a state of heathenism, as, when missionary zeal turned on its light, plainly appeared. Churches, in spite of high-church reverence for the edifice, were sluttishly kept and allowed to fall into decay. A bishop could hold a see in which he was never seen. Bishoprics were treated by statesmen as political patronage, for which ecclesiastics waited and intrigued in the antechambers of power. Even moral reputation was not strictly required. The author of Swift's poems narrowly missed a mitre. Horace Walpole, speaking of the establishment of the Prince of Wales, says, "The other preceptor was Hayter, Bishop of Norwich, a sensible, well-bred man, natural son of Blackburne, the jolly old Archbishop of York, who had all the manners of a man of quality though he had been a buccaneer and was a clergyman; but he retained nothing of his first profession but his seraglio." This was scandal, but it was scandal not incredible in those days. The same writer reproaches Bishop Keene for having failed to fulfil his promise of marrying a natural daughter of Sir Robert Walpole after being paid beforehand by the gift of a crown living. Bishops were grandees; one of them would not go the quarter of a mile from his palace to the cathedral except in a coach-and-four, with servants in full livery. But of the parish clergy and the curates many were very poor, so poor as almost to be compelled to dig and, like Trulliber, to handle swine. There were probably two Trullibers for one Parson Adams. Some of the order became ecclesiastical vagabonds; some of them lived by performing the irregular marriages, called Fleet marriages,

1753 till their trade was stopped by Act of parliament. From the vices of a celibate clergy the English parsons would be free, and they might, as a rule, set a fair domestic example. But as a centre of rural civilization the parsonage could hardly have been worth much more than as a centre of religious life. When later in the century there came a religious revival led by a great evangelist and organizer in the person of John Wesley, it found the masses barbarous as well as without religion. Born and cradled in the establishment, Methodism could there find no abiding home. The new wine of the Gospel burst the old bottle of state religion, and the evangelist in his own despite was driven forth to found outside the church of England the free church of the poor.

The Anglican establishment continued to be a political idol and a watchword of political party, because it was the bulwark against the hated papist on one side and the hated puritan on the other; but the clergy, personally, seem at the same time to have been unpopular and despised. Marriage with them was disparagement. Chaplains in great houses married waiting-maids, and left the table when the sweets were served. Butler, Clarke, Secker, Fletcher of Madeley, and Law among ecclesiastics, like Johnson among laymen, were stars in a dark night. What there was of clerical intellect and learning took largely the form of apologetics, of which Butler was, and remains, the chief. Paley taught the cold religion of common sense. The Deists were at work; and cultivated society, as we see in the writings of Chesterfield, was feeling the influence of Voltaire. Among the nonconformists there was more religious life. But even among them zeal was growing cold and their numbers seem to have been reduced by the toleration which left them to themselves.

The salt having lost its savour, moral rottenness prevailed. Kings openly kept mistresses; nobles did the same; and bishops connived. A set of rakes somewhat later in the century formed a house of pleasure in Medmenham Abbey, decorated it with lascivious emblems, and made it the scene of unspeakable orgies with obscene imitations of religious rites. Among them was the son of an archbishop. This corruption of private character could not fail to tell on public life. In the towns the bodies and souls of the lowest class were ravaged by gin in dens where they could get drunk and have clean straw for a penny. Hogarth has painted society, high and low, in the eighteenth century. In the middle class it seems that moral principles retained their hold, that honest dealing still prevailed, and that man and wife were true to each other.

In England the resistance of the Jacobites to the accession of George I., the Hanoverian and protestant claimant, was weak. A few fox-hunters rose in the North; but at Oxford and elsewhere Jacobitism confined itself to "magnanimous compotations." Its chief, Sir William Wyndham, Bolingbroke's principal confederate, was promptly arrested by the government. In Scotland Highland clans embraced the excuse for a raid, and re-
1715 ceived some general support from the feeling against
1715 the union, which was still strong. At Sheriffmuir they fought a drawn battle with the Whig clansmen and royalist troops of Argyle. But on invading England, where the fox-hunters joined them, they were easily defeated, and James's son, the Pretender, coming to Scotland to rekindle the flame, turned out a chilling disappointment.

Louis XIV., whom no treaty could have withheld from
aiding the rebellion, just at that time closed by his death 1715
the era of French aggrandizement. Executions followed
the rebellion, but there was no Bloody Assize. The
community must be defended. If a political motive were
to confer immunity on rebels, society would be at the
mercy of every brigand who chose to say that his object
in filling it with blood and havoc was not plunder, but
anarchy or usurpation.

Four years afterwards Spain, galvanized into sudden
life and aggressiveness by the magic touch of the adventurer Alberoni, and finding her ambition crossed by England, took up the Pretender's cause and sent a little
Armada against Great Britain. But the little Armada,
like the great Armada, encountered storms in the Bay
of Biscay, and the small force which it succeeded in
landing in Scotland was at once put to the rout.

George I. did not, like William III., try to form a government without respect of party. He at once frankly
threw himself into the arms of the party which had set
and alone could hold him and his house upon the throne.
All the places in the government were filled by Whigs.
The commissions of the judges still expired on the demise
of the crown, and the Tory Chief Justice Trevor was
dropped, nominally on the ground that his judgeship was
incompatible with a peerage. In a general election the
Whigs were completely victorious. Bolingbroke, Harley, 1715
and Ormonde, the Tory Commander-in-Chief who had
betrayed the allies to France, were impeached; and justly, 1715
for if a packed parliament had approved the Treaty of
Utrecht, it had not approved the conspiracy with the
enemy, or the treacherous betrayal of the allies in the

field. Bolingbroke fled and ratified his own condemnation by entering the service of the Pretender, from which, however, finding himself a clever knave among fanatical fools, he was presently compelled to withdraw. Ormonde also fled abroad. Harley, less deeply compromised, perhaps also more phlegmatic, stayed and outlived the storm.

1718 Tory policy was reversed. The Occasional Conformity Act and the Schism Act were repealed. The Treaty of Utrecht, which could not be repealed, was condemned.

Presently the Lords, to prevent another swamping creation, such as that by which the treaty had been carried, proposed to limit the king's power of creating more peerages to six. This would have closed the book of the British peerage as the Golden Book of Venice had been closed. It would have clipped the prerogative and the influence of the crown, shut the door against ambition, and abolished the only means of compelling the House of Lords in an extreme case to bow to the national will.

1719 The Bill was thrown out by the Commons after affording a fine theme for the grand debating club. The opposition made a hit by saying that if the Bill passed the only access to the temple of honour would be through a tomb. Through what portal other than the tomb of a dead father is the House of Lords entered by the successor to a hereditary seat?

Government, however, was now in the hands of the Whigs. It was still in very serious danger from disaffection. Several years later, encouraged by the birth of a son to the Pretender and by a commercial catastrophe in England, the Jacobites were again at work, and Bishop

1722 Atterbury, the great high-church champion and enemy of nonconformists, who had offered Bolingbroke to proclaim the Pretender, was caught in a treasonable correspondence which led to his banishment from the realm. The Whigs consequently became the party of authority and repression. They upheld the standing army. They passed a stringent Riot Act to restrain the Tory mob which had begun to pull down meeting-houses. They left unrepealed, or rather enhanced in stringency, the tax on newspapers and the cheap press. They repealed the act passed in the time of William, limiting the duration of parliament to three years, and extended the term to seven, which remains the law at the present day. Factitious or secondary reasons were given for this momentous change, such as that it would reduce the influence of the Lords over the Commons, and render less frequent the carnivals of corruption and riot which disgraced elections in those days. But the real object was to lend stability to a tottering government and guard it against the danger of being wrecked, as the great Whig ministry of Anne had been wrecked, by a Tory or high-church typhoon. Members of the House of Commons were arraigned at the time, and have since been arraigned, for voting themselves a term longer than that for which they had been elected by their constituents. Parliament was sovereign and was justified in doing whatever the paramount interest of the state required. A dissolution would have been formally constitutional, but it might have overturned the Hanoverian throne.

1715

1716

The Tories and Jacobites, on the other hand, being out of power and bent on the overthrow of the government, took to courting the democracy, to declaiming against standing armies, to agitating for short parliaments, to posing as the champions of the liberties which in power they had sought, and had they returned to power would again have sought, to destroy. There was once more a foreshadowing of that which is called Tory democracy in our day. The leader of the party, Sir William Wyndham, appears to have been a man of character and merit, though it is difficult to believe that a partisan of the Stuarts, in pandering to democracy, was sincere or had any object other than the disturbance of the existing settlement.

1714   In the opening years of George I., the leadership of the government was divided between Townshend and Stanhope, both of them able and honourable men of business. Stanhope was a good though not a fortunate soldier, a man of liberal mind, who would have carried further the principle of religious toleration, extended it to the Roman Catholics, and repealed the Corporation and Test Acts as well as the Schism Act and the Occasional Conformity Act. With them was Robert Walpole, whose parliamentary ability and knowledge of finance were making themselves powerfully felt. Ministers soon had trouble, as their successors were destined to have, about Hanover, the union of which with the British crown drew Great Britain into continental complications, deprived her of the advantages of her insular position, and forced her to be a military as well as a maritime power. The Act of Settlement, anticipating the accession of another foreigner to the British throne, had restrained his departure from the kingdom, but that restriction had been removed. Far better it would have been to provide that a foreigner succeeding to the British throne should give up his foreign dominions. On a Hanoverian question it was that the two ministers first fell out. Townshend was ultimately

dismissed, carrying Robert Walpole with him into opposi- 1716
tion. Stanhope was left at the head of the government,
with Sunderland, a man of ability but slippery, as his
partner, and kept that position practically till he died.

A great financial crisis brought to the front Walpole,
who, with Townshend, had just rejoined the ministry,
and decided that he should be head of the state. The
grasping desire of growing suddenly rich without labour,
which is the root of all gambling, gave birth to the South 1720
Sea Bubble, a counterpart of the Mississippi scheme in
France, of the tulip mania in Holland, and a precursor of
the English railway mania of later days. The government, lured by the fancy, which has taken more than one
form, of conjuring away public debt without paying it,
entangled itself with the projects of the South Sea Company, which, in reliance on the profits of its trade, undertook to finance a great body of government liabilities.
There was a fabulous inflation of South Sea stock. The
general spirit of speculation was set at work, and, having
no financial press to control it, gave birth to a number of
bubble companies, at last to one of which the object was
"thereafter to be disclosed," and was disclosed by the
disappearance of the projector with all the money. Then
came a terrible crash, with a tempest of public rage and
terror. Members of the government who had compromised themselves were driven from place, and one of
them committed suicide. The foundations of public
credit were shaken, and commerce was in despair.
Robert Walpole's name as a financier stood the highest.
The general voice called for him. By bold and sagacious
measures he stayed the panic, restored public credit, 1721
revived commerce, and made himself master of the state

for twenty years. With Townshend, who at first was his partner in the firm, he quarrelled, as it was his nature to quarrel with any one with whom he shared power. Townshend was eccentric enough, instead of going into opposition, to withdraw to his country seat, devote himself to farm improvement, and introduce the culture of turnips; saying that he knew his temper was hot and that he might be betrayed, as he had seen others betrayed, into factiousness and departure from his principles.

Walpole is the first prime minister properly so-called. Hitherto, the term had been branded as unconstitutional, as well it might be, seeing that it meant little less than king; nor was it even yet deemed inoffensive. George I., a German who was fifty-four when he came to England, who spoke no English, who had little knowledge of English politics, and whose heart was in Hanover, where he had everything his own way, left his minister to govern England, lending him at the same time, so far as appears, a steady support; for though his ability was small and his mind was narrow, he was a man of plain sense and honour. He had mistresses, but they were chosen, in fact, for their restful stupidity; they peculated, but they did not seriously intrigue. His hapless queen being a prisoner in Germany on a charge of infidelity, there could be no court influence of that kind. All sovereigns down to this time had presided in council, Anne like the rest, though probably she dozed. George I., as he could not understand the discussion, let the prime minister preside in his place. The prime minister appointed or dismissed his colleagues in the name of the king. His government rested avowedly on a party which accepted his guidance, was bound to support his measures, looked to him to reward its support with patronage, and was assembled by him in caucus at a crisis in the parliamentary battle. Party allegiance and submission to party discipline were justified by the needs of that time. To keep out the Stuart, with despotism and popery in his train, a good citizen might well waive his personal convictions on all minor issues if thereby united action on the grand issue was to be secured. There was, in fact, still on foot a dynastic war, though generally waged without arms and on the floor of parliament; a different thing from the conventional division of a nation into two camps, one of Blues, the other of Yellows, for the sake of perpetuating the party system and maintaining the ceaseless competition for power.

We have now the cabinet and party system almost full blown. The cabinet, though a body unknown to the law, as it remains to this day, finally supersedes the old constitutional Privy Council, the authority of which, and its responsibility for the acts of the crown, the framers of the Act of Settlement had in vain sought to revive by an article which was presently repealed. The responsibility of ministers for the acts of the king, another essential part of the system, was becoming well established. Criticisms on the king's speech would henceforth be held lawful, the speech being taken as that of the minister. "Let the poor fellow alone," said George II. when he was told that a counterfeiter of the speech from the throne should be soon brought to condign punishment; "I have read both speeches, and I like the counterfeit the best." To the completion of the system there was still lacking the joint and several responsibility of the cabinet ministers, which was not yet fully established.

Not that the king had become a mere cypher. He still named his minister, though the ministry could not live without a majority in parliament. He had still a voice in the distribution of patronage, both civil and ecclesiastical. Ambition still sought his favour, and his mistresses were able to make money by the sale of it, as the mistresses of George I. did on an extensive scale. Above all, he was still, by the forms of the constitution, and in the eyes of the nation as well as in its liturgy, the ruler; and the day might come when he would again desire and try to rule.

Unlike Bolingbroke, who, when he was leader of the party, had taken a peerage, Walpole remained in the House of Commons, thereby recognizing that house as the seat of power. The peers, however, retained much of the power which their own house had lost by the influence which, as territorial magnates, heads of the landed interest, and masters of pocket boroughs, they exercised over the House of Commons; though no longer a fully co-ordinate branch of the legislature, they had still, at least on all subjects but money Bills, a voice in the council of the nation.

Robert Walpole was the son of a squire with a good estate in Norfolk. He had the tastes and habits of his class; was a keen fox-hunter, and opened his gamekeeper's letters first. He was thus in touch with the landed gentry, while his financial skill and knowledge of trade gained him the confidence and the political support of commerce. He was a staunch Whig; had been one of the managers of the impeachment of Sacheverell, and felt the vengeance of the Tories in their day of triumph. Ejected for a time from the ministry in conse-

1717

quence of a rupture between Stanhope and Townshend, he had been recklessly factious in opposition; had leagued himself with Jacobites; had attacked the standing army; had opposed the Mutiny Bill; and had voted against a repeal of the Schism Act, which he had himself denounced as worthy of Julian the Apostate. His morals were loose, his conversation was more than coarse, and when at Christmas he gathered his political followers round him at Houghton, their orgies drove decency from the neighbourhood. But he was strong, clear-headed, and sagacious, all in the highest degree. In the House of Commons he rose with a hale and lusty frame, a genial and cheery countenance. He was a master of debate; thoroughly understood the material interests of the country; and though he grasped power unscrupulously and monopolized it jealously, when it was in his hands he used it well.

The political ideal of such a man was not likely to be high. Walpole, in fact, had no ideal. The aim of his policy was to maintain the Revolution settlement by keeping the house of Hanover on the throne. For this he saw that peace with foreign powers, with France above all, was indispensable, since enemies abroad were sure to ally themselves with the Jacobite enemy at home. Peace, therefore, he did his best to maintain; and not only between England and foreign powers, but, so far as he could, among the masters of Europe, ever wrangling for territory, ever disputing about rights of succession, and ever on the verge of war. In this his skill as diplomatic helmsman was taxed to the uttermost, and did not fail. The Spanish tempest raised by Alberoni had been encountered and dispelled by Stanhope. In cultivating friendship with

France, the government of George I. was greatly helped by the change which had taken place in that country. Louis XIV., the fanatical champion of legitimacy and catholicism, had been succeeded by the Regent Orleans, a sybarite who cared little for catholicism and thought only of the prospect of his own succession to the throne, which might be disputed by the Spanish Bourbon, and with a view to which he desired the friendship of England. So far had the fury of religious war abated, that the Regent's minister, Dubois, owed the cardinal's hat, under which his wickedness grinned, partly to British influence at Rome. Fleury, who succeeded Dubois as minister, was also pacific, as beseemed a septuagenarian, and his heart had been won by Walpole's brother, Horace Walpole, the British ambassador at Paris, who had been far-seeing enough to pay him a visit on the day of his transient disgrace.

1715

1726

The enemy to be disarmed at home was the squire, the member of the October Club, to whom Bolingbroke had shown game, and who, hating nonconformists and the commercial interest, had supplied the strength of the Jacobite or Tory party. Him also Walpole tried to win over by reduction of the land-tax, which he always had in view, as well as by general conciliation. Still it was on the boroughs, a number of them in the power of the crown or close and venal, the commercial classes, and the nonconformists that Walpole's government mainly reposed.

Walpole's motto was "Let Rest"; not the worst of mottoes for a nation which had been politically distracted for a century. Content to give industry and commerce, the natural sources of prosperity, fair play, with such help as finance or diplomacy could afford them, he shrank from all organic change or renewal of political strife. He would willingly have gratified the nonconformists who supported him by the repeal of the Corporation and Test Acts; but this he could not have done without provoking a conflict with the Tory parsons which, having been singed by the flames of the Sacheverell conflagration, he had steadfastly determined to avoid. He therefore put off the nonconformists with a pretext for delay, and at last, pressed to name his time, said frankly that the time would be never. An Annual Indemnity Act, however, did for the dissenters almost as much as would have been done by the repeal of the Test Act. Walpole tried to amend the tithe law for the relief of the Quakers, hundreds of whom had been imprisoned and some had died in prison; but the bishops and clergy were too strong for him. Against the catholics the law, sharpened on the defeat of James II., was made more vexatious by the imposition of the protestant oath of abjuration, and in one year a special tax was levied upon their property and that of the nonjurors. The motive was their assumed sympathy with the catholic Pretender. Walpole was no bigot or persecutor. He partook of the religious laxity of his age. It must be borne in mind that all this time catholics were persecuting where they had the power; that tidings of protestants or heretics, deprived of their liberty of worship, burnt alive, hanged, sent to the galleys, or driven into exile, were still coming in from catholic lands. Stanhope in 1691 had seen in Majorca twenty-seven heretics and Jews burnt; he was to see twenty more next day, and another "festival" of the same kind if he would stay a few days longer. Eng-

1727

land was still the asylum of the persecuted for conscience' sake, and their industries were her rich reward.

Stanhope had rid the Whig government of the organ of hostility to it and to all measures of toleration retained by the clergy in convocation. That body, having long ceased to be assembled for its original purpose as the legislature and self-taxing assembly of the clerical estate, had continued to exist as the cockpit of clerical war and a field for the attacks of the high church and Tory parsons on the Liberal bishops who were appointed by the Whigs. The Bangorian controversy waged between the High Church and the Low Church on a vast scale and with intense heat, though, as those who have explored its records say, without any definite issue, furnished a plausible ground for the final suppression of the assembly. A little dust, to use Hallam's phrase, was scattered over the angry insects. The license of the crown necessary to enable convocation to proceed to business was thenceforth withheld, and convocation practically ceased to exist till it was called to a feeble life by the high church movement of our own times. The established church was thus distinctly stamped as a department of the state.

That Walpole was himself corrupt there is no reason to believe. From his paternal estate, his official salaries, and his fair gains on the stock exchange he may well have had enough to pay for his palace at Houghton, his revelries there, and his gallery of pictures, without dipping his hands into the public purse. A committee of inquiry after his fall searched with all the energy of hatred for proofs of his corruption and found none. To sustain his government, to keep the house of Hanover on the throne, to uphold Revolution principle against Jacobite opposition or conspiracy, he used without scruple or remorse the vast and, according to our ideas, in part most objectionable, influence at the command of the crown; its nomination boroughs; the places and pensions, of which a scandalous number were held by members of the House of Commons; the borough votes of an army of excisemen which increased with the revenue; and patronage, military as well as ecclesiastical and civil. He dismissed officers of the army for voting against him. He bribed the political press. He bribed ambition with peerages; vanity with the Bath, a new order of knighthood. Probably he gave money bribes to public men. Among the men of honour, as they styled themselves in that century, to receive a political bribe was not dishonourable; and a nobleman into whose hand a minister had slipped a bill for three hundred pounds, though he refused the bill, did not feel insulted by the offer, but rather feared that the minister might be insulted by the refusal. All this was bad, but the choice was between this and the Stuart. In the nation at large, at least in its political classes, the party of the Revolution was in a minority; so that the prime minister had to keep the pyramid balanced on its point. To lower the tone of public life was hardly in Walpole's power. The worst that can be said of him is that he shared the general lowness of tone, or let himself down to it, and told young men at their entrance into public life that they would soon have to give up being Spartans and reformers. But he might well scorn the patriotism of his day. "Patriots!" he said, "I can make any number of them in a moment; it is but refusing an unreasonable or insolent demand, and up starts a patriot." "If you will not take the seals," said Walpole to Yorke, "Fazakerley will." "Why, Fazakerley is a Jacobite." "No doubt; but if you have not taken the seals by one o'clock, at two Fazakerley will be Lord Keeper and the staunchest Whig in England."

The charge of having failed to patronize men of letters as the statesmen of Anne had done, will not bear heavily on Walpole's memory. He was scholar enough to lose a bet about a quotation from Horace and to give impertinence the lie direct in Latin; but he was a man of business and might mistrust his own literary judgment. Perhaps he feared that in patronizing one man of letters he would be in danger of provoking the jealous resentment of two. It is doubtful whether English literature has ever owed much to government patronage. Walpole did probably the best he could by respecting the freedom of the press and abstaining from government prosecutions for libel, though libels on government were many and fierce. His employment of hacks was not wise; they degraded him without doing him any good.

In financial and commercial legislation Walpole moved on the lines on which the greatest statesmen in that department have moved since. Free trade was his policy. He took off in one year export duties on a hundred and six articles of British manufacture, and import duties on thirty-eight articles of raw material. He introduced the system of warehousing foreign goods duty free. He reduced the land tax; he reduced the interest on the debt. From the fallacy of the sinking fund he could hardly be expected to be free. Public credit was sustained; commerce flourished under his rule; and wealth was made for his successors to spend in war.

Walpole was prompted to tax the colonies. He said he

would leave that for bolder men than he was, little thinking, perhaps, that such men would come. He discerned that the real value of the colonies to England depended on their commercial prosperity; and in an age of monopoly dared to give them a modicum of free trade. In 1704 the whole colonial trade, Burke says, was little more than it was with the single island of Jamaica in his own time.

The Excise Bill was a good financial measure in the opinion of Adam Smith, who ascribes the clamour against it to the interest of smuggling merchants combined with faction. It would have enabled the minister to abolish or reduce the land-tax, and had such been its declared object it would probably have passed with ease. But the name of excise, odious from its use in the Commonwealth times, enabled the opposition to raise a storm. Walpole's men were ready to stand by him; but he declined, not from lack of courage, but from prudence and good feeling, to levy a tax by force. His decision showed that in spite of all the defects of the representation and the force of government influence in parliament, the minister felt the pressure of public opinion.

Hero-worshippers will not worship Walpole. But if he did not give the nation glory, he helped to give it the material elements of happiness. After all, military glory is not the only sentiment. There is a sentiment attached to prosperous industry and the home. If the people are prosperous, they will be happy; if they are happy, as a rule they will be good; and there are those whose sentiment is satisfied by goodness.

The worst part of Walpole's administration, as of that of other British statesmen of the age, was neglect of Ireland, where, while misery and oppression reigned, danger of disunion was gathering, though rather from the quarter of the dominant than from that of the conquered and down-trodden race. Walpole's attention had been called to that weak point by the storm which ensued upon the circulation of Wood's Half-pence. No wrong was intended nor was much really done by the British government. The dark spot in the transaction was the extortion of blackmail from the patentee by the king's mistress. The storm was raised by Swift, who was eating his heart in Irish exile and despaired of promotion under a Whig government. Yet it was formidable and ominous. Walpole, as was his wont, quietly backed out of the quarrel. Allowance must be made for the risks to which he would have had to expose his government in dealing with Irish questions, political, religious, or commercial; for the anti-popery sentiment which would have been aroused by any approach to toleration; the protectionist jealousy which would have been aroused by any measure of free trade. In this quarter, however, his statesmanship failed.

1724

Scotland was still a difficulty. Scotch feeling against the union and English feeling against the Scotch were still strong. A tax on beer, putting an end to the exemption of Scotland from the malt tax, was met by a combined refusal of Scotch brewers to brew. This collapsed. More serious was the lynching, by the Edinburgh mob, of Porteous, an officer who had hastily fired on rioters. There was indignation in England, but when penal measures were proposed, the Scottish members were all on the side of the Edinburgh mob and the opposition played its regular part. Walpole was cool, and got out of the dilemma with a fair show of vindicating the law. But his hold on the Scotch contingent in parliament appears to have been shaken.

1724

1736

Walpole was near losing power at the death of George I. George II., as heir apparent, had, according to the custom of the family, quarrelled with his father. On his accession he dismissed his father's prime minister, and was putting his favourite, Sir Spencer Compton, a lay figure, into his place. For the reinstatement of Walpole and the steady support of him afterwards, the country was beholden to the queen, Caroline of Anspach, who did excellent service in a quiet way. Caroline had much to bear and bore it well. She had to wink at mistresses, which that age scarcely regarded as disgrace, and daily to undergo the intolerable tedium of her husband's company. His not very valuable heart she left to a mistress, kept her hold on what he had of a mind, and guided him well. She was lettered, interested herself in philosophy, and helped to promote men of merit, among them Bishop Butler. Above all, she kept the king true to Walpole, though the king himself was a soldier and disposed to stand honourably by his servant. On her deathbed, to which, by a concealment of her disease, strange in one not generally delicate, she was prematurely brought, she conjured her husband to marry again that he might have a guide. He, really affected, as it seems, blubbered that he would not marry again, but keep a mistress. " Good gracious!" she replied, "you may do both." England owes much to Caroline of Anspach.

Walpole's weakness is said and seems really to have been a too jealous love of power. He could act with no one who had pretensions to a share of it. He had begun by shaking off Townshend. He presently shook off Pulteney, a first-rate debater, though in no other way first-rate; Carteret, a man of genius, a highly instructed politician, a first-rate scholar, daring, impetuous, and erratic, with an ambitious foreign policy in his head; and Chesterfield, not to be measured by Johnson's overstrained letter, or by his own advice to his son, since beneath the airs and graces of a man of fashion he had the mind of a statesman. The temper of these men was not so well under the control of their patriotism as that of Townshend. Whether Walpole could have acted cordially with any of them may well be doubted; they acted with intense virulence against him. He wanted the sensibility to feel and the tact to affect sympathy with the aspirations of youth, and he thus made deadly enemies of the "boys," as he called them, one of whom was "that terrible cornet of horse," William Pitt. Opposition had its centre in the mansions of two successive heirs apparent, each of whom had quarrelled with his father and gave himself a semblance of importance as figure-head of a cabal against the court. It had a closet leader in Bolingbroke, who, half pardoned through the venal intercession of the king's mistress, had come back to England, pulled the wires of his old party, and helped Pulteney in writing or bringing out *The Craftsman*, the opposition print. But Bolingbroke had not been readmitted to the House of Lords, and he found that wire-pulling without a seat in parliament would not help him to the mark of his ambition. When he tried to approach the king, Walpole foiled him by boldly insisting that the king should give him an audience and hear all he had to say. At last he left the country in disgust. The opposition declaimed against corruption; against the standing army, which had not ceased to be a fine theme for declamation; against the sacrifice of English interests to Hanover. But the minister's obedient majority of partisans and placemen long enabled him to smile at invective, the more so as the opposition was made up of three distinct sections which did not always vote together; the malcontent Whigs styling themselves patriots, such as Pulteney and Chesterfield; the Jacobites, led by "honest" Shippen, who formed a standing conspiracy for the restoration of the Stuarts, and the Tories who, like the Tories of a later day, were the party of the church, the king, and the landed interest. Still the opposition gained strength. Walpole seems never to have quite got over the unpopularity which had been brought on him by the Excise Bill. The death of the queen 1737 deprived his government of a strong support.

At last a quarrel with Spain gave the opposition an opportunity of getting up an agitation which proved fatal to Walpole's policy of peace and to Walpole. Spain had been kept in a state of constant irritation by the retention of Gibraltar, which it was the wish of Stanhope to resign. England had by treaty a right to the trade of a single ship with the Spanish dependencies in America. The restriction was evaded by reloading the ship from tenders when she had discharged her first cargo, and some of the smugglers, it seems, were roughly handled by the Spanish revenue officers. There was no question which diplomacy might not have settled, and leaders of the opposition themselves afterwards, as we learn from Burke, coolly washed their hands of the war. But faction grasped the opportunity of overturning a peace government. One 1739 Jenkins was produced to swear that his ear, which he had kept in cotton and which some believed had been cut off in the pillory, had been cut off by the Spaniards; and he fired the national heart by saying, probably from dictation, that in the hands of his cruel captors he had commended his soul to God and his cause to his country. The nation was worked up to fury, and the king, who was a soldier with warlike propensities and had now no Caroline at his side, shared the frenzy of his people. Spain was popish; she was weak, and her treasure fleets were rich prey. Walpole was unable to stem the raging tide. His proper course was to resign; but he clung to power, probably justifying its retention to himself by thinking that he could moderate what he had been unable to prevent. He went into what he knew was an unnecessary and, therefore, a wicked war, exclaiming that they who were ringing the bells that day on its declaration, would be wringing their hands on the morrow. As a peace minister, known to be opposed to the war, and therefore mistrusted as well as misplaced, he of course failed in its conduct. The war machinery was rusty and out of gear. Patronage had corrupted the army and navy. The naval administration was rotten, and the treatment of the sailor was vile. The leaders of the opposition of course did their utmost to weaken and embarrass the government in the conflict into which they had driven it. Such is always the conduct of faction, politely styled party. Anson, in his attacks on the Spanish treasure ships,

1739 renewed the exploits of Drake and Raleigh. Portobello
1741 was taken, but the attack on Carthagena failed; and in the troop-ships, turned into hospitals, or rather charnel-houses, there were appalling scenes. The shadow of approaching defeat fell upon Walpole. Instead of throwing off the minister at dinner and being the merriest of the company, he sat by the hour silent and with fixed eyes. His sleep was broken. But though his buoyancy

left him, his courage did not. He struggled gallantly and spoke ably to the end. He went into his last election weighted by the miscarriages of the war, by the accumulated discontents of twenty years, by the lingering odium of the Excise Bill, by all the calumnies which faction could invent, and by angry passages with the Scotch. Every engine was plied against him by the fury of an opposition divided in principles, but united in hatred. He came out of the fight with his majority greatly reduced 1741 in numbers, still more fatally in spirit. On the floor of the House he fought with unabated energy and force against Pulteney, Pitt, and all the host of enemies whom his long monopoly of power had made; and his last speeches seem to have been his best. Party in these battles showed its character. The maim, the halt, the blind, were whipped down to vote. Some sick ministerialists being about to be brought in through a private door, the opposition stopped the keyhole with sand. A ministerialist stepped up to a member of the opposition and told him that his son had been lost at sea. The bereaved father recognized the kindness of the intention, and stayed to vote. Cornish and Scottish members left Walpole. His majority fell to three. At last he was beaten on an election petition by one. Then, though his 1742 own heart was still high, he yielded to the pressing advice of friends and retired. 1742

The old idea still lingered that a fallen minister was a public criminal to be punished for his abuse of power, and there was talk of impeachment and even of blood. But all the fury simmered down into a committee of inquiry, which sat long, did its worst, and produced nothing. The king, who had shown on the battlefield that he did not lack courage, and who rather shines as a patriot among the vultures of faction, stood by his faithful servant; and Walpole's only punishment was translation, as Earl of Orford, from the scene of his power to the House of Lords. The sole fruit of this victory of patriotism was a Place Bill limiting the number of offices tenable by members of the House of Commons. "The principles of the opposition," said Chesterfield, "are the principles of very few of the opposers." The principle of the opposers had been the overthrow of the government.

1742
1743

Fortune called on Pulteney; but Pulteney's courage failed him. He pleaded a patriotic vow which he had registered against acceptance of place, declined to form a government, and in the end allowed his fallen rival, who still had the king's ear, to reduce him to impotence by making him Earl of Bath. "I have turned the key on him," said Walpole, making the motion with his hand. "Here we go, my lord," said he to Pulteney, "the two most insignificant men in the kingdom." The House of Commons, originally called to give the government supplies, and perhaps advice, had itself become the government.

1742

The nominal head of the next administration was Lord Wilmington, who, as Sir Spencer Compton, had been minister-designate for the hour between the death of George I. and the re-installation of Walpole; but the real head was Carteret, whose parts, according to contemporaries, were not less amazing than his rants. He once read a love-letter in council, being probably full of claret, which was his general state. A more dangerous pilot the ship could not have, especially in foreign affairs, which were his strong point, and of which he deemed himself consummate master. It had been Walpole's policy to

1742

avoid engagements. Carteret showed his genius and proved Hanover to be a fatal adjunct to the island realm by plunging the nation into continental war. Wilmington died. The ball then rolled into the lap of Pelham, younger brother of the Duke of Newcastle, who came in as secretary of state, and by whose vast parliamentary interest the minister was supported. Pelham was a worthy man and a fair administrator; a very inferior and far less courageous Walpole. He floated rather than steered, but managed to keep clear of the rocks. He was a good financier and effected a large conversion of the debt. He sustained the government by Walpole's means, but he could have sustained it in no other way. 1743

Now, however, was seen the wisdom of Walpole's policy of peace. Once more the house of Stuart found supporters in continental powers at war with England. The young Pretender, Charles Edward, who was more engaging than his father, landed in Scotland, raised the Jacobite clans, or the clans which raided under that banner, defeated a royal force under Cope at Preston Pans by the Highland rush with the claymore, took Edinburgh, was installed in the palace of Holyrood, marched into England as far as Derby, and filled the metropolis with shameful consternation. England was denuded of troops for the foreign war and was compelled to call upon Holland for stipulated aid. Among the people a strange and sinister apathy seems to have reigned. That they would look on and cry "Fight, dog! Fight, bear!" was the opinion of shrewd observers; so little root had the German dynasty yet taken, and so needful had been the cautious policy of Walpole. At length the government rallied and gathered force. The Pretender retreated, and with a Highland 1745 1745 1745

1745-1746 host to retreat was to throw up the game. The Duke of Cumberland came up with the rebel army at Culloden, formed, as encounters with the Gallic rush had taught the Romans to form, in the order necessary to repair a broken front, and by his victory extinguished for ever the pretensions of the house of Stuart. The duke, a German soldier-prince, professionally ruthless, treated the vanquished with cruelty. But the conduct of the government in the punishment of the rebels on the whole showed the progress of humanity. The heir of the Stuart cause, all hope lost, sank into a drunkard, and the house of Stuart

1807 expired in a cardinal, whose characteristic memorial is the convent, room for which was made by the demolition of the temple of Jupiter on the Alban Mount.

"You may now go play, unless you like to fall out among yourselves;" so said the old cavalier to the Roundheads on the final overthrow of his party. The same thing might have been said to the Whigs after the final overthrow of the Jacobites; and the Whigs, like the Roundheads, failed not to fall out among themselves. The Whig party began to split into connections, formed severally around great houses, which struggled against each other for place, and with their selfish cabals and perplexed intrigues ignobly filled the scene. There were shades of difference in the political character of the connections, one being purely Whig, another inclining more to Toryism; but power, which gratified ambition and brought with it an immense patronage, was the animating motive of all.

1754 An early outcome of the struggle was the ascendancy of the Duke of Newcastle, the arch borough-monger and arch place-monger of the day, who by assiduous effort in both those lines of corruption, and by the expenditure of a princely fortune in politics, had laid up a vast stock of parliamentary influence. As a head of the state his Grace was grotesque. His royal master said of him that he was hardly fit to be a chamberlain to a petty German prince. His contemporaries vied with each other in depicting the absurdity of his figure, always fussy and spluttering, hurrying as though he were trying through the day to catch an hour lost in the morning, hastening as if he were the carrier instead of the writer of a despatch, rushing from his dressing-room with his face half covered with lather to embrace the man who brought him the good news that Cape Breton was an island. Insanely craving for power, or rather for the dispensation of patronage, he was yet timorous in the pursuit. He lacked even common veracity, and Walpole said of him that his name was perfidy. At a royal funeral we see him pretending to be fainting with grief, while a bishop hovers over him with a smelling-bottle; then, as his curiosity prevails over his hypocrisy, running round with his spyglass to see who was there. His practised cunning, however, enabled him to outwit far abler men than himself. He was industrious and always ready in debate. He was twice prime minister of England, and held high office for thirty-three years. It is due to him to say that while he spent his life in corruption, and his mansion was its court, he was not himself corrupt. It was the game, not the stakes, that he loved, and in the game he squandered three-quarters of his ducal fortune.

Pelham dying, Newcastle became prime minister. He blundered and failed. He and his feeble leader in the House of Commons, Sir Thomas Robinson, were treated

1754

as butts by his own subordinates, Pitt and Henry Fox, cabinet discipline having as yet been imperfectly established, while Newcastle had no personal power of control. The French Bourbon having come to the aid of the Spanish Bourbon, there was war with both powers. It was misconducted; Minorca was lost, and Newcastle basely sought to appease national indignation by the execution of Byng, the naval commander, for failing to relieve it; shooting an admiral, as Voltaire said, to encourage the rest. The ministry broke down, Newcastle unsuccessfully attempting to sustain it by a union with Henry Fox, a very able and daring adventurer, effective in debate, master of the arts of corruption, a first-rate manager of parliament, and without principle of any kind.

William Pitt was now striding to the front. To him the eyes of the people were turning as the man to redeem them from the oligarchical selfishness, incapacity, and corruption which made a man of sense like Chesterfield despair of the state. Pitt, though allied by marriage to Earl Temple, did not belong to the great houses; he was qualified for the part of the great commoner and the man of the people. He had shown no scruples in cutting his way to power. He had been one of the bitterest opponents and most relentless persecutors of Walpole, and had fully shared the crime of forcing him into the war with Spain. As a subordinate in the Newcastle ministry, he had been wanting in loyalty to his chief. On the other hand, he had nobly protested against the execution of Byng, and he had won golden opinions as Paymaster, by refusing the irregular profits of that office, which were eagerly grasped by Fox. By the king he was hated as an opponent of the payment of Hanoverian troops, and as having spoken most contemptuously of Hanover and of the subjection of British to Hanoverian interests. But the king was forced to give way, ejaculating, with a flash of insight, that ministers were king. Under the nominal premiership of the Duke of Devonshire, Pitt became secretary of state and the real head of the government. Fresh energy was at once infused into the war department. Fresh hope was awakened in the national heart. But the government could not command the majority in parliament, which was in the hands of the great parliamentary jobber, the Duke of Newcastle. Weighted at the same time by the king's prejudice against Pitt, it fell; and the country, in time of war, was for eleven weeks without a government. Meantime the nation had marked its man, and gold boxes, with the freedom of cities in them, were showered upon Pitt. 1756 1757

At last, the mediation of Chesterfield effected a coalition between Newcastle and Pitt; Newcastle furnishing the majority, Pitt the capacity; Pitt taking the government absolutely to himself and disdainfully leaving the patronage to the duke. Pitt had compared the union of Newcastle with Fox to that of the languid Saône to the impetuous Rhone. He might now have found a fresh use for his simile. He had an independent source of strength in the enthusiastic attachment of the civic democracy of London, the head of which, Beckford, a somewhat inflated city potentate, served as his political tender, supplying him with the popularity which he disdained to seek for himself. 1757

For four years Pitt is dictator. The House of Commons bows, almost cringes, to his personal ascendancy sustained by the oratoric fire, of which only a few flakes remain. His will is done, and all the money which his vastly expensive policy demands is voted without a word. He had boasted that he alone could save the country. War was his panacea; he avowed himself a lover of honourable war. His grand aim was to humble France, strip her of her colonies, and destroy her commerce, thereby, as he and the traders of that day believed, making British commerce flourish. His policy was thus the very opposite of that of Walpole. Of economy and finance he was alike ignorant and regardless. For Scotland and for the union he did much when he gave effect to the wise advice of Duncan Forbes by raising Highland regiments. For the general administration, for the reform of abuses, for Ireland, he did nothing. But he was the greatest of war ministers. He had the eye to discern merit in the services, and to promote it over the head of seniority and in defiance of routine. He infused his own spirit into all. It was in Hawke, when on a stormy sea and on a dangerous coast, he replied to the sailing-master who had warned him of the peril, "You have done your duty in warning me; now lay me alongside of the French admiral." It was in Wolfe when he scaled the precipice of Quebec. No one, it was said, ever entered Chatham's closet without coming out a braver man. Promotion by merit in the army and navy was an example for the public service generally. The most signal and the happiest instance of it was the bestowal of high command on Wolfe, whose character, combining tenderness and home affection with high aspiration, valour, and chivalry, was an assurance that with much that was unsound there was something still sound in the nation.

Pitt's character was a strange compound of littleness

with greatness. His egotism was intense, and by it and the waywardness that attended it he was more than once fatally led astray. His arrogance was unbounded; the Commons bore it, but the Lords would not. The great commoner never allowed his under-secretaries to sit down in his presence. Yet to the king, even to a king who was a mere boy, his language was almost abject; a peep into the royal closet intoxicated him, and it was said that when he bowed at the levee you could almost see his hooked nose between his legs. He was always lofty, even in his letters, always theatrical; never so much himself, it was said, as when he was acting a part. Genius might and did dwell with such infirmities. It is hard to believe that wisdom or the clearest sense of duty could.

Pitt's continental ally in the war was Frederick of Prussia. That philosophic and philanthropic disciple of Voltaire, having inherited from the military maniac, his father, an incomparable machine of war, had been tempted, as he coolly avows, to use it for the purpose of making himself a name. This he had proceeded to do by a felonious attack on the dominions of Maria Theresa, the young queen of Hungary, afterwards the empress-queen, whose weakness exposed her to aggression. A deadly struggle was thus opened between him and the injured empress. The wrath of the Pompadour, who ruled France, was drawn down on him by the quips of his Voltairean tongue. In the same way he made the Czarina his enemy. He thus formed against himself an overwhelming coalition; and, without the aid of Pitt, he and Prussia with him, in spite of his military genius and the superior drill of his army, must have fallen. In the dance of European discord there had been a change of

1756

partners; England had gone over from Austria to Prussia, and France, swayed by the affronted Pompadour, had thrown herself into the arms of Austria, her immemorial foe. The flame of war, thus kindled, enveloped the whole of Europe and America, and raged over them for seven years. At Torgau, the last great battle, twenty thousand Austrians and thirteen thousand Prussians were killed or wounded, and the wounded were left untended on the field through a night of frost. Torgau was one of a score of battles, some of them hardly less murderous, fought to make Frederick famous, while death and sorrow entered hundreds of thousands of peasant homes. Of Prussians, Russians, Austrians, and French together there had been slain, as Frederick reckoned, six hundred and forty thousand, and worse than the carnage were the desolation of whole districts, the famine, and the pestilence. An officer, riding through seven villages of Hesse, found in them one man, a clergyman, who was boiling horse-beans for his dinner. Frederick, the idol of those who worship force, bombarded a city for several days, destroying life and property, to mask the fact that a secret treaty had been made.

1760

To act with Frederick, Pitt had to throw over all his protests against payment of Hanoverian troops, continental entanglements, and the giving of subsidies to foreign powers. But he was conquering America, he said, in Germany. America, Canada at least, he did conquer. He conquered other French colonies. He destroyed for a time the maritime power and the commerce of France. Bells were always ringing for fresh victories, and the nation was in a delirium of pride and joy. Such was the mood, at least, of the governing classes. What was said or felt in the cottage we cannot tell.

1759

CHAPTER VI

GEORGE III

BORN 1738; SUCCEEDED 1760; DIED 1820

ONCE more the course of victory abroad was arrested and reversed by a political catastrophe at home. The old king, who had fought at Dettingen and liked the war policy, died. Frederick, his eldest son, had closed by an early death a silly and unfilial career. His grandson, George III., ascended at the age of twenty-two the throne which he was destined to fill through fifty-nine years, for the most part terribly eventful. 1760 1751 1760

The name of George III. cannot be penned without a pang, can hardly be penned without a curse, such mischief was he fated to do the country. The effect even of his personal and domestic virtues was evil, in so far as they sanctified his prejudices and gave him a hold upon the heart of the people. Whatever good he did by the example of a moral court was largely cancelled by the conduct of the sons whom he brought up unwisely, and by the Royal Marriage Act, depriving members of his family of their natural freedom of marriage, which was his personal work. The moral improvement of the nation, which by this time had begun, was due less to the influence of the court than to that of Methodism, with which assuredly the court had little to do, and of the evangelical movement within the establishment which

Methodism set on foot; perhaps also to the alarm which the spread of scepticism had given the clergy, and to a recoil from the impiety and immorality of the Voltairean school. But it was no fault of George III. that the part cast for him by destiny was not that of a ploughman, for which he had strength and virtue; or that of a soldier, for which he had courage; but that of a ruler of his kind.

George's education had been royal. He was brought up by courtly tutors of Tory leanings who seem to have taught him nothing that could open his mind, while they instilled into him their political sentiments. His mother, full of the despotic notions of her native Germany, was always saying to him, "George, be a king!" It is probable that Bolingbroke's ideal of a patriot king, putting all parties under his feet and ruling for the good of the whole people, had found its way into his mind. At all events, on being a king and not only reigning but governing, he was bent. The liturgy and the law were on his side. If he looked into a book of constitutional law, such as Blackstone's "Commentaries," the manuscript of which is believed to have been borrowed for his use, he would have found it clearly laid down that it was the right and the duty of a youth of twenty-two with an ominously low forehead and prominent eyes, ignorant, inexperienced, narrow-minded, and with a taint of insanity in his blood, himself to govern the country; to make appointments, civil, ecclesiastical, judicial, military, naval, and colonial; to grant all honours; to call and dismiss parliament; to exercise a veto on all legislation; to direct foreign policy; and by his fiat to make war and peace. Such was the legal constitution; such is the legal constitution at this day.

The moment was propitious to George's game. The cause of the Stuarts was dead. The Tory devotees of divine right were ready to transfer their allegiance to a throne legitimized by two descents, and the occupant of which could say he was born a Briton. Jacobites began to attend the levées. The group of Whig houses which had overtopped the crown was discredited by its cabals and its corruption. The country was weary of their rule, which was no longer needed to keep out the Stuarts. They were quarrelling among themselves, so that they could be played off against each other.

George opened the game by having his declaration to the privy council drawn up without consulting his ministers, and by commanding authorities in Ireland to listen in certain cases to his instructions alone. He did not revert to the practices of his earlier predecessors by presiding in council; but he intended that instead of a prime minister with a party cabinet there should be what came to be called government by departments, without a prime minister, the head of each department holding his place solely of the crown, and all of them being under the personal but irresponsible control of the king. The king was to control the treasury boroughs, the pension list, and the other secret engines of power, to which George soon learned to add what he called "golden pills" for elections or the purchase of votes in parliament; and on a pretty large scale, as debts on the civil list, heavy and unaccounted for, showed. In time there was formed in parliament a set of "king's friends," whose votes were ever at the beck of the king, ready to trip up any minister who had crossed his will. Thus out of the grave of government by prerogative, government by influence was to rise. To carry this plan into effect and get rid from time to time of ministers who refused submission, aptitude for intrigue was required, and with this as well as with tenacity of purpose George was by nature endowed.

It unfortunately happened, however, that the part of patriot king was filled. To enthrone George it was necessary first to dethrone William, and put an end to the pursuit of conquest and glory. To get rid of Pitt the king brought forward and introduced into the government, as an earnest of the preference of merit to party, his groom of the stole and lord of the bedchamber, the Scotch Lord Bute, the special favourite of the Princess Dowager, a courtly and dignified gentleman of high monarchical principles, with a fine leg and a solemn elocution. An opportunity for the revolution soon presented itself. The Spanish Bourbon showed that he was 1761- coming to the aid of the French branch of his family. 1762 Pitt proposed to strike him before the Spanish treasure fleet could come into port. He was outvoted by the Bute section of the cabinet and forced to resign. The king and Bute were wise enough to disarm him, and at the same time to allay public wrath, by heaping on him rewards and honours. With tears of gratitude and in language of astonishing self-prostration he accepted a pension of three thousand a year for himself and a peerage for his wife. Then he ostentatiously sold his carriage horses and offended taste by turning the cheers from the king to himself in a procession to the City. The dismissal of Newcastle soon followed. The old jobber fell honourably after all, refusing a pension, though he had expended far the greater part of his estate in the public service. Bute 1762 became, under the king, the head of the government.

Bute had after all to justify Pitt by declaring war against Spain, and in his own despite he took Havana. 1762 But, like Bolingbroke, he sued to the vanquished for peace. Preliminaries of peace were framed. England 1762 kept Canada with consequences presently to be revealed, Minorca, some sugar islands, and some settlements in Africa which drew her more deeply into slavery and the slave-trade; as well as her winnings in India, where her merchant conquerors had meantime been gaining ground. This was what she got for the expenditure of blood, the war taxation, eighty millions of additional debt, bringing the total up to a hundred and fifty millions, and, what proved to be a heavy item on the wrong side of the account, a renewal of deadly enmity with France. Pitt, his City worshippers said, had made commerce flourish by war. To create a factitious prosperity by the destruction of a rival marine and by war expenditure was possible. To create permanent prosperity by the destruction of wealth was not. England and France were the natural customers of each other.

The preliminaries had now to be forced through parliament. For that or any other political operation, Bute had neither aptitude nor experience. He applied to Henry Fox, who stood for hire in the political market, and for very high pay readily undertook the job. Fox bought a 1762 large majority for the court and the treaty by bribery and by a use of patronage and of official terrorism in the way of sweeping dismissals unparalleled even in that era of corruption. Bribery included the allotment of public loans on scandalously gainful terms to the friends of the government. Such was the elevation of public spirit produced by war. War as a cure for internal vices and domestic discord is not less futile than immoral. Mean propensities are not expelled by violent passions. The contractor is not turned into a hero.

1763 To the general surprise Bute, after securing his majority, resigned. He was breaking down under the burden of state and under a load of public hatred. As the supplanter of Pitt, as the author of a dishonourable peace, and perhaps still more as a Scotchman, he was so detested that his life was not safe and he had to go about guarded by bravoes. That he was the paramour of the Princess Dowager was the belief of the people, playfully expressed by burning a petticoat and a jack-boot. His ministry was weak. His chancellor of the exchequer, Dashwood, who had supplanted the able Legge, was a jest, a bad omen for the opening of a reign of merit. Suspicions of Bute's secret influence continued to cast a shadow over the scene and to form the subject of stipulations and protests somewhat peevishly addressed by the responsible ministers to the king. But for these suspicions there seems to have been not much ground. So ended the first essay of George III. to play the patriot king. Though baffled, he was not subdued. Neither his hatred of the Whig oligarchy which had overmastered the crown nor his struggle to restore personal government ceased. He had his golden pills and was enlisting his king's friends.

1763 For the present the king found himself in the hands of a ministry formed of a coalition, Whig in name but largely Tory in character, of which George Grenville was the head and the Duke of Bedford was the patron. Grenville was an honest, industrious, and capable man of business, but narrow-minded, a legal and constitutional formalist, fitter to be speaker of the House of Commons, his darling sphere, than chief of the state. Bedford was a Tory in grain, always on the arbitrary side.

Government now became involved in two great contests. Of these contests, the first was half comical. John Wilkes was a born demagogue. His face was that of a Thersites, with a horrible squint. Morally he was a scamp and one of the debauched brotherhood of Medmenham Abbey. From principle and conviction he was entirely free, and when all was over he could jauntily tell the king that he had never been a Wilkite. At the same time he was extremely clever and daring as well as restlessly vain, and he possessed in the highest degree the arts of popularity both political and social. He could even throw his spell over Johnson, who regarded him politically as a limb of Satan, by paying skilful homage to the dictator, and helping him to the brown of the veal. Wilkes had assailed Bute, the hated Scotchman, in the forty-fifth number of his *North Briton.* The secretary of state issued a general warrant for the apprehension of the authors and printers of the number, giving no names. This led to a long battle, with actions and counter-actions in the courts of law, about the legality of general warrants, which ended, as it could not fail to end, in their condemnation. But a second issue was raised by the expulsion of Wilkes as a libeller from the House of Commons, of which he was a member. Besides the libel on Bute the government found among his papers an obscene parody of Pope's "Essay on Man," entitled an "Essay on Woman," with mock notes by Bishop Warburton, the worshipper of Pope. This impudent squib was read to the horrified House of Lords by Sandwich, who was himself one of Wilkes's fellow-rakes, and was made a second ground of prosecution. The House of Commons, obedient to the wishes of the court and the government, expelled Wilkes as a libeller. That House, severed as it was from the people by the defects of the representation, was not less given than kings had been to assertions of its prerogative and stretches of arbitrary power. It not only expelled Wilkes, which it had a right to do, but went on to disqualify him perpetually for election. The question thus raised as to the right of constituencies gave birth to a great constitutional fray, in which the thunders of Pitt were heard on the side of popular right, though he disdained the demagogue and denounced hatred of the Scotch. Wilkes was outlawed, returned, underwent a triumphant imprisonment, presented himself as a candidate for Middlesex, and was elected by an overwhelming majority after a tempest of excitement and riot. He was again expelled from the House of Commons. He was again elected after another storm of agitation, when the House gave the seat to Luttrell, the court candidate, who had received the smaller number of votes. Like some other political struggles, this became a combat between the democratic city of London and the oligarchical House of Commons. In the end the House of Commons, weakened by other reverses, succumbed, and erased the proceedings against Wilkes from its journals. Wilkes meanwhile became the idol of the hour, was elected to the highest offices of the city, and touched the civic skies with his impish head. On this as on all occasions, the king was for arbitrary measures; his temper got the better of his policy and, instead of posing as the guardian of public

1768

1769

1782

right against the encroachments of the House of Commons, he pressed the prosecution of Wilkes, thus spoiling his own game if his intention was to play the patriot king. In fact he could play the king but not the patriot.

The other contest, far from being comical, was the most tragical disaster in English history. The thirteen American colonies of England now stretched in a line of seventeen hundred miles along the coast of the Atlantic from bleak Massachusetts to the sunny South. They were of different origin, but had for the most part been founded by religious or political exiles, who carried with them the spirit of resistance to oppression. In the north was the descendant of the exiled Puritan; in the south was the descendant of the exiled Cavalier; in Maryland the Roman Catholic had sought a haven of refuge from the penal laws; in Pennsylvania the Quaker had found freedom from a state church. To these had recently been added Irish Presbyterians, fugitives at once from the tyranny of the Irish episcopate and from British restrictions on Irish industry. The Puritan, though he had lost much of his religious fire, had kept his political republicanism, and had added to it a spirit of litigation, fostered by the lawyers, who were his social and political chiefs. The descendant of the Cavalier was a slave-owner, with the haughty pride of that character and a Roman love of liberty for the master class. As in origin, the colonies differed somewhat in constitution; some were royal; some were proprietary, a remnant of sovereignty remaining in the heir of the founder; some were chartered; but all had acquired something like a counterpart in miniature of the parliamentary government of England, and were instinct with British ideas of liberty, of the Great Charter, and of the Statute against Arbitrary Taxation. The political connection with the mother-country was maintained through governors sent out by the crown or the Proprietary. The colonies had felt in some measure the tyrannical aggressions of the later Stuarts, but from these they had been delivered by the Revolution. They fully enjoyed the personal liberties of Englishmen; on the whole they had been left to develop themselves as commonwealths in beneficent neglect; and though there was a certain amount of chronic friction between their local assemblies and the governors, who were often corruptly appointed, they had politically little cause for complaint, nor did they seriously complain. Governors were sometimes useful in controlling the indiscretions of young communities, notably with regard to the issue of paper currency.

Commercially it was far otherwise. The colonies generally were treated by the mother-country, according to the notion universally prevalent in those protectionist days and accepted by Montesquieu, as existing for her commercial benefit. They were forbidden to manufacture articles which she manufactured, to buy of anybody but her, and to carry their goods to any but her market. Their shipping industry was also restricted by her navigation laws for the benefit of her carrying trade and her navy. Colonists could not export their sugar, their tobacco, their cotton, their indigo, their ginger, their dyeing woods, their molasses, their beaver, their peltry, their copper ore, their pitch, their turpentine, their masts or yards, their coffee, pimento, cocoanuts, raw silk, hides, skins, potash and pearlash, or with some exceptions their rice, to any place but Great Britain, not even to Ireland. Nor might any foreign ship enter a colonial harbour; nor, with certain exceptions, of which the principal were salt and wines, could the colonists import from any country but Great Britain. The American colonists were debarred from the free sale, and thus practically from the manufacture, of cloth, from the manufacture of hats, though theirs was the land of the beaver, from iron manufacture of the higher kinds, though their country abounded in ores, as well as in wood and coal. While their free labor was thus discouraged they were forbidden to put a limit to the slave-trade as, from economical motives, though not from motives of humanity, they desired. Trade, even with British dependencies, was granted them as a special boon and in sparing measure. Commercial privileges, it is true, supposed to be countervailing, were conceded to them. But these privileges did by no means countervail, and the colonial system of England, though liberal compared with the Spanish system, and practically mitigated by contraband trade, was still so galling that in spite of the ties of race, history, and a common flag, there would probably have been a rupture long before had the colonies not been bound to the mother-country by a strong tie of another kind.

Such a tie there was in the need felt by the colonists of Britain for protection against French ambition which threatened them from its citadel at Quebec. They outnumbered the French thirty to one, and were certainly not inferior to them in natural valour. But they were farmers and traders, while the French-Canadian was as much of a bushranger as either, and was backed by the army of France as well as aided by the tomahawk of the Indian savage, to him a too congenial ally. The French forces were wielded by the single hand of a despotic governor, while the English colonies were disunited, and the most warlike, those of the southern slave-owner, being farthest from the point of danger, were the least willing to take arms. Confederation for the common defence had been essayed, but, owing to mutual jealousies, it had been essayed in vain. The colonists, therefore, were glad to be sustained by the mighty arm, and to be united under the leadership, of the mother-country. After the conquest of Canada there was an outburst of loyal affection, and Pitt was as much idolized in British America as in Great Britain. But, as shrewd observers at the time foresaw, when the fear of France departed attachment to England cooled. From that time there was among the republicans in Massachusetts a party which aspired to independence and was ready to embrace the first occasion of breaking the chain. Its apostle was Samuel Adams, who, finding himself unfitted for trade, had turned his mind to political agitation. Thus Pitt's glorious conquest brought in its train calamity, poorly compensated by the acquisition of a French colony which England failed to assimilate, and which added nothing to her wealth or to her real power.

The war being over and the day for payment having come, George Grenville, then minister, resolved to do that which the prudence of Walpole had shrunk from doing. He resolved to tax the colonies. He wanted to lay on them a part of the burden contracted partly for their behoof, and to make them maintain for their common defence a standing force, independent of local parsimony or caprice. It did not occur to him that they were already being heavily taxed by commercial restriction and the navigation laws. The pressure of the commercial restrictions he, just at the wrong moment, aggravated by issuing orders for stricter enforcement and the suppression of smuggling, thus closing the safety-valve of the most dangerous discontent. Grenville's object was purely fiscal or military. He was constitutional, though a political martinet; he intended no aggression on colonial liberties, nor is there good reason to suppose that he was originally inspired by the king. In fact, he was not on the best terms with the king, whom he bored with his tedious homilies in the closet. But he was a parliamentary pedant who took the statute book for policy as well as law. He pitched upon a stamp tax, after consulting the agents of the colonies, as the least odious form of taxation. He tried to gild the pill with commercial boons. But Massachusetts was ripe for revolt. Samuel Adams and his circle had leavened her with his doctrines; lawyers were her political pastors; her taverns were full of political debate and agitation. She rose at once in angry protest, forcibly resisted the execution of the Act, levelled the stamp office, wrecked the house of the stamp distributor, compelled him to resign his office and swear never to resume it, burnt the records of the admiralty court, rifled the houses of its officials, and gutted the mansion of the Lieutenant-Governor, who barely escaped with his life. Her lips continued to speak the language of loyalty, but her hand had raised the standard of rebellion. Pitt, now out of office, applauded her in his unmeasured way, saying that three millions of people, if they allowed themselves to be made slaves, would be fitted to make slaves of the rest. He drew a distinction between internal taxation and external taxation or anything which could be described

1765

as regulation of trade, asserting the right of parliament to lay any impost or restriction it pleased on colonial commerce, to prevent the colonists, if it chose, from making a nail for a horseshoe, but denying its right to levy internal taxes such as the Stamp Act. The difference between one mode of taxation and the other was, according to him, the difference between freedom and slavery. It was clear enough that the supreme power of legislation must carry the power of taxation with it. Whether the power of taxation could be justly or prudently exercised was another question. The colonies were unrepresented in parliament. So it was said, and with bitter truth, was a great part of the people of England. But then the people of England were on the spot; without having votes they might influence parliament; in the last resort they might reform their representation. The general interests of all Englishmen, enfranchised or unenfranchised, were the same. Adam Smith, indeed, had proposed that the colonies should be represented in parliament. But diversity of interest and character as well as a six weeks' voyage stood fatally in the way of that solution. Wisest were they who, like Dean Tucker, said, " If the colonies refuse to contribute to the burdens of the empire, let them go; we have nothing to gain by keeping them against their will." The fact was that the colonial system was fundamentally unsound; it had its source in the feudal idea of personal allegiance; there was no reason why countries on the other side of the Atlantic and capable of self-government should be dependencies of a European power at all; they ought to have been free and followed their own destinies from the beginning. The only sound reason at least for the retention of the tie was the danger to which these colonies, unshielded by the mother-country, might have been exposed from the aggressive ambition of France; while, if left to themselves, they would with greater readiness have combined for their own defence and they would have enjoyed exemption from imperial wars.

For the present the storm was laid. Grenville went out in consequence of a misunderstanding with his master about a Regency Bill which had been rendered necessary by the first appearance of mental malady in the king. He was succeeded, after the usual round of intrigue and cabal among the different aristocratic connections, and the usual struggles for the emancipation of the royal power on the part of the court, by Lord Rockingham, a sporting grandee of second-rate ability, and so bad a speaker that one who attacked him in debate was upbraided for worrying a dumb animal, but sensible, liberal, and a man of honour. Pitt unfortunately refused to join. He was too much under the sinister influence of his brother-in-law, Lord Temple, an arch-intriguer, who wanted a Grenville ministry. But Pitt himself was wayward, and hated the connections. His ideal, like that of George III., was a patriot king, putting faction and oligarchy under his feet, only that Pitt's king was to be William and not George. At his side Rockingham had a man far more memorable than himself, Edmund Burke, the Irish adventurer, as members of aristocratic connections called him, without a landed estate, or any capital but genius and learning, who had done Rockingham the honour to select him as his political patron. By Rockingham's ministry the Stamp Act was repealed, to the delight not more of the loyal colonists than of British merchants,

1765

1766

who, having suffered by colonial boycotting of their goods and the withholding of colonial debts, thronged the portals of the House of Commons on the eventful night, and, says Burke, beheld the face of General Conway, who had moved the repeal of the Act, as it had been the face of an angel. At the same time, to salve the wounded honour of parliament and satisfy the arbitrary temper of the king, an Act was passed declaring that the British legislature had power to bind the colonies in all cases. Such a settlement, theoretically inconsistent, but in appearance at least practically wise, savours of Burke, who in this as on all occasions maintained that government was a matter not of abstract principle, but of practical wisdom. He would be willing to waive any question about principle so long as the practical grievance was removed. The sequel showed, however, that abstract principles sometimes require attention. Burke might have found it difficult to say what a legislative supremacy was worth when it was not to be exercised, and, generally, what was the meaning and value of the connection. Had he not been a free trader, he might have pointed to the imperial monopoly of trade as a warrant for the colonial system; an argument which is wanting to the maintainers of the system at the present day, when a colony if it pleases can treat the mother-country as a commercial enemy and lay protective duties on her goods. The colonies, however, glad to be rid of the tax, acquiesced in the theoretic declaration, and peace for a time returned.

Not for a long time. The Rockingham ministry, weak in itself, and frowned upon in waywardness if not in selfishness by Pitt, soon fell. The king had to go back to Pitt, who formed a ministry after his own pattern without regard to connection or party; a mosaic, as Burke, a liegeman of the Rockingham connection, called it, of pieces taken from all political quarters, diverse in their colour, and totally strange to each other. The nominal head was not Pitt, but the Duke of Grafton, a somewhat indolent grandee, who spoke of the affairs of the turf as more important than those of state, and shocked public decency by his open immorality; yet honourable and sensible, as well as devoted to Pitt. Pitt himself sank into the office of Privy Seal. More than that, he sank into a peerage, leaving his oratoric throne in the House of Commons and passing into the limbo of the upper House as the Earl of Chatham, not without loss of his hold upon the people. His health was failing. Presently suppressed gout, not unmingled, perhaps, with the influence of that uncontrolled egoism which is the source of moral insanity, reduced him to a condition in which he could not be approached by his vicegerent Grafton, or even by the king, but lay, as scoffers said, on his back at Hayes talking fustian, while the ship of state was left to drift without a helmsman. It drifted into the maelstrom. Chatham being out of the way, the strongest, or at least the most aspiring and active, member of the government was Charles Townshend, a reputed man of genius, the leading wit of the day, the author of the famous champagne speech, and light and frothy as the beverage by which that speech was inspired. Partly, it seems, to redeem a reckless pledge, Townshend determined to repeat Grenville's experiment in another and, as he thought, a safer form. He laid duties on tea and some other articles imported by the colonies. This, he thought, would be external, not internal, taxation, while none of the duties were heavy, or, for the revenue

1766

1767

which they would produce, at all worth a dangerous experiment. Nevertheless, the winds which had slumbered in the colonial cave were again let loose. At once Samuel Adams was joyously at work. Again Massachusetts protested and rebelled. Again there was a reign of riot and outrage, this time more violent than before, culminating in the burning of the king's revenue-cutter and the tossing of a cargo of tea into the water. No government could bear this tamely. But the measures of repression were violent and unwise. The port of Boston was closed; the charter of Massachusetts was forfeited; an odious statute of Henry VIII. for transporting persons accused of treason beyond sea to England for trial was revived on the motion of the Duke of Bedford; and though no action was taken on it the wound inflicted by the insult was deep. Troops were sent to Boston, where there had before been a collision between the soldiery and the people, attended by the loss of a few lives, and styled by popular wrath the Boston Massacre. Sinister events now marched apace. Attempts at reconciliation were still made. All the duties except the duty on tea were repealed, and assurance was given to the colonists that no more would be imposed. There seems reason to believe that full satisfaction would have been given had not Hillsborough, who was for coercion, falsified the minute of the cabinet. On the colonial side there were men like Dickinson who desired peace with justice; but there were also men like Samuel Adams who, though they still found it politic to wear the mask of loyalty, were resolved that there should be no peace. Of the two men who might have mediated, Chatham was lying on his back, Franklin, the American Solon, had discredited himself by the use of stolen letters, a heinous offence in the eyes of men of honour, however loose their morality might be, and had been estranged by the abuse showered on him on account of that misdemeanour before the privy council by the coarse lips of the sycophant Wedderburn. The temper of the king had now been fatally awakened, and he had a great body of opinion on his side. The pride of the imperial people had taken fire at the insulting violence of colonists whom their arrogance regarded as subjects. The clergy preached everywhere against rebellion; so did Wesley; and the Tory squires were all for vigorous repression. On the American side platform and pulpit spouted patriotic fire. Burke, in pamphlets pregnant with undying wisdom, pleaded for reason, moderation, and peace; but against the storm of passion he pleaded in vain.

Soon the colonies unfurled the standard of open rebellion, took arms, united in a continental Congress, and set up a revolutionary government for the conduct of the war. The first gun was fired at Lexington, near Boston, 1775 on which the royal troops having marched to destroy revolutionary stores, suffered heavy loss from the rifles of the American volunteers; a presage of the general character of the conflict and of its destined issue. There presently followed the famous Declaration of Indepen- 1776 dence, drawn up by the Virginian Jefferson, whom the Democratic party in the United States revered as its father. This document, commencing, in the metaphysical spirit of that age, with abstract propositions of human equality and inalienable rights, penned by a slave-owner, proceeds to level charges against the king and his government, some of which were well founded, while others injure by their untruthfulness or exaggeration the cause in which they are employed. Measures of repression, taken after insurrection and outrage, are described as normal and characteristic acts of British government. In Jefferson's draft there was a virulent clause fixing upon George III., who was no monster of inhumanity, the personal responsibility for slavery and the slave-trade. The framer of that clause never emancipated his own slaves. The Declaration of Independence, however, is memorable as closing in politics the era of tradition and opening that of speculative construction. It was to be followed by the French declaration of the Rights of Man.

1768 Chatham having at last in a fit of waywardness resigned, upon a nominal pretext, and afterwards turning against his own ministry, the ministry fell, and its fall was followed by the usual chaos of cabal. But in the absence of any first-rate or leading man, the king was able to put at the head of the government a man of his own, Lord 1770 North, whose ministry unexpectedly, and for the country most unhappily, proved strong. With Bute, a mere favourite, the king failed; with North, thanks to the selfish discord of the connections and the decrepitude of Chatham, he succeeded. Instead of cabinet government, under the supremacy of the prime minister, there was now what George desired, government by departments under the supremacy of the king. The patronage and parliamentary influence of the crown sufficed to secure a majority for the administration. North, round whose head a historic aureole of infamy has gathered, was neither bad nor wanting in capacity. With an unwieldy and ungainly figure, protruding eyes and sputtering utterance, he had great aptitude for business, great industry, great tact and readiness, as well as imperturbable good humour in debate. Through the storm of invective he tranquilly dozed between his law officers Thurlow and Wedderburn, the twin pillars of his administration. So he is depicted by Gibbon, who was one of his regular supporters, and to whom, as a Voltairean monarchist, his political character was congenial. He was very happy in repartee, as when he complimented a member who presented a petition from Billingsgate and accompanied it with violent abuse of the minister, on having spoken not only the sentiments but the language of his constituents. Nor, though the King's nominee and a minister of prerogative, was he by any means himself disposed to violent or tyrannical courses. His easy good nature was his fault. His crime was compliance with the arbitrary and obstinate temper of the king, at whose bidding he carried on a struggle to which he was himself disinclined, and which, had his hands been free, he would have closed. His infamy shows that amiable weakness is criminal in a statesman.

The advocates of armed coercion said that the king had a large party in the colonies on his side, and that the colonists would not fight. In the first belief they were right. The loyalists were at least as numerous as the pronounced revolutionists, and they had amongst them a large proportion of the wealth and education, though combined with elements from the other extreme, while the strength of the revolution lay chiefly in the yeomanry and middle class. Their number was presently reduced, and the zeal of many of them was cooled by the arbitrary violence of the king's officers and the excesses of his hireling troops. Yet to the end of the war it remained large, and their constancy testified to the comparative mild-ness and beneficence of the British rule. The belief that the Americans would not fight was a mistake. As riflemen in irregular warfare they fought well. But in pitched fields the king's troops, though many of them were hired Germans, and though they were led by such generals as Gage and Howe, conquered, and an army which cannot hold its own in the open field must in the end succumb. Had the lazy or half-hearted Howe pressed the advantage which, early in the day, fortune threw into his hands, the revolution would probably have been defeated for a time, and Great Britain would have recovered a supremacy which, after the fatal estrangement of the colonial heart, would have been but her weakness and her bane. When from patriotic oratory or the tarring and feathering of Tories it came to real war, and that war opened with reverses, colonial fire began to cool. Men compared the cost of the conflict with its cause. Discontent, disunion, defalcation, and cabal set in. The militiaman would fight for his own homestead but not for the common cause. Bodies of militia, when their time was up, marched away from the camp on the eve of battle. The edicts and requisitions of congress were disregarded. The purchasing power of the paper money which it issued in volumes sank to zero. At last

1780 despair begot treason, and Benedict Arnold conceived the design of playing Monk. The salvation of the colonial cause was its leader, who by a happy choice had been taken from Virginia; a wise propitiation of the slave-owning aristocracy of the South, which would hardly have accepted a leader from mercantile New England. Washington's patriotism, constancy, and courage rose serene, not only over disasters in the field, but over the still more trying embarrassments of his situation, and, united to his powers of command, held together the half-clothed and ill-fed army which was the last hope of the cause in the winter camp of Valley Forge. With difficulty he persuaded Congress, instead of a local militia which was always moulting, to set on foot a continental army under regular discipline. In him, as in Cromwell, amid the deepest gloom hope burned as a pillar of fire. Yet at last even Washington almost despaired.

The turning point was the disaster of Burgoyne, who had marched from Canada down the Hudson and was to have met Clinton moving from New York. The combination failed, owing, if tradition is true, to the insolent carelessness of Lord George Germaine, North's incompetent war minister, who, having been dismissed the army for misconduct at Minden, had by his rank and interest forced his way into political office, where his worthlessness was still more fatally displayed. Burgoyne, surrounded in a tangled country by swarms of riflemen, was compelled with his whole army to surrender. France 1777 now grasped her opportunity of revenge for the loss of Canada and all the humiliations inflicted on her by Chatham. Already Lafayette, a light-headed young aristocrat, caught by the revolutionary theories which were presently to guillotine his order, had gone forth as a knight-errant to fight for American independence. For some time it had been apparent that France meant mischief and that her disclaimers were lies. She now impudently threw off the mask and sent a fleet and army to the assistance of the Americans. Chatham would 1777 have dropped the colonists and turned on France. But

1778 Chatham had passed away after a dramatic death-scene in the House of Lords, still upholding the American cause, yet still protesting against the severance of the imperial tie, and the court had shown the aversion which, mingled with fear, it had felt for him by refusing to take part in his funeral and deprecating the erection of a monument to his memory. North, after a feeble and hopeless attempt at reconciliation, went on with the war, success in which was no longer possible, since by the accession of the French navy to the American side England had lost the free command of her sea base. The nation finding itself disappointed of the speedy victory which had been promised, was growing weary of the war, and it was with difficulty that troops were raised. North, in fact, had long had the good sense to see the folly of prolonging the struggle. But the king was still obstinately bent on coercion, and North, instead of resigning, stayed in office to do his master's will. This he fancied was loyalty; it showed the unsettled state of the constitution. The king and the war party were practically confirmed and seconded in their policy of coercion by the violence of the opposition. The leader of the opposition, Charles Fox, the favourite son of Henry Fox, the master of corruption, had shown when he was little more than a boy miraculous facility as well as astonishing assurance in debate. His mind was highly cultivated as well as powerful; while his warmth of heart, generosity, and joviality, combined with his brilliant ability, had attached to him a large circle of devoted friends. But he was a gambler and a debauchee, losing enormous sums in play, spending whole nights over the bottle; and he carried the gambler's recklessness into public life. He set out as a violent upholder of prerogative and of the arbitrary action of the House of Commons. No one was more forward in the tyrannical treatment of Wilkes. Thrown to the other side by personal resentment, he showed the same violence in his new camp. Fox had human sympathies, broad and warm. For his own country he seems to have had no predilection. He could rejoice in her defeat, and lament her success if the defeat damaged and the success strengthened his political opponents. Not only did he oppose the war and denounce the ministers in the most unmeasured terms; he displayed indecent sympathy with the enemies of the state, wearing the colours which they had assumed and openly exulting in their victories. Burke, who was at his side, if he did not take part in all this, must have acquiesced. The effect, as a good observer remarked, was to inflame the spirit of the war party and goad its pride to persistence in the war.

All the enemies of England now gathered, vulture-like, round her apparently fainting frame. Spain joined the 1779 league, not from sympathy with the Americans, whom she had reason to fear as neighbours to her American dependencies, but from the passionate desire, which never left her, of recovering her Rock. Holland was drawn in 1780 while she contended against the right of searching neutral vessels for enemy's goods, asserted by England and of vital importance to a maritime state in war with continental powers. Russia and the other Baltic powers formed a menacing league of armed neutrality with the same intent. The British waters saw the British fleet flying before the combined fleets of France and Spain. Never was England so near her ruin. At last, Cornwallis, the one royal general who had shown ability in America, after a run of victory in the field, was cut off on a tongue of land at Yorktown by the united armies of France and America, vastly superior to him in numbers, and a French fleet, and was compelled to surrender. This was a fatal blow. North could go on no longer; the king was compelled to succumb; and the American colonies were free.

The loss was a gain in disguise, so far as military strength, commercial profit, or real greatness was concerned. The colonists had refused to contribute to imperial armaments or submit to imperial legislation. Trade with them, instead of being diminished by their emancipation from the colonial system, greatly and rapidly increased. To suppose that Great Britain could have held even a nominal suzerainty over them to this hour would be absurd. The parting was sure to come. What was deplorable was the manner of the parting, which entailed a deadly schism of the race, and left a long train of bitterness and mutual animosities behind. The children of Spain in the new world, though Spain was a far worse mother than England, forgave or forgot; but the children of England cherished against her a persistent hatred. Much is due to the retention of Canada and the continued presence of Great Britain on the American continent as a political and military power in antagonism to the United States. For this, however, Americans have themselves to thank. There were at the time Englishmen who would gladly have withdrawn from the American continent altogether; and had it been a mere question of policy, those counsels might have prevailed. But policy was controlled by honour. Instead of closing the civil war with amnesty, the victorious party in America chose to expel the vanquished, and thousands of loyalists, Tories, as their enemies called them, testified by going into exile their unshaken attachment to the mother country. For these a home was to be found under the British flag, and it was found in Canada, Nova Scotia, and New Brunswick. Congress rejecting or evading by an ironical reference to the States a claim for indemnity, Great Britain gave the loyalists indemnity to the extent of three millions and a half.

A struggle, calamitous in itself and in its result, closed not ingloriously to Great Britain. War with France, Spain, and Holland was not a war with kinsmen, and the spirit of the nation rose again to the combat with its ancient foes. By the repulse of Spain from Gibraltar, by her defeat in the first battle of St. Vincent, and by Rodney's victory over France in the West Indies the honour of the flag at least was saved. Of all the parties concerned the French monarchy in the end suffered most. The reward of its vindictive and hypocritical league with American rebellion was bankruptcy followed by revolution.

1779-1783
1780
1782

George III. had thrown himself vehemently into the war, and had struggled to the last against the recognition of colonial independence. For the protraction of the contest the king was personally responsible. He might well feel that with the interest of imperial supremacy in America was bound up that of prerogative at home. Chatham had said that three millions of Britons, if they were made slaves, would be fit instruments for making slaves of the rest. Yet in fact no great depression of the monarchy ensued on this defeat, and the course of events soon took the opposite turn.

A few years afterwards commenced the British colonization of Australia, the way to which had been shown by Cook. A convict ship was not a *Mayflower*, nor was Botany Bay a Massachusetts; but in time the taint was worked off, and in another hemisphere the loss of colonies was repaired.

The worst political consequence of the American catastrophe was the legislative secession of Ireland. The state of the island under the combined operation of religious intolerance embodied in penal law, commercial restrictions, an alien church establishment, and a government of patronage and corruption had few parallels in the annals of misfortune. It had been treated as an alien dependency, the commerce and manufactures of which, in conformity with the cruel fallacies of the day, were to be repressed in the interest of those of the imperial country; the growth of industrial life and of all its influences, social as well as material, being repressed at the same time. Artificial encouragement of the linen trade was a poor compensation for prohibition of the natural trade in wool. The mass of the population were now cottiers, little above the condition of serfs. They were ground down by the landlord, or, as the landlord was often an absentee, by his middleman, who screwed out his rack-rent, and by the tithe-proctor, who collected tithes for the clergy, also often non-resident, of a hostile church. Refuge there was none; other industries having been ruined by the restrictions on manufactures and trade, there was left to the peasants only the land, for which they competed with the eagerness of famishing men. In addition to all these burdens the peasant had to bear that of paying the priests of his own religion, to which he faithfully clung, while the priests, fitted by celibacy for a lot of poverty and danger, continued their ministrations in face of the penal law, and were the only guides and comforters of the oppressed people. The prohibition of trade bred a general habit of smuggling. The persecution of the popular religion made the people and their guides see enemies of religion in government and law. These are the pleas for Irish lawlessness, which, however, had been not less in the time of the clans. Illicit enlistment for the catholic armies of the continent was constantly going on, and must have carried off much of the best blood and sinew of the country. All catholics being excluded from the Irish parliament and from the franchise, the laws were made by an assembly avowedly hostile to the mass of the population. Persecution was still the rule of Europe. In Ireland there was many a Huguenot who had fled from his catholic persecutor. What was singular and especially hard in the Irish case was that it was a persecution of the vast majority by a minority resting on external power. Persecution in Ireland was also twofold, for the Anglican hierarchy insisted upon imposing on the Presbyterian colonists of the north religious disabilities which, combined with the blighting of trade, drove many of them across the Atlantic. The coincidence of a division of race with a division of religion, and of the two with the internecine struggle for land, put a terrible gulf between the gentry and the peasantry, while of the gentry many were squireens or middlemen, as tyrannical and insolent as they were worthless. Such a combination of curses the world has seldom seen. For food the peasant was being driven to the barbarous and precarious potato. Sometimes there was actual famine. Swift in hideous satire proposed that babies should be used as food. In time the feeling of increased security among the dominant sect and race relaxed the practical rigour of the penal laws, and the Lord-Lieutenancy of Chesterfield, a free-thinker, was a golden era. This was the sole improvement.

1745

But it was not from the enslaved that revolt came; they, thoroughly quelled by their last great overthrow, had sunk into the apathy of despair, and stirred not in 1715 or in 1745, though each time the alarm of the dominant minority produced a fresh spasm of oppression. The revolt came from the ruling race, galled by the commercial restrictions, incensed at the abuse of patronage and the pension list, full of their chartered rights as Britons, and stimulated by American example. In striking against the short-sighted avarice of the British trader the Irish parliament had reason and justice on its side; in striking for legislative independence it was in the awkward position of a minority, holding by virtue of its connection with the imperial country a monopoly of power with which it did not mean to part. Swift out of mischief, Molyneux and Lucas inspired by a more genuine patriotism, had written in favour of legislative independence. The success of the American rebellion and the prostration of Great Britain set the spirit of disunion at work. North made commercial concessions on what, for that day, was a liberal scale. But these did not satisfy the Irish patriots. Under pretence of defending the island against French invasion, they raised a force of fifty thousand volunteers, and demanded the severance of the two bonds of dependence, Poynings's Act, passed in the reign of Henry VII., which put Irish

1778-
1781

legislation under the control of the English privy council, and the Act of George I., affirming that the parliament of Great Britain had power to legislate for Ireland. A moderate regular force would probably have sufficed to put down the volunteers with their somewhat bombastic and very bacchanalian leaders. But the British government was hard pressed by opposition at home as well as by a host of enemies abroad; it gave way and granted Ireland legislative independence. Grattan, the eloquent chief of Irish patriotism, in a passionate burst of rhetoric adored the risen nation before a parliament from which five-sixths of that nation were excluded. The only constitutional link now left between the two islands was the crown. But the crown had its nomination boroughs in Ireland; it had a vast fund of patronage, both civil and ecclesiastical; and an Irish patriot was seldom a Cato. Above all, the oligarchy of protestant landowners was at heart conscious what, if the tyrannical arm of Great Britain were really withdrawn, its fate would be. Great Britain held by the ears the wolf by which Irish oligarchy would have been devoured. 1781

Against such a course of scandals, parliamentary and administrative, as that which ended in the American catastrophe and Irish secession, if political life was left in the nation, reaction was sure to come. In the British nation political life was left. Public wrath had found utterance in the Letters of "Junius," whose keen and glittering weapon was sometimes the sword of patriotic indignation, though more often it was the dagger of personal malice. Mystery, combined with daring personalities, invested a writer whose excellence is not far beyond the reach of a clever journalist of the present day, with an exaggerated interest, 1769-1772 so that even Burke spoke of him with awe. A far grander and nobler advocate of reform was Burke himself, with his "Thoughts on the Present Discontents," denouncing as the source of the evil court influence, which, with its mercenary phalanx of king's friends, and its vast patronage, parliamentary and official, had taken the place of prerogative. Burke's remedy was the revival of party, which he idealizes as a body of men united on a particular principle for the promotion of the national interest, while he would no doubt have found for it a practical basis in his own, that is the Rockingham, connection. To diminish court influence Burke moved for an economical reform, abolishing sinecure offices, setting a limit to pensions, reducing the preposterous expenses of the royal household, and retrenching a civil list on which there was a debt of six hundred thousand pounds contracted partly by waste, partly, there can be little doubt, by the administration of the king's golden pills. Dunning actually carried, in the House of Commons, a resolution that "the influence of the crown has increased, is increasing, and ought to be diminished." Chatham proclaimed the necessity of a reform of parliament, proposing, not to abolish the rotten boroughs, an attempt which, bad as the system might be, he appears to have deemed hopeless, but to increase the representation of the counties, which, though in the hands of the local aristocracy and squires, was comparatively open and pure. The Duke of Richmond proposed annual parliaments and universal suffrage, showing that when an aristocrat does break away from the policy of his class he is apt to break away from it with a vengeance, not the less if he is a magnate of the first order and feels that his own position is in any event secure.

Not Liberalism only, but Radicalism was championed in parliament by Wilkes and Sawbridge, outside the House by Horne Tooke, a clergyman self-unfrocked, a man of character, force, and learning, the leading spirit of a society for upholding the Bill of Rights. This, too, is the natal hour of political powers outside parliament, the Platform, the Stump as Americans call it, and Organized Agitation. At Middlesex elections, where Wilkes was 1768 the candidate, the platform would bellow its loudest. It spoke in accents infinitely more august and memorable by the mouth of Burke, rendering his account to his constituents and defining the true duties of a member of parliament as those of a representative, not a delegate, on the hustings at Bristol. The counties, with their 1777 electoral meetings of freeholders, were organizations ready formed for political action. When the scandals had reached their height, a meeting of the freeholders of Yorkshire, the greatest of these constituencies, was held at York, and was 1780 addressed by the leading men of the district. The example was followed by twenty-eight other counties. Presently the movement burst through the limits of the county or borough and became national. An association to promote economical reform was set on foot with a central com- 1780 mittee, and advantage was taken of the right to petition guaranteed by the Bill of Rights to bring moral pressure to bear upon parliament. Borough-mongers, sinecurists, and king's friends began to quake.

The immediate outcome, however, was not great. The association for economical reform was compromised, as organized agitations are apt to be, by the violence of some of its members, which gave occasion to its enemies to represent it as a seditious attempt to overawe the legisla-

ture and make the people instead of parliament supreme.
When, from promoting economical reform, it proceeded to
take up the reform of parliament, it laid itself open to
a charge of departure from its original object, which lost
it some adherents. Reform of the representation nothing
short of absolute terror could wring from the patrons of
boroughs. To them such reform was political death, while
economical reform was loss of that which made political
life worth living. Dunning's victory was not sustained,
court influence and corruption presently turning the scale
1780 against him. Burke's motion for economical reform was
allowed to pass; but when his party came into power,
and the patronage was theirs, his scheme was cut down
1782 so that the result was only a reduction of seventy-eight
thousand pounds a year, to which Burke himself, being
then Paymaster, nobly added a renunciation of the irregular emoluments of that office. It was, however, a substan-
1782 tial gain when contractors were prohibited from sitting
in the House of Commons, the votes of excisemen, said
to turn seventy elections, were taken away, and a limit
was put to the granting of pensions. The practice of
deciding election petitions by a party vote, from which
the American Congress is not yet free, had been abol-
1770 ished by Grenville, who passed an Act referring those cases
to a judicial committee of the House. The House of
Commons had renounced its usurped power of disqualifying for election. After a violent contest between the
House and the city of London, a by-plot to the drama
of Wilkes, brought on by a futile attempt of the House to
punish a printer for publishing its debates, the liberty of
1771 reporting and printing the debates had been practically
conceded. This no doubt made members more respon-

sible to their constituents and tore away the mask from self-prostitution. On the other hand, when the reporter comes in deliberation must go out. Interchange of thought, suggestion, modification, or withdrawal, such as deliberation requires, become impossible when every word is taken down. Members speak not to the House but to the reporters. From that time, at all events, the House has been not so much a national council as an oratorical battlefield of party, though its debates may furnish a test of ability and give impressive utterance to the opinions of the country.

Liberty of opinion ultimately gained an important step by the agitation of these times. In the course of the political conflict the law of libel had been brought under discussion, and the right of the jury to pronounce on the character of the alleged libel as well as on the fact of publication had been asserted upon one side and denied upon the other, Mansfield's strictly legal intellect taking the illiberal side. For the present the legal decision was suspended; but the jury had morally won the day.

Obstructive prejudice was not confined to the court or the patrons of boroughs. It was strong also, after its kind, among the masses, who by their violent manifestations of it compromised the cause of reform. Roman Catholics, of whom there were still many old families in the north, laboured under a mass of accumulated disabilities, such as, if the law had been strictly enforced, would have deprived them of the rights not only of citizens, but of parents, proprietors, and men; though it seems they had practically been little molested, and had performed their worship, educated their children, and transmitted their estates in peace. Toleration having made way among

men of the world, a Bill abolishing some of the disa-
1778 bilities was carried by Sir George Savile, a steady and
most respectable advocate of liberal legislation. Here-
upon the old popular hatred of popery again broke out,
first in Presbyterian Scotland, where it was most intense,
and afterwards in England. A great anti-Catholic Association was formed under Lord George Gordon, a protestant maniac, who ended by turning Jew. The presentation
by him of a monster anti-Catholic petition was followed
1780 by a frightful uprising of the mob of London. For three
days the great city was in the hands of an infuriated and
intoxicated rabble which revelled in destruction, arson,
and every kind of outrage, though, British savagery having limits, nobody was hanged in a lamp iron, nor were
any heads carried on pikes. Authority was paralyzed and
the metropolis was saved by the decision of the king, who
took it upon himself to order the troops to fire. The
ministers had hesitated and by their hesitation shown
their fear of public sentiment and their respect for the
letter of the law. So strong was still the feeling against
the religion of Bloody Mary and Guy Fawkes, that even
the reform of the calendar, carried by the free-thinking
1751 Chesterfield, was denounced, not only because it robbed
the people, as they said, of eleven days, but because the
reformed calendar bore the name of a pope. The Lord
George Gordon riots would make it far from clear that in
the existing condition of popular intelligence the Duke
of Richmond's scheme of annual parliaments and universal
suffrage, or anything approaching to that scheme, could
work well. In fact, this and other disturbances threw
back the cause of reform.

On the fall of North the Tory king was compelled to go

back to the hated Whigs, and the government was formed by Rockingham, with Burke again as his prompter and Fox as his foreign minister. But Rockingham died, and there ensued a struggle in the cabinet for supremacy between Shelburne, who leaned to the court, and Fox. Shelburne for an hour became prime minister. He represented Chatham's general policy and had a young Pitt at his side. This man is an enigma. He seems highly enlightened for his day; he is a sound economist and a pioneer of free trade. His policy towards America is liberal; he is against coercing her. Afterwards he wishes to heal the rupture with her, as a family quarrel now at an end, to renew the family connection, and amicably share the family inheritance. There appears to be much about him most excellent. Yet he is intensely disliked and mistrusted. He is nicknamed Malagrida, after a Jesuit of sinister visage. By Burke he is compared to a serpent with two heads. Nobody cares to act with him. Pitt, though he has been his chancellor of the exchequer, does not, when he becomes prime minister himself, take him into the cabinet. Fox was evidently resolved to break with him. This he did on a pretext connected with the treaty of American independence, and Shelburne's ministry fell.

Against a return of the detested Whigs to power, by which the king was now confronted, he battled long and hard. He even offered the prime ministership to Pitt, who was then but twenty-three. At last he for the time bowed his neck to the yoke.

There followed under the nominal premiership of the Whig Duke of Portland, a coalition of Fox and North revolting to men of principle and to the nation. Fox had

1782
1782
1782
1783

not only opposed North's policy with the utmost violence, he had denounced him personally as one who in every public or official transaction had shown himself void of every principle of honour and honesty, one with whom he could never have any connection, and with whom, if he allied himself, he would be content to be called the most infamous of mankind. The memory of such language could not be buried by saying that quarrels were transient and friendship was eternal. Nor can the infamy of such a coalition cast a shade upon any union of statesmen who, though previously differing in opinion, have respected the characters of each other. The basis upon which the coalition was formed, and which was supposed to palliate its flagrancy, was cabinet government, withdrawing all real power from the king, as opposed to government by departments with the king supreme. Composed as the House of Commons then was, each of the leaders was able to bring his contingent with him, and the coalition had a large majority in the House, though from the first it was condemned by the country. The king hated all the Whigs politically; Fox he hated personally as a profligate while he was himself morally pure, and as the corrupter of his son; North he hated as a deserter. The coalition was bent on stripping him of power; he was bent on tripping up the coalition.

Before long the king found his opportunity, and the
1783 coalition fell, putting an end by its fall for many a day to the dominion of the Whig houses, which beginning under William III., and interrupted only by the brief triumph of Toryism at the end of the reign of Anne, had lasted for ninety years. The occasion of the catastrophe was an India Bill. While the orb of British empire had been

contracted in the west it had been vastly enlarged in the east, and that career of conquest had begun which, destiny leading on the conquerors step by step, has terminated in the sovereignty of Hindostan. Upon the collapse of the Mogul power at the death of Aurungzeb, 1707 India had fallen into a wild and bloody anarchy, the satraps breaking loose from the central power and warring with each other, while the country was swept by the murderous and devastating raids of the Mahratta horsemen. Order had perished, nationality there had never been; in place of nationality there was only caste. Trading companies which had factories on the coast were constrained in self-defence to become military powers. But the ambition of Dupleix, who was at the head of the French, aspired to nothing less than the empire of Hindostan, towards which he was advancing with great strides, while the British power was brought by his intrigue and force to the verge of destruction. It was saved and brought out of the struggle victorious, alike over French and native enemies, by Robert Clive, who, in the hour of extreme peril, left the desk of a merchant's clerk to 1748 surpass Cortez and Pizarro in arms, while he far surpassed them both in counsel. By Clive was acquired a dominion as large as France, and really independent, though nominally subject to the phantom of Mogul empire at Delhi. Political dominion in the hands of a company of traders or their agents and clerks could hardly fail to be used for the purposes of illicit gain. It led to oppression, corruption, rapine, and the accumulation of scandalous wealth. These abuses Clive had partly repressed by the introduction of something like a regular civil service, the germ of the most marvellous civil service which the world has ever seen. But even after Clive's reform, to leave political dominion in the hands of a company of traders was impossible. Not only was such a body unfit to rule, but there was always the danger of its involving the empire in war. A Bill was brought in by Fox severing the commerce of the company from its political dominion, and transferring the political dominion to seven parliamentary directors elected for four years, while a board subject to the directorate was to control the commerce. The framer, most likely, was Burke, who held a subordinate place in the ministry, and whose imagination had been at once fascinated by the East. The appointment of the members of the board of political control was given for the first turn to parliament, that is, to the masters of the parliamentary majority; in effect to Fox and North. At once a great storm arose. The East India Company protested against the violation of its charter, which it was true the Bill set aside, but which its own acquisition of political dominion had practically cancelled. With more reason it might have complained that the business management of a commercial company was being taken out of its hands. It appealed loudly and not in vain to the fears of other chartered corporations. The unlucky language of a law officer, who had spoken in debate of a charter as a piece of parchment with a seal dangling on it, provoked a general commotion among holders not only of charters but of title-deeds and showed how much mischief a phrase may do. The cry was raised throughout the country against the attempt of the coalition to make itself supreme alike over the crown and the nation by grasping the enormous patronage of Hindostan. Fox was depicted in caricatures as riding triumphant on his elephant into Leadenhall

Street, where the India House then stood. People were ready to believe anything of the profligate and hated coalition. Through the Commons the Bill passed by a large majority; but when it reached the upper House, Lord Temple, a true kinsman of the intriguer who was Chatham's brother-in-law and evil genius, crept to the open ear of the king and received from him a card to be handed about among the Lords, saying that whoever voted for the Bill would be regarded by the king as his enemy. The obsequious Lords threw out the Bill, and the king at once, in a most insulting manner, dismissed his ministry. It is needless to comment on this transaction. If it was constitutional and honourable, why, instead of handing about a clandestine card, did not Temple deliver the king's message openly from his place in the House of Lords? The king might feel that, as the sequel showed, public feeling was with him against the coalition; but this did not warrant perfidy towards his constitutional advisers or disloyalty to the constitution. Temple seems to have been conscious of the character of his act; when nominated for office, as the reward of his exploit, the schemer fled. 1783 1783

The king turned again to William Pitt, and the youth who had before shown his discretion by declining the prime ministership, now showed his courage and his aspiring genius by accepting it. He was a prodigy if ever there was one. He had spent eight years as a student at Cambridge, reading widely it is true, above all reading the newly published work of Adam Smith, but not seeing much of any other than student life; though his father, whose hope he was, carefully trained him in oratory, taught him the arts of elocution, and 1783 fostered the hereditary aspirations which sprang up in the stripling's breast. Yet he came forth at once, not only an accomplished speaker, but a first-rate debater, a ripe politician, a skilful manager of the House of Commons. He owed the prize to an unconstitutional intrigue, of which it is vain to contend that he was guiltless, since he not only accepted its fruits, but threw his shield over it in the House of Commons, not in the most ingenuous way. Nor was this fact without influence on his subsequent career. But he was not, like Bute, the mere offspring of intrigue, and the king, who probably hoped to find in him a servant, was destined to find generally a master. His darling object, the overthrow of the Whig aristocracy, George III. had at last achieved; but in compassing it he in some degree realized the fable of the horse and the stag.

There ensued a desperate struggle in the House of Commons between an overwhelming majority at first commanded by the coalition, and the young prime minister with a minority and single-handed, for he was the only member of his own cabinet in the lower House. Pitt, by his conduct of the battle, earned the praise of precocious skill, resolution, and self-control. But his victory was assured from the beginning. What could the coalition do? It could only in the last resort appeal to the country, and the country was evidently against it. By struggling to prevent a dissolution it doubly ensured its own condemnation. At last its majority melted away.

1784 At the general election which followed, currents of opinion and sentiment usually opposed to each other set together in favour of Pitt. Reformers voted for the heir of Chatham's principles and the advocate of parliamentary reform; Tories voted for the choice of the king and the asserter of the royal authority against oligarchical domination. The coalition was deservedly odious, while the heart of the nation turned to the son of Chatham. At the critical moment Pitt had the opportunity of displaying his disinterestedness by refusing a rich sinecure which he might have taken as a perquisite of his office. The result was the total defeat of the opposition, which lost no less than a hundred and forty seats, and the elevation of William Pitt, in his twenty-fifth year, to a supremacy which he retained, with an accidental break, to the end of his life. Yorkshire, the greatest of the county constituencies, led the way, electing Pitt's young friend, Wilberforce, against the candidate of a great Whig House. It thus appears that in spite of all the defects of the representation, public opinion, when vehemently aroused, could find expression in a general election. Pitt had now an independent support in the nation which put him above subserviency to the court. 1784

So immense was the victory that for a moment it turned the usually strong head of the youthful prodigy who had won it. Fox had been elected for Westminster after a desperate contest, with the usual saturnalia of beer, bribery, and riot, in which the Whig Duchess of Devonshire bought a coalheaver's vote with a kiss. But a partisan high bailiff instead of returning him kept him out of the seat, and put him to ruinous expense by a tricky scrutiny. Pitt so far forgot himself as to support the high bailiff in his iniquity and speak of Fox in language verging on insolence. This was too much for English gentlemen, and Pitt brought on himself a damaging defeat. In that immense and mixed majority 1785 there was, as appeared on this and on after occasions, a good deal of independence.

Of the remnant of the opposition, North being disabled by growing infirmity and blindness, which he bore as cheerfully as he had borne the storm of party denunciation, Fox henceforth was the leader. Among Fox's followers the most illustrious was Burke, of whom, nevertheless, his party never thought as a possible holder of cabinet office. Upon this alleged proof of aristocratic exclusiveness and ingratitude much rhetoric has been expended. Burke was the greatest political philosopher as well as the most magnificent writer of his time, though his philosophy could give way to the Celtic strain which, as his physiognomy showed, contended in his character with the Saxon. But his gifts were not those of a statesman; they were those of a superb pamphleteer. In the House of Commons he was apt to speak pamphlets, which wearied his hearers. Not only so, but his breaches of good taste, and even of decency, were sometimes outrageous and drew upon him contemptuous disgust. His temper was unregulated, and his practical judgment often failed him. He had shown its weakness by a bad departmental scrape into which he got when he was in office under the coalition. To entrust to him a great office of state might well be deemed unsafe. Fox and Burke by this time had with them Sheridan, who, though his name is linked with bacchanalian wit and careless improvidence, seems to have been not only a brilliant speaker but a vigorous and generous if not a high-principled politician.

Pitt set out a Liberal, like his father, in home politics; otherwise he was his father's opposite. His teacher was Adam Smith. He was a peace minister. Economy and commerce were his field. In that field his happier years were spent and his real triumphs were won. His command of it enabled him, like Walpole, to combine the confidence and support of the commercial classes with those of the landed gentry. His great rival, Fox, was too much the gentleman, too classical, and too lazy to attend to finance. Fox used to say that he liked to see the funds fall because it vexed Pitt.

The financial situation, after Chatham's glorious prodigality, North's American war, and a long reign of jobbery, corruption, and chancellors of the exchequer such as Dashwood, afforded abundant scope for reform. There were two hundred and sixty-six millions of national debt for a total population of ten millions. Exchequer bills were at twenty discount. Consols were down to fifty-seven. There was a large deficit. Customs duties were so laid on and so collected that as much went to the smuggler as to the exchequer; the smuggling trade in tea was double the lawful trade. Pitt, with the gospel of Adam Smith in his hand, entered on a bold revision of the system. He successfully applied the principle, 1785 applied after him by Peel, but which he was the first to grasp, that reduction of duties might by increasing consumption increase the revenue; and he transferred to the exchequer the gains of the smuggler. He was enabled at the same time to do away with a number of useless places in customs and excise. He thus, in spite of some waste of money in paying the debts of the Prince of Wales, and of the civil list, turned a deficit into surplus. He reformed the system of placing loans, putting them up to public tender instead of dividing them among the friends of the government, who reaped thereby corrupt gains.

He did the same with contracts. He also reformed a vicious system of keeping public accounts.

1786   He was not so happy in his attempt to conjure away the debt by establishing a sinking fund. Only out of surplus revenue can a public debt be paid. When there ceases to be a surplus the sinking fund must be kept up by borrowing, perhaps at a higher rate of interest than that paid on the debt. Upon the first pressing emergency the savings box is broken open and hands are laid upon the sacred store. The magical operation of compound interest is an illusion into which it is strange that Pitt should have fallen. Compound interest is not a vegetable growth; it is an accumulation of interest re-invested. In the case of a sinking fund the nation which receives the interest on one hand pays it with the other, and gains nothing by the transmission from hand to hand. For an indebted nation there are only three courses: to bear the debt; to repudiate it; to remain at peace, save, and pay.

Pitt, however, saw in national debt a burden of which it is desirable to be rid. That such a nation as Great Britain has prospered in spite of a heavy debt is no proof that a debt is no evil. Is a severe taxation no evil? Is it no evil to have so much dronage quartered on national labour? If, as the optimists allege, in the case of a public debt, debtor and creditor are the same, why not apply the sponge at once? By facility of borrowing, the strongest check is taken from war, as Pitt, in the latter part of his career, was destined most unhappily to show. The day was to come when it would be said Pitt's memory needs no statues; six hundred millions of irredeemable debt are the eternal record of his fame.

Another economical achievement of Pitt, and the glory
of his brighter hour, was a commercial treaty with 1787
France, carried by him against protectionism and against
the national prejudice, to which faction, by the lips of
Fox, appealed. His success was a triumph not only
of free trade, but of good will among nations. In defending the measure, Pitt combated the doctrine that
France must be the unalterable enemy of Great Britain.
To say that any nation must be the unalterable enemy
of any other nation would, he maintained, be a monstrous
libel on human nature. The son of Chatham thus ab-
jured the creed and the policy of his sire.

With Ireland also Pitt tried to inaugurate free trade. 1785
North had given her free trade with foreign countries and
the dependencies, Pitt desired to give her free trade with
England. He would thereby have removed her most
trying grievance, and paved the way for union. But
here he had to encounter not only the malignant avarice
of British protectionism, which sent up from Lancashire
a petition with eighty thousand signatures, but Irish jealousy of British legislation, on which Fox and the opposition, including Burke, to their great discredit, played.
In vain did Pitt conjure parliament to adopt that system
of trade with Ireland which would enrich one part of the
empire without impoverishing the other, while it would
give strength to both. In vain did he liken free trade to
mercy, that attribute of heaven which was twice blessed,
blessing him that gave and him that took alike. In vain
did he implore his hearers to save from further dismem-
berment the remains of the shattered empire. In vain
did he declare with impassioned vehemence that of all the
objects of his political life, this was the most important,

and that he never expected to meet with another which would so strongly rouse every emotion of his heart. His scheme, accepted at first by the Irish parliament, was mangled by the parliament of Great Britain, and rejected on account of the alterations by the parliament of Ireland, which was led to look upon them as derogatory to its independence. Dearly both parliaments paid for its rejection.

1785

The son of Chatham, on his entrance into public life, had declared, as Chatham did, for parliamentary reform. As an independent member he had brought in a Bill, and, though defeated, had a good division. The case was strong. Paley said that half, reformers said that more than half, the members of the House of Commons held their seats by nomination or purchase. He and other optimists might contend that this, in spite of the anomaly, was the best of all possible parliaments, all the leading men of the nation being there and all great interests being represented. They might argue, that if the machine worked satisfactorily, want of symmetry mattered little. But anomaly or want of symmetry so great as to repel respect from institutions is an evil. Burke, however, opposed all change, contending that the British constitution was perfect, or that, if anything, there was already too much of the democratic element; and he might at all events plead for cautious dealing with a constitution which was the only one of importance in Europe. Pitt redeemed his pledges, bringing in a Bill which, frankly treating the nomination boroughs as property, provided for their extinction by purchase. The seats were to be transferred to counties or large cities. The sale was not to be compulsory, but voluntary on the

1785

part of the owners of boroughs. This was mild. But to a borough-mongering parliament, parliamentary reform, even the mildest, was too nauseous to be swallowed, however sugared might be the rim of the cup. Pitt's Bill was thrown out, and here he dropped the question. He might feel that a system which had made him prime minister with an overwhelming majority practically worked pretty well. Besides, management rather than coercion was his line, and he never set himself, perhaps never had the force of will to set himself, against the House of Commons. It is to be noted that defeat of the government, even on so radical a question as parliamentary reform, did not then entail resignation.

If an attempt to reform the parliament of Great Britain was hopeless, still more hopeless was it to attempt to reform the parliament of Ireland. That assembly was at once the political citadel and the political treasury of the dominant race and church. The Roman Catholics, five-sixths of the population, were excluded from seats in parliament and from the franchise. But even as a representation of the protestants the parliament was a mockery. The system of nomination boroughs prevailed even more than in England. In an assembly of three hundred, twenty-five great land-owners returned one hundred and sixteen members. One peer had sixteen members, another nine, another seven. The great jobbing family of Ponsonby had fourteen. A combination of these potentates could dictate to the government. Two-thirds of the House of Commons, however, were attached to government by offices, pensions, or promises. A parliament which the government had bought could be kept in existence as long as the government pleased, there being no limit to its life but the demise of the crown. In the House of Lords, with borough-mongers craving for Castle patronage, was a phalanx of bishops of the established church who were tools of the crown. The system was one of undisguised and almost avowed corruption. Pitt had before him a chart of the Irish parliament confidentially drawn up for his guidance. H. H., son-in-law of a peer, who brings him into parliament, wishes to be a commissioner of barracks, but would go into orders and take a crown living. H. D., brother of another peer, described as a silent, gloomy man, easy to be led if thought expedient, having failed to obtain a specific promise, has lately voted in opposition. L. M., for his skill in House of Commons management, expects one thousand pounds a year. Pitt is warned to be careful of him. J. N., a military man on half pay, wants a troop of dragoons on full pay. His pretensions are fifteen years' service in parliament. He would prefer office to military promotion, but already has a pension. His character, especially on the side of truth, is described as not favourable. F. P. is independent, but well disposed to government. His four sisters have pensions, and his object is a living for his brother. T. P. is brother to a peer, who brings him into parliament. He is a captain in the navy and wishes for some sinecure employment.

The members of the Irish parliament, it is said, were gentlemen; gentlemen they might be, though the social medium in which they lived was one of reckless expenditure, hard drinking, and duelling, challenges being sent upon every affront, not only by members of parliament but by a lord chancellor, by a chief justice, by judges, by the provost of a university. Eloquent speakers they had among them, such as Flood and Grattan, albeit the rhetoric was of a highly full-bodied type and the invective was vehement, as when Grattan compared Flood to "an ill-omened bird of night with sepulchral notes, cadaverous aspect, and broken beak," the broken beak being an allusion to a broken nose. Good things they might do in the way of legislation on subjects outside party or patronage. But a representative assembly they were not. The rejection of parliamentary reform, however, was certain. Corruption, religious exclusion, and the fears of a privileged minority formed a rampart against all measures tending in that direction, which nothing but a political earthquake could overthrow.

Of corruption in England Pitt had cut off some sources by abolition of useless offices and by purifying the mode of contracting loans. But the main evil ceased of itself, at least in its coarser form, on Pitt's elevation to power. A minister with so immense and so sure a majority had no need to bribe. It must be remembered, however, that government still had an enormous mass of patronage, civil, military, naval, colonial, and also ecclesiastical; for bishoprics, canonries, and crown livings were used as rewards for political support. It had also the bestowal of peerages, baronetcies, and orders of knighthood, the most powerful of bribes to men whose wealth placed them above the temptation of money. Of these Pitt made a lavish, not to say an unscrupulous, use. Before he died, one hundred and forty peers, half the House of Lords, owed their creations or their promotions in the peerage to him. Baronetcies and knighthood, the minor bribes of vanity, were scattered with equal profusion.

That Pitt's own hands were clean need not be said.

Far from increasing his fortune, he, through neglect of his private affairs and the dishonesty of his servants, ran deeply into debt. Nor did he stoop to the acceptance of baubles. He refused the Garter, thinking, perhaps, as did a prime minister of a later day, that it would be folly to buy himself with that by which he could buy a grandee.

1792 Pitt was still liberal enough cordially to concur with Fox in a reform of the law of libel, a deferred outcome of the Wilkes affair, establishing the right of the jury to pronounce upon the character as well as upon the fact of the publication. His character would have led him to support measures for emancipation of conscience. Left to himself, he would have voted for the repeal of the Test and Corporation Acts; but he consulted the bishops, who deemed the profanation of the sacrament for political purposes still vital to the maintenance of religion. Under the same influence he refused to grant freedom of conscience to Unitarians, or to release from subscription to the Thirty-nine Articles Latitudinarian clergymen of the church of England. Burke also opposed the concessions to Unitarians and Latitudinarians. He was more willing to grant concessions to catholics, regarding theirs as an ancient and conservative religion. By this time, however, revolution was casting its shadow on the scene, and Burke deemed protestant dissenters revolutionary. It did not occur to the great philosopher that the cause of their revolutionary tendencies was injustice. In legislating for Canada, Pitt recognized Roman Catholicism, which was thus legally tolerated for the first time.

Again Pitt showed his liberal tendencies on the subject of the slave-trade. It seems incredible that men should have gone on talking in high strains of public rights and liberties while they were consenting to the continuance of that trade and to the hideous cruelties of the Middle Passage. The scene of those horrors was distant, but they were clearly presented to the minds of Englishmen by the proceedings in their own courts of law. An action relating to a policy of insurance on the value of certain slaves had been tried in the King's Bench. The question was whether the loss of the slaves had been caused by perils of the sea. A slave-ship with four hundred and forty-two slaves was bound from the coast of Guinea to Jamaica. Sixty of the slaves died on the passage from overcrowding, but in respect of these it was not contended that the underwriter was liable. The captain, having missed Jamaica, found himself short of water, and under the apprehension of scarcity, but before his crew and passengers had been put on short allowance, he threw ninety-six of the sickliest slaves overboard. A fall of rain gave him water for eleven days, notwithstanding which he drowned twenty-six more of the slaves. Ten in despair threw themselves overboard. The ship arrived in port before the water was exhausted. Ill were the wickedness and cruelty of such a system compensated to the nation by the inflow of plantation wealth, the lords of which were often little better than its source, and by their corruption of English society and politics partly avenged the slave.

Wilberforce, who came forward to deliver his country and humanity from the slave-trade, was a representative of that party of evangelicals which, remaining inside the Anglican church, sympathized and co-operated with the Methodists outside, having, indeed, its origin in the same reaction against the vice and impiety of the eighteenth century. His appearance in the House of Commons and

1788

his influence there were among the signs of an improvement in public character traceable to the religious revival as well as to the change in the political position. Pitt supported Wilberforce's movement, and one of the best of his speeches was made in that cause. But, shackled either by political or commercial influences, he failed to put forth the full power of his government, and afterwards, by annexing Sugar Islands which were cultivated by slave labour, he became involuntarily responsible for an extension of the trade.

Fox's India Bill had been thrown out, but the Indian problem still called for solution. To leave an annexed empire, with the power of peace and war, uncontrolled in the hands of a trading company was impossible. Pitt brought in a Bill which, avoiding the rock upon which Fox's measure had split, effected the same object in another way. The patronage which Fox had proposed to transfer to the masters of parliament Pitt left ostensibly in the hands of the company, only giving the crown a veto on the appointment of the governor-general and of some other officers of importance. Nor did he abrogate the company's charter; but he made over the supreme power in reality to a board of control consisting of six privy councillors, including the secretary of state and the chancellor of the exchequer. The company of British traders remained in form and name a great eastern power, and the rulers of the Indian empire were still called directors and writers: but the policy of the company was thenceforth under imperial direction and control. Legally the Indian patronage was left in the hands of the company. Practically it fell to a great extent into those of Henry Dundas, the president of the board of control. Dundas, a very able,

1784

shrewd, and unsentimental Scotchman, skilled in party management, was Pitt's second in command and the adviser on whom he most leaned. Indian patronage in Dundas's gift filled Hindostan with Scotchmen and kept Scotland true to Pitt.

Conquest began to react, as all conquest must, on the conquering nation. To India the coalition government owed its overthrow. Englishmen who had returned with fortunes from Hindostan, Nabobs, as they were nicknamed, were eclipsing ancient houses, buying seats in parliament, giving general umbrage by the display of a wealth which was believed, often rightly, to have been amassed in evil ways. India, in the days of a six months' voyage, was far away, and public indignation was blind in the selection of its objects. It fixed on Clive, the founder of the empire, 1767 and on Hastings, the organizer and preserver. Clive had 1786 not been scrupulous; once, at least, he had stooped to that which in the east was policy, in the west would have been dishonour; but he had been a reformer as well as a conqueror; he had put a stop to rapine by his establishment of a regular civil service, and though he had taken a good deal for himself, he could with justice say that he stood astonished at his own moderation in not having taken more. Unlike the rapacious Greek of old when introduced into the treasure-house, he had filled only his hands, not his boots and clothes, with gold. He escaped 1773 impeachment, but he did not escape hatred and obloquy, which combined with disease to overpower him. In the palace at Claremont which he had built, and the stately rooms of which he paced in his last dark hours, one of the mightiest of Englishmen died by his own hand. The 1774 statesmanship of Warren Hastings and his courage, serene in extremity, had saved, ordered, and extended the empire founded by Clive. His rule, though arbitrary, had been, in comparison at least with native anarchy or tyranny, beneficent, and he was regarded with gratitude by the Hindoo. Of most of the charges against him, notably of the charge of judicially murdering Nuncomar by the hand of Impey, he now stands acquitted before the tribunal of history. In hiring out British troops to a native prince for the Rohilla war, the worst of all his acts, he was yielding to the financial cravings of the company. But he had a deadly enemy in Francis, the venomous writer of the "Junius" letters, who had not only opposed him in council but fought a duel with him at Calcutta. Francis gained the ear of Burke, whose soul was fired by a tale of wrongs done to ancient dynasties and priesthoods, while his warm fancy was always set at work by the imagery of the romantic and gorgeous east.

1786 Burke moved for the impeachment of Hastings. How Pitt, after voting against impeachment on the Rohilla charge, was induced to turn round and vote for it on the charge of extorting an excessive subsidy from Cheet Sing, which now appears less serious, is a mystery; it is probable that he was persuaded by Dundas, who had India in his hands and had before attacked the government of Hastings. His fiat was decisive. There followed the most 1788- important state trial and the grandest judicial pageant 1795 seen in Westminster Hall since the impeachment of Strafford. It ended, after seven years, in an acquittal. But Hastings could truly say that he had given his country an empire, and she had rewarded him with a life of impeachment.

Burke, in the attack on Warren Hastings, behaved

almost like a maniac. He wanted to make Francis, who had fought a duel with the accused, one of the managers of the impeachment. He incurred the formal censure of the House by recklessly charging Hastings with having suborned Impey to murder Nuncomar. His language in Westminster Hall was outrageous. Once at least he was called to order by the lords. He spoke of the illustrious accused as "lying down upon a sty of disgrace, and feeding on its offal," as a captain-general of a robber gang, as a thief, a cheat, a forger, a swindler; as one to be compared, not with Tamerlane, but with the lice which laid waste Egypt. He called him a fraudulent bullock-driver, Hastings having been once concerned in a contract for bullocks. Lord Coke, he said, had done wrong in calling Sir Walter Raleigh "a spider of hell," but he would have been guilty merely of indecorum if he had applied the term to Hastings. Language not less excited he could use in the House of Commons. He had taunted North on personal defects. He compared a minister to an indecent heathen deity. He compared the House when they would not listen to him to a pack of hounds. He spoke of the king, then afflicted with mental disease, in words which shocked his hearers. "Burke concluded his wild speech," said one of his audience, "in a manner next to madness." Magnificent though Burke's gifts were as an orator and a philosopher, it is surely no great scandal that his friends should have feared to trust his practical wisdom. The loftiness and purity of his motives cannot be questioned. Nor can it be questioned that the attention of the nation was called to India and its conscience awakened by the impeachment of Hastings. But violence defeated itself, and injustice to a great public servant was not the best way of reforming the public service.

For a moment Pitt seemed in danger of losing power. The flickering light of the king's intellect was for the second time eclipsed by lunacy. This time the eclipse appeared to be total. Then arose a constitutional question about the appointment of a regency, absorbing in those days, though of little interest in ours, except as the appeal to medieval precedents for its decision marks the unbroken course of the constitution.

It was assumed that the Prince, on becoming Regent, would dismiss Pitt and call in Fox. So much power the crown still retained. Thus on the regency question the two rivals were led to take different lines and lines at variance with the general politics of each. Fox, the Whig, took the legitimist line, contending that the Prince would be Regent of his own right and with the full powers of the monarchy; while Pitt, the Tory, took the constitutional line, contending that it was for the parliament to settle the government during the incapacity of the sovereign, and bringing in a Bill to curtail the powers of the Regent and take from him, among other prerogatives, that of creating peers. Fox and Sheridan, in asserting the Prince's claim, used language so highly legitimist that Pitt could say of one of them that he would un-Whig the gentleman for the rest of his life. They did themselves no small harm, while the Prince, their client, and his brother the Duke of York by unfilial and indecent behaviour provoked general disgust. The king, however, recovered, and a long course of mischief still lay before him. Throughout the kingdom there were rejoicings. Pitt was more firmly than ever seated in power.

Not even yet was it perfectly understood that a ministry was a unit, and that its members must stand or fall together. Chancellors, especially, were still apt to think their tenure permanent. The lord chancellor, Thurlow, a most imposing but rather hollow personage, of whom it was said that nobody could be so wise as Thurlow looked, had made up his mind that though the Pitt ministry might go out the chancellor would stay in. Having beneath an outside of surly honesty no small aptitude for intrigue, when the king's case was supposed to be hopeless he opened an underground communication with the Prince. The ministers, Thurlow among them, went down to hold a council at Windsor. When they were coming away the chancellor's hat was missing, but was presently brought by a page, who told them that he had found it in the Prince's room. Upon the king's recovery Thurlow poured forth his fervent loyalty in the House of Lords. "When I forget my king," he exclaimed, "may my God forget me!" "The best thing that can happen to you," said Burke. "Oh, what a rascal!" said Pitt. "Forget you; he'll see you damned first," said Wilkes. Thurlow, being generally contumacious in cabinet, was presently dismissed. His blatant professions of loyalty had endeared him to the king; but Pitt's will prevailed.

By this complication the character and doings of the Prince of Wales, afterwards George IV., were brought fully into view. It was seen what hereditary monarchy was likely to be when it was relieved of the duties and perils which had been its salt in the middle ages and exposed in irresponsible security to the influences of a royal education, royal luxury, and the flattery of a court. His Royal Highness was wallowing in debauchery and sunk in debt. After the custom of his house, he was at enmity with his father. Affecting Liberalism because the court was Tory, he had thrown himself into the arms of the opposition and made Carlton House its headquarters. Fox and Sheridan were too well qualified to be his boon companions as well as his privy councillors, and by their share in his moral ruin drew on them the deserved hatred of the king. The Prince had fallen in love with Mrs. Fitzherbert, who, to do him justice, was in every way worthy of his love and might have redeemed him if he could have lawfully made her his wife. But she was a Roman Catholic, and by the Act of Settlement marriage with a Roman Catholic was forfeiture of the crown. That forfeiture the Prince would have incurred had his marriage with Mrs. Fitzherbert been valid. But the Royal Marriage Act, passed in the early part of the reign, upon the discovery of two marriages of disparagement secretly contracted by royal dukes, forbade the marriage of any member of the royal family under the age of twenty-five, which the Prince had not reached, without the consent of the crown. The marriage with Mrs. Fitzherbert was therefore invalid, and the Prince by his breach of the second law was saved from the penalty of the first. To say that he counted on the invalidity might be harsh. Coming to parliament for payment of his debts, he was met by an interrogation about his marriage, and the first gentleman in Europe, as he deemed himself, and as in mere manner he might have pretended to be, put up his bosom friend Fox to meet the interrogation with a lie.

So far all had gone well, and more than well, with Pitt. It was still morning with the young statesman, and the morning was almost cloudless. Everything promised him the continuance of a brilliant and beneficent career. He had restored the finances and reformed the financial system. He had converted deficit into surplus. By his commercial treaty with France he had made a great advance towards the realization of Adam Smith's policy of free trade. The total abolition of customs duties even was coming into view. The country was prospering and growing rapidly in wealth. The inventions of Arkwright, Hargreaves, Crompton, Watt, and Wedgewood, together with the invention of smelting iron with coal, had given an immense impetus to manufactures of all kinds, to metallurgy and to mining. Trade, especially with America, had greatly increased. Pitt's hold on the confidence of parliament and of the country had been strengthened. When he rose in the House of Commons with his lean but majestic form, his lofty bearing, and his sonorous elocution, he rose a king.

Pitt's government was one of personal ascendancy supported by the favour of the crown, not of party leadership. His following was made up of different elements brought together by their confidence in the man, hatred of the Whig oligarchy, or attachment to the throne. It followed him but loosely till it was welded by antagonism to revolution. He never appealed to party sentiment, never held counsel with a party. At a crisis of peril he was willing to take his rival Fox into his government and was prevented only by the personal prejudice of the king. It may safely be said that the theory of government by two parties representing opposite sets of principles and alternately rising to power did not present itself to his mind.

Peace was Pitt's element, and the world was and seemed likely to remain at peace. For some years there had been no great war, except that of Russia with the Turks. In Holland Pitt had taken part with Prussia in a successful intervention for the restoration of the House of Orange to power, and the rescue of the country from the grasp of French ambition, which was intriguing with the republican party. He had been on the brink of a war with Russia, whose growing power began to excite alarm, but parliament, deeming the danger too remote, had manifested its independence by drawing him back. In 1792, bringing in his budget, he held out a prospect of relief from taxes within fifteen years; "for although," said he, "we must not count with certainty on the continuance of our present prosperity during such an interval, yet unquestionably there never was a time in the history of this country when, from the situation of Europe, we might more reasonably expect fifteen years of peace than we may at the present moment." He reduced the navy and looked forward to general reduction of armaments, abolition of customs duties, and emancipation of trade. Never was man more bantered, to use Bolingbroke's expression, by fortune. Instead of being on the eve of a fifteen years' peace, Pitt was on the eve of a twenty years' war.

1791 In the discussion of a Bill giving Canada a constitution, which was about the last measure of the Liberal Pitt, the debate had been interrupted by an angry altercation, ending in a rupture of friendship between Fox and Burke on a subject which at this time filled all minds. That subject was the French Revolution.

Pitt, as he scanned the political and social horizon, though he saw no signs of war, could not fail to see signs of change. Everywhere he must have noted that it was coming, in France that it was come. He must have marked that among the educated class scepticism had undermined the established religion. By this perhaps he would not be much disturbed, since, however orthodox in principle, he was not devout, and had let fall his opinion that Bishop Butler raised more questions than he solved. He must have observed the progress made in the conquest of European opinion by the biting wit of Voltaire and the seductive sentimentality of Rousseau; though on this again he might look, if not with complacency, without fear, since Voltaire, though a universal questioner and reformer, was no political revolutionist, while Rousseau's vision of a return to nature might seem a vision and nothing more. American revolution was far away and not propagandist. As a son of light and a friend of humanity, Pitt would view with pleasure the European movement. He would rejoice over the progress of philanthropy, the improvement in jurisprudence and administration, the incipient emancipation of serfs, the mitigation of the criminal law, the tendency to encourage education, the growing tolerance, the suppression of the Jesuits, the reduced power of the Inquisition. Though a thoroughly practical statesman, he would regard with interest and favour the advance of political philosophy, while he could hardly suspect the dire explosiveness of political and social ideals. He would recognize the good done, in spite of standing armies and territorial wars, by Turgot in France, by Aranda in Spain, by Pombal in Portugal, by Leopold in Tuscany, by Tanucci in Naples, by Frederick and Maria Theresa as civil rulers in Prussia and Austria, by Gustavus III. in Sweden, even by Cathcrine in Russia. He would observe that if Europe was still heavily encumbered by the incubus of a feudal aristocracy, which, all its work for civilization having long ago been done, had sunk into an idle, arrogant, reactionary, and grossly oppressive caste, among the kings enlightenment, progress, and beneficence were becoming the fashion, and, as was said at the time, a new political constitution had been born, that of monarchy tempered, not by parliaments, but by opinion. Everything in short might seem to him to promise a peaceful transition from the feudal or absolutist past to a more liberal and happier future.

This is not the place for telling the terrible story of the French Revolution. Louis XIV., taking up again the work of Richelieu, while he was impelled by his own pride and lust of power, had made himself the state and Versailles the country; he had laid low every institution, national or local, which was not a mere instrument of the royal will; he had created an enormous standing army, stamped upon the monarchy an intensely military character, and identified it with the policy of conquest; he had set the example of court expenditure on the most prodigal scale, and of the accumulation of public debt; he had turned the land-owning aristocracy into courtiers, place-hunters, and men of pleasure, domiciled them in his palace, severed them from their tenantry, and divorced them from their rural duties. In the gloomy end of his life, falling under the sway of superstition and of its organs, an intolerant priesthood and a priest-ridden woman, he had sought the favour of his deity by persecution and driven free conscience into exile or sent it to the galleys. The glitter of his system while he lived concealed its rottenness, which in the next reign, that of a voluptuary

1643–1715

1715–1774

ruled by a series of harlots, became apparent as well as
complete. The advent of a young king, well-meaning, 1774
though with little intelligence and no force, seemed
to be a renewal of hope. With it came a roseate dawn
of promise, social, intellectual, and scientific. Abuses
still called for reform; aristocratic privilege and insolence were most galling; the corruption of the church,
especially of the hierarchy, was extreme; the public
debt was heavy, the deficit was large, the financial system
was wretched. Yet the evil was not past cure. Turgot
was in a fair way to cure it when he was turned out of 1776
office, and his measures of reform and economy were
quashed by a court coterie and a pleasure-loving queen.
Then came intervention in America and war with Eng- 1778
land, which completed the ruin of the finances, gave a 1793
stimulus to revolutionary sentiment, and infected with it
the French troops which had served beside American
rebels. Still, a deficit, however large, ought not to have
laid a mighty monarchy in the dust. In the cities, at all
events, there were prosperity and wealth. It is difficult,
even now, to account for the sudden rising of the storm
cloud which overspread the sky, and the simultaneous
boiling up of all the elements of disaffection and revolution, political, social, economical, and religious. Visionary
speculation and practical suffering brought into contact
with each other on the largest scale, it is truly said, could
not fail to be explosive. At a crisis produced by the
financial distress and the administrative rottenness of the
government, the torch of a revolutionary and utopian
philosophy fired the vast mine of material discontent
which ages of wrong and misery had charged. For
something, perhaps for much, bad seasons and scarcity

of bread might account. Hunger, driving men from
the country to the city, would increase the terrible mob
of the Faubourg St. Antoine. In the general spread of
scepticism the government, the ruling class, the priesthood,
had lost faith in themselves and were prepared to fall.
Had the king been strong, the army being at his command, he would have grasped the reins firmly, have himself proclaimed reform, put a stop to waste, beginning
with the waste of his court, lowered the barriers of privilege, abolished oppressive feudal rights by his own legislative power, gone over the country in person looking into
the grievances of the peasants, and if the public creditor
could not be paid in full, have made the best arrangement
possible with him, selling if necessary for the purpose
monastery lands. This he might have done without the
violence displayed in quelling an aristocracy by Gustavus III. of Sweden. To such a policy, welcomed as it
would have been by the masses of the people, the obstructiveness of the parliament of Paris, with its spurious
popularity, could have offered no resistance. Monarchy
itself the French people loved; what they hated and
burned to overthrow was monarchy with a privileged
class, and a state church intolerant and corrupt. Being
not strong, but as weak as he was well-intentioned, Louis
1784– XVI., after trying a financial conjurer in the person of
1787 Calonne, and vainly asking counsel of a narrow Assem-
1787– bly of Notables, called out of the depth of the French
1788 past the States General, and unwisely fixed the place for
1789 their meeting at Versailles, in the contagious neighbourhood of the centre of fermentation. Still, by a frank
policy of concession he might have got on amicably with
an Assembly which, at the outset, was far from hostile to

the crown, and in the end, the country being radically
monarchical, he might insensibly have recovered a good
deal of his power. That hope was blasted by want of tact
on the part of the court and the stupid formalism of court
officials, by the fatal demagogism of Mirabeau, and afterwards by the meddling of the queen and her coterie, who,
like Henrietta and her circle in the English Revolution,
tried to bring up the army for the coercion of the Assembly.
All know the sequel; the legislative babel which ensued
in an Assembly too unwieldy for deliberation, split into a
score of factions, without parliamentary experience; the
construction of an ideal constitution; the flight of the
aristocracy from the post of peril; the death of Mirabeau, 1791
who, with all his profligacy and corruption, was the only
man capable of controlling the Revolution, and whose
departure left the wild steed masterless; while that climax
of enthusiastic folly, the self-denying resolution, put the
operation of the new political machine into utterly untried
hands. Nor is it needful to recount the uprising of a
famished and brutalized people, the burning of chateaux,
the massacres, the defection of the army, the destruction 1789
of the Bastille, emblematic of the downfall of the monarchical and feudal system, the mob invasion of Ver- 1789
sailles, the captivity of the king and queen, their escape, 1791
their recapture, the September massacres, the storming of 1792
the Tuileries, the execution of the king, the domination 1793
of the Faubourg St. Antoine, and the Reign of Terror. 1794

Pitt had viewed with liberal sympathy the first stages
of the Revolution. As it advanced he and Dundas showed
themselves resolved to remain strictly neutral and abstain
from meddling in any way with the domestic distractions
of France, as France had abstained from meddling with

the domestic distractions of England at the time of the great rebellion and the execution of Charles I. The difficulty of holding this course in face of the increasing crime and madness of the Revolution, which filled the most liberal with horror, and the rising tide of anti-revolutionary feeling in the court, the upper classes, and the church of England, was enhanced by the follies of English partisans of the French Revolution who held incendiary language, dallied with revolutionary conspiracy, and exchanged the hug of fraternity with the lunatics of France. It was enhanced by the indiscretion of the leaders of the opposition, especially of Fox, who, when he ought to have held reassuring language and dwelt on the distinction between the case of France and that of England, proclaimed his unbounded sympathy with the Revolution, even when it had begun to carry heads on pikes, and in a debate on the army estimates commended the French Guards for having deserted their duty as soldiers and taken part in the political insurrection. The soldier is still a citizen, and the nation had applauded when the army of James II., at Hounslow, cheered the acquittal of the Seven Bishops. But the conduct of the French Guards had been disgraceful, and Fox's praise of them was most unwise.

Above all, Pitt, in struggling to avert a war of opinion, had to contend against the tremendous impulse given to the reactionary and war spirit by the fiery eloquence of

1790 Burke. The writer of the "Reflections on the French Revolution" may be at once acquitted of apostasy; though an enemy of corruption and court influence, he had always been a friend to monarchy, always an admirer, almost a worshipper, of aristocracy; he had always opposed parliamentary reform. The magnificence of his writings nobody questions, marred though it is by extravagant metaphor and other errors of taste. Nor does anyone question his importance as a political philosopher. Evolutionists of the present day see in him a forerunner of their science of history. Of evolution as a theory he knows nothing. But he carries his hatred of arbitrary innovation and his love of precedent to the length of a worship, not of tradition only, but of prejudice, scarcely leaving reason a place in the formation of institutions. In the "Reflections" he divests himself of the semblance of judicial calmness. Nothing can be more palpable than the partiality with which he glozes over the abuses of the French monarchy, the monstrous privileges and social vices of the aristocracy, the corruption of the French church. Over the condition of the French peasantry, famished, degraded, and brutalized, he passes in silence. He makes no attempt fairly to probe and estimate the situation. No reader would gather from his pages that the French people had grievous cause for discontent. Who can read without derision the lines in which he suggests that a bloated church establishment, with courtier bishops living in luxury while curates starved, was a provision spontaneously made by the charity of peasants who were eating nettles for the spiritual necessities of sorely tempted wealth? How could Burke upbraid French reformers with their temerity in breaking away from the past? What past had they after Louis XIV. wherefrom to break away? How could he charge them with wantonly severing the golden chain of political continuity when there was nothing for them to continue? Had not the French monarchy absorbed all other institutions, then fallen by its own vices? Nothing of the old edifice being left, what could the reformers do but build anew? Did they not, in reviving the States General, reproduce the past, or so much of it as was capable of reproduction, and that with antiquarian fidelity? Particular facts as well as the general picture are distorted by Burke, who sees them all through the mist of his reactionary passion. Had Marie Antoinette only shone with the pure radiance of a morning star? Had she not laid herself open to reproach by gambling in public and by nocturnal frolics in the garden of Versailles? By whom was it that she was first threatened with insult? By the people and the revolutionists, or by the tattlers of the court? The "Reflections," it should be borne in mind, were published in November, 1790, before the Revolution had entered upon its most violent and sanguinary phase.

The most serious charge, however, which we have to bring against the author of this too famous work is one that touched him not as a pamphleteer, but as a statesman. By his own account the revolutionary party in England was not dangerous. He speaks of it with contempt, comparing it to half a dozen grasshoppers chirping noisily under a fern, while thousands of great cattle chew the cud silently beneath the oak; and his description was borne out by the facts. Such revolutionary feeling as there was might have been allayed by a moderate measure of parliamentary reform combined with the repeal of the Test and Corporation Acts and the emancipation of the Unitarians, all of which Burke opposed. The danger which the government was struggling to avert lay in the opposite quarter; it lay in the awakened fears and kindling passions of the king and the governing class; and Burke did all to increase it that his mighty pen could do.

The effect of his pamphlet, especially on the mind of the king, was instantaneous and fatal. Its sale was enormous. The author became almost a European power in himself, inspiring, apart from the government, and in opposition to its policy, the counsels of the exiled French court and the refugees, whose vengeance, when, in accordance with his desire, they should have been restored to power by foreign arms, he was sanguine enough to think that he could keep under his philosophic control. By the effect which his burning eloquence produced on European rulers, Burke may be deemed to have stimulated them to invade France and thus to have been partly responsible for the frenzy which invasion produced, for the September massacres, and for the Reign of Terror.

The Terror is hardly to be laid to the account of the Revolution. It was not political, but cannibal, though the leaders canted in the language of Rousseau. The mob of Paris, unspeakably brutal and savage, had got possession of the government of a highly centralized monarchy, and slaked its lust of riot and blood. Nothing of the kind could have happened in England, nor were English statesmen bound to treat such a catastrophe on the principles of international law or otherwise than they would have treated a hurricane or an earthquake. 1792-1794

Pitt long persevered in his policy of non-intervention. He had nothing to do with the coalition, with the plots of the emigrants, with the conference at Pilnitz, with the expedition or the manifesto of the Duke of Brunswick. By the territorial rapine to which French fraternity at once turned, and the door to which was unhappily opened by the weakness of the surrounding states or provinces; by insolently trampling on treaty rights in the case of the 1791

Scheldt; by aggression upon Holland, the settlement of which England guaranteed; above all by a propagandist manifesto threatening all established governments with subversion, the Jacobins furnished ample grounds for war. But that which is justifiable may not be wise; France was a lunatic whose ravings might be disregarded, whose frenzy would end in collapse. Pitt clung to peace.

He was swept from his moorings at last by the storm 1793 of pity and rage which followed the execution of the king. After all it was not he, it was France that declared war. But war rather came than was declared. Fired by mutual hatred, revolution and monarchy, religion and atheism, rushed upon each other. The British 1793 declaration of war, while it speaks of unprovoked aggressions, referring to Holland and the Scheldt, plainly sets forth as grounds for drawing the sword the internal disorders of France, the anarchy and crimes of the Revolution, the murder of the king, the danger with which all governments were threatened by French example and contagion. It, in fact, proclaims a crusade against the Revolution. It holds out the aid of Great Britain to restorers of monarchy in France. Thus Pitt, in his own despite, was forced into a crusade.

Had he foreseen the twenty years' war, he might still have held back, though it does not seem that with all his loftiness of character and purpose, with all his dignity of bearing, he was the man to hold his own against a heady current of opinion. But he believed that the war would be short; nor without reason. His reliance on the collapse of French finance was ill-founded; bankruptcy cleared France of her debt; rapine supplied her military chest; the transfer of her land from nobles and monks to industrious peasants soon increased her wealth; enthusiasm and conscription filled her armies; all her resources were entirely at the command of a revolutionary government more despotic than that of any king. Yet Pitt would have been well justified in thinking that if the coalition was united and resolute, its armies might at once march to Paris. The coalition was neither united nor resolute. Instead of thinking of the common cause, its members were thinking of their separate interests and their felonious partition of Poland. They behaved, not like crusaders, but like wreckers, fancying that France was going to pieces, and scrambling for their shares of the wreck. Austria took possession of French cities, not in the name of the Bourbons, but in her own. Pitt himself pottered with Dunkirk instead of insisting on a march to Paris. The Revolution in the meantime had put into the field immense armies which, commanded by valour and military genius self-raised from the ranks, and directed by the organizing skill of Carnot, overwhelmed the inferior numbers, mechanical soldiership, and antiquated tactics of the old powers. France conquered the Austrian Netherlands; turned Holland, in which from the first she had a large party, into a vassal state; annexed Savoy; overran the feeble and denationalized principalities of the Rhine; compelled decrepit Spain under the worthless Godoy, not only to cease fighting against her, but to pass over to her side. By the death of Catherine of Russia, whose trade, whatever her philosophy, was to be Czarina, the coalition lost a powerful friend. Prussia, whose councils were in the last degree weak, selfish, and base, at last went over to the enemy. Stolid Austria could be kept in the field only by subsidies. England was left fighting alone.

1796

Why did Pitt continue the war? At bottom, perhaps, because peace was impossible between revolutionary France and constitutional Britain. Royalty, aristocracy, property, the church, were all for war: royalty, aristocracy, and property against democratic levelling; the church against atheism. Pitt has been arraigned for not having boldly invoked the crusading spirit on his side to meet the crusading spirit on the side of the Jacobins. It needed no invocation; it was with him in full force; it was bearing him on more vehemently than he desired. When the pious and gentle Wilberforce raised his voice for peace, the king cut him at the levée. Pitt's formulary at last became "indemnity for the past and security for the future." Indemnity for the past meant the abandonment by France of her conquests, which was hopeless. Security for the future meant restoration of the Bourbons, which then was hopeless also. Pitt held that there was no government in France with which he could treat. From treating with the Jacobin bedlam turned into a slaughterhouse he might well be excused. But the Directory was a government, though it was a strange outcome of a grand effort to regenerate the world. Under it, France was sitting clothed, though not with samite, and in her right, though by no means in a moral, mind. Pitt did then treat for peace, and it was not through his fault, but through the insolent violence of the scoundrels who by military force had got the upper hand in the French government, that the treaty failed. Pitt was even willing to bribe the Directory. Yet when Bonaparte, having afterwards risen to power, made an overture for peace, Lord Grenville was allowed to say in reply, Restore the Bourbons. The retort was ready, Restore the Stuarts. Even George III.

noted the mistake which Bonaparte marked with joy. It is strange that Pitt should have let the despatch go. Lord Grenville, besides being a fanatical enemy of the Revolution, was insular, haughty, wanting in tact, and ill-fitted to cope with Talleyrand. In selecting him as Foreign Minister Pitt showed not much discernment.

Pitt has been damned as a war minister. Assuredly he was no Chatham. Peace, finance, economy, not war, were his field. He had no eye for military or naval merit, no promptness in calling it to the front; he could inspire nobody, nobody could leave his presence a braver man. He twice allowed the fatuous king to entrust the fortunes and honour of the British army to the young and incompetent Duke of York. His continental enterprises failed. His forces were never found on a decisive field. But he might plead that he had no trained commanders, that he had no conscription to furnish him with great armies; that on the sea he had not only been victorious but had annihilated the hostile fleets; that he had taken the French and Dutch colonies and had them to barter for retrocessions on the part of France.

The prime minister, however, must to some extent share with the admiralty the blame of having allowed the condition of the British sailor to be such that he, the most loyal and patriotic of men, the most true to duty, could at last endure his wrongs no more, and rising in a terrible mutiny brought the country to the verge of ruin. The sailor's pay and pensions had not been raised since the time of Charles II., though prices had doubled. He had to complain also of bad rations and short measures, of stoppage of his pay when he was wounded, of want of care and embezzlement of his necessaries when he was sick, of denial of his fair share of prize money, of refusal of permission to visit his home after his voyage, of tyrannical usage by his officers, of a harsh code of discipline cruelly enforced by the lash. Many of the men had been impressed. Never was a mutiny better justified; never was a spirit so good and moderate shown by mutineers. The sailors committed no outrage; never forgot that they were Englishmen; loyally kept the king's birthday; and at once checked the slightest movement towards desertion to the enemy. There was, in fact, no doubt that had the enemy appeared, they would have fought him. A second outbreak of the mutiny headed by Parker, an ambitious demagogue with ends of his own, was more violent than the first. Yet even in this the behaviour of the men was wonderfully good, and the ringleader, when unmasked, was at once deserted, nor was there any other display of revolutionary sentiment; redress of the seaman's wrongs was the sole aim. The government was compelled to negotiate, which it did with dignity and skill, and to grant redress. After the second and more seditious mutiny, there were some hangings and floggings round the fleet, which would have been better bestowed upon the lords of the admiralty and the contractors. In all this history there is nothing brighter than the character of the British tar, with its childlike simplicity, its respect for discipline, its loyalty to the flag. By the British tar, in spite of blundering and jobbery, the country was saved. By his victories was sustained, under all reverses, the fortitude of the nation. Hard was his life and scanty was his reward.

As the seaman was impressed, the soldier was crimped, or recruited in a way little better than crimping. Of course he was of the lowest grade, while French conscrip-

1797

1797

tion took the flower of the people. He was under-paid, ill-fed, ill-housed. He was subjected to a harsh discipline, and to the most cruel and degrading punishments. He had no hope of promotion. He was chained to the service for life. His officers were incompetent, careless, not seldom drunken. During the early years of the war he was under the command of generals described by Grenville as old women in red ribbons. Yet he fought well, and on many a red hillside rolled back the impetuous onset of conquering France. Napier contrasts the lot of the British soldier fighting in the cold shade of aristocracy with that of Napoleon's soldiers "fighting in bright fields where every helmet caught a ray of the glory." The British bumpkin thought not much about aristocracy; he preferred to be led by a gentleman, even if the gentleman was a boy; he did not feel the cold shade when he charged 1811 in his "majesty" at Albuera. Nor can the ray of glory have warmed the French conscript when he had been dragged by the mad ambition of a despot to perish amid Russian snows. It is true, however, that aristocratic privilege, in the way of commissions and promotions, was injurious to the army, and that the navy was better served for being less aristocratic. The nature of the naval service repelled privilege, which might appropriate a colonelcy but would hardly venture to undertake the management of a ship. When invasion threatened, 1794 a large volunteer force was formed. This showed national spirit, but perhaps it was fortunate that the volunteers did not meet on the battle-field of Hastings the trained veterans of France commanded by Napoleon, while the English, if the king's intentions were fulfilled, would have been commanded by George III.

Pitt now wore the appearance at least of sharing the Tory panic, once talked as if his own life were hardly safe from Jacobin poniards, and not only renounced reform, but entered on a course of violent repression. He acted like a changed man. For this he had no valid excuse. In a few hot heads revolutionary ideas might ferment, but the country at large was manifestly loyal and hearty in its support of the government; a few scores of revolutionary grasshoppers might chirp, but they were immeasurably outnumbered as well as outweighed by the conservative kine. The Corresponding Society, which embodied nearly all that there was of pronounced Jacobinism, was reckoned to have only six thousand members, nearly all of the lower class. Paine's answer to Burke might circulate, but its circulation was probably more due to the celebrity of the work to which it was a smart answer than to sympathy with the views of Paine. The golden dawn of the Revolution had entranced young and enthusiastic spirits, such as those of Coleridge, Southey, and Wordsworth. But an illusion, which never kindled sedition, ended with the September massacres and the Reign of Terror. The mob itself was anti-Jacobin; it rose

1791 upon the friends of the French Revolution at Birmingham, and wrecked the house of Priestley, their leading man. Imperfect as institutions were, the nation, comparing them with those of other countries, on the whole was content with them, and was averse from revolution. Danger of disaffection there was, as presently appeared, from the sufferings sure to be caused by war. Otherwise there was none; none, at least, which might not

1794– have been extinguished by moderate and safe reform.
1801 Yet Pitt suspended the *Habeas Corpus* for eight years.

He resorted to a series of repressive measures directed not only against acts but against opinions; a proclamation against seditious writings, a Traitorous Correspondence Act, a Treasonable Practices Act, a Seditious Meetings Act. The Treasonable Practices Act was a sinister enlargement of the definition of treason, though without the capital penalty; while the Seditious Meetings Act precluded even peaceful assemblings for objects of constitutional reform. A swarm of informers was called into activity by the government. Men were prosecuted for loose or drunken words, of which no man of sense would have taken notice, and for speculative opinions with which government had no right or reason to interfere. An attorney named Frost for saying in a coffee house, where he could not have meant to conspire, that he was for equality and no king, was tried before Lord Kenyon, a high Tory judge, and sentenced to six months' imprisonment, to stand in the pillory, to find security for good behaviour, and to be struck off the rolls. Another man, imprisoned for debt, having vented his spleen in what was plainly a mere lampoon, was sentenced to three years of imprisonment in Newgate, to stand in the pillory, and to find security for good behaviour for five years. For selling Paine's works and a political satire called "The Jockey Club," a respectable bookseller was sentenced to four years' imprisonment and to a heavy fine. Courts of quarter sessions, with benches of Tory squires, were empowered and employed to try political cases for the government, to which their character as tribunals must have been well known. Associations were formed under government patronage for the detection and prosecution of sedition. The impartiality of the jury was

[margin: 1793, 1795, 1795, 1793]

thus tainted at the source. There was a Tory reign of terror to which an increase of the panic among the upper classes might have lent a darker hue.

In Scotland, where there was scarcely even a mockery of the representation of the people, the Tory reign of terror was worse than in England. Thomas Muir, a young advocate, was a champion of parliamentary reform, as any man with a spark of patriotism in Scotland must have been, for in Scotland such was the state of the representation that election was but a name. He had been a delegate to the Edinburgh convention of the Friends of the People. He was indicted ostensibly for sedition.
1793 In reality, as he with reason asserted, he was brought to trial for promoting parliamentary reform. The Lord Justice Braxfield, another Jeffreys, confirmed this assertion by charging the jury that to preach the necessity of reform at a time of excitement was seditious. The judge harangued the jury against parliamentary reform. The landed interest, he said, alone had the right to be represented; as for the rabble, who had nothing but personal property, what hold had the nation on them? Another judge said, if punishment adequate to the crime of sedition were to be sought for, it could not be found in our law, now that torture had been happily abolished. Of the three Roman punishments, crucifixion, exposure to wild beasts, and deportation, it was said from the bench, we have chosen the mildest. Muir was sentenced to transportation for fourteen years. Efforts were made in parliament to get the sentence reversed, but the government stood by Scotch iniquity. Romilly, who was present at the trial, was greatly shocked and brands as detestable the Scotch administration of justice.

In the trial, ostensibly for sedition, of an advocate of universal suffrage, a judge said in summing up, "Gentlemen, the right of universal suffrage the subjects of this country never enjoyed, and were they to enjoy it, they would not any longer enjoy either liberty or a free constitution. You will therefore consider whether telling the people that they have a just right to what would unquestionably be tantamount to a total subversion of the kingdom is such a writing as any person is entitled to compose, to print, and to publish." The sentence in this case was transportation for seven years.

Was Pitt responsible for all? With pain it must be said that he was responsible for all, notably for the transportation of Muir. Once, in a case in which an indictment for constructive treason was brought against a parliamentary reformer, he was put in the witness-box to own that he had himself advocated reform of parliament. The son of the morning, Chatham's heir, had fallen indeed. He could say that circumstances were changed and that policy must change with them. He might have said that even if circumstances had not changed, a statesman had a right to change his mind, and that the public good required that his avowal of change should be free. But no one has a right, in dealing with others, to repudiate his own past.

Against these invasions of liberty Fox eloquently declaimed. No more could he do. Repelled by his revolutionary attitude, conservative Whigs, with Portland, Grenville, and Windham at their head, had gone over to the government, and the leader of the opposition was left with a feeble troop. Political parties formed themselves anew on the burning question of the Revolution. Of the

1797

forty or fifty members whom Fox could still muster not a few were members for nomination boroughs in the gift of great Whig nobles who adhered to their family traditions. The minister therefore was all-powerful, and a fresh election only increased his majority. Fox, with Sheridan, Grey, and Burke, kept up a war of indiscriminate invective, by which they could only forfeit whatever influence they might otherwise have had and confirm the minister, as Fox by the same conduct had confirmed North, in the policy from which they desired to restrain him. It seems not impossible that Pitt might have been restrained, had he been approached in a better way. That the Liberal was not dead in him, his subsequent conduct on the subject of Catholic Emancipation proved. In 1792 he had said that it was his wish to unite cordially and heartily, not in the way of bargain, but to form a strong united ministry, and that to Fox he had no personal objection, though he feared he had gone too far. At a later period than this he was willing to coalesce with Fox. But by this time to the spirit of party had been added personal hatred, and the counsels of Fox and the Liberals were thus lost to the nation.

A stand more successful and ever memorable was made by Erskine in courts of law. The government, ill-advised by its law officers, brought charges of constructive treason, which could not be sustained, against Horne Tooke, Hardy, Thelwall, and others. Horne Tooke's opinions might be extreme, but he could not be suspected of treason, while his bold and ready wit made him dangerous game, and his trial was little more than a farce. The 1794 accused were defended by Erskine, whose speeches were masterpieces of the advocate's art. To him was opposed Sir John Scott, afterwards Lord Eldon, the genius of irrational law, who vainly strove by prolix and elaborate construction to involve the prisoners in a technical net which at a stroke Erskine rent and flung aside. "How," said a juror, "could I find a man guilty of a crime when it took the attorney-general nine hours to tell us what it was?" Scott, whose love of money earned him afterwards the name of Old Bags, opened a speech with a picture of his own disinterestedness, over which he shed tears. He would have nothing, he said, to leave to his children but his good name. "What," asked a bystander, "is Scott weeping about?" "He is weeping," was the reply, "to think how little he will have to leave to his children." In these trials the government was defeated. It excused an error which brought upon it odium and contempt by pleading the wholesome effect of the political revelations. But to put a man on trial for his life without adequate proof of crime for the purpose of creating a political effect is an abuse of a court of justice. One good fruit, however, the trials bore; they confirmed the confidence of the people in the jury as a sufficient safeguard of personal liberty. The credit of the jurymen was not on this occasion shared by the bench. The chief justice, Kenyon, showed his Tory bias. As a rule English judges, though appointed, till recently, by party, have doffed the partisan in donning the ermine. Regard for professional reputation and the criticism of a strong bar have generally proved a sufficient guard for judicial virtue.

The platform, in spite of the rod held over it, was not mute. A great public dinner in celebration of Fox's birthday was attended by two thousand persons. At this 1798 the Duke of Norfolk, a sort of English counterpart of D'Orleans Egalité in opinion, though not in polish, for he was unwashed as well as drunken, gave as a toast, "Our sovereign's health, the majority of the people." Fox, at a meeting of the Whig Club, repeated that toast, and was struck off the privy council.

1798

The expense of the war, including the subsidies to allies, was immense and taxed to the utmost Pitt's skill as a financier as well as his hold on public confidence. He began by trying to raise supplies within the year. But his expenditure soon exceeded the measure of endurable taxation, and he was fain to cast upon posterity the enormous burden of which the greater part is still borne. At his death the public debt had mounted from two hundred and forty-seven to six hundred and twenty-one millions, and at the end of his war to eight hundred and sixty-one millions, bearing thirty-one millions and a half of interest. His mode of borrowing has been impugned, but he probably got the full value of his consols. The sinking fund to which he clung as the means of ultimate redemption only served by its operation to make matters a little worse. His three per cents fell at one time to forty-seven. He was driven to a suspension of cash payments, followed by the invariable results to commerce and industry, with the inevitable expense of ultimate redemption, so that in fact suspension was an addition at a high rate of liability to the national debt. Did the thought ever present itself to him that the nation might have an advantage in its immortality, and that between an annuity of a hundred years and a perpetuity, while there would be little difference to the mortal purchaser, there would be great difference to the immortal state? To meet the drain, the new manufactures were producing wealth, while trade derived a factitious prosperity from war expenditure and destruction of the enemy's mercantile marine. Commercial men zealously supported the minister. By a unanimous agreement to take bank notes at par they in great measure averted the depreciation of his paper currency. They crowded to subscribe for a Loyalty Loan on terms involving a sacrifice to subscribers. They were ready with free gifts, and one of a firm having put down ten thousand pounds for his firm, without the knowledge of his partner, was told when he apprehended the partner's anger that he might as well have made it twenty thousand.

Foreign grain being excluded by the war, the price of the home product was raised. Land not otherwise worth tillage was brought under the plough. Rents rose, and tithes along with them. In war power there is usually a political element, and British aristocracy showed its constancy in the struggle with France and Napoleon, as Roman aristocracy had shown its constancy in the struggle with Carthage and Hannibal. But its constancy was made easy by high rents. In general it behaved patriotically about taxation, but it resisted the extension of the succession duty from personal property to land. On the common people, small traders, labourers, and mechanics, the burden of endurance chiefly fell; and great their suffering was. In bad years grain rose to almost famine price, and all such palliatives as restrictions on the use of wheat-flour for pastry, or of wheat in the distilleries, were ineffectual, while worse than ineffectual was the attempt to revive obsolete laws against forestallers and regraters, which the chief justice, Lord

Kenyon, in his wisdom, chose to applaud. There were bread riots; Pitt was hooted; the king was mobbed; and when at last a French envoy brought a peace, the people took the horses out of his carriage and drew it through the streets.

Still Pitt's ascendancy in parliament and the country remained the same. A fresh election went in his favour. After each reverse in war, he rose in the House of Commons undaunted, lofty as ever, and with his sonorous eloquence revived the spirits of his friends and restored their confidence in their chief. As the horrors of the Revolution and the indiscretions of Fox and others of its English friends increased, the more moderate Whigs, led by Portland, the former head of the Coalition, went over to the government. Among them was Windham, the model of an English gentleman, in whom high academical culture was combined with a love of prize-fighting and bull-baiting, an indomitable advocate of war.

Fox's following was reduced to fifty, of whom nearly one-half were members for nomination boroughs. He constantly showed his power in debate, but he and his associates damaged themselves and their cause by indiscriminate attacks on the government and unpatriotic bearing. "I will not," said Wilberforce, "charge these gentlemen with desiring an invasion; but I cannot help thinking that they would rejoice to see just so much mischief befall their country as would bring themselves into office." Fox could say, "The truth is I am gone something further in hate to the English government than you and the rest of my friends are, and certainly further than can with prudence be avowed; the triumph of the French government over the English does in fact afford me a degree of pleasure which it is very difficult to disguise." When the news of Trafalgar arrived, his comment was, " It is a great event, and by its solid as well as brilliant advantages far more than compensates for the temporary succour which it will certainly afford to Pitt in his distress." Such is party. How was it possible that a public man, visibly actuated by such feelings, should have influence with a nation engaged in a struggle for its very existence? Fox's avowal that he thought the submission of the people to a repressive law was no longer a question of moral obligation and duty but only of prudence, may pair off as an indiscretion with Bishop Horsley's saying that he did not know what the mass of the people in any country had to do with the laws but to obey them.

Legislation other than repressive and reform of every kind, whether in church or state, stood still. Even the movement of humanity for the abolition of the slave-trade was thrown back by the dread of revolution. The answer to every proposal of reform was that this was not the time; though in truth it was the very time for such reforms as catholic emancipation and the abolition of nonconformist disabilities, which would have extinguished sources of disaffection and united the nation in its hour of peril.

This is deemed the golden age, though not of legislation, of parliamentary eloquence. One who having heard Pitt and Fox listened to the debates of the next generation, though Grey, Plunket, and Canning were then among the speakers, noted or fancied that he noted a marked decline. Reporting being as yet very imperfect, members still spoke more to the House than to the gallery, and as the political press was weak, the editorials of the morning did not take the wind out of the sails of evening eloquence. The themes were in the highest degree momentous and inspiring. Pitt in his oratory as in his statesmanship was the opposite of his father. There was in his speeches nothing of Chatham's lightning. He had a wonderful command of rounded and stately periods, acquired under his father's tuition by the practice of translation at sight. He was grand in argument and in exposition, in financial exposition above all. His voice was musical and his delivery was impressive. Fox had practised from boyhood as a debater and attained the highest perfection. The character of the speaker, the warmth and spontaneity of his utterances, would lend the speech a charm. Each is seen at his best in the debate of February 3rd, 1800, on overtures of peace from France. Pitt's speech, if it was not prepared by pen, is miraculous; almost more miraculous is Fox's reply, made as soon as Pitt sat down, unless he had anticipated, as he well might, some of his antagonist's points. Sheridan's speech upon the impeachment of Hastings, the Begum speech as it was called, received the extraordinary tribute of an adjournment of the House to give the judgment of members time to cool. But it is lost, and we have no means of assuring ourselves that Sheridan could rise so high. Wilberforce was silvery and homiletic. Windham was forcible in debate though liable to escapade. Dundas was not eloquent but practical and spoke for votes. Erskine, so great at the bar, failed in the House. It is doubtful whether, setting Burke aside as a grand essayist rather than an orator, anything remains of the golden age much superior in literary or political value to a great speech of John Bright or Robert Lowe.

One great measure of improvement for which Pitt in his brighter hour had striven to pave the way he was destined in his darker hour to carry, though through the agency of events which left a terrible stain on its record and are for ever to be deplored. That measure was the legislative union with Ireland. 1800

How unworkable was the union of crowns with separate parliaments was seen when on the question of the Regency the Irish parliament flew apart from that of Great Britain and resolved to recognize the Prince of Wales, who called himself a Whig, as Regent in his own right and without limitations, while Pitt and the Tory parliament of Great Britain proposed to confer on him by Act of Parliament a Regency with limited powers. The two monarchies had been held together and the government of the smaller country had been kept in uneasy and precarious unison with that of its greater yoke-fellow only by Irish crown boroughs and the power of an intrusive church establishment, combined with systematic bribery and corruption.

Like the American Revolution, the French Revolution extended its contagion, as well it might, to Ireland. In Ireland there was the old quarrel, still not quite extinct, of race; there was the old quarrel, still living in memory, between the two races, about the land; there was the double religious quarrel, between catholics and protestants, between the state church and Presbyterians; there was the payment of tithe in kind, its most vexatious form, to the griping tithe-proctors of an alien church; there was a parliament of crown or pocket and purchasable boroughs, bought and sold in market overt, which was a mockery of representation; there was a domination of jobbers; there was absenteeism on a large scale; there was a miserable peasantry holding little potato grounds under middle-men who sublet at exorbitant rents, and multiplying with the recklessness of abject and hopeless poverty. The relations between the gentry, at least the lower gentry, squireens as they were called, middle-men as they often were, and the common people were very bad, the squireen being insolent as well as dissolute and lording it over the peasant with the lash. The state clergy, scandalously pluralist and sinecurist, partly absentee, as well as alien and hated, could have no influence over the people. The catholic church, which had great influence, was the natural enemy of protestant ascendancy.

It was not among the catholics, however, or in the quarrel between catholics and protestants that rebellion had its origin. It had its origin in Presbyterian Belfast and in a circle of free-thinkers full of the doctrines of Tom Paine, and fired by the French Revolution. By the catholic clergy, the Revolution, being atheist, was abhorred; the more so as most of them, denied by the penal law places of education in Ireland, had been educated on the continent, and in religious houses which the Revolution had destroyed. The Belfast conspirators, themselves indifferent as free-thinkers to the religious quarrel, assumed the title of United Irishmen, and strove to combine the catholics with the protestants in a political rebellion. They succeeded only so far as to set boiling all the elements in the fatal caldron of Irish discord and distraction. The catholic peasantry organized themselves as Defenders for agrarian insurrection, with perhaps some admixture of religious enmity. The protestants, seeing their immemorial foes in motion, organized themselves on the other side as Orangemen and vied with the catholics 1795 in outrage. Over Ulster, and in a less degree over Munster and Leinster, the reign of a murderous anarchy set in. Belfast conspiracy, meanwhile, was stretching out its hands to revolution in Paris and inviting a Jacobin invasion. It found a leader and envoy in Wolfe Tone, a brave, light-hearted, and dashing adventurer, who, when 1793 set to more serious work, showed ability of a higher kind, and who could boast that with him hatred of England had become an instinct.

Fitzgibbon, afterwards Lord Clare, the leading spirit of the ruling party, a man of boundless courage and great ability, was for the strict maintenance of protestant ascendancy and for unflinching repression. More liberal was the young Castlereagh, now rising into power. Pitt, who in his Irish policy was still Liberal, and Dundas were inclined to go as far as the Tories and the king would let them in the way of reform and conciliation. They were partly in sympathy with Grattan, the great Irish orator and patriot and the father of independence, and his small group of constitutional reformers, who were for complete emancipation and redress of abuses, but thoroughly against revolution and in favour of British connection. In 1793 the Irish parliament, with the 1793 approbation of the government, passed a large measure of catholic emancipation, though against the opinion of Clare. By this measure the elective franchise and the right of sitting on juries were restored to the catholics; their ownership of property was set free from the restraints of the penal laws; the army up to the grade of colonel was thrown open to them, and they were released from ignominious restrictions on their possession of arms and horses; while a subsequent Act partly removed their disabilities in regard to education. Unhappily they were still excluded from sitting in parliament. Thus the brand of degradation was left, and the support of the catholic gentry, who were well disposed towards the government, and whom it ought to have been the first object of the government to unite with itself in the maintenance of order, was, perhaps, more than ever repelled.

1794 In 1794 the Conservative Whigs, Portland, Fitzwilliam, and Windham, having joined Pitt's administration, sought to apply the Liberal principles of the Whig party to the government of Ireland, which was under the Home Office, Portland's department. Fitzwilliam went to Dub-
1795 lin as Lord-Lieutenant, with the besom of administrative reform in one hand and the olive branch of catholic emancipation in the other. Great hopes were excited by his coming. Unfortunately he was rash, and at Dublin outran if he did not contravene his instructions. By proclaiming at once a complete change of system he stirred to desperate opposition Clare and the whole party of ascendancy and Castle rule. He at once dismissed from office John Beresford, the representative of a great jobbing house, which by assiduous accumulation of patronage had made itself a most formidable power. Pitt, pressed no doubt by the Tory section of his ministry as well as by the friends of ascendancy in Ireland, was
1795 obliged to recall the viceroy, while Portland, the head of Fitzwilliam's party, acquiesced in the recall. Fitzwilliam took his revenge, not very nobly, by publishing a confidential paper and doing all the mischief that he could. His mission had not only failed, but by dashing sanguine

hopes had done incalculable harm. He departed amid
public mourning, while his successor, Camden, was received with popular execration. 1795

The next scene in the drama was French invasion.
Hoche, a renowned general of the Revolution, with a
large fleet and army, sailed from Brest. No British fleet, 1796
to bar its way, appeared. In Ireland there was no force
capable of coping with the invasion. The country was
saved by a storm which separated the French commanders from their armament and drove the French fleet
from the Irish coast, when it had ridden for some days
in Bantry Bay. That in Ireland itself rebellion was not
ripe, and that the movement among the peasantry was
rather agrarian than political, appeared from the conduct
of the peasants, who readily boiled their potatoes for the
soldiers. A small French force under Humbert afterwards effected a landing, and once more proved the 1798
superiority of regulars over irregulars, by putting to
ignominious rout a large body of militia at Castlebar.
But in the end it was compelled to surrender. A great
expedition was fitted out by Holland, now the Batavian 1797
Republic, the nation to save which from French aggression England had been spending blood and money. It
was ready to sail when the British navy was paralyzed
by mutiny. But the winds were again faithful to the 1797
Queen of the Seas. They kept the Dutch armament in
port. When it was able to put out, the mutiny was over
and all fear of Dutch invasion was ended by Duncan's
victory at Camperdown. Hoche, who was bent on the 1797
invasion of Ireland, died. Into his place mounted Bonaparte who had no faith in Irish revolution and little
sympathy with revolution anywhere. "They have made

a 'diversion," he said of the Irish to the Directors; "what more do you want of them?" In the negotiations for peace, little thought was bestowed by the French government upon its friends in Ireland.

Foreign aid having failed, nothing was left for the revolutionists but domestic insurrection, however hopeless. For this the United Irishmen had prepared by secret organization, for which the Irish have a strong taste and aptitude, by the administration of secret oaths, and by the clandestine collection of arms. Society broke up. The gentry lost all influence over their tenants and were besieged in their houses, the mansion becoming an object of war, like the chateau. Everything in the shape of a pole was seized, and saplings were cut down, as handles for the pikes, the heads of which patriotic blacksmiths were busily forging. Of the priests only the lowest joined the movement. Those of the higher class and the hierarchy might have sympathized with agrarianism, still more with the religious uprising against heretical domination, but they could hardly sympathize with Jacobinical and atheistic revolution. The government, finding itself beset with perils great and magnified by rumour, proclaimed martial law, and being ill provided with regular troops let loose the yeomanry and Orangemen on the people. Now set in a reign of agrarian outrage and murder on the one side; of flogging, pitch-capping, picketing, and burning of suspected houses on the other. A party of forty or fifty Catholic Defenders enter the house of an excellent and benevolent schoolmaster named Berkeley, who had given no offence beyond that of being a member of a colony planted for the improvement of industry in the district. They stab him in several places, cut out his tongue, and cut off several of his fingers. They mangle his wife in the same way, and hideously mutilate a boy of thirteen. They plunder the house, and then march in triumph along the road with lighted torches. The feeling of the neighbourhood is entirely with them; only one of the culprits is brought to justice; he refuses to give evidence against his accomplices, and goes to the gallows with the air of a martyr. This crime is a specimen of many. As a specimen of what was done on the side of order, we have Mr. Judkin Fitzgerald perambulating Tipperary, and extorting confessions of concealed arms or secret associations with the torture of the lash. He ties up a man named Wright, and gives him fifty lashes. An officer comes and asks the reason of the punishment. Fitzgerald hands him a French note found on the prisoner, saying that though he could not read French himself, the major would find in it what would justify him in "flogging the scoundrel to death." The major reads it and finds it to be an insignificant note postponing an appointment. Fitzgerald, nevertheless, orders the flogging to proceed. Wright is flung, a mass of wounds, into a prison cell, with no furniture but a straw pallet, where he remains for six or seven days without medical assistance. Judkin Fitzgerald was afterwards brought to trial, and was not only snatched from justice, but rewarded and honoured. Sir Ralph Abercrombie, a humane and honourable soldier, being put in command, denounced in 1797 stinging terms the excesses of the yeomanry, and strove to restore discipline. He was thrust from his command by the party of violent repression, and the whole hell-brood of passions, agrarian, social, political, and religious, raged without restraint over a great part of the island.

1798 Finally rebellion broke out in Wicklow and Wexford, where the revolutionary influence prevailed. A host of catholic peasants, armed partly with muskets which they did not know how to use, but chiefly with pikes which they used with good effect, took the field under two savage priests, one of whom, Father Murphy, showed an instinct of command. They defeated and hideously butchered two or three detachments of the troops, took the city of Wexford, and on its bridge killed a long train of prisoners by hoisting them in the air on their pikes and then letting them drop into the water. They formed a great camp on Vinegar Hill, and there committed a series of fiendish murders. But they were presently over-
1798 powered by superior forces, and a bloody reign of vengeance ensued. These orgies of blood were checked by
1798 the arrival in full command, military as well as civil, of the excellent Cornwallis, who has described the state of things which he found. "The yeomanry," he says, "are in the style of the loyalists in America, only much more numerous and powerful and a thousand times more ferocious. These men have served their country, but they now take the lead in rapine and murder. The Irish militia, with few officers and those chiefly of the worst sort, follow closely on the heels of the yeomanry in murder and every kind of atrocity; and the fencibles take a share, though much behindhand, with the others. The language of the principal persons of the country all tends to encourage this system of blood, and the conversation at my table, where you will suppose I do all I can to prevent it, always turns on hanging, shooting, burning, etc. And if a priest has been put to death the greatest joy is expressed by the whole company." On his arrival, Corn-

Wallis says, he "put a stop to the burning of houses and 1798 murder of the inhabitants by the yeomen or any other person who delighted in that amusement, to the flogging for the purpose of extorting confession, and to the free quarters which comprehended universal rapine and robbery throughout the country." He tells us that of the number of the enemy killed a small proportion only are killed in battle; that he is afraid that any man found in a brown coat within several miles of the scene of action is butchered; and that members of both Houses of parliament are averse to all acts of clemency and desire to pursue measures which would terminate in extirpation. The yeomanry and militia, let it be remembered, as well as the members of parliament, were Irish, and this was before the union. There is evidence that the regiments of the regular army were, compared with the yeomanry and militia, a power of mercy. "The respect and veneration with which I hear the names of Hunter, Skerret, and Stuart . . . pronounced, and the high encomiums passed on the Scotch and English regiments under whose protection the misguided partisans of rebellion were enabled to return in safety to their homes, convinces me that the salvation of the country was as much owing to the forbearance, humanity, and prudence of the regular troops as to their bravery. The moment the militia, yeomanry, and Orangemen were separated from the army, confidence was restored." So writes the historian Wakefield, to whom it is no answer to say that his history was not official, and that he wrote fourteen years after events which must have been deeply imprinted on his memory.

The parliamentary government of Ireland had sunk in blood. About the last measure of the oligarchical legislature was an Act of Indemnity for the illegal infliction of torture on suspected rebels. No power of order remained except the British army. It was impossible to leave the catholics in the hands of the protestants, or the protestants in the hands of the catholics. To do either would have been to give the signal for the renewal of a murderous civil war. Union of the crowns without union of the parliaments had proved unworkable, and was sure thereafter to be more unworkable than ever. Nor would there have been any chance of inducing the borough-owners of the Irish parliament to consent to a reform which would evidently have been their own destruction. There was nothing for it but to bring both races and religions, with all the warring sections and interests, whether political or social, under the broad ægis of an Imperial parliament. That course had its drawbacks. It was sure to import a perilous element into the parliament of Great Britain and at the same time to entangle Irish questions with the conflict between British parties. The first of these consequences at least was foreseen at the time, though the shape which the evil would take, that of an Irish party in the House of Commons fighting for its own objects, regardless of Imperial interests and playing on the balance of British parties, was not foreseen; the fear at the time being rather that the Irish would swell the forces of the crown. But the necessity was overmastering.

So Cromwell's policy of a legislative union was revived. Unhappily, the thing could no longer be done in Cromwell's way by direct and simple incorporation. It was thought necessary to obtain the consent of the Irish parliament, and the consent of such a parliament could not be obtained by mere proof of the wisdom of the measure or by methods entirely pure. Cornwallis, therefore, as viceroy, had work to do from which his integrity shrank. Yet it is untrue, however generally believed, that the union was carried by bribery. Compensation was given by Act of Parliament to all owners of boroughs on the principle, then accepted and recognized in Pitt's measure of parliamentary reform for England, that the nominations were property; and it was given to the borough-owners who had opposed as well as to those who had supported the union, some of the largest sums, in fact, going to opponents. For each borough fifteen thousand pounds were paid, and the sum of one million two hundred and sixty thousand pounds was spent in this way; nor is the price reckoned to have been excessive. Money was spent by both parties in the contest, but of pecuniary corruption on a large scale there is no proof, nor does it seem possible to point out the fund from which the means could have been supplied. Peerages or promotions in the peerage, it is true, were lavished on borough-owners as the price of their support. In the short viceroyalty of Cornwallis twenty-eight Irish peerages were created, six Irish peers were made English peers for Irish services, and twenty Irish peers were raised to a higher rank in the peerage. Lord Ely, with his eight nominees, was bought with the promise of an English peerage. This, if not bribery, was corruption, though corruption which cost the state little; and Lord Gosford, who voted for the union, refused an offer that his motives might be above suspicion. But without compensation of some kind it would have been impossible to induce a strong oligarchy to surrender its monopoly of

1798

power and patronage as well as the exclusive field of its ambition. The patronage of the government, civil, ecclesiastical, and judicial, was also used in support of its policy. But this is always done under the party system. Untrue, too, is the assertion that the union was forced on Ireland by a great British army. The yeomanry and militia were not British but Irish. Invasion still impended, and the viceroy reported that though he might have force enough to maintain order, he had not enough to resist invasion. The union may be said to have been carried by political necessity combined with the exhaustion and panic following upon a civil war. Everyone who had a throat to be cut, a wife or a child to be mangled, a house to be burned over his head, or a herd of cattle to be houghed, might well wish to be transferred from the realm of anarchy to that of a government strong enough to keep the peace. The catholic bishops, the best judges perhaps of the interest of their people, were for the measure, and the chief of them took an active part in its favour. Arthur O'Leary, the foremost of catholic writers, though doubt rests on his independence, if not on his integrity, took the same side. The viceroy, after a tour of inspection, could report a general appearance of at least passive acquiescence. Dublin was naturally unwilling to lose its position as political and social centre. Yet the demonstrations even in Dublin were not violent. Grattan, a sincere and honest as well as able advocate of independence, fought with all the force of his eloquence against union, but he hardly measured the change which had come over the scene since the day on which independence was won. It is said that there ought to have been an appeal to the nation by a dissolution of parliament and a new election. But if the appeal was not to be illusory, it would have been necessary first to reform the representation and to admit catholics to parliament. The idea of a plébiscite was by no one seriously entertained. An appeal to the Irish nation in any form was in truth impossible, since Irish nation there was none; there was only a land which formed the scene of a war between two races not merely alien but deadly and immemorial enemies to each other. After a great parliamentary struggle, in which the force of Clare and the skill of Castlereagh were pitted against the vehement eloquence of Grattan, the persuasive art of Plunket, and the powerful reasoning of Foster, the measure passed the Irish Commons by a hundred and fifty-eight votes to a hundred and fifteen, and the Irish Lords by seventy-five to twenty-six. The island realm was united at last.

1800

Through the British parliament the union passed with ease, Pitt being all-powerful there. In duty to party, perhaps to faction, it was opposed by the small band of Whigs. Fox himself stayed away from the House, pouring his denunciations into the bosom of Grattan and leaving the debating to be done by Sheridan and Grey. He never moved for repeal. Grey afterwards as prime minister pledged the sovereign and the Whig party to employ all the means in their power to preserve and strengthen the legislative union as indissolubly connected with the peace, security, and welfare of the nation, expressing his own emphatic opinion that its repeal would be ruin to both countries. Of the two greatest speakers against the union in the parliament of Ireland, one, Grattan, sat acquiescent at least and loyal in the parliament of the United Kingdom; the other, Plunket, sitting in the united parliament and advocating catholic emancipation, avowed that his opinions in regard to the union had undergone a total change, and that he who in resistance to it had once been prepared to go the length of any man, was now prepared to do all in his power to render it close and indissoluble. He had formerly, he said, been afraid that the interests of Ireland, on the abolition of her separate legislature, would be discussed in a hostile parliament; he would now state, and wished that the whole of Ireland might hear his statement, that during the time that he had sat in the united parliament he had found every question that related to Irish interests or security entertained with indulgence and treated with the most deliberate regard.

In its political aspect the union, whether free and honourable or not, was equal. It followed generally the analogy of the union with Scotland. Ireland got her share of the representation both in the Commons, on a mixed basis of population and property, and in the Lords. In the Commons, by the redistribution of the seats, she got a partial reform of her representation. In the case of the Irish peerage, as in the case of the Scotch peerage, the system of representatives elected by their order was adopted, thus again introducing the elective principle, though once more in the mildest form possible, into the House of Lords. Party not being constitutionally recognized, no provision against a party monopoly was made; the consequence of which has been the exclusion from parliament of Liberal Irish peers. With regard to the church the example of the treaty of union with Scotland was followed with a fatal difference. In the case of

Scotland the establishment guaranteed by the treaty of union was the church of the Scotch people; the establishment guaranteed by the treaty of union with Ireland was the church of a dominant minority, alien and an object of most just hatred to the people.

Pitt had intended that the union should be followed by a measure of emancipation admitting the catholics to parliament, by a provision for their clergy, and by a commutation of tithes. The hope of emancipation, held out informally and indefinitely to the catholics, had no doubt helped to win their support for the union, though deliverance from Irish protestant ascendancy might have been inducement enough. To the admission of catholics to parliament Pitt knew the king to be strongly opposed, and he seems to have thought it best, before approaching him, to secure the concurrence of the whole cabinet, which, as some of its members were wavering, took time. Meanwhile he was betrayed by the chancellor, Lord Loughborough, Wedderburn that had been, an intriguer who wanted to play the part of the king's familiar friend. Loughborough crept to the royal ear, revealed what Pitt in confidence had imparted to him, and confirmed a half-insane mind in the fancy that consent to catholic emancipation would be a breach of the coronation oath and a forfeiture of the crown; a notion which the two great Tory lawyers, Kenyon and Scott, had, much to their credit, pronounced baseless. The archbishops of Canterbury and Armagh, with the bishop of London, completed Loughborough's work, and Pitt, when he approached the king, found him inflexible. "It was the most Jacobinical 1801 thing ever heard of," said the monarch, who had been allying himself with the catholic powers of Europe in his crusade against the Jacobins. Whoever voted for catholic emancipation, he said, would be his personal enemy, using his favourite formula, with his usual contempt for the principles of the constitution. If he granted catholic emancipation, his logical mind told him, the kingdom would depart from his house and go to the catholic house of Savoy. Thus catholic emancipation was deferred for many a day with fatal consequences to the union and the realm. Provision for the catholic clergy also fell to the ground. Not even tithe commutation was carried, and the tithe-proctor was left to vex and to provoke outrage as before. Nor was military command thrown open to catholics though the army was full of catholic Irish. Pitt discharged the debt of honour by resignation.

Pitt's relations with royalty had been formal. George must have rejoiced when in place of his haughty and powerful minister came Addington, a courtly mediocrity, who had decorously filled the Speaker's chair, and whose most conspicuous achievement was the recommendation of a hop pillow to the king as a soporific, by which he earned the nickname of the Doctor. Pitt having taken with him the brains of his Ministry, that of Addington was not less weak than its chief. Eldon, the embodiment of high Toryism, of king-worship, of intolerance, and of law's delay, became chancellor. Loughborough, it is pleasant to recount, missed his prize. Clinging to hope and perhaps nursing the fancy that the chancellor was a fixture, he continued to intrude himself, though out of office, into the meetings of the cabinet till Addington showed him the door. Vainly he danced attendance upon royalty; even George III. saw through

him, and when his death was announced, after carefully 1805
assuring himself of the fact, pronounced the obituary,
"He has not left a greater knave behind him in my
dominions."

It was generally felt that Addington was only Pitt's
warming-pan, and scarcely had a change of ministers taken
place when the reason for it was annulled. A fit of the
king's malady was brought on by the crisis. Thereupon 1801
Pitt renounced any intention of reviving the question of
catholic emancipation during the life of the king. His
act is open to sinister construction. But if the king
could not be converted, he certainly could not be over-
borne. His domestic virtue had given him a popularity
which his malady only increased. In character, habits,
and diet, he was a John Bull; his prejudices, notably
that against the catholics, were the prejudices of the
masses. Pitt might remember that the king was twenty
years older than himself and not in the best of health.
He might also think that if there was a chance of softening the king's prejudice it was by touching his heart. It
has been suggested that Pitt's own health was failing and
with it his strength of will. From his boyhood he had
been taught by the family physician to drench himself with
port, and that medicine combined with toil and anxiety
had no doubt done its work. But over the king's prejudice no strength of will could have prevailed. In the
sequel this plainly appeared.

To the resignation of a power so long held, wielded so
ably, and so loved, Pitt may have been partly reconciled by
the necessity, now too manifest, of making peace with little
honour. There was no longer anything to be gained by the
war, or any apparent reason for its continuance. Austria,

1800 after a run of success during Bonaparte's absence in Egypt, had been crushed at Hohenlinden and Marengo, and forced to make an ignominious and disastrous peace. No ally was left to England but Turkey, Portugal, and Naples. French aggrandizement was most dangerous and threatening to the independence of Europe, but its reversal was past hope. Jacobinism, against which the war had been a crusade, the Revolution itself, and even republicanism, had been extinguished by Bonaparte. Instability, such as would constitute incapacity to treat, could not reasonably be predicated of the Consulate. The boundless rapacity and perfidy of the First Consul, which in reality made lasting peace impossible, had not yet been fully manifested and could not be presumed. War expenditure and lavish subsidies to needy, half-hearted allies had piled up the debt to five hundred and forty millions. Commerce felt the disturbance of the currency. The sufferings of the people were great, and were only enhanced by a poor law which fostered pauperism and by giving premiums to early marriages and large families encouraged paupers to multiply their kind. Discontent
1800 began to show itself in riots. Dislike of the war was growing in Pitt's own party and threatening him with mutiny. His warm ally, Wilberforce, had been moving in favour of peace.

1802 Peace was made at Amiens; but it was no peace, as appeared before the ink of the signatures was dry, for Bonaparte's aggressions were not for a moment suspended. He went on laying robber hands upon the neighbouring states of Holland, North Italy, and Switzerland, as afterwards he did on Spain. War, new victories, and fresh glories were, as himself avowed, indispensable to his hold on the French heart. If he pretended to make peace, it was only as a move in his game. France, spent with revolution, had made herself absolutely over to a military despot, with whom it was indeed hopeless to negotiate, with whom the conflict was really internecine. Henceforth the war is not a struggle against republicanism and atheism in the interest of monarchy, aristocracy, and state churches, but a struggle for national independence and for the independence of all European nations against the boundless aggression of a conquering and tyrannical power. Are there in history no accidents such as must baffle science? What science of history could have predicted that with Corsica France would annex Napoleon Bonaparte, a man combining supreme genius for war and for despotic administration with a devouring ambition, and with a character as remote from moral civilization as that of any native of his isle? This adventurer coming to a political field swept clear for him by revolution, having won the greater part of the army by his splendid victories, and sent that part of it which he had not won, Moreau's troops, to perish in San Domingo, was absolute master of France, whose blood and resources, himself never a Frenchman but always a Corsican, he spent ruthlessly for his own aim; an aim which, however grandiose, was not less vulgar and fatuous than it was immoral; for who could imagine that all the nations of Europe would allow themselves to be permanently made dependencies of France? The French people, ever ready for the yoke of a master, whether he be Grand Monarque, Jacobin dictator, or emperor, ever loving military glory and domination abroad more than liberty at home, put themselves slavishly into his hands. Year after year, by the vote of a legislature formed of his own tools, he drew her youth, and at last her boys, into his armies, and with his vast hosts, still animated by something of revolutionary enthusiasm, but by more of the restless spirit of adventure, overthrew the hireling battalions, the effete strategy, and the mouldering dynasties of Europe, till at last his tyranny roused the nations. Peace with him was impossible. He meant nothing less than the subjugation of Europe. Nor could any treaty bind his perfidy. Of moral sense he was totally devoid. No human suffering, no horrors of the battlefield touched his heart; he had, besides his ambition, a savage delight in the game of war. He had not even national interest to restrain him, for he never was a Frenchman. France he treated as the engine of his ambition and the nursery of his armies. Little interest could she have in his Russian expedition. The nation that fought with him was fighting for its life.

1803   Bent on peace as Addington was, he had therefore to renew the war. To its conduct he and his colleagues were unequal. There was a general call for Pitt, who had at first loyally supported Addington, and being no longer able to support him, yet debarred by their connection from opposing him, had ceased to appear in the House. But Addington was satisfied with himself, and George III. was more than satisfied with Addington. The restless and aspiring genius of Canning, who now comes upon the scene, conceived the scheme of dislodging Addington by a round robin. Pitt, of course, put his veto on a device which savoured of conspiracy. Addington at last yielded to gentle compulsion, and Pitt once
1804 more was head of the state. He came in pledged not to revive the catholic question. This was bad; but what

was Pitt to do? He could not convert the king, he could not dethrone him, nor could the ship of state be left without its helmsman in the stormy night on the lee shore. Between monarchical and elective government there was an awkward interval in which the court, having lost its responsibility, retained its influence. In the human body there is an intestine, the survival of a previous stage of development, no longer serving any good purpose, but still serving to generate disease.

Pitt tried to form a broad-bottom ministry of national defence including Fox, another proof that the party system was not his. But Fox the king abhorred, not only as the opponent of the American and the French war, but as the bad angel of the heir. Grenville, Pitt's own Foreign Minister, and the other Whigs refused to join without Fox, though Fox magnanimously left them free. Thus, between the influences of royalty and that of party, the country in its extremity had to put up with a narrow Tory cabinet, in which Pitt and Dundas, now Lord Melville, were the only men of mark. Further to show what party was, Melville, who was doing well at the admiralty, having been guilty of some financial irregularity, was impeached by the opposition for corruption. Through him, faction struck at Pitt. He was rightly acquitted by the Lords, but it was thought necessary to put him out of office. When the motion for impeachment passed the House of Commons by the casting vote of a perplexed Speaker, which, in such a case, ought to have been given in the negative, members of the opposition pressed towards Pitt, down whose usually impassive face tears were flowing, to see how "Billy" would take it; and a circle of friends was formed to screen him

1805

from their malignant gaze. This, when the country was in hourly danger of invasion. As the result of the Melville affair shows, Pitt was no longer supreme master of the House of Commons; his majority was now comparatively small.

To cope with Napoleon, now emperor, and assembling his army on the heights of Boulogne for the invasion of England, Pitt's diplomacy, aided by his money, formed a coalition with Austria and Russia which brought an army fully equal in numbers to that of Napoleon into the field. More he could hardly do. Nor was he to blame for the disaster which followed. He did not sit in the Aulic council. He did not put Mack instead of the Archduke Charles in command, or direct the movement which lost the day at Austerlitz. Nor was it his fault that Prussia, with mean and purblind selfishness, held aloof, and afterwards paid at Jena for her disloyalty to the cause of nations. After Austerlitz, it is said, he folded up the map of Europe, and died. But despair would hardly have killed him had not disease already brought him low. For with the news of Austerlitz had come the news of Trafalgar. The nation's joy at the great victory of her sailors was mingled with deep grief, Nelson, the hero-sailor, having fallen. The sentiment which inspired his last signal was that which had saved the country, and the best of all dying speeches was, "Anchor, Hardy, anchor!" After Trafalgar the island kingdom was safe, and the rage of the enemy beat against it as vainly as the billows beat against its cliffs. Safe also was the trade from which it largely drew the sinews of war. There was no more fear of invasion; the fortification of London might be laid aside, nor were any more Martello towers needed along the steep. The Danish navy, the last save that of Russia left on the continent, was presently seized by a daring yet well-warranted stroke when it was on the point of being put into the enemy's hands. The British tar had never failed to conquer. Villeneuve at Trafalgar knew his fate when he saw Nelson's two columns bearing down.

By sheer dearth of men, strange when the call for them was so loud, the king was compelled to give way and allow the detested Fox, with Grenville, to form a broad-bottomed administration, combining the Whig leaders and Sheridan with Addington and Windham, which was called the Ministry of all the Talents. Fox, now at the end of his days, at last saw through the character and designs of Bonaparte, reconciled himself to the war, and, as Scott said of him, perhaps with a touch of satire, "a Briton died." This ministry approved its liberalism by carrying the abolition of the slave-trade. But it was soon thrown out by the king on a constitutional question. The ministers proposed to complete the military emancipation of the catholics by admitting them to the higher grades in the army. The king's prejudice was once more aroused, and was played upon, as before, by intriguers. He refused his assent. The ministers put their policy on record in a cabinet minute. The king grasped the opportunity of getting rid of them, called on them for a renunciation, and when they refused compliance, taking their stand on the constitutional principle that ministers could never be debarred from offering any advice which they deemed expedient to the crown, he dismissed them from office.

1806

1806

1807

This stroke of prerogative was about the last piece of

mischief done the country by a strictly moral and pious
1810 king. The glimmering light which had more than once
1811 been eclipsed, now expired in final darkness. A regency became inevitable. The Regent was a worthless sybarite; yet the change, though socially much for the worse, was politically rather for the better. Mistresses and maraschino did not much interfere with government, and the reckoning for them, though large, was a drop in the bucket of public expenditure. It is needless to say that the bosom friend of the Whigs did not carry his "predilections" into the regency; he doffed the Liberal and donned the monarch. His perfidy was chastised by the satirical pen of the Whig poet laureate, Tom Moore.

The Duke of Portland had never been more than a second-rate statesman. He was now decrepit and suffering from a painful disease which obliged him to be much under the influence of opium. This man, at a moment of extreme peril, was allowed to place himself at the head
1807 of the nation. In two years he resigned and died. Then
1809 came Perceval, an ultra-Tory and protestant lawyer, a
1809 staunch opponent of catholic emancipation, marching, as Sydney Smith described him, punctually, at the head of his tribe of well-washed children, to church, but of thoroughly second-rate capacity. Perceval, having been mur-
1812 dered by a maniac, was succeeded by Lord Liverpool, whose strong point, besides his experience and knowledge of business, was that his mediocrity, exciting no jealousy, formed a headship under which rival ambitions might unite. United under him were the ambitions, intensely rival, of Castlereagh and Canning.

Pitt's successors do not seem to have improved much
1823 on his war administration. The seizure of the Danish

navy, when the government had proof that it was about to be made over to Napoleon, was a laudable act of vigour. But the force of England was expended in distant and ineffective operations, such as the unfortunate expedition to Buenos Ayres. The Walcheren expedition was more of a body-blow, and might have told on the fortunes of the decisive field; but it was put under the incompetent command of the Earl of Chatham. A better field was opened in Spain, and Providence at last sent the government generals, Moore and Wellington, the second of whom had been formed on the Indian field. Moore was undervalued; Wellington, after his victory over Junot in Portugal, was superseded by cautious seniority and robbed of the fruits of his success. Nor, if we may trust the tenor of his letters at the time, does he seem to have been worthily supported or supplied. By the Whig opposition he was persistently run down. Trained officers he always lacked; but, as commissions were obtained by favour or purchase, trained officers the government had none to send. 1807 1809 1808

Failing to invade the sea-girt realm, Napoleon thought of killing its commerce and industry by a vast embargo which he called his continental system. To his Decrees the British Government responded with Orders in Council proclaiming a general blockade. The Americans, as neutral traders and carriers, had been making no small profit out of the war, and had been practically aiding the enemy of England and of Europe. They resented the Orders in Council, and at the same time the impressment of British seamen found on board their vessels and carried off by British captains, who roughly exercised an odious and very disputable right. They, or the War-hawks, as the 1807

war party among them was called, wished also to grasp
1812 the opportunity of conquering Canada. They declared
war against England, and another formidable enemy was
added to the host against which she was about to enter
the last desperate conflict for her own independence and
that of all European nations. On land the British con-
1814 quered, saved Canada and took Washington, though,
in rashly attacking impregnable defences, they suffered
a bloody repulse at New Orleans. On their own element they were for some time worsted by an enemy of
the same race as themselves, whose seamanship and gun-
nery they at first despised, but found fully equal to their
own. A fratricidal and fruitless conflict was closed at
last by a treaty in which no mention was made of either
of the two ostensible causes of the war. American his-
torians fancy that this was a second war of independence.
Had Napoleon, by the help of the Americans, triumphed
over England and European freedom, would Louisiana
now be a State of the Union? Might not his insatiate
ambition have trampled on the Union itself?

From victory to victory, from annexation to annexation,
Napoleon went on till he had almost made himself emperor
of the West. He formed for the members of his family a
set of satrapies, the corruption of which would have been
like that of the Second Empire or worse, since the Second
Empire was at least national. Over the kings, with their
senile councils, spiritless battalions, and routine commanders, he triumphed for the most part with ease. At last he
roused the nations; first Spain, who, decrepit and almost
moribund as she was, astonished him by springing to arms
against his insolent rapine, and, miserably as her untrained peasantry were led, poor as was the stand which

under fatuous commanders they could make against the
veteran legions of the conqueror, showed him at least
what a national resistance was, and at Saragossa revived 1808
the memory of Numantia. Something like national resistance he encountered in the campaign of Aspern and 1809
Wagram, when Austria, taught by dire experience the
value of the moral forces, appealed for the first time to
German sentiment and made a better stand against him
than she had ever made before. National resistance he
encountered, though on a small scale, in Tyrol, and was 1809
stung by its achievements to his dastardly murder of
Hofer. National resistance he encountered in deserted 1810
and burning Moscow and at last when he met uprisen 1812
Germany at Leipzig. At length he fell, and the civilized 1813
world was free from Corsican domination. Having 1814
staked his last conscript on the gambling table and
lost, the ruined gambler attempted suicide. Treated on
his capture with improvident confidence, and breaking
his word as he was sure to do, he was restored for 1814
a time to power by his soldiery, amid the general curses 1815
of the French people, who would have torn him in pieces
on his way to Elba had he not travelled in disguise.
He was thus enabled to offer one more holocaust of blood
and human suffering to his selfish ambition. Then the
world was rid of him, though not of the evil which he 1815
wrought. He had consumed in his game human lives
unnumbered, besides an enormous amount of the fruits of
human labour; and far from conferring on humanity any
compensating benefit, had left it a legacy of curses. For
to him was due the Holy Alliance; to him the revolutionary violence with which, after that temporary
triumph of reaction, political progress resumed its march;

to him the monstrous development of the military spirit, and of the system of vast armaments under which Europe now groans; to him the rekindling in France of that rapacious ambition which brought on the war of 1870; to him the crimes, corruption, and villanies of the Second Empire. For this the world worships him. Justice would have dealt with the arch-enemy of his kind as he had dealt with Toussaint-Louverture, Palm, or Hofer. Great Britain was left with six hundred millions of debt contracted in the service of European independence, for which and for the vast sums expended in yearly taxation no indemnity was received.

Europe had been lost by the kings and redeemed by the nations, but the nations had been forced to fight for its redemption under the leadership of the kings. Had the interest of the nations dictated the settlement, France would have been made then, as she was made by the Germans in 1871, to pay for her course of rapine and indemnify the nations which she had robbed, on such a scale as would have sickened her for a time of the game. She would then have been left to establish her own government and regulate her own affairs. But the interest of the kings dictated the restoration of the Bourbon throne, which was raised by their bayonets only to fall again, while nothing effectual was done to secure civilization against French ambition. In a few years French ambition was on its path again. The restoration of the Bourbons, with their reactionary aristocracy and priesthood, speedily provoked the fresh eruption of the revolutionary volcano with all the convulsions which followed, bringing a revival of the Napoleonic Empire and its Corsican policy in their train.

Masters of the legions, the kings were in conclave, resettling Europe after their own mind. Europe for an hour was theirs. With their selfish and feeble policy they had fallen before Napoleon, and most of them at last had kissed his feet, nor when their people rose against his tyranny had they very readily drawn the patriot sword. But for the time they engrossed the fruits of victory. Their guiding principles, as they at first proclaimed, in regulating the world, were to be those of the Gospel; Christian charity, peace, and justice, not less binding on the councils of princes than on private men. This programme was the fancy of Alexander of Russia, 1815 at once Emperor of Cossacks and sentimental dupe of a female mystic, Madame Krudener. When it was propounded to the Duke of Wellington, the duke replied that the British parliament would require something more precise. The religious mysticism of Alexander soon gave place in those councils to practical reaction in the person of Metternich, who undertook to make the world stand still. The members of the conclave proceeded to dispose of Europe as though it had been the personal property of kings, cutting and carving as their own interests dictated, handing over the north of Italy to the foreign and hated domination of Austria, forcing alien communities, such as Holland and Belgium, into uncongenial union, and rearranging territory everywhere without regard for the sentiment of nationality or for the wishes of the people. The establishment of a European settlement with a balance of power was the object ostensibly in view. The next care was to extinguish the desire of freedom which the struggle with Napoleon had kindled in the hearts of nations, and to restore absolute monarchy with its congenial priesthood. Hopeless in the end the attempt proved. The spirit of liberalism, once awakened, might be repressed, but would not die. To re-enforce it presently came the spirit of reviving nationality, fostered by historical studies and impatient of the stranger's yoke, such as was that of Austria in Italy, and that of Russia in Poland. We come to the opening of a new era.

CHAPTER VII

GEORGE IV. AND WILLIAM IV

GEORGE IV. BORN 1762; SUCCEEDED 1820; DIED 1830
WILLIAM IV. BORN 1765; SUCCEEDED 1830; DIED 1837

THE Tories had conducted the struggle with Napoleon. They had won Waterloo, at least Waterloo had been won under them. They were left in possession of the glory and the power. The Whigs were justly discredited by their factious opposition to the war and their unpatriotic sympathy with Napoleon, in whose fall they fell. The prime minister still was Liverpool, the experienced and sure-footed administrator, equal to the business of state and not above it, whose respectable mediocrity was now found useful as a centre of union not only for rival ambitions but for divergent sentiments. For in his cabinet there were both advocates and opponents of Catholic Emancipation; there were men who went thoroughly with the absolutist re-settlement of the continent; and there were men who, though enemies to revolution, were British and friends to the independence of nations.

Of the opponents of Catholic Emancipation and of change of every kind the type and chief was the chancellor, Eldon, a great technical lawyer who cherished the very cobwebs of the old law, and whose hesitations and delays amounted to a denial of justice. In politics Eldon clung not only to catholic disabilities and the unreformed House of

Commons, but to every anomaly and abuse, as a stone which could not be removed without shaking the sacred edifice of the constitution. He clung even to the cruel absurdities of the criminal law. He prided himself upon being the special guardian of the protestant church establishment, on the plethoric revenues and the abuses of which he would not let a profane hand be laid. Being little of a church-goer, he was likened to a buttress supporting the church from without. His orthodoxy was refreshed by copious libations of port. He shared with Addington the fond affection of George III., who, when Eldon was made chancellor, buttoned up the seals in the breast of his coat that he might give them, as he said, from his heart. Addington, the "doctor," was now home secretary under the title of Lord Sidmouth, which gilded, without changing, his mediocrity. Like Eldon, he was a thoroughgoing reactionist, and in all questions between the government and the people a believer in prompt and vigorous repression. Not that he was by nature other than a kind and courteous gentleman, but his medicine for the disease of popular discontent was legal grapeshot administered in good time. With Eldon and Sidmouth at present, though destined memorably to break with them and with reaction in the end, was the young Robert Peel, whose father, a wealthy cotton-spinner, had laid the promise of the youth, shown in Oxford honours, on the altar of Toryism. Perceval had welcomed to office the recruit, who thus gained the advantage of early initiation into public affairs, while by swearing allegiance to a party he forfeited the political independence which, as his mind opened, it became the pathetic struggle of his life to regain.

Castlereagh, foreign minister and leader of the House of Commons, was in European affairs as much of an absolutist as a man not devoid of British spirit could be, and on that account an object of detestation to Liberals. By the people, of whom he did not conceal his scorn, he was so intensely hated that after his tragic death by his own hand his corpse was hooted into its grave. His oratory was almost a jest. But he was a high-bred aristocrat, the pride as well as the type of his order, and a man of undaunted courage. When he rose in the House of Commons, with his lofty bearing and blue ribbon, Tories, we can believe, would forgive broken sentences and false metaphors. On the question of Catholic Emancipation Castlereagh was liberal. He was an Irishman, had taken a leading part in carrying the Union, and being a man of great sense was open to light on the Irish question.

With Castlereagh, rather than with Tories like Eldon or Sidmouth, may be ranked the great soldier whose victory over Napoleon had given him an immense ascendancy, not in his own country only, but in Europe. When Wellington, a few years later, became premier, he was reminded of his saying that if ever he accepted the premiership he would be mad. He had, however, undergone political training, having been Irish secretary in his youth, and in his management of men and affairs in Spain, where he had to deal with the impracticable Junta, he had shown, as his despatches prove, in a very high degree some of the qualities of a statesman. In the councils of Europe his authority was great. Nor was there in him the slightest tendency to military usurpation or sabre sway. Strict allegiance to duty fixed the boundary of his ambition. But military command had been the mould in which the political character of the Iron Duke was cast. The part assigned him, he thought, was that of upholding the king's government and the established institutions in church and state. Beyond this he did not look. The idea of parliamentary and cabinet government had not fully dawned on his mind. To him the government was still the king's government, and he was the servant of the king. From the servility of the courtier, however, he was absolutely free, and while he guarded the crown he could mark and scorn the character of its wearer.

At the head of the more Liberal section of the cabinet was Canning, a brilliant son of Eton and Christchurch, the paragon of classical education, who, having in his youth, it seems, shared the revolutionary fever, had been cured of it partly, like many others, by the excesses of the French revolutionists and completely by an introduction to Pitt. To Pitt, who brought him into parliament and office, he was thenceforth devoted. He was a brilliant and effective speaker; but he had served the Tory party hardly less by his wit as the writer of those pasquinades in the *Anti-Jacobin*, of which "The Needy Knife-Grinder" was the most telling. Though bred at an aristocratic school, adopted by a wealthy uncle, and afterward married to a wealthy wife, he was called an adventurer; his parentage was unhappy and his mother had been on the stage; but in those days every one was an adventurer who went into public life without belonging to the landed gentry, or at least to the class of realized wealth. With more show of reason he was regarded as an intriguer; he was at least restlessly ambitious and somewhat given to scheming. He had also the faults of a smart political writer. On his smartness in dealing with the Americans, whom, as a young nation, policy bade him treat with studious courtesy, rests partly the responsibility for the American war. The restlessness of his ambition it was that, making him an object of mistrust, had forced the brilliant orator and man of genius to yield the Tory leadership first to the mediocrity of Perceval and then to so lame a speaker as Castlereagh. Having buried his political allegiance in the grave of Pitt, he regarded himself as free to take his own course, and he had begun to see that the times were changing, and to feel the rising gale of Liberalism in his sails. He had quarrelled and had fought a duel with Castlereagh, who had accused him of an intrigue when they were colleagues in the Portland cabinet, but this quarrel had been closed, to the surprise and disgust of some who held that wounds ought never to heal. With Canning was Huskisson, a politician out of the aristocratic pale, the first apostle in parliament, since the young and liberal Pitt, of enlightened economy and free trade; as well as some younger men, of whom Palmerston was destined to become the most famous, and to carry the Canning tradition with him into far-distant times.

Of the Whig circle of Fox, Lord Grey was the leading survivor. Grey had been the steadfast advocate of parliamentary reform. In that cause he had been more zealous and daring than Fox. He remained, nevertheless, an aristocrat in character and bearing, and true, as he said himself, to his order, the privileges of which he seems to have thought could be reconciled with the sovereignty of the people. Round him were the representatives of the great Whig houses, such as Russell and Cavendish, which, dead as were the issues between the House of Hanover and the Stuarts, had kept their popular traditions and had been disposed to reform by thirty years of exclusion from power. Grey was an impressive speaker while his pure and lofty character commanded general and deserved respect.

Beyond Whiggism now lay Radicalism, aiming not only, like the Whigs, at reform, but in its extreme sections at least, at changes which would have amounted to a revolution; at annual or triennial parliaments, vote by ballot, payment of representatives, the abolition of the state church, perhaps the abolition of the House of Lords, and even of the monarchy itself. These men had imbibed the teaching of Horne Tooke, of Godwin, and Cobbett in politics; of Jeremy Bentham in jurisprudence; the more refined of them, perhaps, of Byron and Shelley in poetry. Bentham's utilitarianism may be said to have been their prevalent creed. They were the heirs of the Constitutional and Corresponding Societies denounced by Burke, and represented, as far as Englishmen could, the ferment of the French Revolution. This party could not fail to be prolific of demagogues and declaimers such as Orator Hunt, who gave his followers the word to cheer for himself. Cobbett, its chief writer, and the great master of the robust and home-spun style, afterwards found his way into the House of Commons, but too late in life to be there in his element. In the House of Commons the Radicals followed Brougham, a great advocate, a marvellous being, endowed with a superhuman energy which revealed itself in the ever-restless play of his face and figure, and enabled him, as his secretary said, to go through a week's work with two hours' sleep each night. With amazing talent, though without genius, Brougham aspired to excellence and pre-eminence in all lines, legal, or rather forensic, political, literary, and even scientific. He at once led the bar and the Liberal party in the House of Commons, and was the reformer not only of the constitution and the law, but of education. He was a most voluminous writer, as well as an orator who made a speech six hours long, and he did not want the courage to read a scientific paper before the French Institute. It was said of him by one of the old lawyers, whom he flouted as pedants, and who hated him, that he knew a little of everything, even of law. Joyously he rode the rising storm. His force, his vivacity, his daring, his omniscience, his vanity, his indiscretion, and his levity, made him a great but half-comic figure on the scene. The radical party had a parliamentary precursor in Whitbread, a wealthy brewer, an honest and able man, true to his class and to the people, who fought fearlessly and strenuously through the long night of reaction for popular government and reform. But he had died tragically at the dawn of returning day.

George III., after some years of death in life, at last 1820 expired. The regent became king. The debauchee was retiring into sybaritic seclusion. Still, it was necessary to reckon with the crown. Ministers were still constitutionally its servants. Without it parliament could not be called or dissolved. Its consent had to be obtained by cajolery or pressure to great measures of legislative change. To great measures of legislative change royalty was still naturally opposed, all the more since it was haunted by the spectre, only half laid, of the French Revolution. George IV. had already, as regent, thrown off his Liberalism, which in fact had never been much more than a phase of his youthful dissipation combined with his hatred of his father. In spite of his illicit marriage with a catholic, he had a languid fear of Catholic Emancipation, not on religious grounds, for religion he had none, but because it boded change. He was untruthful enough to believe his own untruths.

Of the House of Commons, now almost the sovereign assembly, the majority, reformers could assert, was elected by less than fifteen thousand persons. Seventy members were returned by thirty-five places, with scarcely any voters at all; ninety members were returned by forty-six places with no more than fifty voters; thirty-seven members were returned by nineteen places with no more than one hundred voters; fifty-two members by twenty-six places with no more than two hundred voters. The local distribution of the representation was flagrantly unfair. Rutland returned as many members as Yorkshire, and Cornwall was a corrupt nest of little boroughs whose vote outweighed that of great and populous districts. At Old Sarum a deserted site, at Gatton an ancient wall, sent two representatives to the House of Commons. Eighty-four men actually nominated one hundred and fifty-seven members for parliament. In addition to these, one hundred and fifty members were returned on the recommendation of seventy patrons, and thus one hundred and fifty-four patrons returned three hundred and seven members, or a majority of the House; so that the legislative power might possibly be controlled by one hundred and fifty-four persons. In Scotland there was no free representation; the borough franchise there was vested in self-elected town councils, while the county franchise consisted of "superiorities," independent of property or residence, which were bought and sold in the market; so that in one case the candidate called the meeting, proposed, elected, and returned himself. In counties only freeholders voted, copyholders, leaseholders, and tenants-at-will being excluded. In a few boroughs, by old custom, the suffrage was household or nearly universal; but where the constituency was large enough for free voting, corruption was apt to prevail. Seats for nomination boroughs were unblushingly put up to sale, and even so virtuous a man as Sir Samuel Romilly held that there would be absurd scrupulousness in refusing to enter parliament by that gate. A large proportion of the nominations was in the hands of peers, so that the House of Commons was practically much under the control of the House of Lords. The number of contested elections was usually very small, but immense sums, as much sometimes as a hundred thousand pounds, were spent by rival houses in their struggles for the representation of their territorial realms.

Representation had originally been elastic, the crown calling representatives at its discretion from the most important, which were the most taxable boroughs. The prerogative had afterwards been used in the creation of petty boroughs, such as the Cornish group, for the purpose of packing parliament in the interest of the crown. An end having been put to its exercise in the reign of Charles II., the system of representation had been petrified at that point. Thus, the franchise had been completely outgrown by population and new interests, and the upshot was an oligarchy intrenched in an obsolete system of representation, combining survivals from the middle ages with abuses of the prerogative in later times.

Meantime to the agricultural and commercial England another England, that of manufactures, had been added. By a long line of inventors and improvers in different fields, the cotton, woollen, worsted, iron, and pottery manufactures with their auxiliary industries had been developed. Power, first of water, then of steam, had taken the place of hands. On the wolds, once lonely, of northern England there now swarmed a manufacturing population. Migrating, when coal took the place of charcoal for smelting, from the weald of Kent, the iron industry was making its Black Country in the North Midlands. The factory system, with its mighty interests, with its new relation of capitalist and workman, employer and employed, with its great bodies of artisans, democratic in their tendencies, had come into existence. Commercial wealth, as well as that of the East Indian nabob and the West Indian planter, the landed aristocracy had been able socially to capture and politically to annex. Over the master manufacturer, radically alien to it, and dwelling in a realm of his own, its influence did not extend. Nor was he, like the rich trader, the nabob, or the planter, able or disposed, by buying boroughs, to give his interest a representation in the House of Commons. He now demanded for that interest, and for the new and as yet unenfranchised cities which were its seats, political recognition and admission within the pale of the constitution.

By this time, moreover, had come fully upon the scene three powers which by their combined influence could exercise a not inconsiderable control even over a parliament of rotten boroughs. These were Association, the Platform, and the Press. The platform and the press raised, while the association embodied and sustained, a volume of public sentiment which even the representative of Gatton or Old Sarum could hardly defy. The newspaper of that day was poor indeed compared with our political press. Its articles were usually written by hacks; its scale was small. Statesmen of the old school saw nothing in it but license. No statesman would have confessed that he was influenced by it, or owned that he was connected with its writers. Its power, however, was born, and it gained considerably by the reporting of parliamentary debates, which subjected the doings of parliament and of every member of parliament to its comments. The platform is by nature an engine fully as much of popular passion as of reason; but the expression even of popular passion might be useful when selfish and sinister interests were dominating under the forms of the constitution.

It was in the field of foreign policy that Liberalism first showed its new life. Canning, thinking his game lost at home, had accepted the governor-generalship of India. He was at Liverpool, ready to embark. He had made a 1822 farewell display of his oratoric genius in the famous speech in which he describes the dormant power of England under the figure of one of her battleships sleeping on the water, with furled sails and silent thunders, till war gives the word. Suddenly he was recalled to power by the tragic death of his great rival, Castlereagh. He took Castlereagh's place as foreign minister with a more liberal policy of his own.

Spain, in the absence of her Bourbon king, had given

herself a constitution ultra-republican in fact, monarchical only in name, and she had got rid of her Inquisition. The restored Bourbon, Ferdinand VII., a cruel and perfidious idiot, set himself to restore absolutism, the Inquisition, and the Jesuit. He had with him not only the priesthood, but the ignorant and priest-ridden peasantry. Seeing him likely to be overpowered, the restored Bourbon of France came to his assistance and invaded Spain. Canning could only protest. He alleged the division of parties in Spain, which made it a case of civil war, and the absence of any treaty right of intervention, as his grounds for declining to interfere. In fact, he had no means of coercing a great military power. He and England were compelled to witness the assassination of Spanish liberty and the atrocities by which the victory of a bloodthirsty tyrant and his Jesuits was followed. But Canning had resolved that if the Bourbon must have Spain, it should not be Spain with the Indies. When the native monarchy of Spain was overturned by Napoleon, the Spanish colonies in South America had cut themselves loose from the mother-country, and they were now, after American example, though not with American capacity for self-government, setting themselves up as republics. The Holy Alliance was minded to stretch the arm of its Christian charity across the ocean, and put republicanism down in the western hemisphere as well as in its own. Canning, here strong in England's naval power, interposed, warned off interference, and, as he rather too boastfully said, called the new world into existence to redress the balance of the old. He found a hearty ally in his former enemy, the American Republic. Even Jefferson hailed the concert of Great Britain with America in the cause of humanity, and Canning has had the credit, partly at least deserved, of fathering the Monroe Doctrine, that manifesto of the new world's chartered immunity from the interference of European powers. When an attempt was made to extend the counter-revolution from Spain to Portugal, Great Britain having in that case something like a treaty right of interference, Canning interposed with the same promptness and vigour which he had shown in the seizure of the Danish fleet, and the Bourbons shrank from the encounter. In the kingdom of Naples, on the other hand, the British minister was compelled to witness a restoration of Bourbon despotism by Austrian arms, and to see liberty thrust into the Bourbon dungeon, though not for ever. Nor could the British people extend to agonizing Poland any aid but that of unsubstantial sympathy or pecuniary contribution. To Greece, rising against the Turkish yoke, and appealing by her classic memories to all imaginations and hearts, they lent not only sympathy but substantial and effective help. It has been remarked that the end of the war turned loose military and naval adventurers who, like De Lacy Evans in the civil war of Spain and Lord Cochrane in the Chilian insurrection against Spain, served and promoted the Liberal cause beyond the field of British diplomacy or arms.

Great Britain, playing her part still as the balancing power of Europe, having thrown herself into the scale of order against revolution, henceforth passed into the scale of liberty and national independence against the despotic and anti-nationalist reaction set on foot by the Holy Alliance. She was not a military power; the policy of the great military powers she could not control. Beyond the range of the guns of her navy her influence was moral. But her moral influence after her victorious leadership of the nations against Napoleon was great. From the pinnacle to which circumstances had then raised her, above the measure of her actual force, it was difficult to descend.

At home meanwhile, in spite of the great increase of her wealth, she was unhappy. Her people were suffering, malcontent, and disaffected. The waste of a long war, the taxation imposed by a debt of nine hundred millions, the sudden suspension, after the peace, of war expenditure and war industries, the disbanding of soldiers and sailors, combined with the standing evils of a pauperizing Poor Law, the cruel rapacity of employers, especially in mines and factories, and the general neglect of the poor by the rich, to produce a terrible crisis of misery. Bad harvests once more brought dearth of bread. Matters were made worse by speculation crazy enough to send Scotch dairymaids to milk wild cattle in South America and by the failure of a number of banks. Wages fell till the farm labourer and his family had not enough to support life. Men died of hunger after eating wild herbs. Mechanics were working twelve hours for three pence a day. In the mines and factories womanhood and childhood were being ruthlessly sacrificed. Many men were out of work and were wandering in quest of it, while the settlement clause of the Poor Law was driving or carting them back to their own parishes. Even the improvements in machinery, agricultural or textile, the threshing-machine, the spinning-jenny, and the power-loom, as they threw hands out of employment, for the time increased the distress; so that the burning of threshing-machines and the breaking of power-looms, though unwise as well as illegal, was not without a motive or an excuse. Hence widespread agitation, seditions, harangues, wild and fantastic conspiracies, sometimes riots. Hunger was the cause; the cry was for political change; nor was the cry without relation to the cause. The unreformed parliament was the organ of a special and selfish interest, that of the land-owners, who, during the war, having a practical monopoly of the supply of food, had revelled in high rents, and when the war was over, finding their rents fall, had passed Corn Laws to prolong their monopoly by the exclusion of foreign grain. Not only grain was excluded but other farm products. The effect was doubly evil. Great Britain, the continent having been ravaged by Napoleon, stood alone as a manufacturing country, and might have exchanged her manufactures for the food which was the only staple of the other nations, thereby developing her own industries and finding employment for her people, had not protectionism interfered.

The government, however, with its mind still full of the French Revolution, in the writhings and wailings of the starving people could see nothing but political sedition, and thought of no remedy but repression. Even in the speeches of such a man as Canning, who must have had a heart as well as an eye, coercion, not sympathy, is the pervading note. A body of poor sufferers, called from 1817 carrying their blankets strapped on them, the Blanketeers, marched from Manchester to lay their griefs before the government. A great meeting at Peterloo, an open 1819 space in Manchester where now stands the Free Trade Hall, was charged and ridden down by the yeomanry; eleven persons were killed and a large number hurt.

The government, lauding the yeomanry, showed no feeling for the sufferers, and the iron of the Peterloo massacre, as it was called, entered deeply into the soul of the people. Six Acts for the prevention of arming and training, for the repression of public meeting and discussion, for the restriction of the press, and for summary dealing with conspiracy and seditious movements of all kinds, were framed by the home secretary Sidmouth, and enforced with rigour. In their train spies and decoys did not fail to appear. There was fatal enmity and mutual distrust between the government and the people.

Within the ministry, however, one good genius was at work, if not giving immediate relief, preparing for better times to come. This was Huskisson, unaristocratic but thoroughly versed in commerce, finance, and all that concerned the material welfare of the people, a precursor of the Manchester School. By him as far as was possible in a perverse generation and under a reign of landlords, were advanced in all directions sound economical principles, above all the principle of free trade. He considerably relaxed the navigation laws. He tried to restrain the madness of speculation which led to the commercial crisis of 1825. But the grasping desire of growing suddenly rich without labour not even the foresight and wisdom of Huskisson could control. The crisis came. It increased the dangers of the situation and was ascribed by the protectionists to Huskisson's policy of free trade.

Huskisson had the full sympathy of his friend and leader, Canning. He had the sympathy, less full, yet growing, of his younger fellow-worker, Robert Peel, who in 1819, as chairman of the committee on the resumption of cash payments, underwent his first conversion, and becoming convinced that a depreciated currency was the result of the system of paper pursued since 1797, framed an Act for a return to cash payments, and thus restored 1819 the soundness of the currency, the life of trade.

A royal scandal helped to increase the ferment. The Princess of Wales, cast off by her husband, the Regent, had wandered on the continent, and there, not being a woman of refined taste, had, it can scarcely be doubted, fallen into the arms of her courier, Bergami. When her husband became king she claimed recognition as queen and came to England to assert her right. The king 1820 forced his ministers to move for a divorce. There was a trial before the House of Lords in which the king's character was not spared, Brougham, the counsel for the queen, comparing him, not obscurely, to Tiberius. Thanks largely to Brougham's power of bullying witnesses, the king's suit practically failed. Popular feeling 1820 was thoroughly roused in favour of the queen, or rather against the king, and showed itself in riotous demonstrations. The ill-mated pair had one child, the Princess Charlotte, married to the Belgian Prince Leopold, a girl of spirit, on whom the hopes of the nation, still in sentiment monarchical, were fixed. She died in child-bed 1817 amidst universal sorrow, embittered by the thought that the next heir to the throne was then the Duke of Cumberland, a brutal reactionist, and so hated by the people that they could suspect him of a dark crime.

The fear of revolution which was created by disturbance threw parliamentary reform for the present into the background. Catholic Emancipation, with Canning and Plunket for its eloquent champions, was carried in 1821 the Commons, only to be defeated by Eldon in the Lords. Samuel Romilly, a noble servant of humanity, pushed, with slight success, reform of the criminal law in the teeth of Eldon, who did not want the effrontery to allege in favour of the retention of the death penalty for minor offences that it gave the judge opportunities of showing the grace of mercy by remission. Hangings by scores and the condemnation of a boy of ten to death for stealing were enough to move anyone but Eldon. For the Gordon riots three boys under fifteen had been hanged. Juries, unwilling to send a man to the gallows for a trifling fault, acquitted against evidence, and thus excessive penalty bred impunity of crime. The House of Lords, however, threw out Romilly's bill abolishing the death penalty in case of a petty theft, seven bishops voting in the majority.

1827 After being premier fifteen years, Liverpool was struck with paralysis. The two sections of his cabinet, the pro-catholic and the anti-catholic, the reactionary and the more progressive, the Tories and the Conservatives, as we may already call them, naturally fell apart. The question then was whether Wellington, the head of the reactionary section, with Robert Peel still at his side, or Canning, the head of the more progressive section, should form and lead the next government. Here something depended on the king, and the king, a worn-out debauchee, caring for nothing but his ease, was distracted between his political leaning towards the Tories and his fear of Canning. After a farcical vacillation, Canning received the royal command to form a government. The resig-
1827 nation of Wellington, Peel, Eldon, and the rest of that section followed of course, without conspiracy or even

concert. Peel, who as home secretary was responsible for the government of Ireland, could least of all serve under a prime minister opposed to him on the catholic question. The suspicion which a sinister imagination has cast upon him of dishonourable conduct towards his rival is dispelled by a speech of Canning acknowledging Peel's loyalty in the strongest terms. If there was anything like manœuvring in the transaction, it was probably on the part of Canning himself. The new ministry was joined by some of the Whigs. There followed, of course, a breach between Canning and the Tory wing of the party, with angry denunciations of the "seceder" by hot-headed and irresponsible Tories; but Canning's bitterest assailant was the Whig leader, Grey, who not only refused to coalesce, but denounced Canning as a false pretender to the championship of civil and religious liberty, pointing to his share in all the measures of repression and his opposition to the repeal of the Test and Corporation Acts. Canning was so stung that he thought of transferring himself to the House of Lords to answer the attack in person. Death closed the affray. 1827 Canning, febrile by nature and worn out with contention, died. What he would have done had he lived, or how he would have fared, who can say? His pledges to uphold the Test and Corporation Acts and to oppose parliamentary reform were too deep to be renounced, yet in fulfilling them he must have fallen.

On Canning's death, after a faint attempt to prolong the life of his ministry under the feeble and lacrymose Goderich, the ball rolled back to the Tory and anti-catholic section. Wellington became prime minister, but 1823 at his side was Peel. As Irish secretary, and afterwards

as home secretary, Peel had now displayed his administrative power and shown his tendency, which was always to administrative reform and against organic change. He had also established his power as a debater, in which line he had presently no peer, as his chief opponent thought, and his skill in managing the House, on which it was said at an after day that he could play as on an old fiddle. In knowledge of commerce and finance he had no rival among the political leaders except Huskisson, with whom, in that field, he had rendered the country the highest service by leading it safely back to cash payments. All administrative or legal abuses Peel was prompt and able to reform. As a signal that the door of law reform was opened, Eldon was dropped from the administration. A vigorous policy of retrenchment in the offices of government was set on foot. Improvements were made in police and criminal law. It was thus that Peel hoped to avert organic change. But the need of organic change and the demand for it were now too strong. First fell the Test and Corporation Acts. Their
1828 repeal was moved by Lord John Russell, a scion of the illustrious Whig house the representative of which had fallen a martyr to patriotism by the side of Algernon Sidney under the tyranny of Charles II. To this Wellington and Peel submitted, both of them probably nothing loath; for men of their sense, however attached to the church establishment, could set no value on a law which, its teeth having been drawn by periodical Acts of Indemnity, had become a mere standing insult to a large and worthy section of the community.

In Ireland, after the union, rebellion had sunk to abor-
1803 tive conspiracy. About its last spasm had been the murder

of an unpopular judge in the streets of Dublin. Plunket, once the most eloquent opponent of the union, had, as a member of the united parliament, avowed his conversion to it, and Grattan had sat as member of an English borough and voted for a coercion Bill. But the rent and tithe war still went on. The rent war was intensified by the subdivision of the land into small freeholds, falsely so-called since they were held by sufferance, to multiply vassal votes for the landlord, and by the increase of absenteeism, an evil sure to follow the union, unless the great land-owners would learn, what wealth and leisure seldom learn, the necessity of social duty. In the collection of rents for absentee or unloved landlords, still more of tithes for an alien church, the officers of the law and the law itself were made hateful to the people, and agrarian conspiracy under wild and fantastic forms, such as Whiteboyism, widely prevailed. Hideous atrocities, such as the carding of rent-collectors or tithe-proctors, were committed by a savage peasantry fighting for the land, which was their life. The potato continued to beget low culture, uncertain harvests, periodical famines, and at the same time a reckless increase of population. Not the greatest or the most deeply seated of all the evils, though the most patent, was the exclusion of catholics from parliament and the offices of state, already condemned by Pitt and the best of English statesmen, as well as by reason and justice.

Now there arose for the catholic Celts of Ireland a leader of their own race and after their own heart. Daniel O'Connell, who first made his mark as the prince of advocates in jury cases, was a genuine son of Erin and a devout catholic. He was a man of burly figure, with a typically Celtic face, a voice so mighty that he could make himself heard by vast multitudes in the open air, a boundless flow of what to peasant ears seemed eloquence, and a thorough mastery of the passionate Irish heart. That the Liberator, as his followers styled him, was a patriot, and earned, at the hands of his countrymen, the lofty monument which rises over his grave at Glasnevin, there can be no doubt. If he was foul-mouthed, untruthful, and somewhat perfidious, if he had in him a strain of the savage, and it could be justly said of him that in any case in which his vanity or his passion was excited you might as well have to deal with an Ashanti chief, this was less his fault than the fault of those who had long oppressed and degraded his race. 'Base,' 'brutal,' and 'bloody' were words familiar to his lips. His violence of language had brought on him a duel in which he by chance killed his man, and a challenge from the hot-blooded Peel, then Irish secretary, whom he had reviled. A great Catholic Association had been formed in Ireland to enforce the catholic claim. On the other hand, in the protestant north of Ireland had been formed for the maintenance of protestant ascendancy the Orange lodges, not aptly named after one who had ever been the politic friend of toleration, though instinct with the spirit that had closed the gates of Derry. Orangism was extended to England; it found its way into the army; it put at its head the hated Duke of Cumberland; it was suspected of designs on the succession to the throne. In the minds of a large part of the British people still lived the memories of Smithfield and Guy Fawkes, still burned the hatred of popery which half a century before had burst forth in the Lord George Gordon riots. The king's brother, the Duke of York, a debauchee, whose scandalous loves with a harpy had given rise to a parliamentary investigation which forced him to resign the commandership-in-chief and lent some impetus to the reform agitation, registered in the House of Lords a solemn vow that in whatever situation he might be, in other words, if he should succeed his brother on the throne, he never would consent to Catholic Emancipation. His words were printed by the Protestants in letters of gold.

When Canning, a friend of emancipation, became minister, the Catholic Association was dissolved. It was revived under the leadership of O'Connell when in Canning's place came the anti-catholic ministry of Wellington and Peel. Soon it took decisive issue with the government. At the election for the county of Clare Mr. Vesey Fitzgerald was the candidate of the government and the landlords. The peasant freeholders, catholics and Celts, broke away from their landlords, followed their priests, and elected O'Connell, who, being a catholic and unable to take the oaths, could not sit. The order and discipline maintained by the peasantry during the contest were noted by shrewd observers as a proof that the revolutionary feeling was deeply seated. Wellington and Peel, Peel perhaps more distinctly than Wellington, saw that the hour for concession had now come. The great soldier shrank, as he said, from civil war. A few battalions would have easily disposed of any army which the Catholic Association could have put in the field. It was moral and not physical force that failed the government. The better mind of England was now, as Peel must have keenly felt, on the side of emancipation. Winged by

1825
1828

1828

public opinion, even the light arrows of satire shot by Tom Moore and Sydney Smith had told. At the back of the movement in favour of toleration was the force of the general movement in favour of reform. To the Duke of Wellington, little concerned about the number of the sacraments or the identity of anti-Christ, retreat from a position which had been turned presented itself as a strategical operation, though when he was taunted with apostasy, the man of honour was aroused in him and he forced the offender to fight a duel. To the dismay and horror of all high protestant Tories and Orangemen it was announced that a Tory government would grant Catholic Emancipation. Peel, whose conscience was somewhat punctilious, wished to resign, and was prevented only by the earnest entreaty of the duke. He did resign his seat for the University of Oxford and was defeated on standing for re-election by Sir Robert Inglis, a protestant beyond reproach. Oxford, it should always be remembered, was then not so much a university as a citadel of the established church, and it was not by learning, of which, saving theology, there was little, or by science, of which there was none, but by the wrath of the clergy that Peel was deprived of his seat.

The Bill threw open to catholics parliament and all the great offices except that of regent, that of the lord-lieutenant of Ireland, and that of the chancellor, who appointed to crown livings and kept the conscience of the king. The crown remained limited to the protestant line by the Act of Settlement, which could not have been altered without civil war. To qualify concession and as sops to the opposition, two riders were annexed. By one the Catholic Association was suppressed; the other took away the franchise from the forty-shilling freeholder whose electoral insurrection in Clare had decided the day. The act gave the electoral franchise to English catholics from whom hitherto it had been withheld.

Catholic Emancipation, said the shrewd and cynical Melbourne, was a question in which all the clever fellows were on one side, and all the damned fools on the other, and the damned fools were right. Right the fools could not be in upholding gross injustice, while the fear of divided allegiance and political subserviency to a foreign pope, which formed the only rational motive for exclusion, has by experience been almost dispelled. That the result so far as Ireland was concerned was a disappointment, that she remained disaffected, disturbed, in constant need of coercion acts, is too true. Concession had been robbed of its grace by delay and enforcement; granted by Pitt it would have been welcomed as a boon, and would have knit the heart of Ireland to the union. After all, it was not full, since the state church of the protestant minority continued to wring its tithes from the catholic people. But, above all, the statesmen of that day were mistaken in thinking that in the religious disabilities lay the chief seat of the malady, and that religious emancipation would, therefore, be a sovereign cure. The chief seat of the malady lay, as the sequel clearly showed, not in the religious disabilities, but in the tenure of land, and in the relations between landlord and tenant, bad in themselves, and embittered by the vengeful memories of a disinherited race. In their misery and hopelessness the peasantry multiplied recklessly, fearfully over-peopled the country and overflowed into England, lowering the wages and the condition of the labourer there. In Scotland, at the time of the union, there was no question like the Irish land question; respect for the Scotch religion, therefore, sufficed. Concurrent endowment of the two churches, the catholic and the protestant, might, as some thought, have bound the catholic priesthood to the support of government and order. Some project of that kind seems to have suggested itself to Pitt. But the consent of English and Scotch protestantism could hardly have been obtained to the endowment of the church of anti-Christ.

All the more because it had incurred among its party the reproach of weakness by yielding to the repeal of the Test Act and of apostasy by its conversion on the catholic question, did the Tory government set its face as a flint against parliamentary reform. There was yet time for a moderate measure of concession which would probably have averted sweeping change. But Wellington closed that door by declaring, in the House of Lords, that the constitution was humanly speaking incapable of improvement, and that he would be no party to the slightest alteration. It is probable that he was carried further than he meant to go. Master of the eddies of battle, he was not so complete a master of the drift of his own speech. Surprised at the extraordinary impression which he at once saw that his words had made, he, as he sat down, asked a colleague at his side what he could have said to create such a sensation, and was answered with a gesture and an ejaculation of dismay. He was, however, inflexible, if not blind. A second retreat was too much. Huskisson, the friend of Canning, and half a Liberal, had, with some other friends of Canning, passed into the Tory government. It was moved as a mild measure of reform to transfer the franchise from East Retford, a borough convicted of corruption, to the great manufacturing city of Birmingham. The question was declared open by the government. But Huskisson, having voted for the Bill, and finding himself opposed to his leader, weakly put his resignation in the duke's hand, not meaning it to be accepted. The iron hand closed upon it; Huskisson was dropped from the cabinet; with him departed the other Canningites, and the last hope of concession. So it is that systems, when worn out and condemned, prefer, as it appears, death to reform. In truth, the owners of a rotten-borough parliament, with all its power and patronage, might not without reason think that for them reform was death.

1828

By accepting the repeal of the Test Act the government had estranged churchmen. By granting Catholic Emancipation it had estranged protestants. By its retrenchments it had estranged those whose salaries it had retrenched. To wreak their vengeance the malcontents allied themselves with the opposition, and the last Tory government fell. The tide of general agitation was, by this time, running high, and in the heart of the suffering classes there had sprung up a passionate hope of deliverance by political change. The country was full of ferment and of political clubs which were at last united in a national association. In the more intellectual classes political and social speculation had awakened from the trance into which the struggle with Napoleon had thrown it. On the continent revolution had rolled away the stone which the Holy Alliance had laid upon its sepulchre, and had recommenced its march by overturning the reactionary monarchy of the absolutist

Bourbons in France, and substituting the citizen monarchy of Louis Philippe, the son of Égalité. England felt the contagion; nor was she this time repelled by Jacobin crimes. Her own crown had passed from the sybarite Tory, George IV., to the sailor, William IV., a man of homely character, and inclined to play the popular king.

CHAPTER VIII

PARLIAMENTARY REFORM

THE hour had struck, and Grey, with his Whig following, came in to carry parliamentary reform. Reforming the government was, but it was still aristocratic. Tradition and the chances of political war together had done for the British aristocracy what the deepest policy might have dictated, dividing it between the political parties, giving it the leadership of both, and putting progress under its control. Whig magnates were lords of pocket-boroughs which they sacrificed to the country and their party. Democracy was represented in the cabinet, if at all, by Brougham the chancellor, who with all his volatility and violence, proved in the end no untamable patriot. The leader in the Commons was Lord Althorp, the chancellor of the exchequer, an excellent man of business, noted and trusted as a paragon of downright honesty, all the more perhaps because he was somewhat bovine and lacked the gift of speech. Lord Durham, Grey's son-in-law, wayward and overflattered, showed how an aristocrat might throw himself into a popular cause, court the people, and be a high aristocrat still. Palmerston and other followers of Canning joined the government, though Canning had been a sworn opponent of parliamentary reform. They adhered to their master's general liberalism without the particular and almost unaccountable exception.

1831   On the memorable 1st of March, 1831, the Reform Bill was brought in by Lord John Russell, chosen for that honour, though he was not in the cabinet, on account of his devotion to the cause, in which he had already moved, and his historic name. It was a drastic measure, and to Tories sounded like the knell of doom. Grey was no revolutionist, but he thought that to be final, his measure must be complete. In England the Bill made a clean sweep of the rotten boroughs; deprived a number of petty boroughs of one member; gave representation to Manchester, Leeds, Birmingham, and other large towns and metropolitan districts; gave a large additional representation to the counties; in the counties gave copyholders and leaseholders as well as freeholders votes; for the towns established a uniform ten-pound household suffrage, abolishing the more extended suffrage in the few boroughs in which by custom it had prevailed. Corporations were deprived of their electoral monopoly.

On Scotland, in place of representation by superiorities or corporations, elective representation, nearly on the same scale as that of England, was bestowed. In Ireland the boroughs were taken from the close corporations and given with the same qualifications as in England to the citizens at large.

1831   There followed, inside and outside parliament, an immense debate, in which every tongue and pen was called into play. Outside parliament, reform had its thundering organ in the *Times*, which founded a power destined largely to sway opinion down to our own day. In argument, reform easily swept the field. Who could devise a rational defence of the representation of a mound or an old wall; the return of ninety members by forty-six places, with less than fifty voters each; the nomination of one hundred and fifty-seven members by eighty-four men; the election of the majority of the House by fifteen thousand out of three million male adults; the exclusion of copyholders and leaseholders; or the existence of the beggarly and corrupt nest of Cornish boroughs? Who could plausibly maintain that the manufacturing interest ought to be denied its share of political power? The Tories pointed to the number of eminent men who, through the nomination boroughs, had found entrance to public life. There was force in the argument where the patron was generous and allowed his nominee to be independent; but nominees generally were bound to go with their patrons, while for one young Pitt or Canning there were nominated a dozen mere retainers and agents of private designs. It was alleged that all great interests were practically represented. The manufacturing interest, whose seats were new-born cities, was hardly represented at all, while the overwhelming preponderance of the landlord interest was attested by corn laws, game laws, and laws of every kind framed for the benefit of the land-owner. Gross anomaly, had there been nothing more, would have called for reform, since it deprived the constitution of respect.

The only real defence, or rather the plea for caution and forecast, was that on which the Duke of Wellington touched when he asked how, with a House of Commons elected on democratic principles, the king's government was to be carried on. The House of Commons was no longer the mere representation of the people, one of two co-ordinate branches of the legislature, and subject to the supreme authority of the crown. It had drawn to it the sovereign power, executive as well as legislative, since the ministers were the creatures of its choice. How sovereign power was to be wisely and safely exercised by an assembly of six hundred and fifty-eight men elected by popular suffrage, was a problem to which in these great debates attention was not sufficiently directed, and which still remains unsolved. Popular representation may give expression to the will of the people, though distorted by the passions, the corruption, the trickery, and the various accidents of elections; but what is wanted is government, not by will, but by the reason of the community, the ascendancy of which popular representation without safeguards can hardly be trusted to secure.

In the parliamentary debates Lord Grey is dignified and impressive, he speaks with the weight of age and long devotion to the cause of reform. To the Lords he speaks as one of their own order with which he stands or falls. Macaulay is lucid and very brilliant in exposition of a clear case. But, on the whole, the debates are somewhat disappointing to one who looks in them for great lessons of statesmanship. There will hardly be found in the speeches of the framers a distinct forecast of the practical effects of their measure, or a clear idea of the polity which they expected and intended to produce. They seem scarcely to be aware that they are profoundly altering the practical constitution. Nor do they dwell, as might have been expected, on that necessity of admitting the newly-born interest to a share of political power which was not the least obvious or the least pressing reason for the change. The speeches on the other side were either carping attacks on the special provisions of the Bill, or vague declamations against democracy and predictions of revolution and ruin. Some attempted to misapply the principles of private property to the franchises and charters of the rotten boroughs, and contended that to justify forfeiture delinquency must be proved; as though power intrusted by the state for a public purpose could not by the same authority be resumed. The delinquency was proved by the record of misgovernment. As in early days the crown had chosen at its discretion from time to time the boroughs to be represented in the House of Commons, the wisdom of our ancestors was really on the side of free selection. The defenders of rotten boroughs of course vowed that, though opposed to the plan before them, they were not enemies to all reform. Why had they resisted the transfer of the franchise from East Retford to Birmingham? Croker and Wetherell, who did most of the fighting on that side, were mere mouthpieces of prejudice or of the vested interests of abuse and corruption. In their criticism there is nothing statesmanlike or instructive.

Peel was fettered by Wellington's fatal declaration and by his party ties. Had he been free, it may be surmised that instead of opposing the measure he would have accepted it with a good grace and amended it in the conservative sense, as, with the forces at his command, the House of Lords being entirely with him, he might certainly have done. His large mind could not possibly share the reactionary fanaticism of Croker and Wetherell or have been deluded by the sophistries of chartered right. His speeches are wanting in elevation and breadth. His own apology for hopeless resistance is its salutary impressiveness as a lesson against light tampering with the constitution. This is the weakest part of his career.

In temper the debates did no dishonour to the political

character of the country. Considering the vast interests, personal as well as public, which were at stake, and the passions which were called into play, there was little of violence or disorder. Once or twice, at trying moments, self-control gave way. Once, to prevent a duel, it was necessary to give two members into the custody of the sergeant-at-arms. O'Connell's tendency to vituperation could not be altogether suppressed. But, on the whole, the spirit of men of sense and of English gentlemen prevailed, and parliamentary decorum was preserved. It was a good omen of future re-union and patriotic co-operation under the altered constitution.

1831   The Reform Bill passed its second reading in the House of Commons by three hundred and two to three hundred and one, a majority of one. Even with that unreformed parliament the voice of public opinion which called upon it to put an end to its own existence had been powerful enough to prevail. But the measure met with defeat in committee on a motion against the proposed diminution of the existing number of representatives for England and Wales.

1831   An appeal to the country followed. With some difficulty the king, whose fears had by this time been excited, was induced to dissolve parliament. It appears that a protest of the Tories against dissolution, which seemed to him to touch his prerogative, at last decided his consent. Scenes of extreme excitement were being enacted in both Houses when he came down to the House of Lords and summoned the Commons to the bar. The sound of the cannon which announced his coming was the death-knell

1831   of oligarchic government. In the election, reform everywhere swept the free constituencies and sent the government back with its numbers overwhelmingly increased. The Bill was now carried in the House of Commons by three hundred and sixty-seven to two hundred and thirty-one, a majority of one hundred and thirty-six. From the Commons it passed to the Lords. Had the Lords been wise and known their hour they might in all probability still have secured important amendments in their own favour. Not being wise or knowing their hour, they threw out the Bill by one hundred and ninety-nine to one hundred and fifty-eight, a majority of forty-one. It was remarked that of those who voted against the Bill most were peers not of old creation but of new. The Commons, voting confidence in the government by a great majority, brought their House into direct collision with the Lords.

The country was in a state of excitement verging on civil war. The Bill, the whole Bill, and nothing but the Bill was the cry. Language, threatening not only to the House of Lords but to hereditary monarchy, was held. In England, as in France, the bishops and clergy, suspected as the black soldiery of reaction, were the special objects of popular hatred. The National Union threatened to stop the payment of taxes. Riot broke out in several places, Wellington's windows were smashed, and the iron shutters of Apsley House long remained the duke's mute appeal against popular ingratitude. The scene of the most violent outbreak was Bristol, where the mob sacked and burned the Mansion House, the bishop's palace, and a number of private houses; while authority, civil and military, paralyzed by the dominant spirit of revolution, looked on helplessly at the havoc. Still the Lords held out in spite of the electric appeals of

Brougham, though he literally conjured them on his knees. That thunderbolt of debate found a doughty opponent in Lyndhurst, who, once a radical in sentiment, and still a radical in temperament, having taken the Tory shilling, boldly, unscrupulously, and effectively served that cause. Eldon could only wail.

The Bill, having again passed the Commons by a great majority, was allowed to pass its second reading in the Lords House, but was killed by a hostile motion in committee. The ministers then applied to the king for leave to overcome the opposition of the Lords by a swamping creation of peers, like that which had carried the Treaty of Utrecht, but on a larger scale. The king 1832 demurring, the ministers resigned. The king then called on the Tories to form a government and frame a Reform Bill of their own. Wellington, ever loyal, deemed it his duty to his sovereign to throw himself into the breach. "Run for gold and stop the duke" was then the cry. But Peel's wisdom prevailed. The Whig ministers returned to office with their royal master's permission to create 1832 peers. The peers then surrendered and allowed the Bill to pass in a thin House. They had done the worst they could for themselves by obstinately holding out, instead of coming to terms, and at last giving way to a threat. Thus the great oligarchy passed to its long account in history. Immense rejoicings followed. The light of hope had dawned on the cottage. Machine-breaking and rick-burning ceased. The golden age had begun.

The general election which ensued gave an overwhelming majority to the reformers, though rather to the Whigs than to the Radicals, whose comparative disappointment showed that the excitement was already abating.

The number of six hundred and fifty-eight members for England and Wales, which the first Bill had reduced, was in the last restored. A further respite was given to the abuse of the freemen's vote in boroughs. The county franchise was extended to fifty-pound tenants-at-will, otherwise the Bill, after its stormy course, passed nearly in its original form. The net result for England and Wales was the disfranchisement of fifty-six nomination boroughs; the withdrawal from thirty boroughs of one member each, and from Weymouth and Melcombe Regis of two out of their four; the grant of a member apiece to twenty-two large towns or metropolitan districts, including the great manufacturing towns of Manchester, Birmingham, and Leeds, and of one member apiece to twenty smaller towns; an increase of the number of county members from ninety-four to one hundred and fifty-nine; a ten-pound franchise for the boroughs; while in the county constituencies to the forty-shilling freeholders were added copyholders, leaseholders for terms of years, and tenants-at-will paying a rent of fifty pounds. In Scotland the result was a county constituency of ten-pound property holders and some classes of leaseholders; a borough constituency like the English, of ten-pound householders practically elective in place of nomination. In Ireland the union had done the work of disfranchisement. But the ten-pound household franchise was extended to the boroughs. Both in Scotland and in Ireland the number of members was slightly increased beyond the union settlement; an indication that the union was regarded, not as an unalterable compact, but as a fusion of two nations into one with united powers of self-organization, though with ancient boundaries, political, legal, and ecclesiastical, which it was still necessary to respect.

The amendment extending the franchise to fifty-pound tenants-at-will, called from the mover, Lord Chandos, heir of the Duke of Buckingham, was of the highest importance. The tenant farmers, to whom it gave votes, were under the influence of the landlord, and their interest was bound up with his. This was the one great Tory victory, and it won back for the land-owning aristocracy and gentry, with the seats for the counties, not a little of the political power which, by the Bill as originally framed, they would have lost.

To lessen the abuses, expenses, and riot of elections, the Act introduced regular registration, improved the arrangements for polling, and reduced the number of polling days from fifteen to two. An improvement was afterwards made in the constitution of committees for the trial of election petitions, with a view of checking the corruption of which the small free boroughs were the chief seats. But corruption is protean in its forms. Bribery at elections is expelled, only to give place to bribery between elections. Where public principle is weak, ambition and cupidity will find a way.

Here the tide of parliamentary reform was stayed. Radicals made attempts to go further; to extend the franchise yet more widely; to shorten the duration of parliaments; to introduce the ballot, a name of revolutionary terror in those days; but in vain. Whiggism showed its aristocratic and conservative side, and it received the loyal support of the leader of the Tory opposition in its resistance to democratic innovation. The borough-mongering oligarchy had fallen; a large share of political power had been transferred to the middle class; the manufacturing interest had been admitted to its place in the representation; these were the grand results. The working classes, both in town and country, most completely in the country, were still left outside the political pale. From them had been taken, by the abolition of the popular suffrage, which in a few boroughs had by custom prevailed, such representation as they had. The Whigs had better have sacrificed symmetry, and left scot-and-lot and potwallers alone.

The peers had been deprived of their nomination boroughs, and with them of much of their influence over the popular House. The Duke of Norfolk had lost his eleven members, Lord Lonsdale his nine, Lord Darlington his seven, the Duke of Rutland, the Marquis of Buckingham, and Lord Carrington each of them his six. Still the Lords had many sons and nephews in the Commons. As a House they had undergone coercion on the demand of the Commons, and could no longer be deemed a co-ordinate branch of the legislature. On questions of first-rate magnitude no more was left them than a suspensive veto. On secondary questions their power of obstruction remained the same, and continued to be exercised almost as freely as before. They were still a House of hereditary land-owners, unfit in that respect for the impartial revision of legislation, especially when it affected the landed interest. What is called parliamentary reform had been reform only of the House of Commons, and of that only by extension of the franchise. Statesmanship would perhaps have prescribed a simultaneous re-organization of the two Houses so as to keep them in unison with each other and preserve the balance of the constitution. But a comprehensive revision of the constitution is an idea which has never been entertained, and which, while the predominance of party continues, it would be hopeless to entertain. Loud cries which, when the lords threw out the Reform Bill, had been raised for the abolition of a hereditary peerage, died away when the Bill had passed. The people had gained their substantial object and they are not easily moved to theoretic innovation.

The working classes generally had welcomed the Bill, thinking it would bring relief to their sufferings, while the more democratic among them hoped that the ball of political change, once set rolling, would roll on. They, however, did not fail to see that this was a middle-class measure, or to give vent to their class jealousy and distrust. Hence presently arose Chartism, the agitation for the people's charter, the six points of which were universal suffrage, vote by ballot, annual parliaments, payment of representatives, equal electoral districts, and abolition of property qualification. Chartism, however, fell into bad hands, allied itself with protectionism, and after signing monster petitions and leading to some outbreaks of violence went to its grave. Socialism as yet had hardly reared its head in the political field. Its prophet was the visionary Owen. Francis Place, the arch-Radical, though an extremist in political reform, was not a socialist. Individual liberty and political equality were his creed. He supported a Poor Law Amendment Bill framed on strictly economic lines.

The crown also had succumbed in regard to the matter of the creation of peers, to which the king manifestly consented against his will. It lost by whatever increased the authority of the Commons as the representation of the people. Nor were representatives of the people so likely to become courtiers and "king's friends" as the wealthy purchasers of nomination boroughs.

Croker, when the Reform Bill had passed, left the House of Commons, saying that it was no longer a place for a gentleman. It was no longer a place exclusively for the landed gentry with their social recruits from commerce and their borough nominees. The manufacturer had found his way there, though as yet on a small scale. So had popular leaders, demagogues the gentry called them, such as Cobbett, the sledge-hammer pamphleteer, and Hume, the rude apostle of retrenchment. One man had found his way there who had been a prize-fighter, perhaps not more disreputable than his backers. Yet it was still a House of landed gentlemen. They had regained, or were soon to regain, the counties; the tenants-at-will, enfranchised under the Chandos clause, everywhere voting with the landlord. They had influence over the rural boroughs, and they had still the spell of rank and social position, powerful with the middle classes even in a party election. The really democratic element in the new House was very small. It was unrepresented in the cabinet, of the fourteen members of which eleven bore the title of Lord, one that of Baronet. Grey could say that he never read the newspapers. The House was still governed by the gentleman's sentiment and manners. Latin quotations were still in fashion. The unclassical Hume, to conform to that fashion, called omnibuses *omnibi*. The commercial policy of the country, so far as it affected the land-owners' rents, remained protectionist, and he was a Whig statesman who denounced as madness the proposal to repeal the Corn Laws. The class, or combination of classes, educated at the two great universities remained in fact the predominant influence, the standard of public principle, the practical motor of the political machine. Against the inroad of extreme democracy upon the House of Commons the non-payment of members was the surest safeguard. To remove this no serious attempt was made. On the other hand, the theory that the member is the mere delegate and mouthpiece of his constituency, against which Burke had nobly protested, had made way, and may be regarded as a detraction from the power of the House of Commons. At a meeting of the liverymen of London it was resolved that "for one man to represent another means that he is to act for that other and in a manner agreeably to his wishes and instructions, and that members chosen to be representatives in parliament ought to do such things as their constituents wish and direct them to do." Strictly construed, this would mean that the representative was a messenger and that the only citizens who were to have no opinion or voice of their own were those who formed the great council of the nation.

To this period of legislative change perhaps may be traced the idea, now prevalent, that legislative change is a normal function of a government, and that a government which allows a session to pass without some measure of innovation betrays unworthiness to rule.

In the party system of government there had been a break during the early autocracy of Pitt. The French Revolution had once more drawn the party lines, yet they had been disregarded under the pressure of public danger in the formation of the Grenville administration. By the

Reform struggle they were again sharply drawn, though on both sides there were marked shades of difference among the sections of which the parties were composed.

In the reform of abuse so flagrant, and, with revolution abroad in Europe, so plainly dangerous, men by interest and character conservative had in great numbers taken part. These men might with literal truth say that they were for the Bill, the whole Bill, and nothing but the Bill. From the first sign of general change they recoiled, though that sign was nothing more revolutionary than a proposal to devote a part of the worse than useless wealth of the Irish hierarchy to the purposes of national education. Upon that question the Whig government was deserted by Mr. Stanley and Sir James Graham, the first of whom soon turned the fire of his rhetoric, which was very hot, on his old friends.

After this defection, the tide of reaction was so evidently rising that the king, now cured of his brief fancy for popularity, and sensible that royalty was his trade, ventured on a stroke of personal government, destined probably to be the last of its kind, and to prove by its failure that the ministry now was the ministry of the Commons, not of the king.

Grey, old, weary, being, by an indiscretion of his Irish secretary, Littleton, embroiled with O'Connell, and having thereby lost Lord Althorp, whose character was the mainstay of the government in the Commons, had resigned. He had been succeeded in the premiership by 1834 Lord Melbourne, an easy-going man of the world, sagacious though not brilliant, little troubled with convictions, and affecting to be less troubled by them than he was. The indispensable Althorp, after returning to the chancellorship of the exchequer, was by the death of his father, Lord Spencer, transferred from the Commons to the Lords, and thus practically killed as an effective statesman. The weakening of the government in the Commons gave the king a pretext, though not a constitutional ground, for dismissing his ministers and putting the premiership in the hands of the Duke of Wellington, by whom it was passed to Peel. Peel, looking for no crisis, was then in Italy. Had he been on the spot it is probable that his caution would have condemned the venture as premature. As it was, his sense of duty to his sovereign prevailed. He went to the country and, thanks largely to the operation of the Chandos clause, came back with a gain of seats which showed that reaction had set in. In England he had a decided majority, but Scotland and Ireland turned the scale. Beaten on the Speakership, he yet continued to hold office for three months, during which his main objects, the reconciliation of his party with the new order of things and the promulgation of its amended programme, had been gained. He definitively accepted for himself and his followers the settlement of the Reform Bill. He opened an attractive budget of practical reform, including commutation of tithe, reform of the ecclesiastical courts, a measure for legalizing the marriages of dissenters, an inquiry into church revenues with a view to their better distribution, and a promise of municipal reform. He re-baptized his party, which thenceforth was not Tory, but Conservative. He took up for it a new position as the party of practical improvement opposed to political innovation. To be leader of such a party no one was better fitted than himself. Heir of a great manufacturer and great land-owner, thus representing both the interests, early trained in office, thoroughly master of the public business, especially in the department, now so important, of finance and trade, a first-rate debater and a skilful manager of the House of Commons, courageous yet cautious and patient, thoroughly conservative yet an open-minded reader of his times, Robert Peel seemed sent to his party by its good genius to steer it through the inevitable transition, regain for it the confidence of the nation, and guide it back to power. He was not without his weak points. His failings were a shyness, strange in one who swayed a great public assembly, which impaired his personal influence, and made him sometimes close when he had better have been communicative; an excess of caution, the result of critical positions as well as of a youth passed in office; and an over-sensitiveness about his own character which betrayed itself not only in unnecessary vindications, but, as his temper was hot though generally under strict control, led him to challenge more than one assailant to a duel. Nor was he equally popular with all sections of the party. Stiff old Tories of the Eldonian school might still withhold their confidence. Aristocracy might not quite forget that Peel was a cotton-spinner's son. Yet the mass of Conservatives saw the value of their leader and when upon the passing of a resolution in favour of the secularization of part of the surplus revenues of the Irish church he announced his resignation to the House, the cheers of sympathy, not from his own side alone, amidst which he sat down were morally the voice of victory.

CHAPTER IX

THE FRUITS OF PARLIAMENTARY REFORM

1834   THE Melbourne Ministry was now restored to office, but hardly to power. The Whigs, its only assured following, were outnumbered in the House of Commons by the opposition consisting of Tories and Conservatives. For its majority it was dependent partly on the Radicals, who lent it a cold, uncertain, and somewhat contemptuous support; partly on O'Connell and his "tail," whose support was not only uncertain, especially on Irish questions, but highly compromising in British and protestant eyes, so that the alliance with him, nicknamed the Lichfield House Compact, was morally a heavy drag on the government. A precarious union was enforced among these sections by the formidable force of the common enemy, whose return to power would have been fatal to them all. The Prime Minister, shelved in the House of Lords, could do little more than show his good temper and discretion in the leadership of a hopeless minority. Liberal in creed, but Conservative in grain, in all things a sceptic, not having sought the premiership, but liking it when events had wafted him into it, he wanted no more change than was needful for the filling of his part as the Reform premier and would gladly have put off all change to the morrow. Brougham had been excluded from the reconstructed cabinet by indiscretions and escapades which passed all bounds; he had played most fantastic tricks in a tour of vanity through Scotland. Fortunately, however, for his former colleagues his electricity at first found vent in combats with Lyndhurst rather than in vengeful attacks on the administration. The leader in the House of Commons, the soul of the government in home affairs, was Lord John Russell, who for the present proclaimed the finality of his Reform Bill, though he was in the sequel fain once more to woo for his flagging sails the breeze which had first borne him into power. Lord John was a good tactician, but no match for Peel, whose ascendancy in the House had now been completely established. With a powerful minority in the Commons and a Tory House of Lords, Peel had a veto on legislation. His own tendency and policy were not obstruction but moderation. In practical reform he would probably have been willing to go further had he not been checked by the Tory section of his party in the House of Commons and by the Toryism of the House of Lords. Over the Toryism of the House of Lords he maintained a somewhat precarious control through the Duke of Wellington, who, though opposed to change, was a practical strategist and generally recognized in Peel the commander-in-chief of the party. Peel's ambition was very cautious, and he had no intention of precipitating the fall of the Whig government that he might go on another forlorn hope.

Bound up with reform of parliament and sure to attend it, was municipal reform. The close corporations had in fact been the chief organs of electoral abuse and corruption. Commissioners of inquiry to prepare complex subjects for parliament were becoming instruments of government. A commission of inquiry into the state

of the municipal corporations reported that there was
crying need of reform. Under cover of antiquated
charters self-elected municipalities had become gangs of
public thieves, misgoverning the towns, stealing the corporate property, abusing it for political purposes or
wasting it in revelry, jobbing the appointments, and
selling the parliamentary representation, sometimes for
a regular sum. The basis of the city constituency,
instead of tax-paying, was the freedom of the city, a relic
of the commercial middle ages, now a figment and a cover
for abuse. There were cities in which only a trifling
minority of the ratepayers were members of the corporation. A city council might be made up of a borough-
mongering magnate, two members of his family, three or
four of his dependents, and an officer of the corporation.
Of the charitable funds three-fourths or more might go to
the Blue party. The judicial powers of the corporations,
owing to medieval accident, varied absurdly, and were
often vested in untrustworthy hands. Peel and Wellington consented, Peel no doubt most willingly, to reform.

1835 Elective government on a ratepaying basis was given to
all boroughs, including cities such as Manchester and
Birmingham hitherto unincorporated, and to such as
might thereafter apply for it. The charitable funds and
the judicial power were respectively placed in trustworthy
hands. The city of London alone by its grandeur repelled
reform and retained its ancient government, its Gog and
Magog, the pomp and banquets of its Mansion House,
and those sumptuous survivals of medieval trade, its
guilds, with their vast wealth and its then equivocal application. The Tory Lords would gladly have thrown out
the Bill; they entered, in fact, on what would have been

an endless course of delay ; but, discountenanced by their chiefs, they ventured only to mutilate by respiting here again the evil privileges of the freemen and by other reactionary amendments. Their conduct throughout this period is marked, it must be said, by blind and factious opposition utterly unlike the prudent afterthought which is the supposed function of their House.

In passing the Municipal Reform Act, its authors thought that they were not only purifying municipal government, but studding the country with little commonwealths, to be the schools of good and active citizens. A borough in the middle ages was indeed a little commonwealth, political as well as commercial, asserting its liberties against king, lord, or abbot. It was ruled by its chief merchants, who lived in the heart of it, mingling constantly with their fellow-citizens. The main duty of its rulers, besides the defence of its liberties, was the regulation of its handicrafts and trades. The modern problems of city administration were then almost unknown. The police were the citizens, called to arms at need. Public works were done by common labour. Sanitary regulations were unborn; the street was the sewer. The only school was the monastic or charitable foundation. The almshouse and private alms provided for the poor. A great city in these days needs an administrative and not a political organization. Its leading men usually live apart from the masses, and have not time to spare from their own business for the work, now serious, of city management. The citizens do not know each other and have no means of combining for the selection of city officers. Hence the ward politician, whose reign over American cities warns the world.

1835

Great expectations had been raised of the lightening of the public burdens by the reduction of expenditure in the offices of government and the establishments which was to follow the reform of parliament. Retrenchment found an indefatigable, pertinacious, and most unsentimental advocate in the Radical member of parliament, Joseph Hume. But it turned out that the administration of Wellington and Peel, in its effort to lighten the ship on the approach of the political tempest, had pretty well made jettison of everything that could be spared. Some scandalous sinecures and pensions, products of the oligarchy, remained; but vested rights protected them during the lives of their holders. The army and navy were, up to a certain point, fixed charges so long as Europe remained in arms. Nor, considering the responsibilities of ministers and the social position which they had to maintain, were the offices of state by any means overpaid. The salaries of English judges were and still are large; but the money is well spent in placing on the bench men who have full command over their courts and can make justice swift as well as respectable and sure. That underpayment of public servants and judges is false economy America has good reason to know.

The bishops had voted against the Reform Bill, which, unluckily for them, had been defeated by the exact number of their votes. Scenting restriction of clerical privilege, the clergy had everywhere opposed political reform. The anger of the people had been kindled against them, so that it was hardly safe for a bishop to walk the streets in the dress of his order. Nor was the church in a state to repel rude treatment by her command of popular respect and affection. Methodism, which she cast out; evangelicism, on which she frowned; and growing peril, had done something to awaken her to her duties. Still the vices of a rich establishment prevailed. Sinecurism and pluralism abounded. It is found that under the primacy of good Archbishop Sutton, seven Suttons shared among them sixteen rectories, vicarages, and chapelries, besides preacherships and dignities in cathedrals; while one of his daughters carried as her marriage portion to her husband eight different preferments, valued together at ten thousand pounds, in the course of as many years. The nepotism of Tomline, Pitt's tutor, had been conspicuous. The inequalities of income and the disparities between the work and the payment were still intense. Patrons of livings treated the cure of souls as provision for the younger members of their family, or sold it in market overt. Hunting parsons were still common. The poor in many districts were neglected and abandoned to heathendom and vice. The churches themselves were often in a slovenly condition. At the same time the privileges of the state church were odious, and made every nonconformist her enemy. Grey had warned the bishops to set their house in order. The Radicals would have set it in order with a vengeance, and strong measures would have been welcomed by the people. But the Whigs, though thorough Erastians, were staunch upholders of the Establishment. Their prophet, Macaulay, vindicated it on the ground that the state, besides its cure of bodies, which was its primary duty, might well undertake as a secondary object the cure of souls. All attempts at disestablishment, or even at the removal of the bishops from the House of Lords, made by champions of religious liberty such as Mr. Ward, were totally defeated by the combination of Whigs and Tories. A proposal to secularize the surplus funds of the plethoric Irish church cost the government the secession of four of its members. Reform was limited to the appointment of an ecclesiastical commission, which set the house internally in order by the abolition of the most flagrant abuses such as pluralism and sinecurism, by the partial equalization of incomes, rectification of dioceses, and other reforms of a practical kind. Reform in this sense was promoted by statesmanlike prelates, such as Blomfield, Bishop of London, who understood the crisis and saw that the cry of sacrilege could not avail to hallow abuse. The hand of reform was not laid on the private patronage of livings, nor was anything done to prevent the sale of the cure of souls.

1834

Some points, after much struggling with the obstructiveness of the Lords, were gained for religious liberty. Dissenters obtained permission to marry after their own fashion instead of being compelled to marry with the service of the church. The commutation of tithe into a rent charge rendered its collection less galling to the nonconformist conscience. Quakers were permitted, on taking their seats in parliament, to substitute an affirmation for the oath. The franchise was still withheld from the Jews, but in their case it was not wholly or chiefly a question of religion. Religion, even in the middle ages, had told less than is commonly supposed. The real difficulty lay in the political incorporation of a race which everywhere cherished a separate nationality accentuated by a tribal rite, refused intermarriage, held aloof, regarded other races as the stranger is regarded under the Mosaic

1836

1833

law, was kept united in itself and separate from other nations by a cosmopolitan tie, and was everywhere naturally disposed to use its vast financial influence for objects of its own. It is hard to say whether the transportation of the negro or the dispersion of the Jews has been most serious in its consequences to mankind.

Registration of births, deaths, and marriages was transferred from the church to the state. This again was a step in the divorce of church and state, and the thorough secularization of the state.

The connection between church and state had now become a manifest and, to earnest churchmen, a revolting anomaly. Since the suspension of convocation, parliament had been the only legislature of the national church. Parliament had once been Anglican. It was now a medley of men of all religions and of none. The union with Scotland had introduced a body of Presbyterians. Catholic Emancipation had introduced a body of Roman Catholics, mortal enemies to the church of England, and little likely to be restrained by any formal renunciation from the use of their power for her subversion. The political tide seemed to be setting towards a withdrawal by the state of its support from the church. Some of the clergy began to look about for another basis of their authority. They found it in apostolical succession, to which was presently to be added the sacerdotal theory and sacraments, and in time the "whole cycle of Roman doctrine." Thus commenced the Tractarian movement, upon which, after its catastrophe through the secession of its leaders, the Ritualist movement has followed. Oxford, with her medieval colleges, half monastic, clerical, and celibate, furnished a natural centre for an attempt to return to the beliefs and to restore the church authority of the middle ages; while the movement was limited by the marriage of the Anglican clergy and their rectories, combined with the rooted protestantism of the mass of the people. Tractarianism, as the Romanizing movement was called, found its natural end in a secession to Rome. Again, as soon as life awoke in the church, the Elizabethan compromise broke down. It broke down always because the proper sphere of compromise is interest, not conviction. But it must be repeated that Oxford and Cambridge at this time, especially Oxford, were not so much universities as centres of the clerical interest, which was intrenched in the statutes of the ecclesiastical middle ages.

Nonconformists had been excluded by religious tests from the national universities and upbraided for the lack of culture which was the consequence of their exclusion. A measure of emancipation passed the Commons, but as a matter of course was thrown out by the Lords. The nonconformists, however, succeeded in obtaining a charter for the free University of London, which bestowed the power of conferring literary and scientific degrees. Conscience continued to be mocked in the old universities by the imposition of religious tests, at Oxford the Thirty-nine Articles, on the consciences of boys. Statesmen failed to see the political advantages of identifying the great national universities with the nation, and educating the youth of the governing class under the same academical roof. Yet the nonconformists had more reason to fear for their young men the witchery of the ancient seats of learning, than the ancient seats of learning had to fear the subversion of their religious character by the admission of nonconformists.

1836

An attempt of the government to get rid of the church rates, with the scandals and vestry wars which they bred, by a compromise in the shape of a substituted charge on the land-tax, had miscarried, the clergy being resolved to keep all they had, the nonconformists refusing to be satisfied with anything but total abolition.

Another measure of the Whigs, passed under their first government, was a new Poor Law. Of this they alone, 1834 perhaps, as aristocratic yet unsentimental economists, could have been the authors. The Tories would have been too sentimental; the Radicals too democratic. The law as it stood, by prodigal distribution of outdoor relief, had to a fearful extent pauperized the labourer. By proportioning alms to the number of children, it had encouraged that reckless increase of population, to the dangers of which attention had been called by the alarm-bell of Malthus. The poor-rate had for some time been increasing three times as fast as population, and amounted nearly to eight millions. Farmers had been taking to the employment of pauper labour paid by the parish in the shape of public alms instead of giving proper wages to the labourers. The property of ratepayers who were not farmers was being devoured. The self-reliance, self-respect, and industry of the poor were being fatally undermined. Pauperism, as might have been expected, became hereditary. A Bastardy Law, which enabled abandoned women to swear their bastards to any man they chose, was filling parishes with illegitimate children. A senseless Law of Settlement penned the poor in their native parishes and prevented labour from seeking its best market, besides breeding incessant litigation. Rural England was sinking into the slough of mendicity and parochial jobbery combined, though the best of the labouring class still pathetically struggled against degradation. A commission of inquiry having reported on these evils, a great measure of reform was introduced. The workhouse test of indigence was established, and relief was denied to all, except the sick or hopelessly infirm, who would not come into the poor-house and submit to its discipline. The Bastardy Law was amended by charging the children on the mother; an enactment apparently harsh, but effective in restoring chastity. The law of settlement was amended; unions of parishes were formed; boards of guardians were created to administer the new system; the whole being an important step in centralization. The measure worked well, and the plague of pauperism was stayed. Peel and his Conservative following concurred with the Whigs in this legislation, which, however, was specially creditable to the Whigs, who risked their popularity by a measure sternly economic. The new "Bastilles," in truth, were and are ugly features in the lovely English landscape, though their grim forms preach, to the peasant at least, the wholesome doctrine that he who will not work shall not eat, and they may claim to be regarded rather as bulwarks of industry than as cruel counterparts of the Bastille. Strong opposition, however, was made to them by a party, or rather a circle, which combined Toryism with a strain of Chartism, and of which the leading spirit was John Walter of the *Times*. It is a blot on the escutcheon of the great journal that it long continued its bitter attacks on this most salutary measure. The system of public poor-relief was so rooted, that the question of falling back on voluntary charity, raised by Brougham and other economists, could not be entertained.

1834

Democracy, whatever its political weaknesses, is humane. It is not to be charged with the French Reign of Terror, which was a paroxysm of blood-thirsty madness in the leaders of the Parisian rabble. It sets equal value on all human life, and recognizes in every human form the dignity of man. Its influence on jurisprudence was now felt, and had begun to be felt as soon as, the great war being ended, Liberalism was restored to life, when Romilly, and after him Mackintosh, laboured to reform the criminal law. Peel's growing Liberalism had been shown in the same field. The hideous list of capital crimes which an oligarchical legislature had bequeathed was reduced to murder and a few other offences of the most heinous kind. Further reduction was vetoed by the House of Lords. In the case of capital punishment a merciful interval was interposed between sentence and execution. Counsel was allowed to be heard for the accused in cases of felony, a piece of common justice, which, if English law had not been the slave of custom, it would be startling to find so long delayed. An end was put to imprisonment for debt, under which, to the disgrace of English jurisprudence, tens of thousands had languished, not a few of them for life. Inspection of prisons was instituted to prevent a repetition of the sickening horrors and brutalities which had moved the heroic efforts of Howard.

Something was done to give practical effect to the promise of the Great Charter that the crown would not delay or deny justice. In chancery, delay, above all when Eldon was chancellor, had practically amounted to denial. So had the cost, which was such that no one could be advised to sue in chancery for any sum less than five hundred pounds. Small debts were almost irrecoverable.

So it had been till the machinery of justice was improved by Brougham. The landed interest was so far reduced in power that it had to allow its estates to be made liable for its common debts. Registration of its titles was, under the inspiration of the family solicitor, resisted with success.

1833 The great act of humanity, however, was the abolition of slavery, which had taken place under the government of Grey. It was honourable to the people that the boon which they demanded next to their own enfranchisement was the emancipation of the slave. They had, perhaps, an instinctive feeling that there might be white slaves as well as black. The time for emancipation was now come. Slave colonies, with the whip, the branding-iron, and the general brutality, were a hell, and they had been growing still more hellish as the declining profits of the planter led him to press more ruthlessly on the slave. Slavery was abolished, twenty millions being paid as indemnity to the slave-owners. Wilberforce just lived to see the day and to utter his *Nunc Dimittis*. Parliament, seeing the dangerous gulf which lay between slavery and free labour, sought to bridge it with apprenticeship. But this failed, and before the term had expired full freedom was conferred. The planters of Antigua did themselves honour by forwarding emancipation; the planters in general, as was natural, opposed it, more bitterly because on the approach of freedom the slave had begun to shake his chains, and disturbances had broken out. The abolition of slavery by Great Britain gave an impulse to the abolition of slavery throughout the world, notably in the United States. The slave-trade was already under the ban of nations; but it was carried on by contrabanders, with horrors in the packing of negroes on board slave-ships aggravated by the danger of capture. Great Britain maintained a crusade against it which, purely disinterested and philanthropic though it was, by the jealousy of other nations was ascribed to her lust for domination, and might, under the conduct of Palmerston, now master of the foreign office, assume an imperious and offensive form.

Military flogging, that foul stain on the honour of the British army, and the impressment of seamen, both morally received their death-blow, though the practice of military flogging died a very lingering death.

Freedom of trade had undying advocacy in the "Wealth of Nations," while apostles of it, such as Huskisson, Brougham, and Horner, did not fail. Huskisson, as a minister under Wellington, had effected some reciprocal reductions of duties and a relaxation of the navigation laws. For deliverance from the Corn Laws there was nothing as yet to be done. The landed interest was still too strong in parliament; the argument that the country must produce its own bread, not be dependent on the foreigner, had great weight; and the Whig premier had declared that to propose repeal of the Corn Laws would be madness. At last there arose a great power opposed on this question to the landed interest, and strong enough, when circumstances favoured, to cope with it in the political field. The manufacturer wanted more hands and cheaper bread to feed them. He set on foot a crusade against the bread tax; founded an Anti-Corn Law League; and enlisted in its service the eloquence of Bright and Cobden. There was war between the manor-house and the factory. The land-owner exposed the cruelties of the factory system; while the manufacturer

1836

exposed the misery of the underpaid tiller of the soil, and in the Free-Trade Hall, which rose on the scene of the Peterloo massacre at Manchester, exhibited the nether garments of a Dorsetshire labourer standing upright with patches and grease.

1834 As a free-trade victory, may be reckoned the abolition, on the renewal of the East India Company's charter, of the Company's monopoly of the China trade. The monopoly of the Indian trade having been abolished on the last renewal of the charter, here is the end of that great system of commercial monopolies which, having served its purpose when there was no peace on the sea, and commerce needed everywhere to go armed, had now survived its usefulness, and become a mere obstruction to the growth of trade.

In the Factory Acts the legislature enlarged its sphere and verged on socialism; so at least it appeared to strict economists, who viewed this legislation with misgiving, as well as to the manufacturers and coal-owners whose personal interests were touched. Yet government does nothing socialist or beyond its rightful sphere in protecting those who cannot protect themselves. The factory system, while it was adding vastly to the wealth of the nation, was showing its darker side in its ruthless employment of infant labour. Children had been sent, by parishes which wished to get rid of them, to distant factories as little slaves, and manufacturers had sometimes covenanted to take one idiot in every twenty. Nor was the cruelty much less when the supply of infants was produced on the spot. Children eight years old or even younger were kept at work for twelve or thirteen hours a day, in rooms the air of which was foul and the moral atmosphere equally tainted, to the certain ruin of their health as well as of their character and happiness. Attention had been drawn to the evil and something had been done for its mitigation under George III. ; but the voice of philanthropy was little heard amid the din of the great war. Stubborn was the struggle made by avarice against humanity, which in the person of Lord Ashley pleaded for mercy to the child. Labour for children under thirteen was in the end reduced to eight hours a day, and factory inspectors were appointed.

1833

The Factory Acts presently led on to similar acts, also due to the efforts of Lord Ashley, in favour of the people employed in coal mines, in which women were used as beasts of burden, children were even more cruelly treated than in the factories, and women and children were made to crawl on all fours in the passages of the pits dragging carts by a chain from the waist passed between the legs, immorality as well as filth surrounding all.

Medieval statutes of labourers had compelled the labourers to work at wages fixed by the employer class. Later, combination laws forbade labourers to combine for an advance of wages. On the motion of Joseph Hume, inspired by his Radical mentor, Francis Place, combination laws had been relaxed and trade-unions had been made legal. But some farm labourers in Dorsetshire, where the lot of the labourer was very wretched, having banded themselves together as a union, six of them were indicted, nominally for administering an illegal oath, and sentenced to seven years' transportation. A demonstration of the trades in their favour, on so large a scale and so menacing as to call out soldiery and artillery, brought about their pardon and recall to their native land.

1833 A beginning was made, on a small scale, of national education by forming a committee of the Privy Council for its promotion with an annual sum of twenty thousand pounds, which was distributed through two school societies, one Anglican, the other undenominational and regarded with jealousy by Anglicans. This was Brougham's great subject, and other philanthropists, such as Lancaster, Bell, and Raikes the founder of Sunday-schools, had been labouring in the same field. It was assumed that the chief cause of popular vice and crime was ignorance, which popular education would dispel. Perhaps in the discussion the distinction between popular education and state education was not kept distinctly in view; nor was it very clearly seen what principles the adoption of state education involves. That the community is bound to provide education for all the children whom anybody chooses to bring into the world; that the provident who defer marriage till they can support a family are bound to pay for the improvident; that one class is bound to provide education for another class; are not undisputed propositions. Nature, some contend, pronounces that the duty as well as the right of educating children belongs to the parents, or those to whom the parents may intrust it. It is also to be observed that in a community divided in religion the state can hardly take to itself the duty of education without practically establishing secularism; recognition of religion by giving its ministers access to the children at certain hours being not of great value, since what religion demands is the whole life of the child. Nor is it likely that a state system of education would be free from the defects of a machine. The common schools of primitive New England and

even those of Scotland in early days were probably less
unparental than state schools in the present day, nor was
there in those communities any sectarian division to prevent the school from being religious. The voluntary
system might be the best, as it apparently is the most
natural, if it had power to do the work. But the need
was urgent; the object, if education was really the sovereign remedy for vice and crime, was of transcendent
importance. Security of some sort for the voter's intelligence was the indispensable safeguard of an extended
franchise. The state system, at all events, at this time
introduced in germ, has continued to grow till at last
its complete ascendancy seems assured.

When the franchise was extended a cheap political
press for the instruction of the new voters became a
manifest necessity of the state. The Whig government
proceeded to reduce the stamp duty on newspapers from 1836
fourpence to a penny, and to reduce the excise on paper
at the same time. The Tories urged that greater relief
would be afforded to the people by a remission of the
duty on soap. In the eyes of a true Tory a newspaper
press was a vulgar organ of evil speaking and sedition.
'The lowering of newspaper stamps would tend to introduce a cheap and profligate press, one of the greatest curses that could be inflicted on humanity.' 'The
poor man, as it was, could have a sight of a newspaper in a
coffee-house for three halfpence.' The reduction of the
stamp and excise could not fail to enlarge the realm of
the new-born power. Circulation was speedily doubled.
Nor was the benefit confined to newspapers; it extended
to the Penny Cyclopædia and other conduits of cheap
knowledge. Such a power as journalism, wielded anony-

mously, and therefore without personal responsibility, may seem dangerous, and in fact is not free from danger to the state. But political party at once found its way up the back stairs of the editorial room and got the power into its hands.

1839 With the cheapening of newspapers as well as with the general progress of intelligence may be connected the introduction of the penny post, achieved by Rowland Hill after a long struggle with the official inertness and mistrust of change, which, even when public servants are most upright, are apt to put public services at a disadvantage in comparison with private enterprise, which is stimulated to improvement by the hope of gain.

This was generally a time of intellectual and scientific activity, of adventure, discovery, and hope; a time in which frivolous amusements gave way to serious pursuits, in which card-playing was renounced for conversation. It was a time in which it has been jocosely said everything was new, everything was true, and everything was of the highest importance.

"Ireland is my difficulty," said Peel, when his time for taking office drew near. It was not his difficulty only, it was equally that of the Whigs, and must have been that of any British government set to rule Ireland on the principles which still prevailed. The union of the kingdoms had been politically equal, Ireland receiving her full share of representation in the united parliament. But Ireland, instead of being thoroughly and heartily incorporated, had continued to be administered as a dependency through the lord-lieutenant and the Castle, while protestant ascendancy had continued to be the rule of government. Catholic Emancipation, long-delayed and at last enforced, had lost its grace. Nor had it been followed by real equality. Catholics, their leader O'Connell among the rest, were still treated as social pariahs, and though admitted to parliament and there wielding power in the national councils, were excluded from the offices of government and even from the honours of the bar. Tithes continued to be levied for the detested church of the minority and the conquest, while its members were a mere fraction of the people and its clergy were often without congregations, in many cases non-resident. War was waged between the people and the tithe proctors, and on the side of the people with the paroxysms of cruelty to which Celtic character is prone. The peasantry were a vast conspiracy against the law, which to them was a code of oppression. Murder and outrage stalked in their most horrible forms through the land, while the arm of justice was paralyzed, since none dared to bear witness against the assassin. In Kilkenny, within a twelvemonth, there had been thirty-two murders and attempts at murder, thirty-four burnings of houses, five hundred and nineteen burglaries, thirty-six houghings of cattle, and one hundred and seventy-eight assaults with danger of loss of life. In Queen's County during the same period there had been sixty murders, six hundred and twenty-six nightly attacks on houses and burglaries, one hundred and fifteen malicious injuries to property, and two hundred and nine serious assaults. There were also in one year two thousand and ninety-five illegal notices. One case especially had impressed Peel, when in his earlier days he was administering Ireland, as a proof of the pitch which deadly passion had attained. Assassins entered a house in which were a man, his wife, and their little daughter. The man was found by the assassins on the ground floor. The woman in the room above heard them murdering her husband below. She put the child into a closet from which what was passing in the room could be seen, and said to her, "They are killing your father below, then they will come up here to kill me; mind you look well at them while they are doing it, and swear to them when you see them in court." The child looked on while her mother was being murdered; she swore to the murderers in court; and they were convicted on her evidence. The Orange Lodges in England disbanded on an appeal from the throne. In Ireland they remained on foot and met with equal ferocity the savage hatred of the catholic Celt. Macaulay, when O'Connell threatened the government with civil war, could reply, "We are past that fear; we have civil war in its worst form already."

O'Connell remained master of catholic Ireland. To deal with him was most difficult. While he ostensibly preached respect for law and order, he was always doing his utmost to inflame the passions of his people. His language, not only in speaking of opponents such as Wellington and Peel, but of friends, such as Grey, who thwarted his will, was incredibly foul. "Is it just," he said of Grey, "that Ireland should be insulted and trampled on merely because the insanity of the wretched old man who is at the head of the ministry develops itself in childish hatred and maniac contempt of the people of Ireland?" He proceeded to denounce Grey, his family, and his colleagues, as plunderers of the public, and implored his brother reformers to come forward and teach "the insane dotard, who was at the head of the administration," that Englishmen and Scotchmen were alive to the wants and sufferings and the privileges of the people of Ireland. Attempts to put the law in force against him, amidst the people who worshipped him, he defied. With such a man, even if his cause was right, it was hardly possible to act without dishonour. If the step of justice to Ireland was slow, this man's attitude and conduct, which inflamed every prejudice against his race and religion, must, in part at least, bear the blame. Rather, perhaps, as a menace, than with a hope of any practical result, he commenced, and to the end of his life fitfully kept on foot, an agitation for the repeal of the union. This, both houses of parliament had met with a resolution recording "in the most solemn manner their fixed determination to maintain unimpaired and undisturbed the legislative union between Great Britain and Ireland, which they considered to be essential to the strength and stability of the Empire, to the continuance of the connection between the two countries, and to the peace, security, and happiness of all classes of his Majesty's subjects." A brave resolution if only the right measures could have followed.

Something was done in the way of pruning the monstrous exuberance of the Irish state episcopate, and tempering the more flagrant scandals of the parochial system. By commuting tithe into a rent-charge on the land, that impost was rendered, though not less unjust, less directly galling to the people. Secularization of the surplus revenues of the church, on which the Whigs had defeated Peel and supplanted him in office, they were compelled to abandon, not without loss of honour, that they might carry the commutation of tithes. While the catholics were still excluded from the national university of Dublin, a grant was made to their ecclesiastical seminary at May-

1838

nooth. Irish cities received a measure of municipal self-government, maimed by the constant fear of allowing a catholic majority to gain the upper hand, as though it had been possible to frame elective institutions in which the majority should not prevail. The fancied necessity of upholding protestant ascendancy pervaded and vitiated all government and legislation. Suspension of Habeas Corpus, martial law, prohibition of public meetings, trials for sedition, formed the staple of Irish administration, whether it was in Whig or in Tory hands. The abolition of the Irish state church, the reform of the land law, the levelling of all barriers of race and religion, the substitution, in short, of a genuine union for a union of ascendancy, dependence, and exclusion, were the necessary conditions of a solution of the Irish problem ; and to the level of such a policy the statesmanship of that time had not risen ; nor, if it had, could it have carried with it the English and Scotch people. It is always to be borne in mind that catholicism in countries where it prevailed, such as Italy and Spain, was still less tolerant than was protestantism in Great Britain and Ireland.

The suffering classes, meantime, had not ceased to suffer. They had learned agitation in the struggle for the Reform Bill, and their golden hopes had been disappointed in the result. They also had a press with a wide circulation. They treated universal suffrage as "a knife and fork" question, and demanded for every freeman plenty of bread and a good home. To enforce this demand they signed monster petitions, met in great conventions, and threatened violence. To put the people down was not congenial work for a Liberal government. Yet it was work for which Melbourne was qualified by the calmness of his temper, and his half cynical, half sympathetic view of the errors of mankind. The Chartists injured their cause by attacks on the new Poor Law and opposition to free trade.

The Whig government, however, weak in men, weak especially in finance, harassed by the termagant patronage of O'Connell, ill-supported by the Radicals, dominated by Peel, embarrassed by the Irish difficulty, loaded with promises and expectations which could not be fulfilled, was on the point of falling, when the lingering influence of royalty was once more displayed, and the ministry was respited by the demise of the crown. William IV., who by this time had become thoroughly reactionary and hated his reform ministry, died, and was succeeded by a lady whom the law held, by reason of her birth, qualified to govern an empire at eighteen. The young queen, brought up at a distance from her uncle's court, fell at once under the influence of her Whig ministers, especially of Melbourne, who was well fitted to win her attachment, treated her with consummate tact, and took up his residence at Windsor, where, we are told by Greville, he passed several hours every day in her company, and two every evening at her side, forgoing his habits of lounging ease and his wonted expletives. The sovereign's name was still one wherewith to conjure, and the Whigs conjured with it liberally and with effect. There was, not for the first time, a reversal of parts, the Whigs becoming intensely loyal, while the Tories became enemies of the court. A Tory member of parliament even used language so uncourtly as to move a Whig to show his loyalty and chivalry by provoking the blasphemer to the field.

This restorative, however, was presently exhausted, and, on a question respecting the constitution of Jamaica, its

1837

majority having been reduced to vanishing point, the Whig government fell. Yet once more it lifted itself from the ground by grasping the petticoats of the Ladies of the Bed Chamber. The incident was called the Bed Chamber Plot. The Whigs had surrounded the queen with their women. The women ought at once to have resigned with the government; but they clung to their places, and their mistress naturally clung to her companions. Melbourne having resigned, Peel was called upon to form a government. He insisted that, as a proof of the confidence of his sovereign, the principal ladies of her household should be changed. The queen resisted, and was countenanced in her resistance by the Whigs, who, though they had resigned office, did not scruple to meet as ministers and advise the crown. Peel then refused to form a government, and once more, as in the time of Anne, the Bed Chamber Ladies turned the day. That Peel was constitutionally in the right is not disputed. Even one so loyal to the crown as the Duke of Wellington had no doubt upon that point. It is probable that the Whig ladies might have been able to give trouble; probable also that they would have given it if they could. It is not likely, however, that Peel would have yielded to such an obstacle if he had felt that his time for taking office was fully come. He was determined not to take office without power.

The Melbourne government returned weaker and less respected than ever. A motion of want of confidence, moved by Sir John Yarde Buller, into which Peel was probably hurried by the uncontrolled eagerness of his following to pounce on the expiring prey, was defeated by a small majority. But a serious financial deficit, the most unpardonable of faults in the eyes of a middle-class constituency, finally settled the fate of the Whig ministers. Vainly in the article of death they sought to save themselves by raising the question of the Corn Laws, to the maintenance of which they had committed themselves no less deeply than their opponents. No regard was paid by the nation to so transparent a device. A resolution of want of confidence was passed by a majority of one. Appealing to the country, the Whigs were totally defeated. A resolution of want of confidence was carried in the new House by a majority of ninety-one. The Whigs then resigned. The Conservatives, with Peel at their head, came into power, and the epoch of the parliamentary Reform Act of 1832 was closed.

1841

CHAPTER X

THE EMPIRE

MEANWHILE the United Kingdom had been expanding into the British empire, embracing at this day, besides the thirty-nine millions of people in the two islands, three hundred millions in India and twenty millions, more or less, in colonies scattered over the globe. Instead of being sea-girt, England has an open land frontier of four thousand miles, allowing for indentation, in North America, besides the whole northern frontier of Hindostan. To hold this empire, she has to maintain a fleet not only for her own defence and that of her trade, but for her command of all the seas.

An empire this vast aggregate of miscellaneous possessions is called. To part of them the name is misapplied, and its misapplication may lead to practical error. Empire is absolute rule, whether the imperial power be itself a monarchy, like the Persian or the Spanish; an aristocracy, like the Roman or the Venetian; or a commonwealth, like Athens of old and Great Britain at the present day. In the case of the British possessions, the name is properly applicable only to the Indian empire, the crown colonies, and fortresses or naval stations, such as Gibraltar and Malta. It is not properly applicable to self-governing colonies, such as Canada, Australasia, and the Cape, which, though nominally dependent, are in reality independent; do not obey British law; do not contribute to British armaments, and are at liberty even to wage commercial war against the mother-country by laying protective duties on her goods.

The word "colony" too is used in a misleading sense, as if it were synonymous with dependency or were limited to colonies retaining their political connection with the mother-country. The colonies of England, which now form the United States, did not cease, on becoming independent, to be English colonies.

In the feudal notion of personal fealty which led the colonist to think that even at the ends of the earth he remained indefeasibly the liegeman of the British king, combined perhaps with the notion, also feudal, of the crown as supreme land-owner, we probably see the account of the political tie between the British colonies and the British crown. The *Mayflower* exiles, in their compact before landing, described themselves as loyal subjects of King James, who had undertaken, for the glory of God, the advancement of the Christian faith, and the honour of their king and country, to plant the first colony in the northern parts of Virginia. Had the exiles of the *Mayflower* been citizens of a Greek republic, they would have taken the sacred fire from the hearth of the mother city and gone forth to found a new commonwealth for themselves, owning no relation to its parent but that of filial respect and affection.

Of the self-governing colonies, the chief and the type is Canada, whose political history may be said almost to include those of the rest. When Canada was conquered 1759 by the British, Voltaire openly rejoiced over its transfer from the realm of despotism to that of liberty. A little newspaper, the herald of a free press and political discussion, soon appeared, and trial by jury was introduced, though it seems not to the satisfaction of the French who preferred French ways. The conqueror appears at first to have doubted how to deal with his conquest. Had he wished to Anglicize it, there would have been little difficulty in so doing, the population being under seventy thousand, and its social leaders, mostly official and military, having departed. But the storm rising in the American colonies, whose secession was the certain and predicted consequence of the destruction of the French power on that continent, seems to have determined him the other way. Conciliation of the French Canadians through the priesthood which controlled them became his aim; and this policy, seconded by the priests' hatred and fear of the New England Puritan, kept Canada faithful to the king's cause during the Revolutionary War. The Quebec Act secured to the French Canadians their civil law and recognized their religion, confirming the secular clergy in their position and in their reception of tithes from the catholic population, subject to tests of allegiance. The monastic orders, though excepted by the Act, were yet left in possession. The signorial tenures created by the French monarchy remained untouched. The Act was little pleasing to staunch Protestants or to the British who had begun to settle in Quebec for commercial purposes, and expected to carry with them British institutions, and though they were a small minority to stalk as conquerors in Quebec.

But the British element in Canada and the other North American possessions of Great Britain presently received

1765–1784

1774

a large addition from the influx of United Empire Loyalists, who, at the close of the Revolutionary War, had been 1783 driven from their homes by the blind vindictiveness of the victorious party, disregarding the advice of its best leaders. For these exiles Great Britain was bound in honour to find new homes beneath her flag, otherwise she might, after resigning her American colonies, have taken the advice of those who would have had her altogether withdraw from the continent. A set of families designated by the crown for special honours, and constituting almost a social caste, was thus formed in Canada under the name of United Empire Loyalists, to transmit the memory of the ancestral feud and combine fervent attachment to the British flag with traditional antagonism to American connection. Nor has the spirit of United Empire Loyalism yet entirely died out, though of the descendants of the original exiles not a few are now to be found in the United States.

The French Revolution had passed its first stages when Pitt framed an Act for the permanent settlement of Canada. 1791 To put a bar between the two races Canada was divided into two provinces; Lower Canada, now Quebec, for the French, and Upper Canada, now Ontario, for the British, thus perpetuating the French nationality. To each province was given a constitution on what was taken to be the British model, with a governor for king; a legislative council appointed by him in the name of the crown, for the upper house of parliament; and for the lower house an assembly elected by the people. The governor, however, was intended not only like the constitutional king to reign, but to govern; to appoint his own executive council, not to have it designated for him by the assembly; and to frame his own policy subject to the instructions of the Colonial Office, to which, not to the colonists, he was to be responsible. The members of the legislative council were to be appointed for life. Power was taken to make the tenure hereditary with titles of honour, and thus to endow Canada with a peerage; this project, however, together with great landed estates and primogeniture, the democratic spirit and the economical conditions of the new world repelled. To complete the constitutional imitation, on each province was bestowed something like a counterpart of the state church of England in the shape of a "protestant" church, with an endowment out of the crown lands. In both provinces the criminal law of England, with Habeas Corpus, was established, but to the French provinces the civil law of France was left. The right of imposing duties on commerce or navigation, the exercise of which had led to the quarrel with the American colonies, was reserved to the imperial parliament, but the duties were to be applied to the use of the province.

During the early years the settler in British Canada was too much engaged in his victorious battle with the wilderness to think much about politics; while among the simple peasantry of Quebec, whose life was divided between their tiny farms and their church, politics had 1812 not been born. Then came the American war and the invasion of Canada, which turned all thoughts and energies to arms. Once more the French Canadians were kept true to Great Britain by their priests, who saw in her the antagonist of the French Revolution and had sung *Te Deum* for Trafalgar. This was the time at which it might have been said that the last gun in defence of British dominion on the American continent would be fired by a

French Canadian. A quarter of a century later Lord 1838
Durham, as the British commissioner of inquiry, could
report that an invading American army might rely on the
co-operation of almost the entire French population of
Lower Canada. Before the war commerce and intercourse, with a certain amount of American immigration,
had been exerting their softening influence on the relations between the two sections of the English-speaking
race, and it would appear from the complaints of the
British governor and the British commander-in-chief that
the Canadians were at first not eager to take up arms,
though when attacked they made a very gallant and
memorable defence. The war revived the antagonism in
full force, doing for the traditional feeling of Canada
towards the United States what the Revolutionary War
had done for the traditional feeling of Americans towards
Great Britain; the opposition of New England to the war
going for no more with Canadians than had the opposition of the Whigs to the coercion of the American colonies
with the people of the United States. The treatment of
the Canadian question from first to last seems little creditable to American statesmanship.

In time, however, there was political trouble in both 1837
provinces. In both it took the same form, that of a struggle of the elective assembly to establish its control over
the policy of the governor and over the executive and legislative councils nominated by him; in other words, to introduce in place of the formal British system the real British
system, which was that of government responsible to the
nation. But the cause of quarrel was different in the
two provinces. In Quebec the cause was race. The
"habitants" were a surviving segment of the French

peasantry before the Revolution; kindly and good, but simple-minded, uneducated, unprogressive, primitive even in the farming which was their only pursuit, and governed by the priest, to whom had passed all the power once shared by the king and the signor, saving what might fall to a few old French families or to the notary. They were invaded and confronted by Englishmen and Scotchmen, active-minded, educated, and aggressive, who engrossed the sources of wealth and bore themselves as the imperial race. The French, still Frenchmen, French-Canadians at least, to the core, found their nationality threatened with suppression in its own home. Their jealousy was aroused, and a political war of races ensued. The British had the governor and the offices of government in their hands. They were intrenched, not only in the executive council but in the legislative council appointed by the governor which formed the upper house of the parliament. In the lower and elective house the French had a great majority. The chief bone of contention, as in the contests between the crown and the Commons in England, was the control of the revenue, part of which the crown drew from crown lands and sources other than grants of the assembly. But the signories with their vexatious incidents; the tenure of the judges, which was during pleasure, and their appearance in the political arena; restrictions placed, in the interest of French monopoly, on banking; formed with other minor issues secondary causes of the political war. The war was waged on the part of the French, untrained in constitutional tactics, with irregular and sometimes misdirected fury. Prominent members of the government or judiciary were made the objects of personal attacks. The ignorance of the "habitants," which was such that of eighty-seven thousand persons who signed a petition, only nine thousand could write their own names, combined with their jealous nationality, made their masses an easy field for patriotic agitation. Their leader was Papineau, a popular orator and little more. At his side was Wolfred Nelson, a man of greater force, one of the few Englishmen who on radical grounds took the French side. The Colonial Office, wishing to do right, but in those days of slow communication ill-informed, not discerning that the source of the quarrel was race, but taking it to be political and fiscal discontent, strove in vain by instructions and commissions of inquiry to arbitrate and to lay the storm. It succeeded only in showing the impracticability of a system which sought to combine the parliamentary with the unparliamentary principle and self-government in a distant colony with the continuance of imperial control. That imperial control should continue, and that the governor who represented it should be a viceroy, choosing his own ministers, shaping his own policy, and responsible to the colonial office alone, not a constitutional figure-head, with a ministry imposed upon him by the colonial Commons, was the fixed idea of British statesmen; and not of Tories only, but of Liberals like Lord John Russell.

In the British province, on the other hand, the contest was purely political, the object of the movement there being to put an end to arbitrary rule and introduce the British system of responsible government. Power, office, and public emolument had in British Canada been engrossed by an oligarchy nicknamed the Family Compact, though with little reason, since family connection among its members there was none. The Family Compact was a political ring composed of United Empire Loyalists, with other early settlers and some retired British officers who had received grants of land, and having, not much to their discredit, failed in the battle with the wilderness, were fain to quarter themselves on the state. This oligarchy, which gave itself the social airs of an aristocracy, was, like the English oligarchy at Quebec, intrenched in the nominee House and had the governor and the government in its hands. It monopolized public emolument, handled all public money, and helped itself to the public lands. In opposition to it was the body of the more recent settlers from England, Scotland, and Ireland, exiles often of discontent, together with some immigrants from the United States who brought with them and disseminated republican ideas. With the Family Compact was allied the Anglican church, endowed, privileged, and everywhere Tory, the head of which, Bishop Strachan, a seceder from Presbyterianism and, as his enemies said, from ecclesiastical ambition, was a too active partisan. Of the special questions on which battle was joined, the most burning was the disposal of the clergy reserves, which the Anglican church was resolved to keep for herself, while the opposition sought to divide them between the Anglican church and the church of Scotland; to divide them among all the protestant sects; or, which was the thoroughgoing Radical policy, to appropriate them for the purposes of the state. The reservation of these lands was felt as an obstruction to settlement in addition to the religious injustice. Other questions were the control of all the revenues of the province and the disposal of the public lands, law reforms, the power to impeach public servants, exclusion of judges and clergy from parliament, and the abolition of primogeniture. But the main issue was responsible government; in other words the control of an elective assembly over the appointment and policy of the ministers of the crown. Of the opposition there were different sections. On one hand were constitutional reformers, still attached to British connection and desirous only of a complete measure of British institutions. Of these, forming far the most numerous section, Robert Baldwin was the chief. On the other hand there were the thorough-going Radicals, with a leaning to the American republic, of whom the leading spirit at the critical moment was William Lyon Mackenzie, an excitable and peppery Scotchman, courageous and honest, but not wise. Between Lyon Mackenzie and the Family Compact there was deadly war. The Compact tried to crush him by legal means and five times expelled him from the assembly, while their hot-headed youth broke into his printing office and wrecked the press of his patriotic journal. The governor, Sir John Colborne, was a good old soldier and a martinet of duty, but incapable of reading the times. He regarded political agitation as mutiny, gave popular deputations a chilling reception, and to the numerously signed petitions of an indignant public for the reform of abuses returned the military answer, " Gentlemen, I have received the petition of the inhabitants."

At length in both the provinces came civil war; for 1837 civil war it was rather than rebellion against the British crown. In Quebec the leader of the insurrection was Papineau, who, being a mere orator, at once collapsed and fled. Nelson showed more force and at first gained a slight success over the royal troops. The priests at first stood aloof, their nationality and religion inclining them to the French side; but they knew that incorporation with the American republic, which loomed in sight, would be unfavourable to their ascendancy, and they at last threw their weight into the scale of government. With their moral aid, and that of the British in arms added to the regular troops, the British commander easily suppressed the insurrection, and the province, its constitution suspended, lay at the feet of the government. There was little concert between the two insurrections; in fact, the feeling of the British insurgents in Upper Canada would, on the supreme question of race, have been against the insurgents of Quebec.

In Upper Canada the outbreak was due largely to the eccentricities of Sir Francis Bond Head, a governor devoid of political experience, whom the colonial office had sent out apparently because it was supposed that, as an adventurous traveller, in which character he had made his mark, he would be likely to suit the backwoods. Head threw himself into the arms of the Tory party, the core of which was the Family Compact, and used all the influence of government in favour of that party. In a general election, after a contest of the utmost violence, the Tories won the day, largely by intimidation and corruption. The extreme reform party, now hopelessly outvoted in the assembly, was driven to despair and flew to arms. The governor, confident in his moral influence and puffed up by his victory in the election, had ostentatiously denuded the province of troops and disdained all military precautions. Mackenzie brought before Toronto a force sufficient to take it with the aid of his friends within the city. But he was no general; a belated and almost farcical attack on which at last he ventured failed;

the loyalists rallied; and Mackenzie with most of his political associates fled, while two of them went to the gallows. A desultory and ineffectual war was for some time kept up with the aid of American filibusters on the border, and revived the angry passions of the war of 1812. A party of Canadians burned the filibustering schooner *Caroline*, and the arrest of one of them afterwards in the United States, where he was put on trial for his life, threatened to bring on war.

In Great Britain Liberalism was now in the ascendant and had carried parliamentary reform. As its envoy, and in its mantle, Lord Durham, the son-in-law of Lord Grey, the Radical aristocrat, the draftsman of the Reform Bill, came out as governor and high commissioner to report on the disease and prescribe the remedy. He over-rated his position and his authority, moved about, Radical though he was, in regal state, assumed the power of banishing rebels without process of law, fell into the clutches of Brougham, with whom he was at feud, was censured and resigned. But he had brought with him Charles Buller, an expert in colonial questions, with the help of whose pen and that of Gibbon Wakefield, he framed a report which by its great ability and momentous effects forms an epoch in colonial history.

1838

The Durham report recommends the union of the two provinces and the concession of responsible government, that is, of a government like the British cabinet, virtually designated by the representatives of the people and holding office by the title of their confidence. "To conduct their government," says Durham of the Canadian people, "harmoniously, in accordance with its established principles, is now the business of its rulers; and I know not how it is possible to secure that harmony in any other way, than by administering the government on those principles which have been found perfectly efficacious in Great Britain. I would not impair a single prerogative of the crown; on the contrary, I believe that the interests of the people of these colonies require the protection of prerogatives, which have not hitherto been exercised. But the crown must, on the other hand, submit to the necessary consequences of representative institutions; and if it has to carry on the government in unison with a representative body, it must consent to carry it on by means of those in whom that representative body has confidence." What Durham meant by his saving words about the prerogative is not clear; nor has he explained how supreme power could be given to the colonial parliament without taking away prerogative from the crown. No effect, at all events, has ever been given to those words.

"We can venture," said the Tory periodical of that day in a notice of the report, " to answer that every uncontradicted assertion of that volume will be made the excuse of future rebellions, every unquestioned principle will be hereafter perverted into a gospel of treason, and if that rank and infectious report does not receive the high, marked, and energetic discountenance and indignation of the imperial crown and parliament, British America is lost." If resignation of authority is loss of dominion, the prediction of the writer in the *Quarterly* that British America would be lost, can hardly be said, from the Tory point of view, to have proved substantially unfounded.

The avowed object of union was the extinction of French nationality, which the authors of the report hoped would be brought about without violence by the political subjection of the weaker element to the influence of the stronger. "I entertain," says Durham, "no doubts as to the national character which must be given to Lower Canada; it must be that of the British Empire; that of the majority of the population of British America; that of the great race which must, in the lapse of no long period of time, be predominant over the whole North American Continent. Without effecting the change so rapidly or so roughly as to shock the feelings and trample on the welfare of the existing generation, it must henceforth be the first and steady purpose of the British government to establish an English population, with English laws and language, in this Province, and to trust its government to none but a decidedly English Legislature."

Union was accepted in Upper Canada. On the French province, by which it would certainly have been rejected, it was imposed, the constitution there having been suspended. For the united provinces the constitution was in form the same as it had been for each of the provinces separately, with a governor and his executive council, a legislative council appointed by the governor and a legislative assembly elected by the people; but with "responsible government," the understanding henceforth being in Canada as in Great Britain that the governor should accept as the members of his executive council and the framers of his policy the leaders of the majority in parliament. The upper House was afterwards made, like the lower, elective with constituencies wider than those for the lower House. The same number of members in the legislative assembly was assigned to each of the two provinces, though the population of Quebec was at this time far the larger of the two.

The constitution thus granted to the colony was in reality far more democratic than that of the mother-country, where, besides a court actually present and a hereditary upper · House, there were the influences of a great land-owning gentry and other social forces of a conservative kind, as well as deep-seated tradition, to control the political action of the people.

Not without a pang or without a struggle did the Colonial Office or the governors finally acquiesce in responsible government and the virtual independence of the colony. Poulett Thomson, afterwards Lord Sydenham, 1839 sent out as governor by the Melbourne ministry, showed some inclination to revert to the old paths, shape his own policy, and hold himself responsible to the colonial office rather than to the Canadian people; but he was a shrewd politician and took care to steer clear of rocks. 1841 His successor, Bagot, though a conservative and appointed by a conservative government, surprised everybody by discreet and somewhat epicurean pliancy to the exigencies 1843 of his political position. He reigned in peace. But Metcalfe, who followed him, had been trained in the despotic government of India. Backed by the Conservative government which had sent him out, he made strenuous efforts to recover something of the old power of a governor, to shape his own course, and make his appointments himself, not at the dictation of responsible ministers. The result was a furious storm. Fiery invectives were interchanged in parliament and in the press. At elections stones and brick-bats flew. Canada was for several months without a government. The fatal illness of the 1846 governor terminated the strife. Lord Elgin, when he 1846 became governor, heartily embraced the principle of responsible government, and upon the demise of the ministry sent at once for the leader of the opposition. He flattered himself that he was able to do more under that system than he could have done if invested with personal authority. That he could have done a good deal under any system by his moral influence was most likely, for he was one of the most characteristic and best specimens of imperial statesmanship. But moral influence is not constitutional power. About the last relic of the political world before responsibility was Dominick Daly, who deemed it his duty to stay in office, any changes in the ministry and principles of government notwithstanding.

The other North American colonies, Nova Scotia, New Brunswick, and Prince Edward Island, went through a similar course of contest for supreme power between the governor with the council nominated by him and the elective assembly, ending in the same way. On them also the boon of responsible government was conferred. In the case of Prince Edward Island the political problem had been complicated by an agrarian struggle with the body of grantees among whom the crown, in its feudal character of supreme land-owner, had parcelled out the island.

Liberalism now gained the upper hand in the united Canada and ultimately carried its various points. Exiled rebels returned. William Lyon Mackenzie himself was in time again elected to parliament, and Rolph, another fugitive, was admitted to the government. The clergy 1853 reserves were secularized, university education was made unsectarian, and religious equality became the law. The signories in the French province were abolished, 1854 compensation being given to the lords. The passions of the civil war were for a moment revived when an Act was passed awarding compensation to those whose property had suffered in the suppression of the rebellion. This the Tories took to be payment of rebels. They dropped their loyalty, as Tories are apt to do when Liberals are in power, stoned the governor-general, Lord Elgin, who had assented to the Bill, and burned the parliament-house at Montreal. But Lord Elgin, calmly wise and well sustained at home, restored peace.

1850

As an attempt to suppress the French nationality, union signally failed. The French, the mass of them at least, clung together more closely than ever, and, the other race being split into factions, held the key of the political situation. They enforced the repeal of the clause in the Union Act, making English the only official language. A candidate for the speakership was rejected on the ground of his ignorance of French. At most the French politicians became half Anglicized, as their successors do at present, for the purposes of the political field. It came to be recognized as a rule that government must have a majority of both sections. To the antagonism between English and French was added the strife between Orangism, which had been imported into Canada, though rather in its political than in its religious character, and the catholics, French or Irish. The population of the British province having now outgrown that of the French province, agitation for representation by population commenced on the British side. There ensued a series of cabals, intrigues, and faction fights which lasted for about a quarter of a century, all intelligible principles of difference being lost in the struggle for place, though one question after another was taken up as a counter in the

1823

game. The only available statesmanship was address in
the management of party. In this John A. Macdonald   1817–
was supreme, and gained the ascendancy which made him   1891
ruler of Canada for many years.

Durham, in his report, had spoken freely of the sad
contrast between the wonderful prosperity of the United
States and the comparative backwardness of Canada. The
contrast was still more felt when by England's adoption
of free trade Canada lost her privileges in the British
market, while she was excluded from the market of her
own continent. A petition signed by three hundred and
twenty-five persons, including the chiefs of commerce pro-   1849
posed among other remedies, "a friendly and peaceful
separation from British connection, and a union upon
equitable terms with the great North American Confederacy of Sovereign States." To open a safety valve
for this discontent, Lord Elgin went to Washington and
negotiated a reciprocity treaty with the United States.   1854
The Democratic party, that is the party of slavery, then
dominant would be ready enough to do whatever would
prevent Canada from entering the union and turning the
balance against slavery. At the same time that Canada
lost her privilege in the British market, British privilege
in the Canadian market was virtually given up, and the
colony received fiscal independence.

Faction, cabal, intrigue, and the antagonism between
the British and the French province ended in a political
deadlock, from which the leaders of parties, combining for
the moment, agreed to escape by merging their quarrels
in a confederation of all the British provinces of North   1867
America. Into this confederation Upper or British
Canada, now called Ontario, and French Canada, now

called Quebec, came at once. New Brunswick came early and freely. Nova Scotia was drawn in by questionable means. Prince Edward Island came in later of her own accord. The vast Northwest was afterwards purchased of the Hudson's Bay Company and added to the confederation after the American model as a set of territories to be received, when peopled, as provinces of the Dominion. British Columbia was ultimately incorporated by the construction of the Canadian Pacific railway across the continent. Some of the authors of confederation would have preferred a legislative to a federal union. This was precluded by the jealous nationality of the French province and its adherence to its own civil law.

1873

1870

1871

Federation this process was called, but the form of polity comprised in the British North America Act is not that of federation proper; it is that of a nation with a federal structure. There is a wide and important difference between the two. In federation proper, which has usually been the offspring of union for common defence, the several states remain sovereign. The federal government is formed of delegates from the several states. Its powers are confined to the objects of the bond, security from without and peace within; it has the power of requisition only, not of taxation; nor has it any general legislative powers. The American colonies during their struggle for independence were a federation proper; having afterwards adopted their present constitution, they became a nation with a federal structure; if any doubt remained upon that point, it was dispelled by the war of secession. The political parties are national; they extend into state politics, and there has been a general tendency of the national to prevail over the federal element. In the case of Canadian confederation the national element was from the first stronger than the federal in this respect, that the residuary power which the American constitution leaves in the states was by the Canadian constitution assigned to the Dominion. On the other hand, the geographical relations of the Canadian provinces, which are stretched in broken line across the continent, and separated from each other by great spaces or barriers of nature, so that there is not much natural trade or interchange of population, are a bar to the ascendancy of the national over the federal element. Provinces send their delegations to Ottawa charged with provincial interests, especially with reference to the outlay on public works; and it is necessary to have thirteen members in the cabinet in order to give each province its share, while a cabinet, or, to speak more properly, an administrative council, of eight suffices for the population, fourteen times larger, of the United States. Political parties, however, extend over all the provinces and generally into provincial politics, though in the remoter provinces, with a large element, and in British Columbia with a predominance, of local objects. On the two old Canadas, now Ontario and Quebec, but chiefly on Ontario, have lain the stress and burden of confederation. Ontario has paid more than sixty per cent. of the taxes.

The imperial element in the Canadian constitution is represented, besides the appointment of the governor-general and the commander of the militia, by an imperial veto on Canadian legislation, which, however, is becoming almost nominal; the appellate jurisdiction of the privy council, which has been partly pared away; and the subjection of Canadian relations with foreign countries to the authority of the imperial Foreign Office, which again is gradually giving way to Canadian autonomy, though with British responsibility and under the protection of the British army and navy; a colony having no means of asserting its claims by war. Nor must we forget the influence of imperial titles and honours which on colonial politicians is great. The Canadian constitution, moreover, though framed in the main by Canadian politicians, is embodied in an imperial Act of Parliament, subject to repeal or amendment only by the same authority by which it was passed. A community living under a constitution imposed by external authority, and without the power of peace or war, can hardly be said yet to have attained the status of a nation.

1867

The monarchical element consists of the governor-general, representing the British sovereign and equally divested of personal power, with lieutenant-governors of provinces appointed nominally by the governor-general, really by the prime minister, and figureheads like their chief, the places being in fact retiring pensions for veteran politicians.

There is an upper House in the shape of a Senate, the members of which are appointed for life, ostensibly by the crown, really by the leader of the party in power. If the appointments were really in the crown, there might be some opening for the general eminence of which a model Senate would be the seat. As it is, these appointments merely form an addition to the patronage fund of party. The illusory name of the "crown" reconciles people to the exercise, by party leaders, of powers which might otherwise be withheld. A certain number of places in the Senate is assigned to each province; so that whatever power the Senate has may be reckoned among the federal elements of the constitution.

The Canadian constitution, with its cabinet of ministers sitting in parliament and controlling legislation, its prerogative exercised formally by the crown, really by the prime minister, of calling and dissolving parliament, adapts itself to party government, for which the American constitution, with its election of a president for a stated term, and its separation of the administrative council, miscalled a cabinet, from the legislature, is a manifest misfit. Party takes its usual form and proceeds by its usual methods, though the necessity of holding together provinces geographically and commercially disunited, so as to form a basis for the government, induces a special resort to the influence of federal subsidies for local works.

The exact relation of a colony on the footing on which Canada now is to the imperial country it would be difficult to define, though definition may presently be needful if misunderstanding is to be escaped. The crown, by the British North America Act, renounces its supreme ownership of the land by handing over the lands to the provinces. The personal fealty of the colonists to the sovereign of Great Britain remains.

Australian federation so called, is like that of Canada, not a federation proper, but a nation with a federal structure. It seems to postulate cabinet and, therefore, party government. But how are Australian parties to be formed? How is the cabinet to be evolved? The machine has been constructed with care and doubtless with skill. But what is to be the motor? In the case of the Canadian confederation, parties were taken over from the two united provinces which formed the core of the Dominion, and are still in some measure founded on the opposition between French and English, though the dividing line has grown very indistinct, and the conflict has long since become almost entirely one of electioneering tactics with the usual accompaniments of that game.

The political history of Canada is in its main features that of the self-governing colonies in North America, Australasia, and South Africa. All have passed from the state of dependencies ruled by a governor representing the colonial office to that of self-government and virtual independence, for which some now propose, over-riding geographical conditions and difference of circumstance, to substitute a federal bond. Recent developments, such as the socialism and feminism of Australasia, fall not within the compass of this work. A specially important part has been played in Australasian politics by the land question, the source of which, as has been already said, is the doctrine, handed down from feudal times, of the crown's lordship of all land.

South Africa, a Dutch colony conquered by Great Britain, has been the unhappy scene of a struggle between the British and Dutch races and between each of them and native tribes, some of them powerful and warlike. This again falls not within the compass of the present work.

The West Indian colonies as a group, and notably the most important of them, Jamaica, may be said to have held a place intermediate between self-government and the government of the crown. But the political history of all those islands is slavery.

It is not likely that there was any scruple about slavery

in the mind of Cromwell, whose belief in the Old Testament was uncritical, and might mislead him, not on this question alone. But in attempting the conquest of Hispaniola and in conquering Jamaica his main object probably was, by advancing the outposts of England and Protestantism, to break into the Spanish monopoly of South American lands and waters. He put down secession in Barbadoes, but gave that colony articles of liberty commercial and fiscal as well as political, such as if given to the North American colonies would have averted the American revolution.

All-powerful at sea while she was weak by land, Great Britain found herself after each war the mistress of more sugar and slave islands and more deeply implicated in their unhallowed trade.

There is abundant evidence to show that Jamaica was in the days of slavery full of cruelty and vice. Johnson described it as "a place of great wealth and dreadful wickedness, a den of tyrants and a dungeon of slaves." " Here's to the next insurrection of the negroes in the West Indies!" was the toast which this high Tory gave to a party in high Tory Oxford. Flogging and branding were the ordinary, hanging, burning and gibbeting alive, were the extraordinary, modes of enforcing submission. Killing a negro was long even by law no murder. It was an open question among slave-owners whether it was better to rear or to buy slaves. Of the proprietors the principal were resident in England, where they corrupted society, bought seats in parliament, and there, with their compact phalanx, upheld slavery and the slave trade. The island was left in the hands of slave-drivers, who were sure to be the vilest of mankind. The decencies of civilized life were of course denied to the slave, and if Methodists or Baptists dared to preach religion to him, they were summarily put down. It was in Jamaica apparently that the system was at its worst.

Jamaica and the other West Indian islands had constitutions varying in some respects, but of the general colonial type, with a governor and an elective assembly, the assembly of course consisting exclusively of whites, and the governor having probably as a rule practically more power than he would have in a white colony, though, as Johnson said, "The loudest yelps for liberty were heard among the drivers of negroes."

1833   Emancipation found the negro totally incapable of political self-government. Apprenticeship, even if it could have been carried into effect, would not have sufficed to bridge such a gulf. To this day the negro has nowhere developed a capacity for active citizenship. In San Domingo he had a bad start, it is true, his commonwealth having been born in one of the most fiendish of servile wars. But in the hundred years which have since elapsed he has made little, if any, progress in self-government. A series of usurped dictatorships has been his history. There were, moreover, a physical chasm between the white man and the negro, a social chasm between the deposed master and the liberated slave, and a contemptuous hatred of the black on the part of the white man, which made their union in a commonwealth hopeless. The attempt to form a united commonwealth of whites and blacks has hideously failed in the United States. If it was possible, the negro should have been treated in both cases as a ward of the state without political power, but with personal and industrial rights, and with superior authority to guard them.

Scarcely had emancipation been completed when the restiveness of the assembly of Jamaica constrained the Whig ministry to propose the suspension of the Jamaican constitution. In the attempt to carry the Bill the ministry fell, and when restored to power it failed to pass an effectual measure. But the union of the races in Jamaica was hopeless, though in the lesser islands, with their small white populations and under economic conditions more conducive to negro industry, the friction was not so great. At last, after a period of brooding mistrust and hatred, with political wrangling in the Jamaican assembly, a war of race, violent and bloody, broke out. A local and accidental riot among the blacks, caused by the unpopularity of a district magistrate, was mistaken by the whites, or they pretended to mistake it, for a general insurrection. They made the governor proclaim martial law, and carried on a reign of terror, hanging and flogging both men and women and burning their houses, which brought a serious stain upon the honour of England, where the governing classes, swayed by imperialist sentiment, and many of them by Carlyle's gospel of force, shut against mercy the gate of justice. The governor, however, was recalled; the constitution of Jamaica was suspended; and a royal governor went out, invested with power to hold the balance of equity between the races. Since that time there has, at all events, been peace.

1839

1865

Crown colonies and fortresses have no political history. But one of the fortresses, besides having a military history of extraordinary interest, has exercised a momentous influence on the policy of the country. England did not in the first instance come fairly into possession of Gibral-

1713 tar. It was taken, not in a war with Spain, but in a war in support of a claimant to the Spanish throne, in whose name and interest all captures were supposed to be made. The possession, however, was afterwards amply recognized and confirmed. It brought England, and was sure to bring her, the undying enmity of Spain. On this account principally English statesmen, Townshend, Stanhope, Shelburne, and even Chatham, were willing to resign it. But it had taken the hold on the popular imagination which Calais had in former days, and which two memorable sieges confirmed. Again and again, Spain, sinking into decay, dragged her enfeebled limbs to the attack. She was as far as possible from being inclined to help into existence an American republic in close and dangerous neighbourhood to her own South American possessions; but in the hope of regaining Gibraltar, she joined the league of maritime powers which brought Great Britain to the brink of ruin. Gibraltar, with the subsequent addition of Malta, has drawn with it the policy of ascendancy in the Mediterranean, the acquisition of Egypt and Cyprus, and in some measure the antagonism to Russia as a power striving to force her way into that sea. Ascendancy in the Mediterranean must depend on the ability of Great Britain to maintain an overwhelming sea power. This, again, must depend on the continuance of her superiority in wealth, and, therefore, on her supremacy in manufactures and trade. But we do not presume to lift the veil of the future. Among other things, who can foretell what effect the progressive invention of tremendous instruments of destruction may hereafter produce on war power and all that depends upon it, particularly at sea?

The British empire in India is an empire in the true sense of the word; yet it is unlike all the empires of history. It is held on the other side of the globe by sea power, and in a climate in which the natives of the imperial country must always be sojourners and can never make their home; the races subject to it are absolutely alien, not in blood, form, and colour only, but in mind, sentiment, and religious belief, to the conquering race; while the professed aim, which in no small degree really rules the practice of its government, is the welfare not so much of the conqueror as of the conquered. The Carthaginian empire was held by sea power, but in that respect alone resembled the British empire in India, which it did not approach in scale and still less in beneficence. The Roman empire, though vast, was still in a ring fence. Romans could make their abode in any part of it, and the effete religions of the old world presented no such social obstacle to a tolerant conqueror as the caste of the Hindoo, while the population probably did not amount to two-fifths of that of Hindostan. Spain held a transatlantic empire in South America. But that empire was in no respect a counterpart of the British empire in India. With regard to unselfishness and beneficence of aim, it was not a counterpart, but a contrast.

When, in the latter part of the eighteenth century, the Mogul empire, of which the jewelled throne was at Delhi, having reached its zenith of greatness under Akbar, having declined under his immediate successors, having under Aurungzeb veiled its growing weakness beneath its bloated pomp, at length received its mortal wound from the murderous invasion of Nadir Shah, three great trading companies had their privileged factories on the coast of 1738

Hindostan and faced each other, as competitors for the command of the Eastern trade. All were armed, as the lawlessness of the seas in those times and the hostile relations into which they were often brought by wars among the home governments required. At an earlier period Portugal had aspired to supremacy in the Indian seas; marvels had been wrought by her adventurous mariners under Vasco de Gama, Cabral, and Albuquerque. But she had not strength to hold an empire on the other side of the globe, and at the critical moment she fell into the grasp of Spain. Of the three rival powers left in the field, Holland, it has been remarked, had the advantage of undivided devotion to the aims of commerce; but to her, again, strength was wanting, and she was crippled by the attacks of France, who thus unwittingly played the game of England. Of England's rivals France was the most formidable. But the prize was to the greatest sea power, and England was the stronger upon the sea. France, moreover, was a despotism sinking into decay, ruled by harlots, ungrateful to its best servants. It could requite the zeal of Lally in the contest for India, by sending him to
1766 death, after a secret trial on a fictitious charge, in a common cart, with a gag in his mouth. The English adventurer had to back him a parliament and the spirit of a free as well as largely commercial nation. He had also in dealing with the heathen the advantage, like the Roman, perhaps even more than the Roman, of religious indifference; he could scrupulously respect the faith and rites of the Hindoo even to the extreme, for a long time, of tolerating suttee; he could swear to a treaty by the sun and moon, and furnish a guard to the temple of Juggernaut. He took no missionaries with him, but long discouraged

their coming; whereas the commander of a Portuguese expedition took with him eight friars to preach the catholic faith, and orders to carry fire and sword into every district which would not listen to their preaching.

France, nevertheless, had nearly grasped the prize. The imperial and unscrupulous genius of Dupleix, who knew the secret of dealing with native powers and had learned to make use of native soldiery, was on the eve of decisive victory over the English when Robert Clive, a youth of twenty-five, and bred a clerk in a commercial office, by his native genius for war and diplomacy, which was recognized with happy penetration by the mercantile head of the establishment, turned the scale in favour of his own countrymen. Presently the Dutch also were driven off the field. With the name of Clive, as the founder of the empire, must be linked those of Lawrence, the father of the Indian army, Eyre Coote, and Forde.

1748

In Hindostan there was no nationality, no spirit of national resistance to foreign conquest. The Hindoo population was a vast expanse of social tissue, of which the life was caste and the organization was the communistic village, a remnant of the primeval state. In the realm of the Mahrattas was a spirit of race, in the Sikhs a spirit of religious fraternity; and it was in the Mahrattas and the Sikhs that British power was destined to find its doughtiest foes. None of the dynasties carved by usurping satraps out of the wreck of the Mogul empire had any seat in the heart of the people. The Mogul empire itself had been founded by foreign invaders from the mountains of the north, whence conquest had repeatedly descended on the enervated people of the sultry plains. The Hindoos were ready with perfect indifference to bow to any government; any power of order, however alien, they were ready to welcome when plundering usurpation or anarchy filled their land and over it swept like whirlwinds the Mahratta raids. In such a chaos British dominion could not fail even in its own despite to grow. War power enough to enable the company to hold its ground against its rivals had always been necessary. Sir Josiah Child, the dictator of the India House, under William III., had desired that his company should be a military power. The sage Sir Thomas Roe, on the other hand, had conjured the company to content itself with factories and trade. Roe's advice the company was always inclined to follow, its heart being set on dividends. But the finger of manifest destiny pointed the other way. Brought inevitably into collision with one barbaric power after another, the company's government was compelled to conquer, and having conquered, to annex. With the exception of Scinde, where the impetuosity of Sir Charles Napier made the British power the aggressor, the conquests of which the empire is built may be said to have been made in defensive war.

1756 Surajah Dowlah, Nabob of Bengal and an insolent barbarian, attacked Calcutta, took it, and through his officers perpetrated the hideous tragedy of the Black Hole. Clive came to the rescue, at Plassey virtually conquered Bengal, though a puppet nabob was kept upon its throne, and opened to the greedy eyes of the company's servants the glittering treasury of the East. During his absence in England, merchants' clerks on small salaries being let loose upon a ravishing field of plunder, a scene of the foulest corruption and most iniquitous oppression ensued; fortunes were made in scandalous ways and carried home to buy rotten boroughs, degrade the legislature, and alarm the conscience of the nation. There is hardly a darker stain on the honour of England. Clive returned, restored order, arrested abuse, and strove to prevent it for the future by giving the company's servants regular and sufficient salaries, and forbidding the acceptance of presents. For clandestine and irresponsible influence over Bengal he, by taking a formal grant from the phantom at Delhi, substituted avowed and responsible dominion. A trading company thus became king of the richest of all Indian domains, with revenues bearing no mean proportion to those of the imperial country. The first step towards empire had been taken and it determined the march. As a necessary instrument of dominion, the Company began to form, in addition to the British troops at its disposal, an army of sepoys or native soldiers, easily recruited in the swarms of mercenaries of which the unhappy land was full.

The eyes of the home government were now anxiously turned to the growth of a political dominion in the hands of a trading company with an army and a diplomacy of its own, making wars and alliances without much reference to the king's government, which, nevertheless, was compromised; while reports of gross misdoings found their way to England and were confirmed by the sinister wealth of the "nabobs." In 1773, after a wrangle of the government with the directory, which had a tower of strength in British respect for charters, a Regulating Act 1773 was passed establishing a governor-general, whose authority was to extend over all the Indian possessions of Great Britain, with an advisory council of four, each of whom was to have a vote; an impolitic division of the command. At the same time was established a supreme court of justice for the administration of English law, better than lawlessness but ill suited to the meridian of Hindostan.

1774 The first governor-general was Warren Hastings, to whom it fell to organize and preserve what Clive had won. With consummate ability he performed both tasks; the second with the calmest courage in face of gathering perils, aggravated by the extremity to which the conflict with the American colonists had brought the mother-country, and by a coalition of the great maritime powers against her which endangered her indispensable supremacy at sea. At the same time he was contending, not merely with factious opposition, but with the bitterest personal enmity in his council, and could carry his vital measures only by his own casting vote. Out of his ebbing revenues he had at once to meet his own political necessities and to satisfy the commercial cravings of his company. This was his excuse for hiring out a British force to the Vizier of Oude to serve against the Rohillas, though there were also reasons of British policy for the measure, and the Rohillas, instead of being an idyllic and poetic race, were a dominant tribe of Afghan free-booters, whose overthrow and partial eviction would be a relief to the subjugated Hindoo. The same dire necessity dictated the exaction at a crisis of extreme peril of what would otherwise have been an exorbitant aid from a feudatory, Cheyt Sing, the Rajah of Benares, and the impounding of a treasure which had been appropriated by the Begums of Oude, but to which, it seems, they had no title, while for the force applied by native cruelty to them and their attendants Hastings was at most indirectly responsible. Not one of the acts taken at the worst could warrant Burke in saying that Hastings had in his whole course "manifested a heart dyed deep in blackness, a heart gangrened to the very core." In all Burke's torrent of invective nothing is more unjust than his assertion that Hastings' ruling motive was thirst of money. Hastings had, at all events, a soul above sordid gain. He saved British dominion in India, for which a life of impeachment was a poor reward. The abandonment of Hastings to his enemies, whatever was the motive, is a blot upon Pitt's fame.

The coalition government of Fox and North, inspired no doubt by Burke, whose generous heart had been wrung, and whose vivid imagination had been fired almost to frenzy, by the wrongs done to ancient dynasties and fanes, had brought in a pair of Bills, drawn probably by Burke's hand, by which, if they had passed, the whole government and management of the territorial possessions, revenues, and commerce of the Company would have been vested in seven directors named in the Act, that is, by the leaders of the majority in parliament, for a term of four years. There was to be a subordinate board of nine directors qualified by holding two thousand pounds of the Company's stock for the special direction of commerce. All monopolies were to be abolished, acceptance of presents was to be prohibited, a state of inheritance was to be secured to the native land-holders, and servants of the Company and agents of native princes were to be excluded from the House of Commons. A cry at once arose that the coalition was grasping the dominion of India with patronage which would seat it permanently in power on the ruins of the constitution. The Company appealed to reverence for charters; an argument futile when the subject was not a private privilege but a public

1783

trust, yet telling, and driven home by the imprudent words of that advocate of the Bill who scoffed at a charter as a parchment with a piece of wax dangling from it, a description not less applicable to the title-deeds of estates. To the assumption of commercial management by a government there was a manifest objection. But the Bill in reality was killed by the unpopularity of the coalition, which enabled the king to defeat it, to trip up the ministry which had framed it, and to call the youthful Pitt to power.

A change, however, there had to be. Burke, if he had failed as a legislator, had been magnificently successful as a preacher; and such a reign of corruption and extortion as was presently revealed by his immortal speech on the Nabob of Arcot's debts no statesman could permit to continue. One of the first measures of Pitt was an India 1784 Bill, leaving the commercial management in the hands of the Company, but placing the government, with all its functions, political, diplomatic, military, and fiscal, under the control of a board of six members of the Privy Council appointed by the crown, with a cabinet minister for that department at its head. The appointment of the governor-general remained, in accordance with the Regulation Act, legally vested in the court of directors, but he was practically selected by the crown. The patronage generally was left to the Company, though by amicable understanding much of it went to the government, and, being administered by Dundas, helped largely to keep Scotland Pittite.

The Bill having passed, Lord Cornwallis went out, the 1785 first of a line of governors-general invested with the full authority of parliament and with the delegated dignity of the crown. Cornwallis was an excellent man and a noble example of the class of statesmen formed in the service not of party but of the empire. He found the Indian civil service still in a degraded and corrupt state; freed its members from temptation by raising salaries to the proper mark, and by his influence and example improved its social tone. Less happy, though not less well intentioned was his "permanent settlement" of the vital questions of land ownership and taxation. Bent on conferring upon India the blessings of a squirarchy, he thought to find squires in the zemindars, who were really collectors of the revenue, though often with a permanent interest, and made them proprietors in fee, only paying a quit rent to the government. There was no such tie between these men and the cultivator as there was in England between landlord and tenant, and the result was the oppression and impoverishment of the peasantry of Bengal. Warned by the failure, later legislators have recognized in the cultivator the proprietor of the soil.

1793

Pitt's Act of 1784 embodied the declaration that to "pursue schemes of conquest and extension of dominion in India were measures repugnant to the will, the honour, and the policy of the nation." It prohibited the governor-general in council from declaring war, entering into any treaty for making war, or guaranteeing the possessions of any native princes or states, except where hostilities against the British nation in India had been actually commenced or prepared, without express command and authority from the home government. With these injunctions Cornwallis, himself moderate and cautious, would gladly have complied. But compliance in that seething and tossing element of anarchy, usurpation, and rapine was beyond his power. In Mysore, among a population then warlike, a plundering sultanate had been founded by Hyder Ali, an able and unscrupulous adventurer who had formed a powerful army, and at one time had inflicted a serious defeat on the British and threatened the existence of their power. The conflict was renewed with Hyder's heir Tippoo, a frantic despot spurred on not only by his own rapacity and pride, but by the inspirations of Bonaparte, who ceased not himself to hanker for a career of Oriental conquest, and hoped here to strike England by land as he could not strike her by sea. Cornwallis conquered, and showed his respect for the rule of moderation by leaving to Tippoo half his territories and his fortress capital of Seringapatam.

1784

England was now in India a great power. She was not yet paramount. For a paramount power capable of maintaining a general peace, such as in his day Akbar had maintained, the torn and distracted country yearned. Gravitation towards a new centre had begun. Wellesley, who succeeded Cornwallis as governor-general, was a "glorious little man" of a thoroughly imperial cast of mind, fond even of the trappings of empire, brimful of energy and daring, regardless of the commerical objects in comparison with the political objects of his government, and somewhat scornful of "the cheese-mongers of Leadenhall Street," who, on their side, watched the play of his genius with alarm. He distinctly resolved to make England not only a great but the paramount power, extending her peace over the continent, rendering the native principalities subsidiary to her military force, and bringing them under her diplomatic control. To effect this he had to overthrow the sultanate of Mysore and the Mahratta confederacy, which alone of the native powers retained

1798

formidable force. Grounds of war in both cases were
given or easily found. Mysore, he overthrew by the 1799
hand of General Harris, the Mahratta confederacy by the 1805
hand of his brother, Arthur Wellesley, the conqueror of
Napoleon that was to be. A set of subsidiary treaties
ranged the native principalities as military dependencies
under the British government; the British peace was
established over India; and Great Britain as a paramount,
though not as an indigenous, power filled the vacant
throne of the Mogul. In the train of the Mahratta confederacy had prowled a jackal horde of Pindarees, free-
booters of the vilest kind, whose extinction followed in 1817
due course.

Nothing in the exploits of Cortez and Pizarro, or even
those of Alexander, is more wonderful than the victories
of the British armies in India. Plassey was won by four
thousand men against sixty thousand; Assaye by four
thousand five hundred against fifty thousand in a strong
position with a hundred pieces of cannon. The arms
were equal; the natives had sometimes been trained by
European officers; the British soldier had to fight and
march, sometimes to make forced marches, in pursuit of
a nimble enemy, beneath the Indian sun, probably in the
old-fashioned accoutrements and without the palliatives
which he has now. Most Englishmen still know little
of the achievements or the heroes. They have heard the
names of Clive, Lake, and Wellington, perhaps those of
Lawrence and Eyre Coote, but not those of Pattinson and
Pottinger. Wellesley affected to doubt whether the reward of a policy so little in accord with the golden rule
of moderation would be requited with honour or with the
gallows. Whatever the cheese-mongers of Leadenhall

Street would have done, the national government requited it with honour. Resolutions condemning him were moved by the party of moderation in both houses, but were overwhelmingly defeated.

By the circumstances of his reign Wellesley had been deeply impressed with the necessity of a trained civil service. Merchants' clerks, educated only for the counting house, could not be fit instruments of government for the paramount power of Hindostan. Wellesley set up a training institution at Calcutta. The measure was regarded with an evil eye by the Company, which perhaps scented a transition from commercial to political interests and aims. The upshot, however, was the college at Haileybury, of which Wellesley, a fine classical scholar and a first-rate writer of Latin verses, selected the motto, *Redit a nobis aurora diemque reducit*. By this combination of special training with adequate salaries and early responsibilities was formed by far the greatest civil service that the world had ever seen.

1806

So far the Company had retained its monopoly of the Eastern trade and the spirit of the trader therewith. Its dividends had been uppermost in its mind, and in their interest it had been interfering with the action of the governor-general even in his hour of peril. It had jealously excluded European settlers from the country. It had prohibited Christian missions, lest a shock should be given to the religious prejudices of the Hindoo, so that it might be said that the only religion which could not be preached in India was that of the ruling race. But in 1813, on the renewal of the charter for twenty years, the monopoly of the Indian trade was abolished, and that of the trade with China alone was left. The

1813

India House, through its forty members in the House of Commons, struggled hard, and of course predicted ruin. Its predictions were, of course, signally falsified by the growth of a free trade. Lord Grenville would have gone further; he would have made over India entirely to the crown, obviating the danger to the constitution from the increase of crown patronage by throwing the civil service open to competition. Governments, he held, were always bad hands at trade, and traders were always bad hands at government. Public sentiment prevailed over India House prejudices, mistaken, though not unnatural. India was opened to European settlers and to the missionaries, without bad effects in either case. The Hindoo, though intensely jealous of his caste, is tolerant of religious speculation. Christianity presently made its appearance in the angelic form of Heber.

1822

In passing from the control of the Company to that of parliamentary ministers, India became exposed to the influences of political party. From these, however, it has suffered little, governors-general having doffed the party politician when they donned the viceroy, retaining at most their general tendencies, progressive or cautious, Conservative or Liberal. The Marquis of Hastings, who was an ex-governor-general, had, as Lord Moira, been a fighting Liberal in the British parliament and a resolute opponent of the policy of coercion for Ireland. As governor-general he remained Liberal, perhaps to as great an extent as a government of conquest could bear. He gave India a free press, which the European settlers, now admitted, were ready to set on foot, proclaiming that "it was salutary for government, even when its intentions were most pure, to look to the control of public opinion." Leadenhall Street quaked, and might perhaps have argued that these principles were suited to the British meridian, and that it was not upon public opinion that the power of a conqueror was based. Hastings also flouted the belief that much light was not good for the conquered by striving to promote education, though Leadenhall Street might still have its misgivings as to what, by the light afforded it, a conquered population might see.

1833 In 1833, among the fruits of parliamentary reform, came, with the renewal of the charter, an Act which took away from the Company its remaining monopoly, that of the China trade, discharged the magnificent fleet of clippers which had been its pride, finally divested it of its commercial character, leaving only the mercantile names, and made it simply the administration of the Indian empire under the board of control. It is not denied that from that time the policy of the Company was liberal, and directed entirely to the maintenance of the empire and the welfare of the people of Hindostan. Lord William
1828–1835 Bentinck, who at this time was governor-general, could enter on a bold course of social reform with a perfectly free hand. He ventured to abolish suttee, and no convulsion followed. He took measures for the education of a class of natives in Western literature and science. He advanced natives to official positions. He promoted the settlement of Europeans in India, the investment of European capital, and the extension of steam communication. In his time, with the aid of Macaulay, was framed a code which combined the principles of European justice with regard for Hindoo custom. By the acting governor-general, who after him held the reins, unrestricted freedom was given to the press. Bentinck's rule was marked

also by the suppression of Thuggee, a hideous brotherhood of murder, the existence of which, with the fiend goddess of its worship, was almost enough in itself to prove that conquest was a blessing.

At the Sutlej it was believed that the empire had reached its Rubicon. Beyond it, in the Punjaub, was the domain of the Sikhs, a sect of religious purists formed into an army, dissenters from Brahminical caste, and at the same time deadly enemies to Mahometanism, which persecuted them to the death. Under the able and unscrupulous leadership of Ranjit Singh, they had become a formidable force, trained by European officers, with a powerful artillery. After the death of Ranjit, who left no strong successor, anarchy ensued, and the Khalsa, as the Sikh brotherhood was called, inflamed with fanaticism, pride, and lust of conquest, crossed the Sutlej and hurled itself 1845 on the British dominions. There ensued a series of desperate battles in which the empire fought for its life, while England waited with throbbing heart for tidings of the war. Nothing in our military history is more impressive than the night of Ferozeshah, when, after the doubt- 1845 ful struggle of the day, the British regiments lay down almost under the Sikh guns; while Lord Hardinge, who, with a noble sense of supreme duty, had laid aside the governor-general, went to and fro over the field reviving the spirits of the troops for the renewal of the battle on the morrow. Having measured their strength with the Englishman and found him their master, the Sikhs took his pay and became the best of his native soldiers.

By the annexation of the Punjaub, marvellously organ- 1849 ized under the hand of Lawrence, the empire reached its final boundary. Invasion no longer threatened from the mountains on the north. The settled and strong, though rude, confederacy of the Afghans had barred that gate. But though Moguls were no more to be dreaded, Russia, in nervous apprehensions, took their place. Russian dominion had grown in central, like British dominion in southern Asia, by collision with a series of barbarous powers which were successively annexed, and there was nothing to prevent the two empires from resting in peaceful neighbourhood with the wall of independent tribes between them. Yet there were British statesmen who always imagined that they saw an invading army of Russians issuing from Herat. The result was the ill-starred expedition to Cabul, ending in the most disastrous of those defeats of the British, the memory of which, it seems, is ominously cherished by the Hindoo. Neither from invasion nor from insurrection among a people, long disarmed, and divided among themselves into Mahometans and Hindoos, did danger thenceforth impend over British empire in India. If danger now impends, it is from the impossibility of acclimatizing the ruling race; from the difficulty of holding open the road to India in the face of all the maritime powers; from the financial difficulty of administering a poor though gorgeous country on the footing demanded by European opinion ; above all, from the growing pressure of multiplying myriads of human sheep, helpless and reckless, with their plagues and famines, upon the energies and resources of a paternal government.

1837- 1842

The conqueror's moderation had left a fifth of Hindostan under native princes, whose position was that of feudatories of the empire, bound to aid it in war, to respect its peace, to contract no alliances without its sanction, to receive each of them at his court a Resident as the organ of imperial authority and supervision. To the prince the empire guaranteed his throne so long as he governed well or not intolerably ill. For intolerable misgovernment the native remedy was dynastic revolution. The power, which by its protectorate deprived the people of that remedy, was bound to provide a remedy in its place. Lord Dalhousie, as governor-general, was probably disposed to territorial extension; but he was only doing his duty in deposing the imbecile despot whose foul train of sycophants, buffoons, and harpies was holding a reign of the most insufferable misrule in Oude. That he was equally wise in proceeding to the annexation of Oude is less certain. He thereby at all events helped to charge the mine, of which a terrible explosion followed. 1856

The great mutiny of the native army of the Company, which shook the empire to its foundations, was the last of a series caused by suspected attacks on caste. The great mutiny at Vellore, in which the native troops massacred their European officers, had been caused by a suspected attack on caste in the regulation of the soldier's headgear. Brahmin regiments had mutinied on being ordered to cross the sea, which their caste forbade. Of the great mutiny the immediate cause appears to have been a suspicion that caste was being furtively attacked by the introduction of the fat of cows into the cartridges. But the Bengal army of the Company, recruited from the higher castes, had become too confident in its own strength, while the proportion of British troops was too small, and too many European officers were withdrawn to the general staff. The circle of the deposed tyrant and those who had subsisted by the tyranny in Oude were prepared for mis- 1857 1806 chief, if not actually plotting, while in the people of Oude at large there may have been some dislike of annexation. The opportunity was seized by the outcast Nana Sahib of avenging a wrong which he fancied he had received in the disallowance of his claim to an inheritance by the Hindoo title of an adopted son. The feudatory princes, on the other hand, when the crash came, remained faithful to the hand which held them on their thrones. The newly-conquered Sikhs fought not only well but savagely on the British side. The people in general did not stir; they had long lost warlike tendencies or qualities and probably regarded almost with apathy the struggle for dominion. The outbreak in this case, therefore, has been truly described as a mutiny, not a rebellion. At the same time caste was the immediate cause, and caste is the nationality of the Hindoo.

Horrible atrocities were committed in the rising, atrocities not less horrible in its suppression. England paid in the effect upon her own character the worst of all the penalties of conquest. The panic rage of the dominant race and its hatred of the conquered broke forth with fearful violence. "It is a terrible business," says Lord Elgin, who witnessed the scene, "this living among inferior races. I have seldom from man or woman since I came to the East heard a sentence which was reconcilable with the hypothesis that Christianity had ever come into the world. Detestation, contempt, ferocity, vengeance, whether Chinamen or Indians be the object. There are some three or four hundred servants in this house. When one first passes by their *salaaming* one feels a little awkward. But the feeling soon wears off, and one moves among them with perfect indifference, treating them, not as dogs, because in that case one would whistle to them and pat them, but as machines with which one can have no communication or sympathy. Of course those who can speak the language are somewhat more *en rapport* with the natives, but very slightly so, I take it. When the passions of fear and hatred are engrafted on this indifference, the result is frightful; an absolute callousness as to the sufferings of the objects of those passions, which must be witnessed to be understood and believed." The government had removed some commissioners, who not content with hanging all the rebels they could lay their hands on, had been insulting them by destroying their caste, telling them that after death they should be given to the dogs. A reverend gentleman could not understand the conduct of government; could not see that there was any impropriety in torturing men's souls; seemed to think that a good deal might be said in favour of bodily torture as well. "These," exclaims Lord Elgin, "are your teachers, O Israel! Imagine what the pupils become under such leading!" A British soldier sought permission to burn alive and impale. The cries for more blood will not be forgotten by those who heard them.

When the news of the mutiny reached England the public horror was enhanced by the thought that Lord Canning was the governor-general. He had little reputation for ability; was believed to have been advanced in public life out of regard for his father's memory; was even supposed to have been sent to India to relieve the cabinet of his vexatious pertinacity. But in the hour of need his pertinacity became firmness, with which he controlled the passions of the dominant race and in some measure saved the honour of the country.

The native army, on which the dominion of the Company rested, had now broken down; and the Company's rule had become a hollow form in the retention of which there appeared to be no use. The empire of India was united to the British crown, the wearer of which presently adopted the title of Empress, on the understanding, however, that it should never be used in her constitutional realm.

Thus closed, by final transformation into an empire, the wonderful and romantic history of the East India Company. Some misgivings were felt as to the political effect both on the imperial country and on the dependency. They may perhaps have been re-awakened by the action of extremely liberal governors-general on one hand and by the appearance of Hindoos as Radical candidates for seats in the British parliament on the other. Any political danger that there might have been from the transfer of the mass of Indian patronage to the crown has been averted by the adoption of the competition system; and though success in a literary contest is no proof of practical ability or vigour, competition does not seem to have produced less of either than were produced by nomination. The Indian service remains a fine field for British youth; that it supplies England with her best men has been said, but cannot be maintained. Life when it has been spent in the Indian service cannot be begun again. Even of the governors-general, whose term is only five years, Lord Wellesley alone has played a leading part in England after his return.

What had been commenced before the transfer has been carried on with unabated, perhaps with increased, vigour since. The extension of railroads has united the country, quickened industry and production, improved the distribution of population and of food. Other works of utility have been performed. It cannot now be said of the British as it was said in former days that if they gave up India they would leave behind them no monuments but empty beer bottles. Education has been liberally promoted. European culture and science have been imparted. Laws and the judiciary have been improved. Christianity has been freely preached, and has perhaps been gaining some ground in Hindostan, while it has been losing ground among the educated classes at home. Efforts have been made to teach regard for public health. Municipal government has been promoted. Natives have been admitted to office both administrative and judicial as far as the conditions of conquest would permit, and great freedom has been allowed to a press sometimes childishly seditious. All, in short, that the most beneficent of conquerors could do has been done. But the most beneficent of conquerors, while he may make himself respected and trusted as well as feared, cannot make himself beloved. Nor can he fill the gulf of sentiment between himself and the conquered. The estrangement sadly noted by Lord Elgin has been rather increased than diminished since steam and the overland passage have brought the Anglo-Indian into closer communication with his own country and prevented him from identifying himself with the subjects of his rule so much as he did when it was a six months' voyage between him and his home.

Once more, it is not for history to attempt to raise the veil of the future.

INDEX

A

Abbeville, i. 215.
Abbey of Reading, i. 67.
Abbot, George, Archbishop of Canterbury, i. 444, 451, 462, 475.
Abbots, reason of their sitting in parliament, i. 174; mitred, removed from the House of Lords, 334.
Abercrombie, Sir Ralph, ii. 289.
Aberdeen, University of, focus of presbyterianism, i. 505.
Abhorrers, the, ii. 45.
Abjuration oath (13 Gul. III. c. 6), ii. 127; renewed by Anne (1 Ann. c. 2), 139.
Absolution, the priestly, i. 346.
Accursi, Francesco, i. 181.
Acre, taken by Richard I., i. 112.
Act of Oblivion passed (1652), i. 590.
Adams, Samuel, ii. 206, 207, 212.
Addington, Henry, first Viscount Sidmouth, takes office, ii. 248 et sq.; makes war on France, 302.
Adela, Countess of Blois, effects a reconciliation between Henry I. and Anselm, i. 65.
Adjutators, i. 559.
Adrian IV., Pope, grants the king of England dominion of Ireland, i. 99.
Adventurers, how they were paid, i. 583.
Adwalton Moor, battle of, i. 541.
Affinity, degrees of, i. 318, 319, 320.
Aghrim, battle of, ii. 97.
Agincourt, battle of, i. 259, 280.
Agreement of the people, Ireton's, i. 574, 605.
Agriculture, change from, into sheep-farming, effect of, i. 352, 353.
Aidan, i. 7.
Aids, feudal (temp. William II.) i. 45.
Albemarle, George Monck, first Duke of, his conduct compared with that of the Marquis of Argyle, ii. 8; defeats the Dutch, 32; his vice-regency in Scotland, 625; defeats Lambert, 647.
Alberoni, Giulio, ii. 165.
Albigenses, extermination of, i. 442.
Albini, William d', i. 140, 141.
Alcuin i. 22.
Alderman, the, in Saxon times, i. 9.
Alençon, Francis, Duke of, i. 383.
Alexander, Bishop of Lincoln, i. 72.
Alexander III., Pope, i. 86.
Alexander II., king of Scotland, sides with the barons, i. 141.
Alexander III., king of Scotland, i. 194.
Alexander I. of Russia, ii. 311.
Alexander IV., Pope, wrings money from English clergy, i. 155; releases Henry IV. from the provisions of Oxford, i. 159.
Alexander VI., Pope, i. 280, 287, 313.
Alexander, the mason, i. 126.
Alfred, King, i. 12.
Almains, i. 282.
Alphonso X. the wise, i. 181.
Altar, changed to the communion table, i. 346.
Althorp, John Charles Spencer, Viscount, and third Earl Spencer, ii. 311, 355.
Alva, Fernando Alvarez de Toledo, Duke of, i. 377, 388.
America, war with (1812), ii. 307 et sq.
American revolution, compared with the civil war (1642-1649), i. 599.
Amiens, peace of, ii. 300.
Anabaptists, persecuted by Henry VIII., i. 318, 348, 377, 395, 476, 545.
Andrewes, Lancelot, Bishop of Winchester, i. 439, 451.
Angles, emigration of, i. 3.
Anglesey, i. 189.

Anglicanism and puritanism compared, i. 495 et sq.
Anglo-Saxon race, characteristics of, i. 3.
Angoulême, Ademar, Count of, i. 119.
Angus, Archibald Douglas, fifth Earl of. See Douglas.
Anne, Queen, of England, brought up a Protestant, ii. 43; her character, 128, 129; characteristics of her age, ii. 128.
Anne of Bohemia, wife of Richard II., dies, i. 241.
Anne of Brittany, wife of Louis XII. of France, i. 408.
Anne of Cleves, married to Henry VIII., i. 338.
Anne of Denmark, wife of James I. of England, secretly inclined to Rome, i. 440.
Anne, wife of Prince George of Denmark, sides with William III., ii. 77.
Annexation of Canada to the United States mooted, ii. 401.
Annual Indemnity Act, the (Geo. II. st. 2, c. 23), ii. 175.
Anselm, his character, i. 48; his birth and early life, *ib.*; enters the Abbey of Bec, *ib.*; as theologian, *ib.*; as educator, *ib.*; as a spiritual director, 49; visits England, *ib.*; is nominated Archbishop of Canterbury, *ib.*; consecrated and enthroned, 50; offers the king £500, *ib.*; endeavours to curb the effeminacy of the nobles, 51; prays the king for a restoration of religion, *ib.*; asks leave to go to Rome, *ib.*, 54; before the Grand Council at Rockingham Castle, 52; contributes £200 towards the loan to Robert of Normandy, 54; before the second Grand Council, 55; leaves for Rome, *ib.*; is received by the pope, *ib.*; attends the Council of Bari, *ib.*; his attitude towards William during his exile, 56; retires to Lyons, *ib.*; recalled by Henry I., 58; sides with Henry against Robert, 61; refuses to do homage to Henry, 61, 62; his quarrel with Henry referred to the pope, 62; then to the great council, 63; again to the pope, *ib.*;

refuses to consecrate Henry's appointees to bishoprics, 63; sets out for Rome, 64; betakes himself again to Lyons, 65; goes to Normandy, *ib.*; returns to England, 65; his triumphant reception, *ib.*; a compromise effected, 66; devotes himself to ruling his church, 66; his character as painted by his biographer, *ib.*; holds a reforming synod, *ib.*, 425.
Anson, George, Lord Anson, ii. 184.
Anti-Catholic Association, ii. 230.
Anti-corn law league, the, ii. 371.
Antinomians, i. 545.
Anti-Sabbatarians, i. 545.
Anti-Scripturists, i. 545.
Anti-Trinitarians, i. 545.
Apostolical succession, i. 373.
Aquinas, St. Thomas, quoted by Fortescue, i. 277, 279, 425.
Arabella Stuart, Lady, i. 453.
"Areopagitica," the, makes an era, i. 577.
Archbishop of Canterbury, representative of the papal power (*temp.* William I.), i. 32.
Archbishops, struggles between, i. 86.
Archers, the British, i. 216.
Archery, British, i. 248.
Architecture, Scotch, i. 409; ecclesiastical, 287; Gothic, giving way to Grecian, 279.
Argyle, Archibald Campbell, first Marquis and eighth Earl of, leader of Scottish rebellion against Charles I., i. 499, 527; defeated by Montrose, 550; execution of, ii. 8; his conduct defended, *ib.*, 585.
Argyle families, the, i. 410.
Argyle, the Earl of (McCallum More), ii. 93.
Aristocracy, the (*temp.* William I.), i. 28; a guardian of liberty, 38; in the baronial "army of God," character of, 131; (*temp.* George I.), ii. 161.
Aristotle, quoted by Fortescue, i. 277.
Arkwright, Sir Richard, ii. 255.
Arlington, Henry Bennett, Lord, member of the cabal, ii. 27, 30.
Armada, the, i. 377; sails, 386; im-

portance of its defeat, 390; its defeat and flight, *ib.*; share taken by the Dutch allies, *ib.*; a convoy for Parma's army, *ib.*, 415.
Arminianism, i. 428 *et sq.*; the Commons denounce, 482, 500.
Armorial bearings, i. 29.
Army of God and Holy Church, i. 131 *et sq.*
Army, standing, absence of, under the Tudors, i. 296, 297; reason of this, 297, 306; introduced, 356.
Army, the, in Saxon times, i. 10; the Norman, how levied, 25; composition of (*temp.* Edward III.), 217, 218; command of, restored to the king (Charles II.) (13 Car. II. st. 1, c. 6), ii. 10, 11.
Army, the parliamentary (*temp.* Charles I.), remodelled, i. 550. See also New Model, the.
Arnold, Benedict, ii. 216.
Arnold, Matthew, i. 314.
Arran, James Hamilton, second Earl of, and Duke of Châtelherault, i. 415.
Arran, James Hamilton, third Earl of, i. 415.
Arran, James Stewart, Earl of, ii. 434.
Array, feudal, of barons, i. 176.
Art, ecclesiastical, at its height, i. 230; transition in, 279.
Artevelde, Jacob van, i. 218, 219.
Arthur, King, i. 190; his crown, 191, 192.
Arthur, Prince, son of Henry VII., i. 289, 318.
Arthur, son of Geoffrey, i. 118.
Articles, the thirty-nine, framed, i. 346; protestant in doctrine, 343, 371; Charles I.'s manifesto on, 482.
Artillery, adds to the power of the crown (*temp.* Richard II.), i. 248; adverse to aristocracy, 259; comes into use, 280; decides the day at Blackheath (1497), 283; in the hands of the crown, 297, 306.
Arundel, Richard Fitz-Alan, Earl of, i. 241.
Arundel, Thomas, Archbishop of Canterbury, i. 241, 244, 248, 249.
Arundel, Thomas Howard, second Earl of, i. 473, 479.

Ascham, Anthony, assassinated, i. 578.
Ashburnham, John, i. 564.
Ashley-Cooper, Anthony. See Shaftesbury, Earl of.
Aspern, campaign of, ii. 309
Assaye, battle of, ii. 421.
Assemblies, local, i. 175.
Assembly of divines (at Westminster) frame a presbyterian ecclesiastical polity, i. 543; and a confession of faith, 543, 544.
Asiento, the, ii. 150.
Assize or edict of arms, i. 78; enforced by Edward I., 176.
Assize of battle. See Wager of Battle.
Assize of Clarendon, i. 81, 82.
Association for economical reform, the, ii. 227 *et sq.*
Associated Eastern counties. See Eastern Counties' Association.
Astley, Sir Jacob, i. 552, 553.
Asylum, right of, restricted (3 Hen. VII. c. 5, etc.), i. 286.
Atheling, Edgar. See Edgar Atheling.
Athelstan, i. 12.
Attainder, i. 338, 339, 356; act of (7 and 8 Gul. III. c. 3), ii. 125.
Atterbury, Francis, Bishop of Rochester, ii. 166, 167.
Audley, James, Lord, i. 283.
Audley, Thomas, Baron Audley of Walden, lord chancellor, i. 304, 321, 324.
Augustan Age of Anne, its characteristics, ii. 128.
Augustine, St., converts Ethelbert, i. 6.
Aurungzeb, ii. 233.
Austerlitz, battle of, ii. 304.
Australia, colonization of, ii. 222.
Australasia, ii. 406.
Avignon, return of the papacy from, i. 219, 231, 312.
Aylesbury election case, the, ii. 130, 131.
Aylmer, John, Bishop of London, i. 397, 399.

B

Babington conspiracy, i. 442.
Bacon, Francis, i. 281, 285, 287, 383, 401, 402, 409, 417; his ideal of monarchy, i. 432; his large plans, 435;

his greatness and his weakness, *ib.*, 436, 456; his eminence, 459; his fall, *ib.*
Bacon, Roger, i. 37.
Bacon, Sir Nicholas, i. 369.
Badby, Thomas, i. 253.
Bagot, Sir Charles, governor of Canada, ii. 398.
Bagot, Sir William, minister of Richard II., i. 239.
Balance of power, i. 307.
Baldwin, Robert, ii. 393.
Balfour, James, of Burleigh, slays Archbishop Sharp, ii. 24.
Baliol, Edward, i. 211.
Baliol, John de, king of Scotland, i. 193, 195, 196.
Ball, John, i. 235.
Ballads, the Robin Hood, i. 135; patriotic, 219.
Bancroft, Richard, Archbishop of Canterbury, i. 428.
Bangorian controversy, ii. 176.
Bank of England, statute originating the (5 and 6 Gul. and Mar. c. 20), ii. 117.
Bankruptcy law (*temp.* Henry VIII.), i. 336.
Bannockburn, battle of, i. 202, 206.
Bannow Bay, i. 102.
Baptists, first assert the principle of liberty of conscience, i. 543; the English, at Amsterdam, *ib.*
Bar, birth of a professional, i. 182, 183.
Bards, Welsh, i. 191, 192.
Barbarossa (Frederick I.), i. 86.
Bardi, the, i. 222.
Barham Down, i. 127, 162.
Barillon, —, ii. 37.
Barnet, i. 268.
Baron, meaning of the word, i. 29.
Baronetcy, order of, instituted, i. 443.
Barons, the, power of (*temp.* William I.), i. 29; rise against William II., 43; revolt of the, against Henry I., 60; conspire against Henry II., 103; rebel against King John, 130; the cause of quarrel, *ib.*; refuse to follow John to France, *ib.*; Langton sides with them, *ib.*; gather at St. Edmundsbury, *ib.*; their demands, *ib.*; appeal to the pope, 130; advance to Brackley, 131; appear before Northampton, i. 132; occupy London, *ib.*; the greater, 136; the lesser, 136; made leaders of the whole people by the great charter, 139; garrison Rochester castle, 140; turn for aid to France, 142; protest against Henry III.'s abuses, 157; their quarrel with Henry III., 158, 159; the greater, how summoned to parliament, 172; the lesser, how summoned to parliament, i. *ib.*; of the exchequer, significance of the title, 183; the Scotch, rise against Baliol, 196; invade Cumberland, *ib.*; give place to groups of magnates, 203, 204; feudal, supplanted (*temp.* Henry VIII.), 334.
Barons' war. See under Barons; also under Henry III.; also under Montfort, Simon de.
Barrow, Henry, i. 396.
Barry, Thomas, i. 311.
Bartholomew, convent of St., i. 153.
Basinghouse, stands three sieges, i. 638.
Bastwick, John, is set free, i. 514.
Bastwick, Robert, is indicted, i. 503.
Bate, George, doctor, i. 612.
Bate, John, i. 446, 483, 484.
Bath, Earl of. See Pulteney.
Battlements, i. 280.
Baxter, Richard, quoted, i. 611.
Bayonet, its influence at Killiecrankie, ii. 94; improvements in, *ib.*
Beachy Head, naval defeat at, ii. 119.
Beaton, David, Cardinal, i. 412.
Beatrice, wife of Philip Mary, Duke of Milan, i. 325.
Beaufort, Henry, Cardinal, i. 264.
Beauforts, the (see also Somerset), i. 265.
Becket, Thomas à, a champion of church privilege, i. 87; his biographies, 87; his parentage, *ib.*; education, *ib.*; advancement, *ib.*; sent to Rome, *ib.*; takes deacon's maces, *ib.*; invested with archdeaconry of Canterbury, etc., 87; made chancellor, *ib.*; his style of living, 88, ambassador to Paris, *ib.*; taxes the clergy, *ib.*; made Archbishop of

Canterbury, *ib.*; the change in his life and aims, 89; comes into collision with the king, *ib.*; an open rupture ensues, 90; refuses to seal the constitutions of Clarendon, 92; attends the council at Northampton, 93; his threatening demeanour there, *ib.*; leaves England for France, 94; surrenders his archbishopric to, and receives it from, the pope, *ib.*; significance of his ecclesiastical principles, *ib.*; curses his enemies at Vézelay, 95; his miracles, 95, 98; is restored to his see, 96; returns to England, *ib.*; excommunicates the Archbishop of York and others, *ib.*; stirs up the people, *ib.*; preaches a minatory sermon, *ib.*; is slain by four of Henry's knights, 97; his character, *ib.*; his cause, *ib.*; the effects of his death on Europe, *ib.*; on his own fame, 98; his shrine, *ib.*; the esteem in which he was held, *ib.*; its lapse at the reformation, *ib.*; its resuscitation in the nineteenth century, *ib.*; his biography, *ib.*, 244, 247, 286, 313.
Bed-chamber plot, ii. 382.
Bede, the Venerable, i. 7, 22.
Bedford, opens its gates to the barons (*temp.* John), i. 132.
Bedford, Francis Russell, fourth Earl of, i. 479, 512, 520, 521.
Bedford, John, Duke of (regent of France), i. 200, 201, 261.
Bedford, John Russell, fourth Duke of, ii. 200, 201.
Bedloe, William, his infamy and its consequences, ii. 41.
Begums of Oude, the, ii. 416.
Bellesme, Robert de, i. 60.
Belhaven, Lord, ii. 137.
Benefit of clergy lingered long (abolished, 7 and 8 Geo. IV. c. 28, and 4 and 5 Vict. c. 22), i. 344.
Benevolences condemned by Richard III. (1 Rich. III. c. 2), i. 374.
Bentham, Jeremy, ii. 318.
Bentinck, Lord William Cavendish, ii. 424.
Beresford, John, ii. 286.
Bergami, ii. 329.

Berkeley, Sir John, i. 564.
Berkeley, Sir Robert, arrested, i. 514.
Bermingham, Sir John, defeats Edward Bruce, i. 203.
Bernard, St., i. 110.
Berwick, storming of, i. 196; parliament meets at, *ib.*; annexed by Edward III., i. 211, 267.
Bible, translation of, i. 232, 233; proscribed, 314; allowed to be read in English (*temp.* Henry III.), 337; its use restricted (34 Hen. VIII. c. 1), *ib.*; translation of, authorized (*temp.* Henry VIII.), 339; its authority, *ib.*; the sheet anchor of reformation, *ib.*; an appeal to reason, 349; withstood the Marian storm, 362; puritanism its outgrowth, 393; authorized version of James I., 438; as viewed by the Puritan, 497, 498.
Biddle, John, the Socinian, i. 610.
Bigod, Roger, Earl of Norfolk, opposes the king, i. 186.
Bill of right, i. 133.
Bill of rights, the (1 Gul. and Mar. st. 2, c. 2), its assertions and provisions, ii. 81, 82; its effect on monarchy, 85.
Birth, little regard for (*temp.* Edward I.), i. 173, 174.
Bishops, the, in Saxon times, i. 10; cease to sit with the sheriff in the shire court, 31; appointed by the Norman kings under the form of election, 32; reason of their sitting in parliament, 174; made to take out official patents (*temp.* Edward VI.), 345; appointment of (*temp.* Elizabeth), 373; withdraw from the House of Lords (*temp.* Charles I.) (16 Car. I. c. 27), 528.
Bishops' war, the, i. 495.
Black death, i. 226, 231, 233.
Blackheath, Cornish miners defeated at, i. 283.
Blacklow Hill, i. 206.
Blackstone, Sir William, i. 181.
Blake, Robert, i. 593.
Blanche (daughter of the Duke of Lancaster), first wife of John of Gaunt, i. 229.

Blanketeers, the, ii. 327.
Blenheim, battle of, ii. 133, 134.
Blomfield, Charles James, Bishop of London, ii. 364.
Blood, Thomas, Colonel, maltreats the Duke of Ormonde, ii. 34; attempts to carry off the regalia, *ib.*; his subsequent career, *ib.*
Blood-fine. See Were-gelt.
Bloody assize, the, ii. 61.
Bocher, Joan, fate of, i. 348.
Bohemia, Wycliffism carried to, i. 313; religion of, 425; rebels against Ferdinand of Austria, 461.
Bohun, Humphrey de, Earl of Hereford, opposes the king, i. 186.
Boleyn, Anne, i. 304; marries Henry VIII., 323; gives birth to Elizabeth, *ib.*; arrested, 324; her trial, *ib.*; 340; makes a confession, 324.
Boleyn, Mary, i. 320.
Boleyn, Sir Thomas, i. 302.
Bolingbroke, Henry St. John, Viscount, his character, ii. 148; his "patriot king," *ib.*, 149; collapse of his Jacobite plot, 152, 153; impeached, 165, 166; returns to England, ii. 183.
Boniface, of Savoy, made Archbishop of Canterbury, i. 153.
Boniface VIII., Pope, i. 178; his bull forbidding the clergy to pay taxes to the lay power, 180; forbids Edward I. to attack Scotland, 188, 326.
Bonner, Edmund, Bishop of London, imprisoned, i. 344; released from prison, i. 360, 376.
Bonvilles, the, i. 269.
Book of Sports, James I.'s, republished, i. 501; condemned (*temp.* Charles I.), 522.
Books, statute for admission of (*temp.* Richard III.), i. 274.
Borderers, Scotch, i. 408.
Borgia, Cæsar, i. 281.
Borgia, Roderic. See Alexander VI., Pope.
Borgias, the, i. 270, 313, 320.
Born, Bertrand de, i. 104.
Borough franchise, the, ii. 156 *et sq.*
Boroughs, side with the crown (*temp.* Richard I.), i. 115, 116.

Boroughs, small, created by Elizabeth, i. 400.
Borromeo, San Carlo, Cardinal, i. 424.
Boston (England), pillaged, i. 154.
Boston (Massachusetts), port of, closed, ii. 212; massacre, *ib.*
Bosworth, battle of, i. 275, 281.
Bothwell, James Hepburn, fourth Earl of, i. 417.
Bouvines, battle of, i. 129.
Boves, Hugh de, i. 140.
Boyd, house of, i. 405.
Boyne, battle of, the, ii. 97.
Bracton, Henry de, on monarchy, i. 149.
Bradshaw, John, i. 597.
Bramhall, John, Archbishop of Armagh, ii. 22.
Braose, William de, his wife and child captured by John, i. 126.
Braxfield, Lord Justice, ii. 274.
Breakspear, Nicholas. See Adrian IV., Pope.
Breauté, Fawkes de, i. 143, 150, 157.
Brehon law, i. 100, 310.
Brereton, William, i. 324.
Breteuil, De, i. 57.
Bribery, at elections, makes its appearance, i. 400.
Bright, John, ii. 282.
Bristol, i. 38, 146, 294, 536, 541, 552.
Bristol, John Digby, first Earl of, i. 473, 479.
British Columbia, ii. 402.
British North America Act (30 & 31 Vict. c. 3), ii. 401 *et sq.*
Brittany, i. 288.
Broad churchmen, precursors of the, i. 499.
Brocs, the De, i. 96.
Broghil, Roger Boyle, Baron (first Earl of Orrery), is warned concerning Ormonde, i. 613; his administration of Scotland, 625 *et sq.*
Brooke, Robert Greville, second Lord, i. 512.
Brougham and Vaux, Henry, Lord, his character and abilities, ii. 318, 358, 359.
Brownists, i. 395, 443.
Bruce, Edward, tills Ireland with havoc, i. 202; is defeated, 202, 203.

INDEX

Bruce, Nigel (grandson of the Competitor), i. 200, 201.
Bruce, Robert VI. (the Competitor), Earl of Annandale, i. 193, 195, 200.
Bruce, Robert VII. (son of the Competitor), i. 200.
Bruce, Robert de, VIII. (son of Robert de Bruce VII., Earl of Carrick, and grandson of Robert de Bruce VI. = the Competitor), i. 200, 202.
Brunanburg, battle of, i. 12.
Bruno, Giordano, i. 35, 377.
Bucer, Martin, invited to England, i. 345.
Buch, Captal de, i. 220.
Buck, Walter, i. 140.
Buckingham, Edward Stafford, Duke of, i. 304, 306.
Buckingham, George Villiers, first Duke of, i. 434; George Villiers, second Duke of, i. 452, 465, 469, 471, 473, 479, 481.
Buckingham, Henry Stafford, Duke of, i. 275.
Buenos Ayres, expedition to, ii. 306.
Buller, Charles, ii. 395.
Buller, Sir John Yarde, ii. 382.
Bunyan, John, imprisonment of, ii. 19.
Burgesses. See Burghers.
Burgh, Hubert de, i. 144, 150, 152.
Burgher aristocracy, i. 292.
Burghers, first summoned to parliament, i. 162; sit in parliament, 170; importance of, as representatives in parliament, 171; how elected, 192, 298.
Burghley, William Cecil, Lord, i. 368, 396, 399.
Burgoyne, John, General, ii.
Burgundy, John sans peur, Duke of, assassination of, i. 260; Philip the Good, Duke of, i. 262.
Burke, Edmund, his definition of party, ii. 106, 209 et sq.; his "Thoughts on the Present Discontents," 226; proposes economical reform, 228; his capabilities and limitations, 238; his conduct of the impeachment of Hastings, 250 et sq.; his "Reflections on the French Revolution," 262 et sq., 416, 417, 418.
Burke, John, i. 311.

Burley, Sir Simon, i. 239.
Burnell, Robert, i. 181.
Burnet, Alexander, i. 586.
Burton, Henry, i. 503, 514.
Bussy, Sir John, i. 239.
Bute, John Stuart, third Earl of, becomes head of the government, ii. 198; declares war on Spain, 199; resigns, 200.
Butler, Samuel, "Hudibras," ii. 2.
Byng, Admiral, executed, ii. 190.
Byron, Lord, ii. 318.

C

Cabal, the, ii. 27.
Cabinet, the, foreshadowings of, i. 151, 250; replaces the council, i. 342.
Cabinet system, the, ii. 27, 171.
Cabots, the, i. 294.
Cabul, expedition to, ii. 426.
Cade's, Jack, rebellion, i. 266; its political character, ib.; is crushed, 276.
Cadiz, i. 472.
Cædmon, i. 22.
Cæsar's depicture of the Celtic race, i. 5.
Caister Castle, i. 262, 263.
Calais, Edward III. besieges, i. 212; won and retained by the English (temp. Edward III.), i. 221, 262, 291; lost by England, i. 366.
Calonne, Charles-Alexandre de, ii. 260.
Calveley, Sir Hugh, i. 218, 220.
Calvin, Jean, i. 232, 313; his thoroughgoing doctrine, 345; burns Servetus, 348, 394.
Calvinists and Calvinism, i. 426, 428 et sq., 462, 500.
Camarilla, i. 274.
Campeggio, Lorenzo, papal legate, i. 321.
Camperdown, battle of, ii. 287.
Canada, conquered by Pitt, ii. 194, 206; retention of, by England, 220; history of, 385 et sq.; Pitt's Act, settling, 387; war of 1812, 388; rebellion of 1837, 389 et sq.
Canadian Pacific railway, ii. 402.
Canning, George, ii. 281, 302, 306; his character, 316, 317; takes Castle-

reagh's place, 323, 328, 329, 330, 331, 341.
Canning, Charles John, Earl and Viscount, governor-general of India, ii. 429.
Cannon introduced (*temp.* Edward III.), i. 217, 248.
Cannynge, i. 280.
Cannynges, the, i. 291.
Canon law, development of, i. 86.
Cantelupe, Thomas de, Bishop of Hereford, i. 160, 179, 180.
Cantelupe, Walter de, Bishop of Worcester, i. 156, 160.
Canute, a Christian ruler, i. 13; makes a pilgrimage to Rome, *ib.;* divides the country into earldoms, i. 13, 14.
Capel, Arthur, Lord Capel of Haddam, is banished, then condemned to death, i. 566.
Capel, Sir Henry, Lord Capel of Towkesbury, ii. 36.
Carbisdale, battle of, i. 585.
Carew, Sir Peter, rebellion of, i. 359.
Carileph, William. See William Carileph.
Carlisle, restored and fortified by William II., i. 44.
Carmarthen, Thomas Osborne, Earl of Danby and Marquis of. See Danby.
Caroline, wife of George IV., i. 338.
Caroline, the, ii. 395.
Carrickfergus, massacre by the Scotch garrison of, i. 579.
Carteret, John, Earl of Granville, ii. 186, 187.
Carthagena, the attack on, ii. 184.
Cartwright, Thomas, Bishop of Chester, ii. 65.
Cartwright, Thomas, i. 394, 432.
Carucage, replaces danegelt, i. 84, 115, 226.
Cashel, Archbishop of, i. 420.
Castile, princes of, i. 123.
Castles, multiplicity of (*temp.* Stephen), i. 73; losing their strength of defence, 151; give way to the mansion, 280.
Castlereagh, Robert Stewart, second Marquis of Londonderry and viscount, ii. 285, 306; his character, 315; dies, 323.

Caterage, i. 71.
Cateran, statute for the suppression of, i. 410.
Cathedrals, building of, i. 145; form of, makes for high church party, 428.
Catherine of Aragon, wife of Prince Arthur, and of Henry VIII., i. 289; the question of her divorce from Henry VIII., 318, 319; her noble conduct, 319.
Catherine of Russia, ii. 267.
Catholic emancipation, germs of the struggle for, i. 375; (Ireland), ii. 297 *et sq.*, 329, 330, 335 *et sq.*
Catholic league, i. 382, 424, 462.
Catholics (peers), disabled from sitting in the House of Lords (30 Car. II. stat. 2, c. 1), ii. 36: suspected of plots (*temp.* Charles II.), 40.
Catholicism (*temp.* Henry VIII.), i. 317; (*temp.* James I. *et sq.*), i. 440 *et sq.;* usually allied with despotism, 427; a rival to disunited protestantism, 502, 503; a reaction towards, *ib.;* the religion of kings, ii. 25.
Cavalier, the, his religion and character, i. 496, 497; the name comes into use, 528, 536; his morality, 539.
Cavalry, mailed, decline of, i. 259.
Cavendish, Sir William, i. 322.
Cavendish, Thomas, i. 382.
Cavendishes, the, origin and politics of, i. 334.
Caxton, introduces printing into England, i. 279.
Cecil, Robert. See Salisbury, Earl of.
Cecils, the, origin and politics of, i. 334.
Celibacy of the clergy in Saxon times, i. 18; enjoined after the Conquest, 32; Anselm tries to enforce, 66; enforcement of, withdrawn by act of parliament (2 and 3 Edw. VI. c. 21), 343; abolished (*temp.* Edward VI.), 346.
Celts, the, i. 5, 100, 101, 189, 190, 193, 311, 410; ii. 22.
Cerdic, line of, i. 14.
Chalices, discarded, i. 346.
Chalons, Count of, i. 168.
Chambers, Richard, i. 484.

Chancel rail, morally removed, i. 346.
Chancellor, the, chief minister (*temp.* Edward I.), i. 183, 184.
Chancery, court of, claims decision of disputed returns, i. 445; ii. 369, 370.
Chandos clause, the, ii. 350, 356.
Chandos, Sir John, i. 218, 220.
Channel, the. See English Channel.
Charles-Emmanuel II., Duke of Savoy. See Savoy.
Charles I., of England, i. 106, 251, 455; goes to Spain (when prince), 465; compared with Louis XVI., 468; his character, *ib.*, 469; his ideas of monarchy, 469; his motto, *ib.*; his weakness, *ib.*; called to the throne, *ib.*; his forced loans, 471; his war against Spain, *ib.*, 472; his political struggle with parliament, 472 *et sq.*; his religion, 473, 474; levies tonnage and poundage, 478; consents to the petition of right, 479, 480; revolts to ship-money, 492; attempts to coerce the Scotch covenanters, 506 *et sq.*; assents to the sweeping reforms of the long parliament, 515; signs Strafford's death-warrant, 521; goes to Scotland, 524; attempts to arrest the five members, 528, 529; leaves Whitehall, 529; his final rupture with parliament, *ib.*; calls a parliament at Oxford, 534; sets up his standard at Nottingham, 540; sends commissioners to meet presbyterians at Uxbridge, 549; his army sacks Leicester, 551; his letters captured and published, 551, 552; is given up by the Scotch, 553; his journey from Newcastle to Holmby, 557, 558; first negotiations with parliament, 558; in the hands of the independents, 562; sent to Hampton Court, 564; flies to the Isle of Wight, *ib.*; communicates with the Duke of Hamilton, 565; is taken from Carisbrooke to Hurst Castle, thence to London, 568; his trial, 568 *et sq.*; the motive and character of those who tried him, 568.
Charles II., of England (as prince), i. 559; is invited to Scotland, 585; accompanies Leslie in his invasion of England, 589; is defeated at Worcester, *ib.*; escapes to the continent, *ib.*; is recalled, 648; his journey from Dover to London, *ib.*; his restoration, ii. 3; suited his epoch, *ib.*; his character. *ib.*; his notion of kingship, *ib.*; compared with his brother James, 3, 4; his revenue, 11; at heart a papist, 25; his secret league with Louis XIV., 31; closes the exchequer, 33, 34; his last parliament, 46; forfeits civic charters, 49; his death, 54; his character, *ib.*
Charles V., Emperor, i. 307, 308, 320, 321, 322, 331, 364.
Charles V., of France, i. 221.
Charles V., of France, i. 288.
Charles V., of Spain, i. 172.
Charles Martel. i. 107.
Charles Lewis, Elector Palatine, i. 559.
Charlotte, Princess (daughter of George IV.), ii. 329.
Charter, Henry I.'s, provisions of, i. 57, 58.
Charter, the Great, i. 133; its provisions, 134 *et sq.*; its political clauses, 135, 136, 138; how it was to be upheld, 139; republished by Pembroke, 149, 305.
Charter House, monks of the, put to death, i. 330.
Chartism, ii. 352.
Chatham, William Pitt, Earl of. See Pitt, William.
Chaucer, Geoffrey, i. 211, 219, 230.
Chertsey, i. 268.
Chester, Hugh Lupus, Earl of. See Lupus, Hugh.
Chester, Randulph de Blundevill, Earl of, heads the opposition to the king, i. 157.
Chesterfield, Philip Dormer Stanhope, fourth Earl of, ii. 182, 224.
Cheyt Sing, ii. 416.
Chichele, Henry, Archbishop of Canterbury, i. 257.
Chichester, Sir Arthur, i. 420.
Chief, the Saxon, i. 9.
Chiefs, tribal, of Ireland, their character, i. 419.
Child, Sir Josiah, ii. 414.
Chillingworth, William, i. 499.

Chinon, castle of, i. 104.
Chivalry, i. 29; height of, 145; died with the Templars, i. 211; character of, in the reign of Edward III., *ib.*, 280, 381 *et sq.*
Christendom, disintegration of, i. 323.
Christian IV., king of Denmark, defeated by Tilly, i. 495.
Christianity, Britons converted to, i. 4; unifying influence of, 6; spreads over the Heptarchy, *ib.*; its influence on early England, 7; the rallying cry against the Danes, i. 11.
Christ's Hospital, founded, i. 349.
Chronicles, give place to histories, i. 281.
Church, the, in Saxon times, i. 10, 11; character of, 18 (*temp.* William I.), 34 *et sq.*; abuses in, 36, 37; a guardian of liberty, 38; an organ of moral restraint, 41; under William II., 47; under Stephen, 75 (*temp.* Henry II.), 85; salutary influence of, (*temp.* John), 120; occupies the first place in the Great Charter, 134; corruption of (*temp.* Henry III.), 145; nationalization of (*temp.* Edward I.), 177; decadence of (*temp.* Richard II.), 230; its exactions (*temp.* Henry V.), 257; its power (*temp.* Henry VII.), 287; its influence impaired by litigation, 290; its corruption and abuses as causes leading to the Reformation, 312 *et sq.*; attachment of the mass of the people to (*temp.* Henry VIII.), 314; its character (*temp.* Henry VIII.), 340, 341; stamped as a state establishment, 374; *temp.* Charles II., ii. 15 *et sq.*; its condition (*temp.* the Restoration), ii. 21; its political tendencies, 60; (*temp.* William III.), 68 *et sq.*; (*temp.* Anne), 151; (*temp.* George I.), 161 *et sq.*
Church, the Irish, i. 99 *et sq.*, 310, 419 *et sq.*; secularization of the funds of, ii. 364.
Church, the Scottish, i. 409, 411 *et sq.*
Churches, building of, i. 145, 287.
Cicero, i. 279.
Cifford, John, Lord, i. 269.
Cinque ports, the, i. 111; their duties and privileges, 218; thrive under Henry III., 146; side with De Montfort, 160, 261, 260, 291.
Circumspecte agatis, statute of, i. 179.
Cistercian order comes to England, i. 67.
Cities. See also Towns.
Cities, growth of, under Henry II., i. 84; liberties of, secured by the Great Charter, 134, 135; modern, 291; administration of, ii. 361.
Citizen, the duties of (*temp.* Henry VII.), i. 291.
Civil war, the (1642-1649), its prevailing character religious, i. 495; characteristics of the contestants, *ib.*; how waged, 532; political map of England, in time of, 5, 35; division of classes in, 536; the opposing armies compared, 537 *et sq.*; turning point in, 541, 542; weariness of, 554; compared with the French Revolution, 566; compared with the American Revolution, 599.
Clans, Irish. See under Celts.
Clare, John Fitzgibbon, Earl of, ii. 285.
Clare, Richard de, Earl of Pembroke, i. 101, 163, 164.
Clare, Richard de, eighth Earl of Clare, sixth Earl of Hertford, seventh Earl of Gloucester. See Gloucester, Earl of.
Clarence, George, Duke of, put to death, i. 272.
Clarence, Lionel, Duke of, i. 266, 309.
Clarendon, constitutions of, provisions of, i. 90, 91.
Clarendon, Edward Hyde, Earl of, i. 491, 492, 510, 520; Charles II.'s chief minister, ii. 4; his history, *ib.*; his ecclesiastical policy, 13 *et sq.*; the marriage of his daughter, 25; opposes the declaration of indulgence, 25 *et sq.*; his fall, *ib.*
Classical education, approach of, i. 230.
Classics, the Greek and Roman, i. 279.
Clement III., Pope, i. 47.
Clement V., Pope, lays Flanders under an interdict, i. 219.
Clement VII., Pope, and the divorce of Catherine of Aragon, i. 318; Henry VIII. breaks away from, 327.

Clergy, how represented in parliament (*temp.* Edward I.), i. 174; preferred for high offices, 175; claim to be beyond the domain of secular government (*temp.* Edward I.), 180; becoming worldly (*temp.* Richard III.), 230; lose their hold on the people (*temp.* Richard II.), 234, 235; criminal immunities of (*temp.* Henry IV.), 247; restriction of impunity of (*temp.* Henry VII.), 286; hated by inhabitants of cities (*temp.* Henry VIII.), 316; corruption of (*temp.* Henry VIII.), *ib.*; permitted to marry (*temp.* Edward VI.), 346; lose their power and influence (*temp.* Edward VI.), 347; the inferior conform (*temp.* Elizabeth), 375; character of (*temp.* George I.), ii. 163, (*temp.* William IV.), 362 *et sq.*
Clergy reserves, the, ii. 392 *et sq.*; act respecting (3 and 4 Vict. c. 79), 399.
Clerical encroachments thwarted by statutes (*temp.* Edward I.), i. 179.
Clerical immunity, i. 316.
Clerical privilege, i. 86, 90, 92, 97.
Clifford, Sir Thomas, a member of the Cabal, ii. 27, 29.
Clinton, Sir Henry, General, ii. 217.
Clive, Robert, ii. 233 *et sq.*, 249, 413, 414, 415, 421.
Clonmacnoise, i. 101.
Cloth, England exports, i. 292.
Coal in Great Britain, i. 2; taxed, to build churches in London (9 Ann. c. 17), ii. 151.
Coalition of Fox and North, ii. 231, 232.
Coats of arms, i. 174.
Cobbett, William, ii. 318.
Cobham, Lord. See Oldcastle, Sir John.
Cochrane, Thomas, tenth Earl of Dundonald, ii. 325.
Coffee and coffee-houses, introduction of, ii. 12.
Coin, debasement of. See Currency.
Coinage (*temp.* Henry II.), i. 84; reform of (*temp.* Elizabeth), 375.
Coke, Sir Edward, i. 181, 227, 452, 454, 456, 457.

Coke, Sir John, leader for the crown in the Commons, i. 473, 479.
Colborne, Sir John, ii. 363.
Cole, Sir W., i. 579.
Coleman, Edward, ii. 40.
Coleridge, Samuel Taylor, ii. 272.
Colet, John, i. 314.
Collar, order of the, i. 211.
College, Stephen, ii. 47.
Colleges, foundation of, i. 279; Oxford, sequestrated, i. 335.
Cologne, merchants of, i. 84.
Colonies, government of, by the commonwealth, i. 591; the American, their origin and character, ii. 203 *et sq.*; commercial restrictions in, 204, 205; taxation of, 206 *et sq.*; revolt of, 213 *et sq.*; are freed, 220; the self-governing, 385 *et sq.*, 406 *et sq.*
Colony, meaning of the word, ii. 385.
Columbus, Christopher, i. 280.
Combat, the judicial, i. 82.
Commendation, practice of, i. 15.
Commerce (*temp.* Henry II.), i. 84; awakening of, 146; fostered by Edward I., 182; extension of, under Edward III., 224; activity of (*temp.* Henry VII.), i. 280, 292.
Commercial interests, growth of (*temp.* Edward I.), i. 182.
Commissioners, royal, sent over the realm (*temp.* Henry I.), i. 69; transformed by Henry II. into justices in eyre, 80.
Commissions of array, sent by Charles I., i. 539.
Committee of both kingdoms, i. 574.
Committee of safety, i. 574.
Common law, i. 183, 296, 457.
Commons, house of, creation of, i. 173; gains authority (*temp.* Edward II.), 209; representation in, 225, 226, 250; its right to originate money bills, 276; not democratic (*temp.* Richard III.), 278; its character under the Tudors, 298; its character (*temp.* Elizabeth), 392, 397 *et sq.*, 401; a seat in an object of ambition, 400; its struggle with the crown (*temp.* Elizabeth), 430 *et sq.*; (*temp.* James I.), 445 *et sq.*; its usurpation of ju-

risdiction, 461 et sq., 464; (temp. Charles I.), 472 et sq.; its petition of right, 479; temper of (temp. Anne), 483.
Common pleas, court of, i. 137.
Common Prayer, book of, i. 343; Edward VI.'s supplants the breviary, 371; its abolition demanded, 523.
Common recovery, process of, i. 287.
Commonwealth, the, the first national republic, i. 573; how regarded by European governments, 592, 593; the virtues of its rulers, 595.
Commune, French, i. 233.
Communion cup given to the laity, i. 346.
Comprehension, ii. 14, 86.
Compton, Sir Spencer (created Lord Wilmington), ii. 186.
Compton, Henry, Bishop of London, ii. 71.
Compurgation, i. 10, 348.
Comyn, John, Earl of Badenoch, i. 193, 199, 200.
Conan, the rebel of Rouen, i. 59.
Concubinage, common, i. 85.
Condottieri, i. 280.
Confederation of Canada, ii. 401 et sq.
Confiscations, the, of William I., i. 21.
Congregationalism, i. 548.
Connaught, great part of, confiscated by Strafford, i. 488; catholic landowners transported to, 583.
Conquest, the Norman, i. 16, 17, 18, 19, 20; its double character, 17, 18; character of, 21 et sq.; effects of, ib., 31 et sq.
Constantine, donation of, i. 99.
Constitution, the, development of, the chief line along which it moved, i. 30, 31; the rudiments of, 37, 38; the earliest, 133; completed by the statute *de tallagio non concedendo*, 187; development of, under Edward VI., 355, 356; the British, ii. 157, 196; the Canadian, 401 et sq.
Contarini, Gasparo, Cardinal, i. 313, 314, 425.
Conventicles Act (35 Eliz. c. 1), i. 391, 396; (16 Car. II. c. 4), ii. 17, 87.
Convention, the, of 1688, settles the crown on William and Mary, ii. 78, 79, 80.
Convocation, the clerical, origin of, i. 174; brought under royal control, 327; subserviency of (temp. Henry VIII.), 327, 328; declares Henry VIII.'s marriage with Anne of Cleves void, 338; its doctrine of monarchy (temp. James I.), 438, 439; loses its power, 347; protests against the religious revolution (temp. Elizabeth), 374, 482; upholds divine right, 508; practically suppressed (1641), 522; ceases to exercise political authority, ii. 21; practically ceases to exist, 176.
Cony. protests against customs duties, i. 611.
Coote. Eyre, ii. 413, 421.
Copyhold, i. 295.
Copyright, i. 237, 297.
Corn laws, the, ii. 371.
Cornwall, Richard, Earl of, king of the Romans (second son of King John), i. 157.
Cornwallis, Charles, first Marquis and second Earl, surrenders at Yorktown, ii. 219, 220, 290; governor-general of India, 418 et sq.; his "permanent settlement," 419.
Corporation Act, the (13 Car. II. stat. 2, c. 1), ii. 17, 322.
Corresponding society, ii. 272.
Corruption, common (temp. Edward I.), i. 182; parliamentary, ii. 113; (temp. George III.), 245.
Cottington, Francis, Lord, i. 484, 514.
Cotton, Sir Robert, i. 447.
Council, the Great (*magnum concilium regis et regni*), i. 27; a continuation of the witan, 30; meeting of, at Clarendon, 90, 91; at Northampton, 95; its composition, 136; acquires stability, 151; its importance in Henry III.'s minority, ib.; superseded by a true parliament, 170; (temp. Edward I.), 176; (temp. Henry IV.), 251, 342, 508.
Council, the privy, germs of, i. 151, 176, 286, 306; members of, in the House of Commons, 400; enlarges its jurisdiction, 491; begins to give

way to cabinet (*temp.* Charles II.), ii. 27.
Council of Kilkenny, its composition, i. 580.
Council of the north abolished (16 Car. I. c. 10), i. 515.
Council of state elected (1649), i. 574; its composition, *ib.*; resolves to invade Scotland, 587; makes war on Holland, 593.
Court of common pleas, i. 183.
Court of exchequer, i. 183.
Court of king's bench, i. 183.
Court of star chamber. See Star Chamber.
Courtenay, Peter, Bishop of Exeter and Winchester, i. 229, 230.
Courts, character of (*temp.* Henry VIII.), i. 306; struggle between the ecclesiastical and lay (*temp.* James I.), 456.
Courts, ecclesiastical, i. 179, 315, 316.
County court, i. 81.
County, the, i. 30.
Covenanters, ii. 24, 92.
Coventry, parliament meets at, i. 267.
Coventry, Sir John, ii. 36.
Cowell, John, i. 438, 439.
Cranfield, Lionel, Earl of Middlesex, i. 452.
Cranmer, Thomas, Archbishop of Canterbury, i. 323, 336; guides the religious revolution, 344, 348; sides with Lady Jane Grey, 358; attainted, 360; condones persecution, 363, 365.
Crécy, battle of, description of, i. 43 *et sq.*, 215, 216, 220, 233, 238, 246, 259, 280.
Cressingham, Hugh, i. 197.
Crests, i. 174.
Crevant, i. 261.
Crewe, Nathaniel, third Baron Crewe of Stene, Bishop of Durham, ii. 65.
Crichton, house of, i. 405.
Crime, how repressed by Henry II., i. 82, 84; clerical, impunity of, 85; rife in Ireland in sixteenth century, 310, 311.
Criminal code (*temp.* George I.), ii. 159, 160.

Criminal law, i. 81; reform of, ii. 330; amendment of, 369.
Criticism, revolt against (*temp.* Edward III.), i. 220.
Croker, John Wilson, ii. 345, 353.
Crompton, Samuel, ii. 255.
Cromwell, Oliver, his lineage, i. 511, 545; as a military commander, 546; his attitude towards liberty of conscience, 548; re-appointed after the self-denying ordinance, 550; leads the independents, 556; his religious patriotism, 557; his attitude towards the army, *ib.*; his political ideal, *ib.*; subdues Welsh insurrection, 566; defeats Hamilton at Preston, *ib.*; decides to bring the king to justice, 568; takes an army into Ireland, 581; takes the field against the Scotch, 584; invades Scotland, 587; encounters David Leslie, *ib.*; defeats him at Dunbar, 588; defeats Leslie at Worcester, 589; his treatment of the defeated Scotch, 588, 589; manœuvres against Leslie's new army, 589; his administration of Scotland, 591; calls for dissolution of parliament, 596; goes to the House and drives out its members, *ib.*; supreme power in his hands, 598; his aims, *ib.*; compared with Washington, 599; is master of the situation, 599; declared Protector, 608; his first parliament, 609, 610; his advantages and obstacles, 601; calls a convention of Puritan notables, 602; his law reforms, 603; dismisses Barebones Parliament, 604; resorts to personal government, 610, 611; appoints major-generals, 613; calls a second parliament, 614; is offered the crown, 616 *et sq.*; is inaugurated as Lord Protector, 618; dissolves parliament (1658), 620; his speeches, 620, 621; his administration as protector, 621 *et sq.*; his ecclesiastical policy, 622 *et sq.*; his Irish policy, 627 *et sq.*; his law reforms, 630; fosters commerce, 630, 631; his colonial policy, 631; his

foreign policy, 632; his court and state, 639 *et sq.*; his death, 641.
Cromwell, Richard, succeeds, i. 645, retires, 646.
Cromwell, Thomas, i. 304; his early life and character, 326; brings about a severance from the papacy, 327; his political aim, 331; his cruelty, 332, 337; his fall, 338.
Croullé, M. de, quoted, i. 595.
Crucifixes discarded, i. 346.
Crusades, the, influence of, i. 86, 87; what they really were, 107, 145, 164, 203, 280.
Culloden, battle of, ii. 188.
Culpepper, Sir John, i. 510.
Cumberland wrested from Scotland (*temp.* William II.), i. 44; the Duke of, ii. 188, 328.
Cup, the sacramental, given to the laity by statute (1 Edw. VI. c. 1), i. 343.
Curia Regis, the, i. 27; establishment and composition of the, 69.
Curia, the Roman, i. 145, 155, 315.
Currency, debasement of (*temp.* Henry VIII.), i. 335, 336; debasement of, aggravates vagrancy, 352, 356; condition of (*temp.* Elizabeth), 379.
Custom, the merging of, into law, i. 82, 83.
Customs duties, i. 227.
Cyprus, ii. 410.

D

Dacre, Thomas Fiennes, Lord, of the south, i. 340.
Dalhousie, James Andrew Brown, tenth Earl, and first Marquis of, governor-general of India, ii. 427.
Daly, Sir Dominick, ii. 399.
Danby, Thomas Osborne, Earl of (afterwards Duke of Leeds), his policy, ii. 34 *et sq.*; impeached, 36, 71; dies, 118.
Danes, the, character of, i. 11; invasion of England by the, *ib.*; defeated by Edmund the Elder, 12; the English kingdom passes into the hands of, 13; become Christian *ib.*; renew their attacks after Ed

gar's death *ib.*; influence of, on England, 15.
Danegelt, i. 25.
Danelagh, i. 12.
Danish dynasty, end of the, in England, i. 14.
Darien company, the, ii. 136.
Darnley, Henry Stuart, Lord, i. 387, 417.
Dashwood, Sir Francis, Baron le Despencer, chancellor of the exchequer, ii. 200, 239.
David (brother of Llewelyn) is knighted, i. 191; again revolts, *ib.*; is given up by the Welsh, *ib.*; is executed, *ib.*
Davies, Sir John, attorney-general for Ireland, quoted, i. 309, 420, 422.
Davison, William, i. 369, 388.
Debates, parliamentary, contest over the printing of, ii. 228, 229.
Declaration of Independence, the American, i. 134; ii. 213, 214.
Declaration of Indulgence, the, ii. 68.
Declaration of Rights, the, ii. 81.
Decretals, the false, i. 86.
De donis conditionalibus, the statute, i. 177.
Defenders, ii. 284.
Delinquents, the, their estates sequestrated, i. 539; treatment of, 558.
Democracy, character of (*temp.* Edward III.), i. 219.
Denain, battle of, ii. 150.
Derby, Henry Plantagenet, Earl of (also Earl of Lancaster, Leicester, and Lincoln, and Duke of Lancaster), a grandee in the time of Edward III., i. 218.
Derby, James Stanley, seventh Earl of, leads a royalist rising in Lancashire, i. 589.
Derby, Thomas Stanley, first Earl of, i. 275.
Dermot, calls aid of Henry II., i. 101.
De Ruyter. See Ruyter.
Despenser, Henry le, Bishop of Norwich, i. 237.
Despenser, Hugh le (baron and justiciar, killed at Evesham), i. 207.
Despensers, the, i. 206; reign in the

king's name, 207; their political aims, ib.; execution of, 208.
De Vere, Robert. See Vere, Robert de.
Devons, the, i. 269.
Devonshire, William Cavendish, fourth Earl (and first Duke) of, ii. 70, 71.
Devonshire, William Cavendish, fourth Duke of, ii. 191.
Devonshire, Georgiana Cavendish, duchess of (wife of the fifth Duke), canvasses in the Whig interest, ii. 237.
D'Ewes, Sir Simonds, i. 398.
De Witt. See Witt.
"Dialogue on the Exchequer," the. See Nigel, Bishop of Ely.
Digby, John. See Bristol, Earl of.
Diocesan system, i. 11.
Diplomacy (temp. Henry VIII.), i. 307; the zenith of, 383.
Directory, men of the, ii. 28.
Discovery, activity of (temp. Henry VII.), i. 280, 294.
Disestablishment, attempts at, ii. 363 et sq.
Dissenters (see also Nonconformists), their influence on England, ii. 17; effect of the Toleration Act on, 88; marriage of, 364.
Distraint of knighthood, i. 176.
Dobson, William, his portrait of Charles I., i. 469.
Dodwell, Henry, ii. 89.
Dominicans, founded by Innocent III., i. 123, 124, 145, 157.
Donis conditionalibus, the statute, de (13 Edw. I. c. 1), i. 177, 288.
Doomsday Book, i. 28.
Dorislaus, Isaac, assassinated, i. 578.
Dort, Synod of, i. 444, 476, 483.
Douglas, Archibald, fifth Earl of Angus, i. 405.
Douglas, house of, i. 405.
Douglas, William, eighth Earl of Douglas, i. 405.
"Douglas's larder," i. 201.
Dover, treaty of (temp. Charles II.), ii. 31, 33.
Drake, Sir Francis, i. 368, 382, 472.
Drogheda, slaughter at, i. 581.
Drury, Sir Dene, i. 388.

Dudley, Edmund, i. 300; executed, 302.
Dudleys, the origin and politics of, i. 334.
Du Guesclin, Bertrand, i. 221.
Duke, title of, i. 228.
Dunbar, battle of, i. 588.
Duncan, Adam, Viscount Duncan, ii. 287.
Dundalk, battle of, i. 203.
Dundas, Henry, first Viscount of Melville, ii. 249, 303, 448.
Dundee, Graham Claverhouse, Viscount, raises an army in Scotland, ii. 93.
Dunning, John, first Baron Ashburton, ii. 226, 228.
Dunois, Jean, Count of, i. 261.
Duns Scotus, John, i. 279.
Dunstan, St., i. 12, 13.
Dupleix, Marquis, ii. 233, 413.
Durham, John George, first Earl of, ii. 341, 389; sent as governor to Canada, 395; his report, 395, 401 et sq.
Dutch war (temp. Charles II.), ii. 32 et sq.

E

Eadmer, i. 49, 50, 64, 65.
Earldoms, the great, in Saxon times, i. 15; creation of, 82; the great (temp. Edward II.), 204.
Earls, i. 29.
Eastern Counties' Association, i. 546, 550.
East India Company founded (see also India, British Empire in), (9 Gul. III. c. 44), ii. 117, 232 et sq.; Pitt's bill (24 Geo. III. Sess. 1, c. 3), 248 et sq., 372.
East Retford, ii. 339.
Edgar Atheling, i. 15, 20.
Edgar the Pacific, i. 12.
Edgehill, battle of, i. 540.
Edict of Arms. See Assize of Arms.
Edmund, Archbishop of Canterbury, i. 156.
Edmund, Earl of Lancaster, second son of Henry III., i. 157.
Edmund Ironside, i. 13.
Edmund the Elder, i. 12.
Edmundsbury. See St. Edmundsbury.

Education, becomes classical, i. 279; popular, forwarded by protestantism, 349; national (*temp.* William IV.), ii. 374, 375.
Edward the Confessor, i. 14; his character, *ib.;* political history in reign of, 15.
Edward the Elder, i. 12.
Edward, Prince (afterwards Edward I., *q. v.*), first comes upon the scene, i. 159; his conduct at the battle of Lewes, 161; pledges himself to the Earl of Gloucester, 163; joins the last crusade, 164; proclaimed king in his absence, *ib.*
Edward I. (see also Edward, Prince), the greatest ruler of the middle age, i. 165; as compared with others, *ib.;* his reign an epoch, *ib.;* thoroughly English, 166; powerful and respected, *ib.;* his appearance, *ib.;* his character, *ib.*, 167; returns from the crusades, 168; his political aim, 169; his statesmanship and policy, 170 *et sq.;* his military policy, 176; restrains clerical encroachments, 177–180; fosters commerce, 183; banishes the Jews, i. 185; incenses the feudal magnates, 186; his financial straits, *ib.;* resorts to tallage, *ib.;* evokes opposition, 186, 187; embarks for Flanders, 187; confirms to Great Charter, with extensions, *ib.;* his conquest of Wales, 189, 190–192; loses his wife, 192; bears her corpse to London, *ib.;* his attempts to annex Scotland, 193; adjudicates upon the succession to the Scotch throne, 194, 195; subdues Scotland, 196; is called away to France, 197; enters Scotland, 198; defeats Wallace, *ib.;* is again called to Scotland, 199; his treatment of the followers of Bruce, 200; marches towards Scotland, *ib.;* dies, *ib.;* compared to Richelieu, *ib.;* the stability of his government, 209.
Edward, Prince (afterwards Edward II., *q. v.*), i. 194.
Edward II., neglects Scotland, i. 202; is defeated at Bannockburn, *ib.;* his weakness, 203; his appearance, *ib.;* his character, *ib.;* relies on the Dispensers, 206; defeats Lancaster, 207; his end, 209.
Edward III., begins really to rule, i. 210; his capabilities, *ib.;* the character of his reign, *ib.;* invades Scotland, 210, 211; wins at Hallidon, 210; annexes Berwick, 211; his chivalry, *ib.*, 212; invades France, *ib.;* baleful influence of his victories on England, 214; on France, *ib.;* makes an alliance with the democracy of Flanders, 218; stretches the prerogative, 221; renounces his prerogatives, 223; fosters trade, 224; the last years of his reign, 227; dies, 229.
Edward, the Black Prince, i. 212, 213, 220; allies himself with Pedro the Cruel, 227; returns to England, *ib.;* supports his heir, 228, 239.
Edward IV., defeats Margaret's army at Tewkesbury, i. 268; not despotic, 272; his ruthlessness, *ib.;* his arbitrary taxation, *ib.*, 270, 295.
Edward V., proclaimed king, i. 272.
Edward VI., his precocity, i. 343; his protestantism, *ib.*
Edwin, Earl, i. 20.
Egbert, king of Wessex, i. 6.
"Eikon Basiliké," effectiveness of, i. 576.
Eldon, John Scott, Lord, ii. 277; Chancellor, 298, 313, 314, 329, 330, 332.
Eleanor, Queen (of Provence), wife of Henry III., i. 152, 153, 162.
Eleanor, Queen (of Castile), wife of Edward I., i. 166, 167, 192, 201.
Election, principle of, in the succession to the throne, set aside, i. 75; freedom of, modified (*temp.* Edward I.), 172, 173, 276, 400; parliamentary, disputed, referred to a judicial committee of the House (10 Geo. III. c. 16), ii. 228.
Eleven members, the, denounced by the army (1647), i. 563.
Elgin, James Bruce, eighth Earl of, governor of Canada, ii. 398 *et sq.*, 400, 401; quoted, 428, 429.
Eliot, Sir John, i. 446, 462; his character, 476; his political philosophy,

477; his speech in the impeachment of Buckingham, 476, 477; his "The Monarchy of Man," 477; imprisoned, 483.
Elizabeth, Queen of England (as princess), i. 323, 325; Seymour tries to marry, 354; (as queen), i. 367; changing estimate of, *ib.*; her character, *ib.*, 368; her counsellors and favourites, 369; declared supreme in the church (1 Eliz. c. 1), 371; is deposed by the pope, *ib.*; her reign a political gap, 380; the question of her marriage, 383 *et sq.*; her flirtations, 384; her favourites, *ib.*; her rivalry with Mary, 386 *et sq.*, 416; her heart not in the protestant cause, 389; her parsimony, *ib.*; negotiates with Philip II. of Spain, 391; styled overlooker of the church, 395; her recourse to, and treatment of, parliament, 400, 431; refuses to settle the succession, 403.
Elizabeth, Princess (daughter of James I., wife of Frederick V., elector palatine), i. 460.
Ellesmere, Thomas Egerton, Baron, i. 457.
Elpheg, i. 49.
Emigration (*temp.* Charles I.), i. 501.
Empire, the British, ii. 384 *et sq.*
Empson, Richard, i. 300; executed, 302.
Enclosures or commons, laws against breaking into (386 Edw. VI. c. 5), i. 349.
Encyclical, the, of 1864, i. 35, 348.
Engagers, i. 589.
England, no common name for, i. 1; her insular character, 2; condition (*temp.* George IV.), ii. 326, 327; condition of (*temp.* William IV.), 367 *et sq.*
English Channel, influence of, in history of England, i. 1, 2, 3.
English language, supplants French, i. 219.
Englishry, presentment of, i. 21; ceases under Henry II., 119.
Entail, guarded from alienation, i. 177; power of breaking, 288.
Episcopacy, retained where the reformation was monarchical, i. 375; its abolition demanded, 523.
Episcopate, a new, required (*temp.* Elizabeth), i. 375 *et sq.*
Erasmus, Desiderius, i. 313, 314, 328, 329, 425.
Erastianism established, i. 347, 374.
Erskine, Thomas, Lord, ii. 276.
Escheats (*temp.* William II.), i. 45.
Essex, Arthur Capel, Earl of, ii. 36, 48.
Essex, Countess of. See Howard, Frances.
Essex, Henry of, i. 82.
Essex, Robert Devereux, second Earl of, i. 402, 436.
Essex, Robert Devereux, third Earl of, i. 451 *et sq.*, 538; marches from London, 542; defeated in Cornwall, 549.
Établissements, i. 181.
Estates tail, not forfeitable by treason, i. 288.
Ethelbert, king of Kent, converted to Christianity, i. 6.
Ethelred, i. 13.
Eucharist, how regarded (*temp.* Edward VI.), i. 346.
European system, England's relation to, i. 1.
Eustace (second son of Stephen), i. 87.
Eustace the Monk, i. 150.
Evans, Sir George de Lacy, ii. 325.
Evelyn, John, on the execution of the regicides, ii. 6.
Evesham, battle of, i. 163, 207.
Evidence, in trials, primitive views of, i. 81, 82.
Evreux, Bishop of, i. 41.
Exchequer, organization of the, i. 69; funds in the, seized by Charles II., ii. 33, 34.
Excise bill, the, ii. 179.
Exclusion bill, the, ii. 43, 82.
Exeter (town), besieged, i. 349.

F

Factory acts, ii. 372, 373.
Fairfax, Thomas, third Viscount, placed at the head of the new model, i. 551; his accomplishments, *ib.*, 556; takes Colchester, 566; re-

fuses to attend the trial of Charles I., 569; puts down mutiny, 575; his leanings towards Presbyterianism, 587; declines to command the army for the invasion of Scotland, *ib.*; retires to Nun Appleton, *ib.*; results to his retirement, *ib.*
Fairfaxes, the (Ferdinando and Thomas, second and third Viscounts Fairfax), are overthrown at Adwalton Moor, i. 541, 546.
"Fair of Lincoln." i. 150.
Faith, catholic, decay of, i. 279.
Falkland, Lucius Cary, second Viscount, i. 499, 510; supports the attainder of Strafford, 520; killed, 542.
False decretals. See Decretals.
Familists, i. 545.
Family Compact, the, ii. 391 *et sq.*
Famine (*temp.* Henry III.), i. 155, 156; (*temp.* Edward II.), i. 206, 207.
Fasting upheld by the reformers, i. 343; why enjoined, 346.
Fastolf, Sir John, i. 262.
Fawkes, Guido, i. 441.
Fazakerley, Nicholas, ii. 177, 178.
Fealty, age of, passing away, i. 238.
Federation, Canadian meaning of the word, ii. 602 *et sq.*; Australian, 405.
Ferdinand II., of Austria, i. 461, 462.
Ferdinand V., of Spain, i. 281, 284.
Ferdinand VII., of Spain, ii. 324.
Feringdon, Hugh, Abbot of Reading, i. 333.
Ferozeshah, battle of, ii. 425.
Ferrand, Count of Flanders, threatens Philip of France, i. 129.
Feudal system, the, as it existed in France, i. 23; as it was introduced into England by William, *ib.*; origin of, 24; as remodelled by Flambard, 45; (*temp.* William II.), 45, 46; abuses of, 134; disappearance of, 280; the end of, ii. 9.
Fiefs, i. 28, 29.
Fiennes, Nathaniel, i. 541.
Fiennes, William. See Saye and Sele, Viscount.
Fifth-Monarchy Men, i. 515.
Filmer, his theory of divine right, ii. 50.
Finance (*temp.* Henry II.), i. 81.

Finch, Sir John, Baron Finch of Fordwick, i. 514.
Fines, abuses of, i. 134; statute of (4 Hen. VII. c. 24), 287, 288.
Finnian, Count of, Prince Bishop of Salzburg. See Salzburg.
Firearms replace bows, i. 280.
Fish recommended for fast days (283 Edw. VI. c. 19), i. 343.
Fisher, John, Bishop of Rochester, i. 305, 329, 330.
Fitzarthur, Ascelin, i. 41.
Fitzgerald, Judkin, ii. 289.
Fitzgerald, Maurice, i. 102.
Fitzgerald, Vesey, ii. 335.
Fitzherbert, Mrs., ii. 254.
Fitzneale, or Fitznigel, Richard. See Richard of Ely.
Fitzosbert, William (surnamed Longbeard), i. 116, 117.
Fitzpeter, Geoffrey, i. 120.
Fitzstephen, Robert, i. 102.
Fitzwalter, Robert, i. 131.
Fitzwilliam, William Wentworth, second Earl, ii. 286.
Fitzwilliams, the, origin and politics of, i. 334.
Five members, the, proceedings against, i. 528.
Five Mile Act (17 Car. II. c. 2), the, ii. 18.
Flails, protestant, ii. 41.
Flambard, Ranulph, Bishop of Durham, justiciar of William II., i. 45; remodels the feudal system, *ib.*; his encroachments on the church, 46, 47; fills the king's treasury, 47; sues Anselm, 50; imprisoned by Henry I., 58; escapes, *ib.*; debauches the English fleet, 59.
Flanders, i. 293, 425.
Fleet, the, Richard I.'s, opens the history of the British navy, i. 111; Edward III.'s, how raised, 218; (*temp.* Commonwealth), 578.
Fleet marriages stopped (26 Geo. II. c. 33), ii. 162.
Fleetwood, Charles, Colonel, i. 556, 611.
Fletcher of Saltoun, ii. 137.
Fleury, Andre-Hercule de, ii. 174.
Flodden, battle of, i. 308, 407, 408.

Floyd, Edward, i. 461, 462, 504.
Foliot, Gilbert, Bishop of London, pleads the king's cause against Becket, i. 95.
Fontevraud, i. 144.
Ford, John, i. 282.
Forde, Francis, ii. 413.
Forestallers, i. 224.
Forest, John, is burned, i. 363.
Forests and forest law, i. 6, 27, 46, 135, 149, 187; ii. 56.
Fortescue, Sir John, i. 276.
Fouché, Joseph, Duke of Otranto, a product of the French Revolution, ii. 28.
Four tables, the, i. 505.
Fowin, Edward I.'s groom, i. 168.
Fox, Charles, ii. 218, 219, 231, 232; his India bill, 234, 235; his election for Westminster, 237, 275 *et sq.*, 280 *et sq.*, 303, 305, 369.
Fox, Henry, ii. 190, 199.
Fox, Richard, Bishop, i. 300.
France, ravaged by Edward III., i. 214; the conquest of, a mischievous dream, 220; Edward III.'s war with, degenerates into raids, 221; effect of English attacks on, 262; the war in (*temp.* Henry VI.), 264; growing strength of, under Richelieu, 426.
Franchise, the, outgrown, ii. 321 *et sq.*, 342 *et sq.*; as changed by the reform bill, 349 *et sq.*
Francis of Assisi, i. 145, 146.
Francis I., of France, i. 307, 331.
Francis de Sales, St., i. 424.
Franciscans, founded by Innocent III., i. 123, 124, 145; enter the universities, i. 148; influence education, *ib.*, 157.
Franklin, Benjamin, ii. 212, 213.
Frank-pledge, i. 10; defunct, 184.
Fratricide, common in Norman annals, i. 104.
Frederick II., Emperor of the Holy Roman Empire, i. 155, 181.
Frederick V., Elector Palatine, accepts the Bohemian crown, i. 461, 472.
Frederick II. the Great, of Prussia, and the Seven Years' War, ii. 193 *et sq.*
Freehold, forty-shilling, qualification, i. 276.

French-Canadians, the, ii. 390 *et sq.*, 396 *et sq.*, 400.
French language, the, use of (*temp.* Henry II.), i. 78; (*temp.* Edward I.), 166.
Friars, degradation of, i. 231.
Frobisher, Sir Martin, i. 368, 382.
Froissart, Jehan, i. 241.
Fronde, wars of the, i. 302.
Fulk, Count of Anjou, i. 71.
Fyrd, i. 25, 30; reorganized by Henry II., 78, 79, 176.

G

Gaelic, i. 410.
Gage, Thomas, General, ii. 216.
Gaillard, château, i. 114, 120.
Galileo Galilei, i. 35.
Gallowglass, i. 419.
Galway, i. 310.
Gardiner, Stephen, Bishop of Winchester, i. 337; imprisoned, 344; released, 360.
Garnett, Henry, implicated in gunpowder plot, i. 441.
Garter, Order of the, i. 211.
Gascony, retention of, by England, i. 197; lost, 262.
Gatton, ii. 320.
Gauden, John, Bishop of Worcester, i. 576.
Gaunt, Elizabeth, burnt alive, ii. 61.
Gaunt, John of. See John of Gaunt.
Gaveston, Piers, i. 204; banished, i. 206; absolved by the pope and returns, *ib.*; is beheaded, *ib.*; his merits and demerits, *ib.*
Gendarmerie, the, of London, i. 356.
Gentleman, country. See Squire.
Gentry, landed, growth of, i. 392.
Geoffrey, bastard son of Henry II., i. 105, 108.
Geoffrey, Archdeacon of Norwich, starved to death, i. 125.
George I., ii. 154 *et sq.*; resistance to his accession, 164 *et sq.*; clings to the Whigs, 165; leaves government to Walpole, 170.
George II., ascends the throne, ii. 181.
George III., ascends the throne, ii. 195; his education, 196; his policy,

197 et sq.; coerces the colonies, 218, 221; his madness, 306.
George IV. (as Prince of Wales), ii. 253 et sq.; his character, 306; becomes king, 319 et sq.
George, Prince, of Denmark, sides with William III., ii. 77.
Geraldine, Sept of, i. 312.
Germaine, Lord George, Viscount Sackville, ii. 217.
Germany, catholicism and protestantism in, i. 313, 424, 425.
Gerrard, John, his plot, i. 612.
Gesiths, i. 9.
Ghent, besieged by Philip II. of France, i. 129.
Gibraltar, retained by England, ii. 150, 409 et sq.
Ginkell, Godart van, Earl of Athlone, reduces Ireland, ii. 97.
Giordano Bruno. See Bruno, Giordano.
Girard, i. 53.
Glanville, Ranulph de, i. 83, 106, 108.
Glasgow Cathedral, i. 409, 413.
Glaston, the Abbot of. See Whiting, Richard.
Glencoe, massacre of, ii. 136.
Glendower, Owen, i. 192, 248.
Gloucester, Gilbert de Clare, eighth Earl of, i. 160.
Gloucester, Humphrey, Duke of, made Protector, i. 264.
Gloucester, Richard de Clare, eighth Earl of Hertford and seventh Earl of Gloucester, sides with De Montfort, i. 158; falls out with him, 159, 163.
Gloucester, Thomas, of Woodstock, Earl of Buckingham, and Duke of, i. 240.
Gloucester (town), a royal seat, i. 26; (temp. William I.), 38; sacked, 73, 74, 536; besieged, 542.
Gloucester, William, Earl of, i. 119.
Glyn, John, i. 510, 556, 563.
Godfrey, Sir Edmund Berry, murder of, ii. 41.
Godolphin, Sidney, first Earl of, supports the exclusion bill, ii. 43, 107, 131.
Godwin, Earl, i. 11.
Godwin, William, ii. 318.

Golden Fleece, Order of the, i. 211.
Gondomar, Diego Sarmiento de Acuña, Count of, Spain's ambassador to England, i. 453.
Goodman, Godfrey, Bishop of Gloucester, i. 502.
Goodwin, Thomas, i. 535, 544.
Gordon, Lord George, and the riots, ii. 230.
Goring, George. See Norwich, Earl of.
Gosford, Lord, ii. 293.
Government, local, form of, under William I., i. 30; how Henry II. dealt with it, 82; constitutional progress in (temp. Richard I.), i. 114; the three branches of, nearly completed, 183; parliamentary (temp. Edward II.), 209; development of, under Edward III., 210; condition of (temp. Elizabeth), 379; responsible (temp. Elizabeth), 399.
Gower, John, i. 219.
Gowrie conspiracy, i. 434.
Grace, act of ("act of pardon and indemnity"), (temp. William III.), (2 Gul. and Mar. c. 10), ii. 91.
Grafton, Augustus Henry Fitzroy, third Duke of, ii. 211.
Grafton, Richard, i. 274.
Graham, house of, i. 405.
Graham, Sir James, ii. 355.
Grand demonstrance, the, i. 525; the debate on, 526.
Grand jury, trace of primitive mode of presentment found in, i. 80, 81.
Grandmesnil, Ivo de, i. 60, 61.
Grattan, Henry, ii. 225, 245, 285, 294, 295, 333.
Gray, Thomas, i. 191.
Great Council. See Council, Great.
Great Tew, i. 499.
Gregory the Great, Pope, sends Augustine to England, i. 6.
Gregory VII., Pope. See Hildebrand.
Green, Sir Henry, i. 239.
Greene, Robert, i. 377.
Greenwood, John, i. 396.
Grenville, George, head of the government, ii. 200; taxes the colonies, 206 et sq., 268, 269, 423.
Grenville, Sir Beril, i. 539.

Grey, Arthur, fourteenth Lord Key de Wilton, i. 418.
Grey, Charles, second Earl, ii. 281; advocates parliamentary reform, 317 et sq., 341 et sq., 344.
Grey, John de, Bishop of Norwich, i. 121, 126; governs Ireland for John, ib.; death of, 130.
Grey, Lady Jane, i. 358, 360.
Grey, Sir Richard, i. 273.
Grey, Walter de, Bishop of Worcester, i. 142.
Grindal, Edmund, Archbishop of Canterbury, i. 396, 397.
Grindecobbe, i. 237.
Grocyn, William, i. 314.
Grosseteste, Robert, Bishop of Lincoln, i. 156, 158, 177, 315.
Gualo, papal legate, i. 144, 150.
Guesclin. See Du Guesclin.
Guild halls, i. 147.
Guilds, merchant, replaced by full commune, i. 115, 147.
Guilford, Francis North, Lord, ii. 41, 42.
Guises, the, i. 377, 386.
Guitmond, refuses to remain in England, i. 37.
Guizot, François-Pierre-Guillaume, quoted, i. 621.
Gulbert of Hugleville, returns to Normandy, i. 37.
Gunpowder, i. 259.
Gunpowder plot, the, i. 441.
Gustavus Adolphus II., king of Sweden, i. 495; ii. 38.
Guthrie, James, executed, ii. 8.

H

Habeas corpus, i. 133, 138, 296; unknown in Scotland, 407; act, passed (31 Car. II. c. 2), ii. 38; suspended by Pitt (34 Geo. III. c. 54; 35 Geo. III. c. 3; 38 Geo. III. c. 36; 41 Geo. III. c. 26), 272.
Habitants, the, ii. 389 et sq.
Hadrian IV., Pope. See Adrian.
Hadwisa, King John's first wife, i. 119.
Hæretico comburendo, the statute *de* (2 Hen. IV. c. 15, stat. 2), i. 252, 253,
357; re-enacted (*temp.* Mary, 1 & 2 Phil. & Mar. c. 8), i. 361; abolished (29 Car. II. c. 9), ii. 20.
Haileybury College, ii. 422.
Hales, John, i. 499.
Halidon, battle of, i. 210, 407.
Halifax, George Savile, first Marquis of, succeeds Danby, ii. 39, 43, 44.
Hall, Sir Matthew, i. 181.
Hallam, Henry, i. 287, 288, 306, 401, 402; ii. 4, 147.
Hamilton, house of, i. 405.
Hamilton, James Hamilton, third Marquis and first Duke of, i. 506; heads a royalist Scotch party, 565, 589.
Hammond, Robert, Colonel, i. 564.
Hampden, John, refuses to pay shipmoney, i. 492; is condemned, 493, 510, 524; his object in the civil war, 532, 533, 541; ii. 36.
Hampshire, i. 27.
Hampton conference, the, i. 437, 438.
Hanseatic league, formed, i. 146.
Hanse, the, i. 292.
Hardinge, Henry, first Viscount, ii. 423.
Hargreaves, James, ii. 255.
Harlaw, battle of, i. 410.
Harley, Robert, first Earl of Oxford, ii. 131; his character, 147, 148; dismissed, 152; impeached, 165, 166.
Harold Hardrada, i. 19.
Harold, King, raised to the throne, i. 15; defends England against the Normans, 19; opposes Harold Hardrada, *ib.*; conquers the Danes at Stamford Bridge, *ib.*; confronts the Normans in Sussex, *ib.*; takes up a position on the hill of Senlac, *ib.*; disposition of his army, *ib.*; is killed by an arrow, 20.
Harris, George, first Lord, ii. 421.
Harrison, Thomas, Colonel, takes the king to London, i. 568; his execution, ii. 5.
Haro, Luis de, i. 435.
Haselrig, Sir Arthur, i. 510, 620.
Hastings, Francis Rawdon-, first Marquis of, governor-general of India, ii. 423.
Hastings, the battle of. See Senlac, the battle of.

Hastings, Warren, ii. 416; his impeachment, 249 et sq., 416.
Hastings, William, Lord, i. 273.
Hatton, Sir Christopher, i. 384, 389, 402.
Havana, taken, ii. 199.
Hawkins, Sir John, i. 382.
Hay, James, first Earl of Carlisle, his ostentation, i. 450.
Head, Sir Francis Bond, ii. 394.
Hearth-tax, repealed (1 Gul. & Mar. c. 10), (imposed, 14 Car. II. c. 10, and 16 Car. II. c. 3), ii. 86.
Heath, Sir Robert, i. 492.
Heber, Reginald, Bishop of Calcutta, ii. 423.
Henderson, Alexander, i. 506.
Henrietta Maria (wife of Charles I.), compared with Marie Antoinette, i. 468; marries Charles I., i. 470; comes to England, *ib.*; religious difficulties in connection with, 470, 471; her attempt to overawe parliament, 520; betrays the projected arrest to five members, 528; infuses spirit into the war, 537; advises Charles from Paris, 549.
Henry of Essex. See Essex, Henry of.
Henry I., gallops to Winchester on his father's death, i. 57; has himself elected king, *ib.*; publishes a charter, *ib.*; recalls Anselm, 58; imprisons Flambard, *ib*; his character, 58, 59; makes a treaty with Robert, 59, 60; marries Matilda, 60; his preference for Normans, *ib.*; his struggles with the baronage, 60, 61; defeats Robert de Belesme, 61; his quarrel with Anselm, *ib. et sq.*; the question referred to the pope, 62; seizes the estates of the archbishopric of Canterbury, 65; banishes Anselm, *ib.*; his choice of ministers, 68; his resort to espionage, *ib.*; the character of his rule, *ib.*; his services to commerce, 68, 69; goes to Normandy, 70; dies of a surfeit of lampreys, 71; his absences from England, 119.
Henry, Bishop of Winchester (Stephen's brother), his shifting policy, i. 71, 73, 74.

Henry II., his appearance, i. 76; his activity, *ib.*; his disposition, *ib.*, 77; his possessions, 77; his sovereignty, *ib.*; organizes the kingdom, 78; institutes scutage, 79; his political aim, *ib. et sq.*; his finance, 84; his attitude towards Becket, 93; undertakes the conquest of Ireland, 99 et sq.; overthrows conspiracy, 103; takes William, king of Scots, prisoner, *ib.*; his sons Richard and John plot against him, 104; overpowered by them and by the king of France, 105; dies at Chinon, *ib.*
Henry, Prince (son of Henry II.), dies, i. 104.
Henry III., crowned, i. 149; his minority, 151; his character, 151, 152; his predilections and tastes, 152; wars upon Gascony, 154; renews the Great Charter, 157; gets into the pope's debt, 158; pawns his kingdom, *ib.*; swears to the provisions of Oxford, 158, 159; civil war openly breaks out between the king and the barons, 159; defeated at Lewes, 161; ratifies reforms, 164; dies, *ib.*
Henry (son of Richard, Earl of Cornwall), murdered, i. 164.
Henry IV., of England (see also Lancaster, Henry, Duke of), his right to the crown compared with that of William III., i. 243; his coronation, 243, 244; copes with Welsh disaffection, 248; his energy, 249; most constitutional monarch, *ib.*; his character, 245; his struggles with conspiracy, 245, 246; his relations with parliament, 249, 250; his character and government, 253, 254; effects of his policy, 254.
Henry V., i. 249; his character, 255; his claim to the crown of France 258; attacks France, 259.
Henry VI., his coronation, i. 263; his character, *ib.*; murdered, 273.
Henry VII., Richard III.'s rival, i. 274; his title to the crown, 281; his struggles with pretenders to the throne, 282; with rebellion in the north, 283; in Cornwall, *ib.*; with general disorder, *ib.*; his political aims, *ib.*;

his character, *ib.*; his diplomacy, 288; fosters trade, 293; his alliances, *ib.*; his choice of ministers, 299, 300; his craving for money, 300; his exactions, *ib.*; becomes odious, *ib.*; his funeral, *ib.*; his Irish policy, 311, 312; his relations with Scotland, 411.

Henry, Prince, son of Henry VII., afterwards Henry VIII. (*q. v.*), affianced to Catherine of Aragon, i. 289.

Henry VIII., i. 289; his appearance, 301; his character, *ib.*; his extravagance, 302; his popularity, *ib.*; his debts repudiated by act of parliament (21 Hen. VIII. c. 24; 36 Hen. VIII. c. 12), 302, 303; his proclamations declared to have the force of law (31 Hen. VIII. c. 8), 303; his diplomacy, 308; his Irish policy, 312; receives the title of Defender of the Faith, 317; his attitude towards Roman Catholicism, 317, 318: the sole cause of his secession, 318; his attempts to obtain a divorce from Catherine of Aragon, 318 *sq.*; marries Anne Boleyn privately, 322; falls in love with Jane Seymour, 323; declared supreme head of the church (26 Hen. VIII. c. 1), 324, 327; marries Jane Seymour, 325; extorts money from the clergy in the form of penalties of Præmunire (22 Hen. VIII. c. 15), 326, 327; his "Institution of a Christian Man," 328; his extravagance, 336; his wavering religious policy, 337; holds a public disputation, 338; marries Anne of Cleves, *ib.*; authorizes a translation of the Bible, 339; the upshot of his ecclesiastical policy, 340; his creed and ritual, 340, 341; his will, 340, 403; not a religious reformer, *ib.*; bequeaths the kingdom, 342; acts of his executors, 342, 343; futility of his attempts to settle the succession, 357; his dealings with Scotland, 411.

Henry IV., of Germany, i. 86.

Henry VI., Emperor of Germany, captures Richard I., i. 112.

Henry IV., of Navarre, i. 384, 424, 426 *et sq.*, 442.

Henry, Prince, eldest son of James I., of England, i. 455.

Henry, Prince, Duke of Gloucester, third son of Charles I., of England, too young for the throne, i. 559.

Heptarchy, the, i. 6.

Heralds, college of, i. 174.

Heraldry, becomes a science, i. 211.

Herbert, Arthur, Earl of Torrington, Admiral, invites William of Orange over, ii. 70.

Herberts, the, origin and politics of, i. 334.

Hereditary system, instance of the weakness of, i. 263.

Hereford, Henry, Duke of (afterwards Duke of Lancaster and Henry IV., *q. v.*).

Heresy, statutes against, i. 252, 253.

Heretics, treatment of a company of, from Germany (*temp.* Henry II.), i. 98.

Hereward, defeated by William I., i. 20.

Hickes, George, ii. 89.

High commission, court of, how formed (*temp.* Elizabeth, 1 Eliz. c. 1, stat. 18), i. 374; composition of, 396, 401, 491; abolished by the long parliament (16 Car. I. c. 11), 515.

Highlanders of Scotland, i. 193.

Highlands of Scotland, early condition of, i. 410; clan system reigns in, *ib.*; Gaelic the speech, *ib.*; antagonism to lowlands, *ib.*

Hildebrand, i. 18; his designs on behalf of the church, *ib.*; the effect of his ecclesiastical designs in Germany, 18, 19; abets the invasion of England, 19; introduces reforms in England, 31; calls on William I. to do homage to his kingdom, 32; his ambition for the church, 34; humbles Henry IV. of Germany, 86.

Hill, Abigail, supplants the Duchess of Marlborough. ii. 147.

Hill, Rowland, ii. 376.

Hillsborough, Wills Hill, Earl of, ii. 212.

History of England, chief interest of, i. 1.

Hobbes, Thomas, his philosophy, ii. 2; his scepticism, 20.
Hobrigge, Gervase, i. 141.
Hoche, Lazare, invades England, ii. 287.
Hofer, Andreas, murder of, ii. 309.
Hohenlinden, battle of, ii. 300.
Holland, protestantism in, i. 424; hegemony of, 573.
Hollands, the (Sir John and Sir Thomas, half-brothers of Richard II.), i. 238.
Holles, Denzil, i. 510, 556, 563.
Holy Alliance, the, ii. 309, 311, 324.
Holy water, discarded, i. 346.
Home rule, i. 5.
Homildon, battle of, i. 248, 407.
Homilies, the, published, i. 346.
Hood, John, ballads, i. 135.
Hooker, Richard, i. 399, 428.
Hooper, John, Bishop of Worcester, objects to vestments, i. 345, 364.
Hothams, the, i. 540.
"Hotspur." See Percy, Sir Henry.
House-carts, i. 14.
Howard, Catherine, wife of Henry VIII., i. 329.
Howard, John, ii. 369.
Howard, Lady Frances (afterwards Countess of Essex, then Countess of Somerset), i. 451 *et sq.*, 538.
Howard, William, third Lord Howard of Escrick, betrays Russell and Sidney, ii. 49.
Howe, William, General, ii. 216.
Howell, the good, i. 190.
Hubert, Archbishop, i. 118, 120.
"Hudibras," i. 542; delights the court, ii. 2.
Hudson's Bay Company, the, ii. 402.
Huguenots, the, i. 424. 583.
Hugh Lupus, Earl of Chester. See Lupus.
Hugh, St., Bishop of Lincoln, i. 121, 130.
Hull (the town), i. 536; gates of, closed against Charles I., 539, 540.
Humbert, J.-R.-M., general, ii. 287.
Humble petition and advice, i. 617.
Hume, David, i. 191, 612.
Hume, Joseph, ii. 362, 373.
Hundred, the, i. 30.

Hundred court, i. 81.
Huntly, George Gordon, second Marquis of, i. 585.
Husbandry, the care of, i. 350, 351.
Huskisson, William, ii. 317; his policy, ii. 328, 338, 339, 371.
Huss, John, i. 313, 425.
Hutchinson, John, Colonel, i. 496, 497.
Hyde, Anne (daughter of the Earl of Clarendon), marriage of, ii. 25.
Hyde, Edward. See Clarendon, Earl of.
Hyder, Ali, ii. 420.

I

Images of saints, discarded, i. 346.
Impeachment, i. 296; right of, asserted by Commons, 464.
Impositions, the Commons raise the question of, i. 446.
Imprisonment, arbitrary, i. 437.
Indemnity and Oblivion, Act of (12 Car. II. c. 11), dissatisfaction with, ii. 13.
Independents, i. 544; their severance from the Presbyterians, 547; aims of, 555.
India bill (see also East India Company), (of Fox and North), ii. 417; (of Pitt), 418.
India, English rule in, ii. 233 *et sq.*, 411 *et sq.*
Indulgence, declaration of (*temp.* Charles II.), ii. 26, 30.
Inglis, Sir Robert, ii. 336.
Innocent III., Pope, i. 122; his character, *ib.*, 123; his policy, 123; lays an interdict on England, 124; excommunicates John, 125, 127; annuls the Great Charter, 140; suspends Langton, 142; dies, 144.
Inquisition, the, i. 35, 348, 424.
Instrument of government, the, i. 605 *et sq.*
Intendant, king's. See Sheriff.
Intercursus magnus, the, i. 293.
Interdict, the (see also under Innocent III.), i. 124 *et sq.*
Inventions (*temp.* George IV. and William IV.), ii. 322, 326.
Iona, islet of, i. 100.

Ireland, Henry II. undertakes to conquer it, i. 99; escapes Roman and Saxon conquest, 100; obstacles to unification of, 101; invasion of, by Strongbow and others, *ib.*, 102; is annexed by Henry II., 102; governed by John de Grey, 126; its bitter fate, 309; under Henry VII., 312; the war of races, 417 *et sq.*; Strafford's administration of (see also Strafford), 487 *et sq.*; catholic rebellion and massacre of protestants (1641), 524; internecine character of the civil war (*temp.* Charles I.) in, 532, 579; Cromwell's policy with regard to, 627; union of, with England (*temp.* Protectorate), ii. 21; James II.'s policy in, 61, 62; the revolution of 1688 in, 94 *et sq.*; the racial and religious conflict in, 98, 99; condition of (*temp.* Anne), 142, 143; neglected by Walpole, 179 *et sq.*; condition of (*temp.* George III.), 222 *et sq.*; under Pitt, 241, 242; condition of (*temp.* George III.), 283 *et sq.*; united to Great Britain (39 and 40 George III. c. 67), 293; condition of, as described by Cornwallis (*temp.* George III.), 290, 291; after the union, 332; condition of (*temp.* William IV.), 376 *et sq.*

Ireton, Henry, i. 556; draws up the agreement of the people, i. 574.

Irish brigade, the, i. 583.

Ironsides, the, i. 546.

Isabel of Angoulême, i. 119, 152.

Isabella (daughter of Charles VI. of France), second wife of Richard II., i. 241.

Islands, the British, situation of, i. 1, 2, 3; dedicated to freedom, 2.

Italy, untouched by the Reformation, i. 424; republics of medieval, 573.

J

Jacobins, the, compared with those who tried Charles I., i. 568.

Jacobites, i. 334, 335; ii. 101 *et sq.*, 164, 165.

Jacquerie, the, i. 214, 233.

Jamaica, rising in, in 1865, i. 133; ii. 381, 382, 406 *et sq.*; slavery in, 407; insurrection in, 409.

James I., of England (as James VI., of Scotland), i. 417 (as king of England), 432 *et. sq.*; bred a Calvinist, 436; sides with the Anglican hierarchy, 437; his papal leanings, 440; his extravagance, 443; his lavishness towards parasites, *ib.*; his financial embarrassments, 448 *et sq.*; his court, 450, 451; his leanings towards Spain, 453; his foreign policy, 460 *et sq.*; his restoration of Episcopacy in Scotland, 504, 505.

James II., of England (as Duke of York), i. 559; marries Anne Hyde, ii. 25; resigns the office of high admiral, 31; publicly avows his Roman Catholicism, 40; attempted exclusion of, 42, 43; marries Mary of Modena, 43; (as king) his character, 54, 55; his policy, 56, 57, 62; how put into force, 63, 64; revives the court of high commission, 65; his attempts to pack parliament, 69; a son born to him, 70; his change of front on the landing of William, 75; his flight, 77, 78; was virtually deposed, 80; lands in Ireland, 95; his party, 104; dies, 127.

James I., of Scotland, i. 406.

James II., of Scotland, i. 406.

James IV., of Scotland, i. 408.

James VI., of Scotland, afterwards I., of England, *q. v.*

Jedburgh law, i. 408.

Jefferson, Thomas, ii. 213, 324.

Jeffreys, George, first Baron of Wem, judge, ii. 61, 68.

Jena, battle of, ii. 304.

Jenkins, ii. 183, 184.

Jerome, of Prague, i. 313.

Jesuits, the, i. 377, 424, 425 (*temp.* James I.), 440, 441; (*temp.* Charles II.), ii. 40, 55, 56.

Jewel, John, Bishop of London, i. 482.

Jewry, the, a source of revenue, i. 84.

Jews, the, how treated by William II., i. 46; an anti-semitic movement sweeps over Europe, 108; their ad-

diction to usury, *ib.*; an object of religious aversion, *ib.*; generally hated, 109; lived apart, *ib.*; suspected of siding with the infidel, 110; massacred, *ib.*; clauses relating to, in the Great Charter, 137; oppressed by Henry III., 154; banished by Edward I., 185; clip the coin, *ib.*; own land, *ib.*; amass wealth, *ib.*; results of their banishment, *ib.*
Joan of Arc, i. 261.
Joan of Kent. See Bocher, Joan.
John, of Bretagne, i. 199.
John, of Crema, i. 66, 67.
John, king of England (as prince), his father's vicegerent in Ireland, i. 102; plots against his father, 104; (as king), his character, 118, 119; disloyal to his brothers, 106, 119; marries Hadwisa, 119; marries Isabella, *ib.*; loses Normandy, *ib.*; defies the pope, 121; threatened with an interdict, *ib.*; his free thinking and impiety, 121, 122; invades Scotland, 125; is excommunicated, *ib.*; flies to Wales, 126; flies to Ireland, *ib.*; crushes the De Lacys, *ib.*; submits to the pope, 127; musters his forces to oppose Philip, of France, on Barham Down, *ib.*; his abuses and exactions, 128; takes an army to France, 129; temporizes with the barons, 130; meets the barons at Windsor, 132; sends abroad for support, 140; devastates the country, 141; largely deserted, 143; is forced northward, 144; loses his treasure, *ib.*; dies, *ib.*; is buried, *ib.*
John, of Gaunt, Duke of Lancaster, i. 213; marries Constantia, daughter of Pedro the Cruel, 228; his lineage, *ib.*; his Lancastrian claims, *ib.*; his claim to the kingdom of Castile and Leon, *ib.*; seizes the government, *ib.*, 229; leader of the Oligarchs, 239, 243, 265.
John, of Leyden (Johann Bockelson or Bockold), i. 351, 545.
Johnson, Samuel, his estimate of Charles II., ii. 3.
Journalism, political, birth of, i. 539.

Joyce, Cornet, carries off Charles I., i. 562.
Judges, itinerant, i. 137.
Judges, status of (*temp.* James I.), i. 448; arbiters of the constitution, *ib.*; servility of (*temp.* Charles I.), 492; independence of, established, ii. 83; payment of, 362.
Judicature, advance of, i. 137.
Judiciary, the (*temp.* Henry II.), i. 80; (*temp.* Edward I.), 181, 182; (*temp.* Henry VII.), 296; of Scotland, 407; James I. assails the independence of, 458; corruption of (*temp.* James I.), 459.
Judith, niece of William I., i. 39.
Julius II., Pope, i. 313, 320.
"Junius," the letters of, ii. 225, 226.
Juries, untrustworthy (*temp.* Henry VII.), i. 286.
Jurisprudence, birth of, i. 82, 83.
Jury trial, i. 137, 296.
Justices in eyre, established by Henry II., i. 80.
Justices of the peace, i. 184, 227.
Justiciar, the, i. 26; growing influence of, 120, 184.
Jutes, migration of, i. 3.
Juxon, William, Archbishop of Canterbury, i. 486.

K

Kane, Donald, i. 311.
Keble, John, i. 428.
Ken, Thomas, Bishop of Bath and Wells, ii. 89.
Kenilworth, i. 163.
Kenyon, Lloyd, first Lord Kenyon, ii. 273, 277, 280.
Kerne, i. 213.
Kéronalle, Mme. de. See Portsmouth, Duchess of.
Kett, Robert, rebellion of, i. 351; is hanged, 352.
Kett, William, is hanged, i. 352.
Khalsa, the, ii. 425.
Kildare, Gerald Fitzgerald, Earl of, i. 312.
Killiecrankie, battle of, ii. 93.
Killigrew, Thomas, ii. 26.
Kilwardby, Robert, Archbishop of Canterbury, i. 178.

King, functions of the, in Saxon times, i. 8; election of, in Saxon times, 9; mode of coercing (*temp.* John), 139.
"King's cabinet opened, the," i. 551.
King-worship in England (*temp.* Henry VIII.), i. 302.
King's evil, touching for, revived (*temp.* Charles II.), i. 648.
"King's friends," ii. 197.
Kirkaldy, Sir William, of Grange, i. 416.
Kirke, Colonel, ii. 60, 61.
Kitchin, Anthony, Bishop of Llandaff, i. 375.
Knighthood, i. 29.
Knights, protest of, for reforms (*temp.* Henry III.), i. 159; four from each shire summoned to parliament (*temp.* Henry III.), 161, 162, 170, 171, 172, 298.
Knolles, i. 218, 220.
Knollys, Sir Francis, i. 369, 383.
Knox, John, i. 357, 386; his character, 412; organizes Calvinism, *ib.*, 506.
Krudener, Madame, ii. 311.

L

Labour, statutory legislation of (see Labourers, Statutes of), first regulated by parliament in 1349, 226; forced, giving way to hired, 233.
Labourers, the (*temp.* William I.), i. 38; statutes of (23 Edw. III. stat. 2), 225, 233; scarcity of, *ib.*; discontent, 233, 234; statutes of (*temp.* William IV.), ii. 373, 374.
Lafayette, Marquis de, ii. 217.
La Hogue, victory of, ii. 119.
Lake, John, Bishop of Chichester, ii. 90.
Lake, Sir Thomas, i. 452.
Lally, T.-A., Count of, ii. 412.
La Marche (Hugh IX.), Count de, i. 119, 152.
La Mare, Peter de, i. 229.
Lambert, John, Henry VIII. argues with, i. 338.
Lambert, John, Major-General, i. 611.
Lambeth Articles, the, i. 345, 476, 482.
Lambeth, treaty of, i. 150.
Lancaster, Henry (son of John of Gaunt), Duke of (afterwards Henry IV.), his quarrel with the Duke of Norfolk, i. 212; is banished, *ib.*; returns, 243; mounts the throne as Henry IV. (*q. v.*), *ib.*
Lancaster, John of Gaunt, Duke of. See John of Gaunt.
Lancaster, line of, i. 268; its adherents, 269; were leaderless, 271.
Lancaster, Thomas, Earl of, grasps at powers, i. 205; his party splits, 207; is defeated, *ib.*; is venerated by the people, *ib.*
Landed aristocracy, growth and importance of, ii. 154 *et sq.*
Landen, battle of, ii. 119.
Land tax. See Carucage.
Lanfranc, Archbishop, i. 91; his character, 33; his fitness for his post, *ib.*; crowns William II., 42; curbs William II., 44.
Langland, William, i. 219; his description of his era, 233.
Langside, battle of. i. 417.
Langton, Stephen, i. 121; goes to Pontigny, 124; releases John from excommunication, 127; the political movement against John, 128, 129; produces a copy of Henry I.'s charter, 130; mediates at Windsor between John and the barons, 133; his influence in the framing of the Great Charter, 138; leaves England, 142; goes to Rome, *ib.*; is suspended, *ib.*; steadfastly upholds the cause of order, 150.
Language, the English, effect of the Conquest on, i. 21, 22, 23.
Latimer, Hugh, Bishop of Worcester, quoted, i. 295, 350; driven from his see, 338; his character, 344; condones persecution, 363.
Latimer, Thomas Osborne, Viscount. See Danby, Earl of.
Latimer, William, fourth Baron, i. 229.
Latitudinarians, ii. 86.
Laud, William, Archbishop, i. 479; his religion, 484, 485; his appearance, 485; his rise, *ib.*; pope of the state church, 486; head of the government, *ib.*; puts ecclesiastics into secular offices, *ib.*; the character of

his government, 489, 490, 494; sets about the suppression of Puritanism, 500; extends uniformity to Scotland, i. 504 *et sq.*; is impeached, 514; is executed, 545.
Lauderdale, John Maitland, second Earl, and first Duke of, his administration of Scotland, ii. 23, 27, 29.
Law, in primitive times, i. 28; emergance of, 82, 83; the study of, 83; development of (*temp.* Edward I.), 180, 181; forms of, preserved (*temp.* Henry VIII.), 305.
Law, Brehon. See Brehon Law.
Law, canon. See Canon Law.
Law, common. See Common Law.
Law, ecclesiastical, new code proposed, i. 348.
Law, Jedburgh. See Jedburgh Law.
Law, Scotch, as compared with English, i. 415.
Lawrence, Sir Henry, ii. 413, 421.
Laws, penal. See Penal Laws.
Laws, sumptuary, i. 226.
Lawyers, the feudal, i. 83; exasperation against (*temp.* Richard II.), 236.
Laymen, ousting ecclesiastics in high offices, i. 220.
Learning, birth of, in England, i. 7.
Leeds, Thomas Osborne, Duke of. See Danby, Earl of.
Legates, papal, appear in England, i. 31; introduce reforms, *ib.*, 67.
Legislation (*temp.* Henry II.), i. 82, 83; advance in (*temp.* Edward I.), 180, 181; commercial (*temp.* Edward III.), 224.
Leicester, Philip Sidney, third Earl of. See Lisle, Viscount.
Leicester, Robert Dudley, Earl of, goes as commander to the Netherlands, i. 384, 389.
Leicester (the town), sacked, i. 532, 551.
Leighton, Alexander, indicted, i. 503.
Leighton, Robert, Archbishop of Glasgow, his futile attempts at mediation, ii. 24, 25.
Lenthall, William, speaker of the House (*temp.* Charles I.), i. 529, 554.
Leo X., Pope, i. 313, 317.
Leofric, the house of, i. 15.

Leon, princes of, i. 123.
Leopold, Duke of Austria, captures Richard I., i. 112.
Leopold, Prince, of Belgium, ii. 329.
Lerma, Francis de Roxas de Sandoval, Duke of, i. 435.
Leslie, Alexander, first Earl of Leven, i. 506.
Leslie, David, i. 546; defeats Montrose at Carbisdale, 585; encounters Cromwell at Dunbar, i. 588; forms a new army, i. 589; invades England, *ib.*; is defeated at Worcester, *ib.*
L'Estrange, Sir Roger, made censor of the press, ii. 12.
Levellers, the, i. 555; their demands, 559, 560; the most formidable disturbers, i. 575; mutiny amongst, 575, 576.
"Leviathan," Hobbes's, ii. 2.
Lewes, occupied by Henry III., i. 160; battle of, 161.
Lewis, Charles, Elector Palatine, i. 533.
Libel, prosecution for, ii. 39; reform of the law of, 246.
Liberals, the (*temp.* Charles I.), neither Laudian nor Puritan, i. 490.
Libertines, sect of, i. 545.
Liberty, the first great documents of English, i. 133; personal, as secured by the Great Charter, i. 137, 138.
Liberum veto, the Polish, i. 136.
Licensing Act (14 Car. II. c. 33), the lapse of, gives freedom to the press, ii. 38, 39.
Lichfield House Compact, ii. 358.
Life, shortness of (*temp.* Edward III.), i. 213.
Lilburne, John, indicted, i. 503; his influence, 575; his character, 555, 578; tries to upset the government of the commonwealth, *ib.*; how Cromwell dealt with him, 614.
Limerick, siege of, ii. 97.
Limitation, bill of, ii. 44.
Limoges, siege of, i. 212.
Linacre, Thomas, i. 314.
Lincoln, "fair" of, i. 150.
Lincoln, John de la Pole, Earl of, i. 282.
Lionel of Antwerp, Duke of Clarence, third son of Edward III., i. 215.

INDEX 461

Lisle, Alice, beheaded, ii. 61.
Lisle, Philip Sidney, Viscount (afterwards third Earl of Leicester), i. 611.
Lisle, Sir George, condemned to be shot, i. 566.
Literature, birth of, in England, i. 7; revival of, under Henry I., 58; has a new birth (*temp.* Edward III.), 219; (*temp.* Henry VII.), 279.
Littleton, Edward John, first Baron Hatherton, ii. 355.
Liturgy, Cranmer's English Protestant, i. 345, 346; a compromise, 371, 372.
Liveries, statutes against, i. 284.
Liverpool, Robert Banks Jenkinson, second Earl of, ii. 306, 313.
Livingstone, house of, i. 405.
Llewelyn, marries Eleanor de Montfort, i. 191; rebels, 190, 191; surrenders, 191; revolts, *ib.*; slain, *ib.*
Local government in Saxon times, i. 11.
Locke, John, his political philosophy, ii. 57.
Lockyer, Robert, the pomp of his funeral, i. 575, 576.
Lollardism, i. 239; attitude of the church towards, 251; (*temp.* Henry V.), 256, 314, 412.
Lollards, acts against, repealed, i. 348.
Lombard, Peter ("master of the sentences"), i. 279.
London (*temp.* William I.), i. 38; receives a charter of liberties, *ib.*; its fidelity to Stephen, 74; massacre of Jews in (*temp.* Richard I.), 110; progress of (*temp.* Richard I.), 116; its first lord mayor, *ib.*; its government, *ib.*; riots in (*temp.* Richard I.), 117; occupied by the barons, (*temp.* John), 132; treated on the footing of tenants-in-chief, 135; laid under an interdict, 142; thrives under Henry III., 146; liberties and companies, 147; tallaged by Henry III., 154; sides with De Montfort, 160; Watt Tyler occupies, 236; sides with Anne Boleyn, 320; sides with the Puritans (*temp.* Charles I.), 512; its council shares legislative power (*temp.* Charles I.), 534; the core of the Puritan cause (*temp.* Charles I.), 535, 536; threatened by Charles I., 540, 541; sides with the Presbyterian party after the civil war, 556; its charter forfeited (*temp.* Charles II.), ii. 49.
Londonderry, defence of, ii. 96.
Longbeard. See Fitzosbert, William.
Longbow, the, i. 198; compared with the firearm, 216, 248, 259, 407.
Longchamp, William of. See William.
Longsword, William, Earl of Salisbury, captures a French fleet, i. 129; death and burial of, 146.
Lords, House of, hereditary right to a seat in, i. 173; its constitution traceable to Edward I., *ib.*; composition of (*temp.* Henry VII.), 298; as a tribunal (*temp.* Henry VIII.), 306; diminution of spiritual element, 334; settles down into a conservative house, 401; its character and composition (*temp.* James I.), 444, 445; dwindles into an appendage to the Commons (*temp.* Charles I.), 534; fall of (*temp.* Commonwealth), 572; (*temp.* William III.), ii. 111.
Lords of articles, the, i. 407; ii. 23.
Lords of the congregation, i. 413.
Loretto, house of, i. 334.
Lorraine, Charles III., Duke of, i. 537, 552.
Lostwithiel, capitulation of, i. 549.
Loughborough, Alexander Wedderburn, Lord (afterwards first Earl of Rosslyn), betrays Pitt, ii. 297, 298.
Louis VII., of France, countenances Becket, i. 96.
Louis VIII., of France, lands in England, i. 143; enters London, *ib.*; denounces John, *ib.*; many declare for him, 143; defeated at the fair of Lincoln, 150; retires from England, *ib.*; annuls the provisions of Oxford, 160.
Louis IX., St., of France, i. 181, 263.
Louis XI., of France, i. 281, 284, 408.
Louis XIV., of France, i. 272; his despotism, 302; expels the Huguenots, 583; his secret alliance with Charles II., ii. 31; his paramount object as regards England, 37; his intrigues, ii. 40, 258.

Louis XVI. of France, compared with Charles I., i. 468; his trial compared with that of Charles I., i. 568; ii. 260, 261.
Louis Philippe, ii. 340.
Lovel, Francis, Viscount, i. 282.
Lowe, Robert, ii. 282.
Lowlands of Scotland, i. 410.
Loyalists of America, ii. 215, 216, 221.
Loyalty loan, the, ii. 279.
Loyalty, personal, in Saxon times, i. 9; birthday of, i. 297.
Loyola, Ignatius, i. 425.
Lucas, Sir Charles, condemned to be shot, i. 566.
Lucy, Richard de, i. 96, 103.
Ludlow, Edmund, Colonel, i. 556; ii. 91.
Lumley, Richard, first Earl of Scarborough, ii. 71.
Lunsford, Thomas, appointed governor of the Tower, i. 528.
Lupus, Hugh, Earl of Chester, i. 49.
Luther, Martin, i. 232, 313, 328, 394.
Lutheranism (*temp.* James I.), i. 462.
Lutherans, i. 329, 426.
Lutter, battle of, i. 495.
Lützen, battlefield of, i. 494.
Luxury, repression of, i. 226.
Lydgate, John, i. 219.
Lyme, fury of the women of, i. 532.
Lyndhurst, John Singleton Copley, *jr.*, Lord, ii. 348.
Lyons, Richard, Edward III.'s financial agent, i. 229.

M

Macclesfield, Lord Chancellor, ii. 160.
Macaulay, Thomas Babington, Lord, ii. 344, 424.
Macdonald, John A., ii. 401.
Machiavelli, Niccolo, i. 270, 280, 326.
Machiavellism, i. 254.
Mackay, General, defeats Claverhouse, ii. 93, 94.
Mackenzie, William Lyon, ii. 393, 394, 399.
Maclonghlin, Turlough Oge, i. 311.
Magdalen College, i. 274.
Magna carta. See Charter, the Great.
Maguinness, Donald, i. 311.

Maguinness, Hugh, i. 311.
Mahrattas, the, ii. 413, 420, 421.
Maidstone, John, quoted, i. 643.
Maitland, William, of Lethington, i. 416.
Major-generals appointed, i. 613.
Malcolm III. of Scots, called Canmore, i. 60, 166.
Malet, Robert, i. 60.
Maletolt, i. 223.
Malignants, the, i. 533.
Malplaquet, battle of, ii. 144.
Malta, ii. 410.
"Malvoisin," i. 144.
Manchester, Edward Montague, second Earl of, his conduct at the second battle of Newbury, i. 550; refuses to sit in Cromwell's upper House, 619.
Manny, Sir Walter, i. 218, 220.
Manor, the (*temp.* William I.), i. 31.
Manor court, the, i. 81.
Manor, lord of the, how curbed, i. 170, 177.
Manorial system, requisites of, i. 234; finally replaced by land-ownership and hired labour, 350; the new (*temp.* Elizabeth), 380, 381.
Mansell, John, i. 153.
Mansfeld, Ernst von, i. 462; loses the Protestant cause, 472.
Manufactures, advance and spread of (*temp.* Henry VII.), i. 292.
Manwaring, Roger, quoted, i. 474, 475, 482.
March, Edmund Mortimer, Earl of, i. 243, 245.
March, Roger Mortimer, Earl of. See Mortimer, Roger.
Marche, Count de la. See La Marche.
Marengo, battle of, ii. 300.
Margaret, daughter of Alexander III., King of Scotland, i. 19.
Margaret, daughter of Eric of Norway, i. 411.
Margaret (daughter of Henry VI.), marries James IV. of Scotland, i. 289.
Margaret, Duchess of Burgundy, i. 282.
Margaret, of Anjou, wife of Henry VI., i. 264, 266, 267, 268, 269, 271.

INDEX 463

Margaret, wife of Malcolm Canmore, i. 166.
Maria Theresa, attacked by Frederick the Great, ii. 193.
Marie Antoinette (wife of Louis XVI.), compared with Henrietta Maria, i. 468, 471.
Marisco, Adam de, i. 158.
Maritime enterprise, awakening of, i. 146.
Marborough, parliament of, i. 164.
Marlborough, John Churchill, first Duke of, his importance in the revolution of 1688, ii. 76; his character, 76, 77; completes the victory in Ireland, 97; his perfidy, 103; his ascendancy, 129 et sq.; his politics, 131; his army, 132, 133; compared with Hannibal and Napoleon, 134; dismissed and disgraced, 149.
Marlowe, Christopher, i. 209, 377.
Marriage, indissoluble in church of Rome, i. 318, 319.
Marshall, Richard, third Earl of Pembroke and Striguil, takes arms against the king, i. 157; is slain, *ib.*
Marshall, William, first Earl of Pembroke and Striguil, sides with the king, i. 132; acts as mediator, 133, 146; crowns Henry III., 149; is regent, 150.
Marston Moor, battle of, i. 546, 547.
Marten, Henry, i. 511, 555.
Martial law proclaimed (*temp.* Charles I.), i. 472.
Martin Marprelate, i. 397.
Martinitz, Jaroslas von, i. 461.
Martyr, Peter, invited to England, i. 345.
Martyr, Catherine (Peter Martyr's wife), i. 360.
Marvell, Andrew, quoted, i. 602; his incorruptibility, ii. 35, 36.
Mary (sister of Henry VIII., daughter of Henry VII., wife of (1) Louis XII. (2) Charles Brandon, Duke of Suffolk), i. 358.
Mary, Queen of England, i. 319; the lawful heiress, 358; naturally an enemy of the Reformation, 359; not naturally cruel, *ib.*; the motive of her persecutions, *ib.*, 363; her character and appearance *ib.*; her difficulties, 359; marries Philip II. of Spain, 362; her chagrin at her barrenness, 363; her attitude in the counter-reformation, 363; the significance of the epithet "bloody" applied to her, 366.
Mary Stuart (daughter of James V., of Scotland), Queen of Scots, i. 343, 368, 370; the legitimate heir, 386; assumes the royal arms, *ib.*; her Catholicism, 387; her pitiful plight in Scotland, *ib.*; takes refuge in England, *ib.*; her conviction and trial, *ib.*, 388, 411, 414; the question of her marriage, 416; her attachment to Catholicism, *ib.*; marries Darnley, *ib.*; marries Bothwell, 417; is imprisoned, *ib.*; resigns, *ib.*; is defeated, *ib.*; and beheaded, *ib.*
Mary of Guise (wife of James V. of Scotland), i. 412, 414.
Mary, Princess, daughter of Charles I., i. 524.
Mary, of Modena, ii. 43.
Mary (daughter of James II. of England, afterwards queen), marries William, Prince of Orange (afterwards William III.), ii. 35; brought up a protestant, 43; her influence in the Revolution of 1688, 79; ascends the throne, 82; dies, 120; her character and influence, *ib.*
Massachusetts, founders of, i. 649; rebels, ii. 207, 212.
Massey, John, ii. 65.
Massinger, Philip, i. 459, 496.
Matilda, married to Henry I., i. 59; rejoices at Anselm's reinstatement, 65; set aside for Stephen, 71; married to Fulk, Count of Anjou, *ib.*; lands in England, 73; enters London, 74; is expelled, *ib.*
Matthew Paris. See Paris, Matthew.
Maud. See Matilda.
Mauleon, Savary de, i. 140.
Maximilian, Duke and first Elector of Bavaria, i. 462.
Mayflower, the, ii. 385.
Maynard, John, i. 510, 556, 563.
Mayor, Dorothy and Richard, i. 590.
Mazarin, Jules, Cardinal, i. 435, 537;

his envoy to the Commonwealth, 595.
McMahon, i. 311.
Medmenham Abbey, ii. 164.
Melbourne, William Lamb, second Viscount, ii. 355 *et sq.*; his ministry, 358 *et sq.*, 381.
Mellent, Robert de, i. 55; excommunicated, 65.
Melrose Abbey, i. 409.
Melville, Andrew, i. 436, 506.
Mercenaries come to the aid of John, i. 140.
Merchants, foreign, protected by the Great Charter, i. 135; statute of (11 Edw. I.), 183; rival the aristocracy (*temp.* Henry VII.), 280.
Merchant adventurers, i. 292, 293.
Mercia, i. 6; resists Christianity, 7.
Merton, Walter de, i. 148.
Mercury, newspaper, i. 539.
Metcalfe, Charles Theophilus, Baron, governor of Canada, ii. 398.
Methodism, influence of, ii. 163, 195, 196.
Mexico, effects of the discovery of silver in, i. 336.
Middle ages, end of, i. 230; end of the Catholic, 279.
Middleton, John Middleton, first Earl of, his administration of Scotland, ii. 53.
Militia, national (see also Fyrd), reorganized by Henry II., i. 78, 79, 176, 217.
Millenarians, i. 545.
Millenary petition, the, i. 437, 438.
Milton, John, combines Puritanism and culture, i. 497, 540, 541; among the moral anarchists, 545; on liberty of conscience, 548, 549; replies to the "Eikon Basiliké," 576; is made Latin Secretary, *ib.*; becomes the state pamphleteer, *ib.*; his controversy with Salmasius, *ib.*; his "Areopagitica," 577; his advice to the long parliament, 595; his sonnet to Cromwell, 599; his fidelity to Cromwell, 612; his advice to the rump parliament, 647; escapes the fate of the regicides, 8.
Minerals, of Great Britain, i. 2.

Mines, act forbidding women and girls working in (586 Vict. c. 99), ii. 373.
Ministers, responsibility of, to parliament (*temp.* Charles I.), i. 473.
Ministry of all the talents, the, ii. 305.
Minority, parliament empowers cancellation of laws passed during (*temp.* Henry VIII.; 28 Hen. VIII. c. 17), i. 303.
Minstrelsy, Welsh, i. 191, 192.
Mirabeau, Count de, ii. 261.
Miracles performed by Becket, i. 95.
Mise of Lewes. See Lewes.
Missionaries, Irish, enterprise of, i. 100.
Mitton, battle of, i. 206.
Moats, disappear, i. 280.
Mogul empire, ii. 233, 411, 413.
Moleyne, Adam, Bishop of Chichester, i. 265.
Mompesson, Sir Giles, i. 459.
Monacute. See Montague.
Monarchy, the Norman, in England, character of, i. 24; functions of, 25; a new element added to the right to, 60; the scope and functions of, in the reign of Henry I., 67, 68; growth of, its stability and power under Henry II., 106; evidences of its strength under Richard I., 114; strong under John, 120; elective system of, 147; Bracton on, 149; Matthew Paris on, 148, 149; constitutional, principles of (*temp.* Henry III.), 148; De Montfort puts it in abeyance, 162, 163; restored after De Montfort's defeat, *ib.*; the ruling power (*temp.* Edward I.), 169, 175; element of chance in, 203; constitutional, vital principle of, 256; becomes partially despotic after the War of the Roses, 281; the Tudor, rested on the middle classes, 289; placed on a firm and enduring basis by Henry VII., 296; the five chief checks on, *ib.*; other checks, *ib.*; deprived of the support of Catholicism (*temp.* Henry VIII.), 327; government deemed to be in the crown (*temp.* Elizabeth), 399; parliament-

ary and Protestant (*temp.* James I.), 429 *et sq.*; begins to cast the burden of government on a vizier, 435; convocation formulates the absolutist creed, 438, 439; modern idea of, 558; effect of the Bill of Rights and the Mutiny Act upon, ii. 85.

Monasteries, founded by Henry I., i. 67; their influence on civilization and learning (*temp.* Henry I.), *ib.*; their chronicles, *ib.*; their influence on church art and music, *ib.*; suppression of (lesser 27 Hen. VIII. c. 28, and greater 31 Hen. VIII. c. 13), 329 *et sq.*; Cromwell recommends dissolution of, 331; commissioners want, 332; their use and abuse, 331, 332; give place to universities and schools, 332; their value in the north, *ib.*; expenditure of the fund derived from, 334; usefulness of, 335; dissolution of, increases vagrancy, 352; dissolution of, lands derived from, 361, 362; dissolution of, give rise to the landed gentry and yeomanry, 392.

Monasticism, extension of, in England (*temp.* Henry I.), i. 67; flourishes under Stephen, 75; beyond resuscitation (*temp.* Mary), 362.

Monck, George, first Duke of Albermarle. See Albermarle.

Money bills, origination of, i. 276, 401.

Money-power in politics (*temp.* William III.), ii. 318.

Monks, effect of the dissolution of the monasteries upon, i. 336.

Monmouth, James Fitzroy (*alias* Scott, *alias* Crofts), Duke of, invades Holland, ii. 33, 44.

Monopolies, i. 398; declared illegal (*temp.* James I., 21 Jac. I. c. 3), 459; abolished by the long parliament, 514.

Monroe Doctrine, the, ii. 325.

Montagu, Charles, Earl of Halifax, one of the junto, ii. 109; his character, *ib.*; improves the coinage (7 & 8 Gul. III. c. 1), 116; funds the debt, *ib.*

Montague, Edward. See Sandwich, Earl of.

Montague, Henry Pole, Lord, executed for treason, i. 329, 331.

Montague, Richard, Bishop of Chichester, i. 474, 482, 502.

Montéreau, i. 260.

Montesquieu, Baron de la Bride et de, i. 458

Montford, Eleanor de, i. 191.

Montfort, Robert de, i. 82.

Montfort, Simon de, i. 123, 158; an adventurer, *ib.*; highly religious, *ib.*; sent as governor to Gascony, *ib.*; leads the opponents of the king, *ib.*; calls a parliament, 162; is slain, 163; hymn to, *ib.*; the fate of his sons, 164, 207.

Montrose, James Graham, fifth Earl, and first Marquis of, i. 198, 524; his brilliant victories over Argyle, 550; defeated at Philiphaugh, 552; is defeated at Carbisdale, 585; is executed, *ib.*; his career, *ib.*; his death, 586.

Moore, Sir John, ii. 307.

Morcar, Earl, i. 20.

More, Barry, i. 311.

More, Sir Thomas, i. 281, 305, 314; his crime, 328, 329; his character, 328; made chancellor, 329; resigns, *ib.*; is executed, *ib.*, 330; quoted, 351.

Mortalists, 545.

Mortimer, Edmund. See March, Earl of.

Mortimer, Roger, i. 208, 209, 210.

Mortmain, statute of (Edw. I. c. 2), i. 179; attempts to elude, *ib.*, 315.

Morton, John, Archbishop, i. 300, 369.

Moscow, burning of, ii. 309.

Mountjoy, Charles Blount, Earl of Devonshire, and eighth Lord, Laud panders to, i. 490.

Muggletonians, i. 545.

Muir, Thomas, ii. 274.

Municipal life, awakening of, i. 147.

Municipal Reform Act (5 & 6 Gul. IV. c. 76), ii. 359 *et sq.*

Munster, i. 351.

Münzer, Thomas, rising of Anabaptists under, i. 348, 545.

Murphy, Father, ii. 290.

Murray, James Stuart, second Earl of, and of Mar, i. 415.

Mutiny Act, the (1 Gul. and Mar. c. 5), passed, ii. 84; its importance ib.; its effects on monarchy, 85.
Mutiny, the Indian, ii. 427 et sq.
Mysore, ii. 419, 420, 421.

N

Nadir, Shah, ii. 411 et sq.
Nag's head, story of the consecration at the, i. 376.
Namur, taken by William III., ii. 119.
Nana Sahib, ii. 428.
Napier, Sir Charles, ii. 414.
Napoleon Bonaparte, compared with Cromwell, i. 642; ii. 300 et sq., 304; his Berlin decrees, ii. 307; his career, 308 et sq.; falls, 309; his influence, ib.
Naseby, battle of, i. 551; its decisiveness, ib.
National Assembly (French), the, i. 172.
National debt (temp. George III.), ii. 239 et sq.; evils of, 240.
Nationality, i. 7; the grand aim of Edward I., 169; becomes conscious, 171; growth of (temp. Edward III.), 219; rebels against the papacy (temp. Richard II.), 231; (temp. the Tudors), 297.
Navarre (Sancho VII.), the king of, cursed by Innocent III., i. 123.
Navigation Acts of Henry VII. (1 Hen. VII. c. 8; 4 Hen. VII. c. 10), i. 293, 593.
Navy (see also Fleet), how manned (temp. Richard I.), i. 111; imprisonment of, under Edward I., 176; attention paid to, by Edward III., 217; mercantile, growth of (temp. Henry VII.), 292, 306; its influence on English liberty, 382.
Naylor, James, i. 619.
Neile, Richard, Bishop of Durham (afterwards Archbishop of York), i. 439, 451.
Negro, the, ii. 408.
Nelson, Horatio, Viscount, death of, ii. 304.
Nelson, Wolfred, ii. 391, 393.
Neo-Catholicism, i. 428.

Netherlands, persecution in the, i. 35; struggles of Protestantism in, 388; persecution in, 442; almost a monarchy, 573.
Neuilly, Fulk de, i. 123.
Nevers, the Earl of, i. 144.
Nevill's Cross, battle of, i. 221, 407.
Neville's, the, i. 260.
Neville, Sir Henry, i. 452.
New Brunswick, ii. 399, 402.
New College, i. 228.
New England, emigrants to, i. 649.
New model, the, how formed and commanded, i. 551; supports the independents, 556; its character, 557; becomes a political organization, 559; enters London, 563; refuses to disband, ib.; marches to Uxbridge, ib.; denounces eleven Presbyterian members of parliament, ib.; demands that the king shall be brought to justice, 567.
New Orleans, British repulsed at, ii. 308.
Newark, castle of, i. 108, 144.
Newbury, battle of, i. 542; second battle of, 550.
Newcastle (the town), commissioners from the long parliament meet Charles I. at, i. 553.
Newcastle, Thomas Pelham-Holles, Duke of, ii. 188, 189, 191, 198.
Newcastle, William Cavendish, first Marquis (and afterwards Duke) of, holds York for Charles I., i. 546.
Newfoundland, i. 294.
Newspapers, duty on reduced (6 & 7 Gul. IV. c. 76), ii. 375.
Newton Butler, battle of, ii. 96.
Nigel, Bishop of Ely, i. 69, 72; his views on monarchy, 106.
Nithing, meaning of, i. 10.
"No addresses," vote of, i. 565.
Nobility, a new order of, on the merging of chief into king, i. 9; (temp. William I.), 28, 29; predominance of (temp. Richard II.), 239; the old, the part played by (temp. Henry VIII.) 304; character of, ii. 71.
Noblesse, the French, i. 172.
Nogaret, William of, i. 326.

Nonconformity, political, birth of, ii. 17.
Nonjurors, the, ii. 89-90.
Non-resistance, oath of, imp sed by statute (13 Car. II. stat. 2, c. 1), ii. 11; the Lords pass a bill imposing an oath of, 37, 38.
Norfolk, Henry Charles Howard, thirteenth Duke of, is converted to Protestantism, ii. 278.
Norfolk, Thomas Howard, second Duke of, and Earl of Surrey (victor of Flodden), i. 407.
Norfolk, Thomas Howard, third Duke of, i. 324, 337.
Norfolk, Thomas (III.) Howard, fourth Duke of, i. 376.
Norfolk, Thomas Mowbray, Duke of, banished by Richard II., i. 242.
Norman Conquest. See Conquest, the Norman.
Norman, pious and papal character of the, i. 18; and the Saxon, compared, 22.
Normandy, the Duke of, origin of, i. 16; compared with England, 22; falls into anarchy under Robert, 70; a focus of feudal mutiny, 119; much of the time of English kings spent in, ib., 120; its severance from England essential, 120.
Norris, Henry, i. 324.
Norsemen, i. 193.
North Briton, the, ii. 201.
North, Francis. See Guilford, Lord.
North, Frederick, Lord, second Earl of Guilford, head of the government, ii. 214; his character, ib.; coerces the American colonies, 218, 231, 232.
Northampton, the Great Council meets at, i. 93.
Northmen, the, in Normandy, i. 16.
Northumberland, earldom of, sold by Richard I., i. 108.
Northumberland, John Dudley, Duke of, his conspiracy, i. 354, 355.
Northumberland, Thomas Percy, seventh Earl of, i. 376.
Northumbria, Christianity in, i. 7.
Northwest territories of Canada, the, ii. 402.

Norwich, George Loring, Earl of, is banished, i. 566.
Norwich, Kett's insurrection at, i. 351, 352.
Nottingham burned, i. 73; Charles I. sets up his standard at, 540.
Nottingham, Daniel Finch, second Earl of Nottingham, and sixth Earl of Winchilsea, supports the Whigs, ii. 105, 106, 130.
Nova Scotia, ii. 399, 462.
Nunneries, usefulness of, i. 332.
Nye, Philip, i. 535, 545.

O

Oates, Titus, his infamy and its consequences, ii. 41.
Occasional Conformity Act, the, ii. 130, 151; repealed (5 Geo I. c. 4), 166.
O'Connell, Daniel, his appearance and character, ii. 333 et sq., 346, 378.
October Club, the, ii. 145.
Odo, Bishop of Bayeux, i. 40, 44, 91.
O'Dogherty, rebellion of, i. 422.
O'Kane, Donald, i. 311.
Old Sarum, ii. 320.
Oldcastle, Sir John, i. 256, 257.
O'Leary, Arthur, ii. 299.
Olivarez, Gasparo de Guzman, Count of, i. 435.
O'Neill, Owen Roe, i. 580.
Ontario, ii. 387, 401, 403.
Opposition, a parliamentary, regularly organized (*temp*. Charles II.), ii. 36.
O'Quillan, i. 311.
Orangeism, ii. 334; introduced into Canada, 400.
Oratory, parliamentary (*temp*. Elizabeth), i. 398; begins to be a power in politics, i. 520.
Ordeal in trials, i. 10; its use restricted, 81, 82; in Henry II.'s legislation, 119.
Orders of Knighthood, i. 211.
Ordinances, imposed upon Edward II. by a committee of lords and prelates, i. 205; their provisos, ib., 206; are overthrown, 207, 208; the concessions demanded by them practically confirmed, 208.

Orford, Edward Russell, Earl of. See Russell, Edward.
Orford, Robert Walpole, Earl of. See Walpole, Robert.
Orkney, Elizabeth Villiers, Countess of, land grants to, ii. 123.
Orleans, the Regent, succeeds Louis XIV., ii. 174.
Orlton, Adam, Bishop of Hereford, i. 209.
Ormonde, James Butler, twelfth Earl, first Marquis, and first Duke of, deputy in Ireland, i. 579, 580; returns to London, 613; ii. 4, 34; impeached, 165, 166.
Orombelli, Michael, i. 325.
Orrery, Roger Boyle, first Earl of. See Broghill, Baron.
Otho IV., of Brunswick, i. 123.
Otho, papal legate, i. 156.
Oude, annexation of, ii. 427.
Oudenarde, battle of, ii. 143.
Overbury, Sir Thomas, i. 457 et sq.
Overbury trial, the, i. 436, 451 et sq.
Oxford, John de Vere, Earl of, i. 285.
Oxford, Robert Harley, Earl of. See Harley.
Oxford (town), the base of Charles I.'s operations, i. 536; surrenders, 552.
Oxford, University of, birth of, i. 58, 147; students of, assault of the, 156; side with De Montfort, 160.

P

Paget, Sir William, quoted, re Somerset's policy, i. 354.
Paget, William, first Baron Paget of Beaudesert, Secretary of State, i. 302, 304, 360, 361.
Paine, Tom, ii. 272.
Palatinate, the recovery of (temp. Charles I.), i. 470, 471, 478 et sq., 494.
Pale, the Anglo-Norman, in Ireland, i. 309 et sq.; atrocities of, 418.
Palmerston, Henry John Temple, third Viscount, ii. 317.
Pamphlets (temp. Elizabeth), i. 397; shoals of (temp. Charles I.), 539; (temp. William III.) ii. 115.
Pandulph, papal legate, i. 127, 131, 133, 142.

Panzani, Gregorio, papal envoy, i. 502.
Papacy, the (temp. William I.), i. 34 et sq.; morality of the, ib. et sq.; has always been Italian, 35; its encroachments in England (temp. Henry I.), 67; its resort to force, 97; always despotic, 131; practises extortion on English clergy (temp. Henry III), 155; the zenith of its usurpation, 156, 157; unpopularity of (temp. Henry III.), 177; its pretensions (temp. Edward I.), 178; strives to dominate England, ib.; subjection to, being shaken off, 219, 220; transferred to Avignon, 219; its rapid advancement between the reigns of Henry II. and John, 122; causes contributing to this, ib.; its claims (temp. John), ib.; becomes the tool of France, 231; degradation of, ib.; schism in the, 248; corruption of, 312; schisms in, 313; always foreign to England, 361.
Papineau, Louis Jean, ii. 391, 393.
Papists, disabled from sitting in parliament (30 Car. II. stat. 2, c. 1), ii. 36.
Paris, Matthew, i. 118; on the elective system of monarchy, 148, 149.
Parish system, i. 11.
Parker, Matthew, Archbishop of Canterbury, i. 376.
Parker, Samuel, Bishop of Oxford, ii. 65.
Parliament, germs of, in the Great Charter, i. 136; birth of, 145; the name given to the assembly of barons and prelates,154; knights summoned to, 161; representation of the people in (temp. Henry III.), 162; De Montfort's (Jan. 28, 1865), character of, 165; representation in (temp. Edward I.), 170 et sq.; our modern, traceable to Edward I., 173; its primal function of, under Edward I., 175; how this was developed, ib., 176; demands redress of grievances (temp. Edward II.), 205; to be held yearly (temp. Edward II.), 206; growth and power of (temp. Edward II.), 209; ill-informed (temp. Edward III.), 221; struggles against Edward III., 223; enlarges its pow-

ers, *ib* ; activity of (*temp.* Edward III.), 224; its organization pretty complete, *ib.*; definitely divided into two houses, *ib.*; reforms abuses, 225; cancels Richard II.'s charter of manumission, 237; the complaisance of (*temp.* Richard II.), 241, 242; its deposing power, 243; deposes Richard II., *ib.*; settles the succession on Henry IV., *ib.*; latitude allowed to, by Henry IV., 249, 250; its consent is necessary to laws, 255, 256; the powers it had acquired (*temp.* Richard III.), 276; how acquired, *ib.*; its condition in the Wars of the Roses, 275, 276, 277, 278; annual, ordained by Edward II., 278; its influence paramount over that of the city, 291; no tax levied without its consent (*temp.* Henry VII. *et sq.*), 296; no fixed time for election or dissolution (*temp.* Tudors), 298; its weakness its strength (*temp.* Tudors), *ib.*; only seven called by Henry VII., 299; an engine by the government (*temp.* Henry VIII.), 304; its subserviency to Henry VIII., *ib.*; legislative authority of, restored, 356; its independence (*temp.* Elizabeth), 397 *et sq.*; Tudor compared with Lancastrian, 399 *et sq.*; annual, prescribed by statute (5 Edw. II. c. 29; 36 Edw. III. c. 10), 515; growth of the power of (*temp.* Restoration), ii. 10; right of, to deal with the succession to the crown, 43; end of the struggle between king and, 85; character of (*temp.* William III.), 112 *et sq.*

Parliament, the Addled (1614), significance of the elections to, i. 450; its constitution, *ib.*; its dissolution, *ib.*

Parliament, the "Barebones," or "Little," i. 602 *et sq.*

Parliament, Charles II.'s, ii. 7, 10; its opposition to the Declaration of Indulgence, 30; strikes at the Duke of York, 31; its corruptibility, 35; its protests and demands, 36; is dissolved, 39; his second, *ib.*; his Oxford parliament, 46.

Parliament, the "Convention," restores Charles II., ii. 5.
Parliament, Cromwell's, i. 614.
Parliament, the "Good," i. 229.
Parliament of Ireland, i. 310, 312, 422; (*temp.* George III.), ii. 243 *et sq.*; passes Catholic emancipation, 285.
Parliament, the "Long," called, i. 508 *et sq.*; its temper, 512; its reforms, 513; passes a triennial bill (16 Car. I. c. 1), 515; forbids its own dissolution (16 Car. I. c. 7), *ib.*; attaints Strafford, 521; its ecclesiastical reforms, 523; demands the command of the militia, 529; its rupture with the king, *ib. et sq.*; makes war on the king, 533; raises an army, 539; accepts the solemn league and covenant, 543; its severe measures when under Presbyterian domination, 545; remodels the army, 550, 551; publishes "The King's Cabinet Opened," 551, 552; corruption of, 554; opens fresh negotiations with Charles after his surrender by the Scotch, 558; attempts to disband the army, 563; fortifies London, *ib.*; gives way to the army, *ib.*; submits a compromise to the king, 565; sends commissioners to treat with the king at Newport, 567; ceases to be representative of the people, 574; surnamed the "Rump" (*q. v. infra*), 594; perpetuates itself, 596.
Parliament, the "Mad," i. 158.
Parliament, the "Merciless," i. 242.
Parliament, the "Rump," called, i. 647.
Parliament of Scotland, the, i. 406 *et sq.*; remodelled by James I., 407.
Parliamentary government (*temp.* Edward I.), needs of, i. 165; not a solitary birth in England, i. 171.
Parliamentary reform, Pitt's attempt at, ii. 242, 320 *et sq.*, 341 *et sq.*
Parma, Hercules Farnese, Duke of, i. 377, 388, 425.
Parr, Catherine, wife of Henry VIII., i. 339.
Parricide, common in Norman annals, i. 104.
Parties, formation of (*temp.* Edward

II.), i. 204; (*temp.* Henry VIII.), 342.
Party government, origin of, ii. 106 *et sq.*
Party system, the, ii. 171.
Paschal, Pope, i. 62.
Paston letters, i. 262.
Paterson, William, projects the Darien Company, ii. 136.
Pattinson, ii. 421.
Paul III., Pope, his attitude in the question of the divorce of Anne Boleyn, i. 320, 321; excommunicates Henry VIII., 322.
Paul IV., Pope, his treatment of Cardinal Pole, i. 365.
Paulet, Sir Amyas, i. 388.
Paulinus, carries Christianity to Northumbria, i. 6.
Pauperism, growth of (*temp.* Edward VI.), i. 352; (*temp.* Elizabeth), 379.
Peace, the king's, i. 10.
Peacham, Edmond, i. 436, 455.
Peasant, the (*temp.* William I.), i. 31; not freed by the Great Charter, 138; (*temp.* Edward I.), 175.
Peasants' war (England). See Serfs, Revolt of.
Peasants' war (Germany), i. 233.
Peckham, John, Archbishop of Canterbury, i. 178, 179.
Peacock, Reginald, Bishop of St. Asaph and of Chichester, i. 314.
Pedro the Cruel, king of Castile, i. 227.
Peel, Sir Robert, ii. 314; his ability and politics, 331 *et sq.*; as leader, 328, 356 *et sq.*
Peers, i. 173; assembly of, called by Charles I., 508.
Pelham, Henry, ii. 187.
Pembroke, William and Richard Marshall, Earls of. See Marshall, William and Richard.
Pembrokeshire, Flemings posted in, i. 189.
Penal laws, i. 440.
Penda, King, i. 7.
Penitentials, Roman, i. 318.
Pennenden Heath, great suit decided on, I. 30, 91.
Penny post, the, ii. 376.

Penruddock, John, royalists rise under, i. 612, 613.
Penry, John, I. 396.
Perambulation of the forests, i. 187.
Perceval, Spencer, ii. 306, 314.
Percy, Henry, second Earl of Northumberland, son and heir of Sir Henry Percy, called "Hotspur," i. 256.
Percy, Sir Henry ("Harry Hotspur"), i. 246.
Percys, the (see also Northumberland, Earls of), Richard II. estranges, i. 242, 243; ally against Henry IV., 246, 269.
Perrers, Alice, i. 228, 229.
Persecutions, the Marian, i. 363 *et sq.*; number of those who suffered, 364; few gentry and no nobles among the martyrs, *ib.*; its initiation ascribed to Gardiner, *ib.*; its cruelty to Bonner, *ib.*; parliament, queen, and council responsible, *ib.*; not Spain, *ib.*, 365; burnings confined to south and east, 365; by the long parliament, 545 *et sq.*
Perth, North Inch of, clan fight at, i. 411.
Peruzzi, the, i. 222.
Peter the Hermit, i. 127.
Peter's pence irregularly paid in Saxon times, i. 18; paid after the Conquest, 32, 315.
Peterloo, massacre of, ii. 327, 328.
Petition of Right, i. 133, 479.
Petre, Edward, Father, ii. 61, 63.
Philip II., Augustus, king of France, i. 104, 111; prepares to invade England, 127; attacks Flanders, 129; fears the pope, 142.
Philip III. (the Bold), king of France, instigates the Scotch to attack England, i. 213.
Philip II., of Spain, i. 172; marries Mary, queen of England, 362, 365, 388.
Philip IV. ("the Fair"), of France, i. 326.
Philip Mary, Duke of Milan, i. 325.
Philip (Duke of Swabia), the Hohenstauffen, i. 123.
Philiphaugh, battle of, I. 552.

INDEX 471

Philippa, Queen, wife of Edward III., i. 227.
Philosophy, scholastic, the era of, i. 147; is displaced, 279.
Picard, Sir Henry, i. 224.
" Piers Ploughman," i. 253.
Pilate's Stairs, i. 334.
Pilgrimage of grace, i. 330, 333, 335.
Pilgrimages, discarded, i. 346.
Pilnitz, conference at, ii. 265.
Pindarees, the, ii. 421.
Pinkie Cleugh, battle of, i. 343, 411.
Piracy, common (*temp.* Henry VII.), i. 292.
Pitt, William, Earl of Chatham, ii. 182, 185; comes to the front, 190; his qualifications, *ib.*; head of the government, 191 *et sq.*; his policy, 192; his character, *ib.*, *et sq.*, his foreign wars, 194 *et sq.*; his fall, 198; upholds the revolt of the colonies, 207, 208; forms a ministry, 210, 211; raised to the peerage, 211; resigns, 214; dies, 218.
Pitt, William, ii. 231; accepts the premiership, 235 *et sq.*; his early training, *ib.*; his financial policy, 239 *et sq.*, 241, 278 *et sq.*; his treatment of Unitarians and Latitudinarians, 246 ; his East India bill, 248 *et sq.*; his foreign policy, 256 *et sq.*; on the French Revolution, 261, 262, 265, 266; his war with France, 266 *et sq.*; as war minister, 269; his invasions of liberty, 275; his oratory, 281, 282; and the union with Ireland, 295 *et sq.*; resigns, 298 *et sq.*; again takes office, 302 *et sq.*
Pius V., Pope, deposes Elizabeth, i. 377.
Place bill proposed, ii. 110.
Place, Francis, ii. 352, 373.
Plague, the great, of London (see also Black Death), ii. 18.
Plantagenet line, founder of the, i. 76.
Plantagenet, Richard, Duke of York, assumes the name of, i. 266.
Plantations, in Ireland, 422, 423.
Plassey, battle of, ii. 414, 421.
Platform, the birth of the, ii. 227; influence of (*temp.* George IV.), 323.
Plato, i. 279.

Platonists, Cambridge, precursors of the, i. 499.
Plessis les Tours, i. 284.
Plunket, Oliver, Archbishop of Armagh, executed, ii. 41.
Plunket, William Conyngham, first Baron, ii. 281, 296, 329, 330, 333.
Plymouth (town), i. 536.
Poems, political, i. 147, 148.
Poitiers, battle of, i. 213; its influence, 214, 220, 238, 246.
Poitou, conquered by King John, i. 129.
Pole, John de la, Earl of Lincoln. See Lincoln.
Pole, Michael de la, i. 240.
Pole, Reginald, Cardinal, i. 313, 314, 330, 359; made papal legate, 361; his liberality of creed, 365.
Pole, William de la, fourth Earl, and first Duke of Suffolk. See Suffolk, Duke of.
Poles, the de la, i. 291.
Police, in Saxon times, i. 10.
Polity, old English, i. 1–15; Norman, as compared with English, 30; its central idea, *ib.*
Poll tax, i. 235.
Pomfret Castle, Richard III. consigned to, i. 244.
Pompadour, Jeanne Antoinette Poisson, Marchioness of, ii. 193.
Pontefract, Robert de, i. 60.
Pontigny, Abbot of, i. 95.
Poor law, i. 352 (*temp.* Elizabeth), (35 Eliz. c. 4), 326 ; (*temp.* William IV.) (4 and 5 Gul. IV. c. 76), ii. 367, 379.
Poor, relief of, enjoined by statute (1 Edw. VI. c. 3), i. 353.
Pope, the, his claims (*temp.* John), i. 122; rival popes (*temp.* Henry III.), 155; how regarded in England, 314, 315.
Popish plot, the (*temp.* Charles II.), ii. 41.
Portland, William Henry Cavendish, third Duke of, Prime Minister, ii. 231, 286, 306.
Portobello taken, ii. 184.
Port-reeve, i. 38.
Ports, English, safe from attack, i. 2;

liberties of, secured by the Great Charter, 134, 135.
Portsmouth, Duchess of, as Mme. Louise de Kéroualle, sent by Louis XIV. to Charles II., ii. 32.
Pottinger, Eldred, ii. 421.
Poundage. See Tonnage and Poundage.
Poynings, Sir Edward, i. 312.
Præmunire, statute of (16 Rich. II. c. 5), i. 220, 313, 315, 326, 361, 373.
Prayer Book. See Common Prayer, Book of.
Prayers for the dead discarded, i. 346.
Preambles of statutes, i. 305.
Prerogative, the king's (temp. William I.), i. 25 sq.; stretches of, by Edward III., 221, by James I., 457.
Presbyterian party (temp. Charles I.), aims of, i. 555; the Scotch, their attachment to monarchy (temp. Commonwealth), 584.
Presentment of Englishry. See Englishry.
Presentment of jury, primitive form of, i. 80.
Press, the, government censorship of (temp. Charles I.), i. 503; freedom of the, fettered by the Commonwealth, 577; laws restraining (temp. Charles II.), (14 Car. II. c. 33), ii. 12; censorship of, 114, 115; influence of (temp. George IV.), 323; a cheap political, 375.
Preston, battle of, i. 566, 584; ii. 187.
Pretender, Charles Edward Stuart, the young, lands in Scotland, ii. 164, 187, 188.
Pride, Thomas, Colonel, "purges" parliament, i. 567.
Priests, marriage of, i. 338.
Primogeniture in the choice of king in Saxon times, i. 9, 26.
Prince Edward Island, ii. 399, 402.
Princes, the, murdered in the Tower. See Edward V. and York, Richard, Duke of.
Printing is born, i. 279; spread of, 297, 317; ousts copying, 332.
Prisons, inspection of, ii. 369.
Privy Council. See Council, the Privy.
Proclamations, royal, given the force of law, repealed, i. 352, 356; Coke protests against, 457.
Proctors, clerical, i. 174.
Property, statutes limiting free conveyance of (temp. Henry VIII.), i. 303.
Protector, the, functions of, i. 608.
Protectorate, the, interferes with private tastes and habits, i. 635; anarchical state of, after Richard Cromwell's resignation, 646 et sq.
Protestantism (see also Reformation), Henry VIII.'s attitude towards, i. 317, 318; what bound the nobility to, 334; its true birthday in England, 339; zeal of the continental, transplanted to England, 394; diversions in, 426; and political freedom, 427; outburst of (temp. James I.), 461.
Provisions of Oxford, objects of, i. 158, 159; annulled by Louis, 160, 205.
Provisors, statute of (25 Edw. III. c. 6), i. 220, 313, 315.
Prynne, William, indicted, i. 503; is set free, 514; his vengefulness, ii. 6.
Public opinion (temp. George I.), ii. 157 et sq.
Puiset, Hugh de, Bishop of Durham, i. 111.
Pulpit, the, a channel for opinion, i. 297.
Pulteney, William, Earl of Bath, ii. 182, 186.
Punjaub, the, ii. 425; annexed, ib.
Purgatory discarded, i. 346.
Puritan, a, described, i. 496, 497.
Puritanism, an antidote to arbitrary government, i. 381; advent of, 393; compared with Catholicism, ib.; its spirit, ib.; its morality, ib.; its attitude towards culture and education, ib.; its preachers, 396; the germs of its conflict with Anglo-Catholicism, 428 et sq.; compared with anglicanism, 495 et sq., 500; the end of, in England, 649; the reaction from, ii. 1; death of, 17.
Puritans, middle class, described, i. 542.
Purveyance, i. 25, 26; restrained by the Great Charter, 136, 137; Commons attack the abuse of (temp. James I.), 445 et sq.

Pym, John, defends the penal laws, i. 464, 479, 480; frames a remonstrance, 508, 509, 510; advises strong measures, 512, 513; carries the impeachment of Strafford, *ib.*; attempt on his life, 525; his object in the civil war, 532, 533; his death and burial, 541.
Pyxes discarded, i. 346.

Q

Quakers, the (*temp.* Restoration), ii. 19; penal law against (14 Car. II. c. 1), *ib.*
Qualification of electors, i. 276; of member of parliament settled (*temp.* Anne) (9 Ann. c. 5), ii. 152.
Quarterly, the, quoted, ii. 396.
Quebec, i. 402; ii. 386, 387, 388, 392, 393, 402.
Quebec Act, the (14 Geo. III. c. 83), ii. 386.
Quia Emptores, statute of (18 Edw. I. c. 1), i. 177.
Quinn, James, quoted, ii. 6.
Quo Warranto, commission of, i. 177.

R

Racial distinctions, i. 28, 119.
Radicalism, ii. 318.
Ragman's roll, the, i. 196.
Rainsborough, Thomas, Colonel, i. 556; murdered, 568.
Raleigh, Sir Walter, i. 368; his loyalty, i. 381, 382; his plot on behalf of Arabella Stuart, 453 *et sq.*; his trial and imprisonment, 454; his Guiana expedition, *ib.*; his execution, *ib.*; his last poem, *ib.*, 455.
Ramillies, battle of, ii. 143.
Randolph, Sir Thomas, i. 383.
Ranjit Singh, ii. 425.
Ranters, i. 545.
Ranulph Flambard, or the Firebrand. See Flambard.
Reading, judicial combat at, i. 82.
Reading, the Abbot of. See Feringdon, Hugh.
Reciprocity treaty, Lord Elgin's, ii. 401.

Recognitions, sworn, in place of wager, i. 82.
Recovery, common, i. 288.
Recruiters, i. 556.
Recusancy, laws against, made severer (3 Jac. I. cc. 4, 5), i. 440.
Recusants, the, ii. 89.
Reform bill, the (2 Gul. IV. c. 45), i. 173, 502; ii. 342 *et sq.*
Reformation, the, dawn of, i. 156; influences tending towards, 312 *et sq.*; its leaders in Europe, 313, 314; (*temp.* Henry VIII.), 326 *et sq.*, 337 *et sq.*, 341 *et sq.*; (*temp.* Edward VI.), 343 *et sq.*; (*temp.* Mary), 360 *et sq.*; (*temp.* Elizabeth), 371 *et sq.*; in Scotland, 411 *et sq.*; in Ireland, 417 *et sq.*; in Europe, 423 *et sq.*, 427 *et sq.*, 502, 503.
Regency, first regularly created, i. 150; of Richard II., 241, 342; of George III., ii. 209, 252.
Regicides, execution of (*temp.* Charles II.), ii. 5 *et sq.*
Reginald, sub-prior of Canterbury, i. 121.
Registration of births, etc., ii. 365.
Regium donum, the, stopped, ii. 151.
Regraters, i. 224.
Regulating Act (India), ii. 415.
Relief (feudal), i. 45.
Remonstrants, ii. 589.
Renaissance, dawn of, in England, i. 230, 238.
Representation, principle of, often resorted to by kings, i. 162; parliamentary, anomalies of, ii. 320 *et sq.*, 342 *et sq.*
Republicanism of Greece and Rome, influence of, i. 477, 478.
Republicans (*temp.* Charles I.), i. 555.
Republics, comparison of, i. 573.
Rescissory, the act, ii. 23.
Restoration, the, i. 648; transition to, ii. 1, 9, 20.
Revolution, the French, ii. 258 *et sq.*
Revolutions, character of, ii. 53; of 1688, character of, 53, 54; bloodless and peaceful, 90 *et sq.*
Rhé, Isle of, i. 472.
Rhode Island, liberty of conscience in, i. 548.

Rich, Richard, first Baron Rich, i. 329.
Richard (Fitzneale or Fitznigel), Bishop of Ely, Bishop of London, his *Dialogus de Scaccario*, i. 83, 99.
Richard I., i. 104; is crowned, 106; his mode of raising money, 107, 108; his crusade, 112 *et sq.*; his death, 114; his absences from England, 120.
Richard II., i. 228; his ascension, 233, 236, 237; his character, 238 *et sq.*; resumes power, 241 *et sq.*; is imprisoned, 244, 309.
Richard III., i. 272 *et sq.*; his murder of the princes, 274, 281.
Richelieu, Cardinal, i. 201; his policy purely political, 426, 435, 481.
Richmond, Charles Lennox, third Duke of Richmond and Lennox, ii. 226.
Richmond (palace), i. 284.
Ridley, Nicholas, Bishop of London, his character, i. 344, 364.
Rights of Man, the French declaration of, i. 134.
Rinuccini, Giovanni Batista, papal nuncio, i. 580, 582.
Riot Act, the (1 Geo. I. stat. 2, c. 5), ii. 167.
Ritualism, i. 502.
Rivers, Anthony Woodville, Earl, i. 273.
Rizzio, David, i. 387; murdered, 417.
Roads, the Roman, i. 6; improved (*temp.* Henry VII.), 293.
Robert, Earl of Mellent, i. 52.
Robert III., of Scotland, i. 411.
Robert, of Gloucester (bastard half-brother of Matilda), i. 73, 74.
Robert, of Normandy (son of William I.), mortgages his duchy to William Rufus, i. 54; returns from the crusades, 59; invades England, *ib.*
Robert, of Jumièges, i. 14, 18.
Robert the Devil, i. 16.
Robinson, Sir Thomas, ii. 189, 190.
Robsart, Amy, i. 368, 384.
Robsart, Sir John, i. 384.
Rochelle, i. 472, 481.
Roches, Peter des, Bishop of Winchester, i. 151, 152.
Rochester Castle, i. 140.
Rockingham Castle, i. 52.

Rockingham, Charles Watson-Wentworth, second Marquis of, head of the government, ii. 209, 210, 231.
Rocroy, battle of, i. 426.
Roderick, the Irish chieftain, i. 102.
Rodney, George Brydges, first Baron Rodney, Admiral, his victories, ii. 221.
Roe, Sir Thomas, ii. 414.
Roger, Bishop of Salisbury, and his son Roger, i. 69, 72.
Rolph, Dr. John, ii. 399.
Roman Catholicism, how regarded by people and parliament (*temp.* Charles I.), i. 549.
Roman Catholics, disabilities of (*temp.* George III.), ii. 229; some of these abolished, 230.
Roman influence on the English race, i. 4.
Roman law, i. 83.
Rome, the natural centre of the Latin church, i. 34; sack of, 307.
Romilly, Sir Samuel, ii. 274, 321, 329, 330.
Rooke, Sir George, ii. 145.
Root and branch bill, causes a split in the party, i. 523.
Roses, Wars of the, i. 204, 261 *et sq.*
Rosslyn Chapel, i. 409.
Rota Club, the, i. 646.
Round table, i. 192, 220.
Round towers of Ireland, i. 101.
Roundheads, origin of the name, i. 497, 528, 536; their morality, 539.
Rousseau, Jean-Jacques, i. 230, 458.
Roxburgh, castle of, i. 108.
Royal Marriage Act (12 Geo. III. c. 11), ii. 195.
Royal Society, formation of, ii. 20.
Royalists (of the civil war), their armament and forces, i. 537, 538; rise in the north and west (1655), i. 612.
Runnymede, King John meets the barons at, i. 133.
Rupert, Prince, i. 538, 539; his conduct at Edgehill, 540; surrenders Bristol, 552; raises the siege of York, 546; his conduct at Marston Moor, 547; defeats the Dutch, ii. 32.
Rupert's drops, ii. 20.

Russell, Edward, Earl of Oxford, ii. 71; his character, 109.
Russell, Lord John, first Earl Russell, ii. 332, 359, 391.
Russell, Sir John, i. 302, 304.
Russell, William, Lord Russell, ii. 36, 48.
Russells, the origin and politics of, i. 334.
Rutland, Edmund, Earl of, i. 269.
Ruyter, Michael Adrians-zoon van, sweeps the channel, ii. 32.
Rye house plot, the, ii. 48 et sq.
Ryswick, treaty of, ii. 120.

S

Sabbath, the Calvinistic, instituted, i. 346.
Sacheverell, Henry, impeached, ii. 146.
Sacraments, the seven, reduced to two, i. 346.
Sadler, Sir Ralph, i. 383.
Sailor, the British, treatment of (temp. George III.), ii. 269 et sq.
St. Albans, i. 271; battle of, i. 266.
St. Augustine. See Augustine.
St. Bartholomew, massacre of, i. 35, 377, 415, 442.
St. Catherine Cree, church of, i. 501, 546.
St. Drausius, i. 95.
St. Edmundsbury, i. 109, 130.
St. George's Channel, its influence on English political history, i. 2.
St. Giles's Kirk, riot in, i. 505.
St. Hugh, Bishop of Lincoln, 114.
St. John, Oliver, i 510.
St. Pierre, Eustace de, i. 212, 291.
St. Ruth, General, is defeated by Einkell, ii. 97.
Salisbury, Margaret, Countess of, executed, i. 331.
Salisbury, Robert Cecil, Earl of, i. 434, 448.
Salmasius, Claudius, his controversy with Milton, i. 576.
Salzburg, Protestants of, expelled, i. 583.
Samson, Abbot, i. 109.
Sancroft, William, Archbishop, ii. 79, 89.

San Domingo, ii. 408.
Sanctuary, privilege of, i. 316.
Sandwich, Edward Montague, Earl of, his victories over the Dutch, ii. 32.
Sandwich (town), i. 143.
Saragossa, ii. 309.
Sarsfield, Patrick, ii. 97.
Savage, Sir Arnold, i. 249.
Savile, Sir George, ii. 230.
Savoy, Protestants of, massacred, i. 583.
Sawtre, William, i. 253.
Saxons, migration of, i. 3; and Normans, compared, 22.
Saye and Sele, William Fiennes, first Viscount, i. 479.
Scandinavia, i. 293; Protestantism in, 425.
Scepticism, spread of (temp. Restoration), ii. 20.
Schism Act, the (13 Ann. c. 7), ii. 151; repealed (5 Geo. I. c. 4), 166.
Scholasticism, retreat of, i. 230.
Schomberg, Frederic Armand de, Marshal, goes over to Ireland with an army, ii. 96, 97.
Schools, founded by Edward VI., i. 349.
Schwartz, Martin, i. 282.
Sciences, the natural, progress of (temp. Restoration), ii. 20.
Scotland, its union with England attempted (temp. Edward I.), i. 189; a disunited nation, 193, 199, 202, 404; attacks England (temp. Henry VIII.), 308; its constant wars with England, 407 : (temp. Charles I.), 505 et sq.; (temp. Charles II.), 585 et sq.; ii. 21 et sq.; i. 590; (temp. Cromwell), 625 : (temp. Revolution of 1688), ii. 91 et sq.; united to England (6 Ann. c. 11), 134 et sq.; effects of the union, 140 et sq.
Scott, Thomas, i. 620.
Scroggs, Sir William, ii. 41, 42, 47.
Scrope, of Masham, Lord, i. 256.
Scrope, Richard, Archbishop of York, rebels, i. 246; executed, ib., 247, 252.
Scutage, instituted, i. 79, 84, 226.
Seal, the great, a new one made (1643), i. 533, 534.

Sects, religious growth of (*temp.* Charles I.), i. 544, 545; (*temp.* Commonwealth), 575.
Security, act of, ii. 136.
Seditious Meetings Act, the (36 Geo. III. c. 8), ii. 273.
Sedley, Catherine, ii. 63.
Seekers, i. 545.
Selden, John, his book on tithe, i. 458; retracts, *ib.*, 483, 510, 535; supports the independents, 556.
Self-denying ordinance, the, i. 550.
Self-government, Teutonic tendency towards, i. 3.
Senlac, the battle of, i. 19, 20.
Septennial Act, the (Geo. I. c. 38), ii. 110, 167.
Septs, the Irish, i. 310, 418.
Serfdom, i. 38, 39.
Serfs, ordination of, i. 91; condition of (*temp.* Edward I.), 175; revolt of, 233 *et sq.*; emancipation of, 237; drift into cities, 291 *et sq.*
Serlo, mayor of London, i. 147.
Servetus, Michael, burnt, i. 348.
Settlement, act of (Ireland) (*temp.* Charles II.) (14 and 15 Car. II. c. 12), ii. 22.
Settlement, act of (securing the Hanoverian succession) (8 Ann. c. 15), 1709.
Settlement, act of (12 and 13 Gul. III. c. 2), the, ii. 123; provisions of, 123, 124.
Seven bishops, the petition of, ii. 68; trial of, *ib.*
Seymour, Jane (wife of Henry VIII.), i. 323, 325; death of, 338.
Seymour, Thomas, Baron Seymour of Sudeley, i. 302, 354, 355.
Seymours, the, origin and politics of, i. 334; influence of, 340.
Shaftesbury, Anthony Ashley Cooper, first Earl of, a member of the Cabal, ii. 27, 28, 36, 42, 47.
Shaftesbury, Anthony Ashley Cooper, seventh Earl of, ii. 373.
Shakespeare, William, i. 209, 238, 245 248, 257, 259, 264, 368, 377, 380, 381, 383, 394, 461.
Shales, Henry, Commissary-General, his roguery, ii. 102.

Sharp, John, Archbishop of York, murdered, ii. 24.
Shaxton, Nicholas, Bishop of Salisbury, driven from his see, i. 338.
Sheep farms, increase and profits of, i. 350.
Shelburne, William Petty, Earl of, and first Marquis of Lansdowne, his character, ii. 231.
Sheldon, Gilbert, Archbishop of Canterbury, a leader ii. 20.
Shelley, Percy Bysshe, ii. 318.
Sheriff, the, in Saxon times, i. 10, 30.
Sheriffmuir, battle of, ii. 164.
Shilling, value of (*temp.* Henry VIII.), i. 336.
Ship-money, origin of, i. 492; re-imposed by Charles I., *ib.*; abolished by the long parliament, 514.
Shire, the, i. 30.
Shire-reeve. See Sheriff.
Shires, division of the country into, i. 9.
Shrewsbury, Anna Maria, Countess of, seduced by the Duke of Buckingham, ii. 29.
Shrewsbury, Francis Talbot, eleventh Earl of, killed in a duel, ii. 29.
Shrewsbury, Charles Talbot, twelfth Earl, and Duke of, ii. 71.
Shrievalties, the, i. 82.
Sibthorp, Robert, i. 475.
Sidmouth, Lord. See Addington.
Sidney, Algernon, i. 556, 612; ii. 36, 48.
Sidney, Henry, ii. 70.
Sidney, Sir Philip, i. 368, 381.
Sidneys, the, origin and politics of, i. 334.
Siete Partidas, i. 181.
Signories, the French, in Canada, ii. 390, 399.
Sikhs, the, ii. 413, 425.
Simeon trustees, the, i. 501.
Simnel, Lambert, i. 248, 282.
Sinking fund, efficacy of, ii. 240.
Six Acts, the, ii. 328.
Six Articles, statute of (35 Hen. VIII. c. 5), i. 337; repealed (1 Edw. VI. c. 12), 341.
Skippon, Philip, i. 541.
Slave trade, in Saxon times, i. 15; Pitt and the, ii. 246 *et sq.*

Slavery, abolition of (3 and 4 Gul. IV. c. 73), ii. 370, 371; in Jamaica, 407 *et sq.*
Slawata, William von, i. 461.
Slingsby, Sir Henry, his plot, i. 612.
Sluys, battle of, i. 212, 217.
Smeaton, Mark, i. 324, 325.
Smerwick, battle of, i. 418.
Smith, Sir Thomas, i. 286.
Society, demoralized by the French wars, i. 231; character of (*temp.* Henry VI.), 262, 263, 270.
Soldier, the British (*temp.* George III.), ii. 270 *et sq.*
Solemn league and covenant, the, i. 505 *et sq.*
Somers, John, Lord, his character, ii. 109, 121, 130.
Somerset, Countess of. See Howard, Frances.
Somerset, Edmund Beaufort, second Duke of, i. 265.
Somerset, Edward Seymour, first Earl of Hertford, and Duke of (the Protector), i. 343 *et sq.*; sympathizes with the Commons, 353; his fall and rise, 355; his execution, *ib.*; results of his death, 357, 411.
Somerset house, i. 344.
Somerset, Robert Carr, Earl of, i. 434, 451 *et sq.*
Soul-sleepers, i. 545.
South Africa, ii. 406.
South Sea Bubble, the, ii. 169, 170.
Southampton (town), i. 536.
Southampton, Thomas Wriothesley, fourth Earl of, Clarendon's colleague, his character, ii. 4.
Southampton, Thomas Wriothesley, fifth Earl of, i. 570.
Southey, Robert, ii. 272.
Spain, decrepitude of (*temp.* James I.), i. 426; quarrel with (*temp.* George II.), ii. 183 *et sq.*
Spanish marriage (Prince Charles's projected), the, Commons protest against, i. 464 *et sq.*; is relinquished, 469.
Spanish succession, the (*temp.* William III.), ii. 125 *et sq.*
Speaker, the, of the House of Commons, i. 225.

Spenser, Edmund, i. 368, 382.
Sprat, Bishop, ii. 65, 69.
Squire, the, i. 379; (*temp.* George I.), ii. 160, 161.
Stafford, William Howard, Viscount, executed, ii. 41.
Stamford Bridge, battle of, i. 19, 140.
Stamp duty, imposed on pamphlets and newspapers (10 Ann. c. 19), ii. 152.
Stamp tax, Grenville's, ii. 207; repealed, 209, 210.
Stanhope, James, first Earl Stanhope, leader of the government, ii. 168 *et sq.*
Stanley, Sir William, i. 283.
Stapleton, Sir Philip, i. 510, 556, 563.
Star Chamber, court of, instituted (3 Hen. VIII. c. 1), i. 285 *et sq.*, 296, 401; enlarges its jurisdiction, 491; abolished (16 Car. I. c. 10), 515.
States General, the, i. 172.
Statesmen (*temp.* Elizabeth), i. 369 *et sq.*
Steele, Richard, expelled from the House of Commons, ii. 152.
Steinkirk, battle of, ii. 119.
Stephen, takes the throne, i. 71; his character, 71, 72; his reign divided into three periods, 72; defeated and taken prisoner, 74; gets free, *ib.*
Stigand, Archbishop, i. 14, 18, 31.
Stirling, i. 197.
Stoke, battle of, i. 282.
Strachan, J., Bishop of Toronto, ii 392.
Strafford, Thomas Wentworth, Earl of, i. 486; Lord Deputy of Ireland, 487 *et sq.*; his " thorough " policy, 488 *et sq.*, 494; recalled from Ireland, 507; impeached, 513, 516 *et sq.*; executed, 521.
Stratford, Robert, Bishop of Chichester, i. 223.
Striguil, Richard de Clare, second Earl of Pembroke and ("Strongbow"), i. 101, 102.
Strode, William, i. 510.
Strongbow. See Striguil.
Strype, John, i. 380, 395, 397.
Stuart, Lady Arabella, i. 403.
Stuarts, the, i. 302.
Stubbe, John, i. 397.

Suarez, Francisco, i. 425.
Subinfeudation, i. 177.
Subsidies, i. 227.
Succession to the throne, parliamentary settlement of, i. 243; regulated (*temp.* Henry VIII.) (26 Hen. VIII. c. 2; 28 Hen. VIII. c. 7; 35 Hen. VIII. c. 1), 317, 320, 327, 329; (*temp.* Anne) (6 Ann. c. 7 and 8 Ann. c. 15), ii. 139; right of parliament to deal with, 43.
Sudbury, Simon of, Archbishop of Canterbury, i. 236.
Suffolk, Edmund de la Pole, Earl of, i. 284; beheaded, 302, 303.
Suffolk, house of, i. 403.
Suffolk, William de la Pole, fourth Earl, and first Duke of, i. 264, 280.
Summons, to attend the Council, forms of, i. 136.
Sunderland, Robert Spencer, second Earl of, succeeds Danby, ii. 39; supports the exclusion bill, 43.
Superiorities, ii. 321, 342.
Supplies, granting of, far-reaching influence of, i. 175.
Supremacy, act of (1 Eliz. c. 1), i. 329, 374.
Surajah Dowlah, ii. 414.
Surrey, Henry Howard, Earl of, i. 305, 340.
Surrey, Thomas Howard, Earl of. See Norfolk.
Sussex, weald of, i. 294.
Suttee, ii. 424.
Sutton, Archbishop, ii. 363.
Swinford, Catherine, i. 265.
Switzerland, renounces the papal faith, i. 313; Protestantism and Catholicism in, 423, 425; the cantons of, a mere league, 573.
Synods, i. 10.

T

Tallage, i. 25; renunciation of, 133, 186, 187.
Talleyrand-Périgord, ii. 28.
Tantallon Castle, i. 405.
Tasso, Torquato, i. 382.
Tax, poll. See Poll Tax.
Taxation (*temp.* Henry II.), i. 84; constitutional resistance to, 114, 115; (*temp.* John), 125; change in mode of, 226 *et sq.*; (*temp.* Charles II.), ii. 9; (*temp.* George I.), 158, 159.
Taylor, Jeremy, Bishop of Down and Connor, i. 470.
Templars, the, i. 92; dissolution of, 203, 332.
Temple, George Nugent-Temple-Grenville, second Earl (afterwards Marquis of Buckingham), ii. 235.
Temple, Sir William, brings about the Triple Alliance (*temp.* Charles II.), ii. 33.
Tenants-in-chief, i. 29, 138, 173, 177.
Tennyson, Alfred, i. 192.
Tenure, military, i. 30; abuses of, 134; villain, 295, 297.
Test Act (25 Car. II. c. 2), ii. 31; repealed (9 Geo. IV. c. 17), 332.
Teutonic spirit, the, i. 41.
Tewkesbury, battle of, i. 268.
Thane, i. 9.
Theobald, Archbishop of Canterbury, i. 75, 87.
Theodore, of Tarsus, organizes the church, i. 11.
Theresa, St., i. 424.
Thistle, Order of the, i. 211.
Thomas Aquinas. See Aquinas.
Thomas à Becket. See Becket.
Thomson, Edward Charles Poulett, Baron Sydenham, governor of Canada, ii. 398.
Thuggee, ii. 425.
Thurlow, Edward, first Baron, ii. 253.
Tiers État, i. 172.
Tilbury, i. 394.
Tilly, Count von, i. 271, 462, 472, 495.
Times, the London, ii. 368.
Tinchebrai, battle of, i. 70.
Tippoo, ii. 420.
Tiptoft. See Worcester, John Tiptoft, Earl of.
Tithe, payment of, in Saxon times, i. 11; embezzled (*temp.* Henry VIII.), 335; commutation of (6 and 7 Gul. IV. c. 71), ii. 364.
Tithing, the, i. 30.
Toleration Act (*temp.* William III.), (1 Gul. and Mar. c. 18), ii. 87.
Tomline, Sir George Pretyman, Bishop of Winchester, ii. 363.

INDEX   479

Tone, Wolfe, ii. 285.
Tonnage and poundage, i. 478, 492.
Tooke, John Horne, ii. 276, 319.
Torgau, battle of, ii. 194.
Torture, judicial, renunciation of, i. 137; introduced under Henry VI., 296; sanctioned in Scotland, 407.
Tory democracy, ii. 167, 168.
Tory, first use and origin of the name, ii. 45.
Tostig, i. 19.
Tournaments, forbidden by Edward II., i. 205.
Tours, battle of the plain of, i. 107.
Towns (*temp.* William I.), i. 38; frequent sacking of (*temp.* Stephen), 73, 74; advance of (*temp.* Richard I.), 115; attain corporate existence, 147; side with De Montfort, 160; (*temp.* Henry VII.), 290 *et sq.*; Scotch, growth of, retarded, 408, 409.
Townshend, Charles, leader of the government, ii. 168 *et sq.*; taxes tea in the colonies, 211, 212.
Towton, battle of, i. 267, 269, 271.
Tractarian movement, ii. 365, 366.
Trade, extension of, under Henry II., i. 84; secured by the Great Charter, 135; its chief seat (*temp.* Henry VII.), 294; obstacles to (*temp.* Henry VIII.), 336; condition of (*temp.* Elizabeth), 379; (*temp.* Charles II.), ii. 51.
Trafalgar, battle of, i. 390; ii. 304.
Trailbaston, writ of, i. 184.
Treason, defined (25 Edw. III. stat. 5, c. 2), i. 225.
Treason laws (*temp.* Henry VIII.) (26 Hen. VIII. c. 13), i. 202, 303; repealed (1 Edw. VI. c. 12), 352; new added (5 and 6 Edw. VI. c. 11), *ib.*, 355 *et sq.*; repealed (1 Mar. c. 1), 359; severity of, increased (13 Car. II. stat. 1, c. 1), 11; improved, 82, 83; amended (7 Ann. c. 21), 130.
Treasonable Practices Act, the (36 Geo. III. c. 7), ii. 273.
Treaties, commercial (*temp.* Henry VII.), i. 293.
Trent, council of, i. 425.
Trèves, holy coat of, i. 334.

Trevor, Sir John, made speaker, ii. 113; 165.
Trial by battle, i. 28; by ordeal, *ib.*
Trial by jury, germ of, i. 80, 81.
Trials, form of (*temp.* Henry II.), i. 80 *et sq.*; by one's peers, 174.
Tribalism, Irish, i. 101.
Tribunals, ecclesiastical and secular, their respective spheres (*temp.* Henry II.), i. 85.
Tridentine faith, i. 425.
Triennial Act, repealed (16 Car. II. c. 1), ii. 10; (*temp.* William III.), (6 and 7 Gul. and Mar. c. 2), ii. 110.
Triple Alliance, the (*temp.* Charles II.), ii. 33.
Tromp, Martin Harperszoon van, i. 593.
Tucker, Josiah, Dean of Gloucester, quoted, ii. 208.
Tunstall, Cuthbert, Bishop of London, i. 365, 366.
Turgot, A.-R.-J., ii. 259.
Twenge, Sir Robert, i. 156, 177.
Twiss, William, i. 534.
Tyler, Wat, occupies London, i. 236, 351.
Tyrconnel, Richard Talbot, Earl of, i. 420; ii. 62; calls a parliament at Dublin, 94; which passes an Act of Attainder, 95.
Tyrone, Hugh O'Neil, Earl of, i. 420.
Tyrrell, Walter, i. 56.

U

Ulster, lands in, forfeited, i. 422.
Uniformity acts (2 and 3 Edw. VI. c. 1; 5 and 6 Edw. VI. c. 1), i. 343, 346; (1 Eliz. c. 2), 374; (14 Car. II. c. 4), ii. 15, 87.
United Empire Loyalists, the, ii. 387, 392.
United Irishmen, the, ii. 284.
Universities, growth of, i. 147.
Universities, Scotch, i. 409.
University of London, ii. 366.
Urban II., Pope, i. 47.
Usher, James, Archbishop of Armagh, i. 500; ii. 14.
Usury law (*temp.* Henry VIII.), i. 336.
"Utopia," Sir Thomas More's, i. 328.

Utraquism, i. 425.
Utrecht, treaty of, ii. 150.

V

Vagabondage, i. 336, 352, 353.
Vagrancy, laws respecting, i. 237; (*temp.* Henry VI.-Richard III.), 278; necessity of, 336; (*temp.* Edward VI.), 349, 350; cruelty of, 353.
Valence, William de, i. 153.
Van Dyck, Sir Anthony, i. 469.
Vane, Sir Henry (the elder), his notes at Strafford's impeachment, i. 517, 518.
Vane, Sir Henry (the younger), i. 510; a member of the council of state, 574, 575, 578; execution of, ii. 8.
Vaughan, Sir Thomas, i. 273.
Vellore, massacre at, ii. 427.
Venner, Thomas, heads an insurrection, ii. 19.
Vere, Robert de, Earl of Oxford, Marquis of Dublin, and Duke of Ireland, i. 239.
Verneuil, i. 261.
Vestry, the, i. 11.
Vézelay, i. 95.
Victoria, Queen, ascends the throne, ii. 381.
Villain, the, his condition (*temp.* William I.), i. 38, 39; what the Great Charter did for him, 138.
Villanage (*temp.* William I.), i. 38, 39; gradually disappears, 237.
Villani, Giovanni, i. 217.
Villeneuve, Admiral, ii. 305.
Vinegar Hill, camp at, ii. 290.
Vineis, Peter de, i. 126, 181.
Viscount, origin of the title, i. 30.
Viterbo, i. 164.
Vowel, Peter, his plot, i. 612.
Voyages of discovery, i. 294.

W

Wager of battle lingered long (abolished, 59 Geo. III. c. 46), i. 348.
Wages, increased after the black death, i. 233; regulated, 237, 278.
Wagram, campaign of, ii. 309.
Wakefield, battle of, i. 267.

Wakefield, Edward Gibbon, ii. 395.
Wakefield, E., ii. 291.
Walcheren expedition, ii. 306.
Waldenses, persecution of. See Savoy.
Wales, the Norman Conquest advances towards, i. 189 *et sq.*; its bards, 191, 192; though annexed, not incorporated, 192; incorporated with England (27 Hen. VIII. c. 26), 306, 308.
Walker, Obadiah, ii. 65.
Wallace, William, defeats Cressingham at Stirling, i. 197; invades England, *ib.*; is given up, i. 198; executed, *ib.*; his deserts, *ib.*
Wallenstein, i. 271, 472, 495.
Waller, Edmund, conspires for Charles, i. 541.
Waller, Sir, William, his army destroyed, i. 541.
Wallington, Nehemiah, a typical Puritan, i. 499.
Walloons, the Catholicism among, i. 425.
Walpole, Robert, rising to power, ii. 168 *et sq.*; the first prime minister, 170, 171; his birth and character, 172 *et sq.*; his policy, 173 *et sq.*, 176 *et sq.*; financial legislation, 178 *et sq.*; declares war on Spain, 184; his declining influence, 184, 185, 186.
Walsingham, Sir Francis, i. 368, 378, 383, 391.
Walter, Cardinal, Bishop of Albano, i. 53.
Walter, Hubert, Archbishop of Canterbury, i. 114.
Walter, John, ii. 368.
Walters, Lucy, ii. 44.
Waltheof, i. 28; put to death, 39.
War of the Roses, i. 268 *et sq.*
Warbeck, Perkin, i. 275, 282, 284, 408.
Wardship, i. 45, 445 *et sq.*
Warfare, changes in mode of, i. 217, 218.
War-hawks, the, ii. 308.
War power, political element in, i. 210, 217.
Warrenne, Earl, i. 177.
Warwick, Edward, Earl of, executed, i. 284.

Warwick, Richard Beauchamp, Earl of, i. 263.
Warwick, Richard Neville, Earl of, and of Salisbury (the "King-maker"), i. 267; his extravagance, 269; his influence, 270.
Warwick, Sir Philip, i. 511.
Warwick, Thomas Beauchamp, Earl of, 241.
Washington, George, ii. 216 et sq.
Washington (town), taken by the British, ii. 308.
Watch and ward, i. 184.
Waterloo, battle of, i. 390.
Watt, James, ii. 255.
Wayneflete, William, Bishop of Winchester, i. 274.
Wedderburn, Alexander. See Loughborough, Lord.
Wedgewood, ii. 255.
Wellesley, Arthur. See Wellington, Duke of.
Wellesley, Marquis, Governor-General of India, ii. 420 et sq.
Wellington, Arthur Wellesley, first Duke of, ii. 307; his political character, 315 et sq.; former minister, 331, 421.
Welsh disestablishment, i. 5.
Welsh language, the, preserved, i. 308.
Wentworth, Peter, i. 398.
Wentworth, Thomas. See Strafford, Earl of.
Were-gelt, i. 10.
Weshington, Walter de, i. 160.
Wesley, John, ii. 163, 232.
Wessex, the germ of the United Kingdom, i. 6.
West Indian colonies, ii. 406.
Westminster Abbey, i. 152.
Westminster, a royal seat, i. 26.
Westminster Assembly of Divines, i. 534.
Westmoreland, Charles Neville, sixth Earl of, i. 376.
Weston, Richard, first Earl of Portland, his ministry, i. 484.
Weston, Sir Francis, i. 324.
Wetherell, Sir Charles, ii. 345.
Wexford, slaughter at, i. 581; rebellion at, ii. 290.

Wharton, Thomas, Earl of, his character, ii. 108, 109, 130.
Whig, first use and origin of the name, ii. 45.
Whigs, the, in power (temp. George I. and II.), ii. 165 et sq.; split into sections, 188 et sq.
Whitby, synod of, i. 7.
White Hart, badge of the, i. 246.
Whitecoats, the, i. 547.
Whitelock, Bulstrode, i. 510, 594; his description of Cromwell's inauguration, 618; sent as ambassador to Sweden, i. 632.
Whitgift, John, Archbishop of Canterbury, i. 397, 428.
Whiting, Richard, Abbot of Glaston, i. 333.
Whittingtons, the, i. 291.
Wicklow, rebellion at, ii. 290.
Wilberforce, William, ii. 237 : and the slave trade, 247 et sq., 268, 280, 370.
Wildman, John, i. 556.
Wilfrid tries to introduce high church principles, i. 10.
Wilkes, John, his character, ii. 201; assails Bute, ib.; expelled from the House, 202, 227.
William I. (the Conqueror), his birth, i. 16; his ambition, 18; defeats Harold, 19, 20; is crowned, ib.; introduces the feudal system into England, 23; makes a survey of the kingdom, 27, 28; his mode of dealing with local institutions, 30: declines to do homage for his kingdom, 32; a strong and good ruler, 39; his end, 40.
William II., i. 42 et sq.; abuses his prerogatives, 46; falls sick, 47; recovers, 50; sets out for Normandy, 51; recognizes Urban, 53; sends envoys to Rome, ib.; is killed in the New Forest, 56.
William III. (as Prince of Orange), i. 243, 266, 544; marries, ii. 35; invited to England, 70, 71; his character, ib., 100 et sq.; ascends the throne, 82; (as king) wins the battle of the Boyne, 97.
William IV., ascends the throne, ii. 340; dies, 381.

William (son of Henry I.), drowned, i. 71.
William, Bishop-Elect of Winchester, i. 63.
William, Earl Marshal. See Pembroke, William Marshall, Earl of.
William of Carileph, Bishop of Durham, i. 44, 52.
William of Longchamp, Bishop of Ely, i. 111, 115.
William of Nogaret. See Nogaret.
William of Warelwast, i. 53, 64.
William of Wykeham, Bishop of Winchester, i. 228, 230.
William the Lion, king of Scotland, invades England, i. 103; is taken prisoner, *ib.*; does homage for his kingdom, 104.
Williams, John, Archbishop of York, i. 486, 500.
Williams, Roger, i. 548.
Wilmington, Spencer Compton, Lord. See Compton.
Wiltshire, William le Scrope, first Earl of, i. 239.
Winchelsey, Robert, Archbishop of Canterbury, i. 180, 186, 188.
Winchester, a royal seat, i. 26, 38.
Winchester, John Paulet, fifth Marquis of, i. 538.
Winchester School, i. 228.
Winchester, statute of, i. 176.
Windebank, Sir Francis, i. 514.
Windham, William, ii. 275, 280, 286.
Windsor Castle, i. 228.
Winwood, Sir Ralph, i. 452.
Wishart, Bishop of Glasgow, i. 200.
Wishart, George, i. 412.
Witan, the, i. 8, 18, 30.
Witchcraft, in Scotland, i. 414.
Witt, Jan de, ii. 33.
Wolseley, Sir Charles, i. 611.
Wolsey, Thomas, Cardinal, i. 303 *et sq.*, 316 *et sq.*; his fall, 321 *et sq.*, 329, 332, 369.
Women, chivalric regard for, i. 211;
their demeanour (*temp.* Edward III.), *ib.*
Woodville, Elizabeth, i. 267, 272.
Wool, exported from England, i. 146, 218; imports laid on, 222.
Wooton. See Wotton.
Worcester, battle of, i. 589.
Worcester, John Tiptoft, Earl of, i. 270.
Wordsworth, William, ii. 272.
Workhouses, ii. 368.
Wotton, Nicholas, i. 452.
Wotton, Sir Henry, quoted, i. 307.
Wriothesly, Thomas. See Southampton.
Writs, legal, lasting form given to, i. 182.
Wyatt, Sir Thomas, rebellion of, i. 359, 363.
Wycliffe, John, i. 219, 225, 228, 231 *et sq.*, 251 *et sq.*, 313 *et sq.*
Wyndham, Sir William, ii. 165, 168.

Y

Yelverton, Sir Christopher, i. 398.
Yeomanry, growth of, i. 294, 295, 392.
Yeomen of the guard, i. 297, 306.
York (city), i. 38; outrage upon Jews in, 110, 274, 546.
York, Edward, Duke of (afterwards Edward IV.) (*q. v.*), his victories, i. 267 *et sq.*, 271.
York, James Stuart, Duke of (afterwards James II.) (*q. v.*).
York, Richard, Duke of, i. 266, 267, 274 *et sq.*, 281.
York, the line of, i. 269.
Ypres, taken by Philip II., i. 129.

Z

Ziska, John, i. 425.
Zutphen, battle of, i. 381.
Zwingli, Ulrich, i. 313, 394.

THE UNITED STATES.

AN OUTLINE OF POLITICAL HISTORY, 1492-1871.

BY

GOLDWIN SMITH, D.C.L.

With Map. Crown 8vo. $2.00.

PRESS COMMENTS.

" Is a literary masterpiece, as readable as a novel, remarkable for its compression without dryness, and its brilliancy without any rhetorical effort or display. What American could, with so broad a grasp and so perfect a style, have rehearsed our political history from Columbus to Grant in 300 duodecimo pages of open type, or would have manifested greater candor in his judgment of men and events in a period of four centuries? It is enough to say that no one before Mr. Smith has attempted the feat, and that he has the field to himself." — *The Nation.*

" It is a marvel of condensation and lucidity. In no other book is the same field covered so succinctly and so well. Of the five chapters, the first deals with the Colonial epoch, the second with the Revolutionary period, the third and fourth review the history of the Federal Government to the outbreak of the Civil War, and the fifth depicts the era of rupture and reconstruction. We have marked certain passages for extract, but the truth is that almost every page is enriched with striking comments that cause the reader to carefully reconsider, if not to change, his views of historical persons and events." — *New York Sun.*

"To say that nothing comparable with this most instructive and enchanting volume has hitherto come from Professor Smith's pen would perhaps be only anticipating the judgment of its readers." — *Toronto Mail.*

" Professor Goldwin Smith always writes with a trenchant pen, but he has never written anything so incisive in style and so interesting in the points of view taken and the judgment of men and things as his essay of three hundred pages on the United States, the scope of which is well described in its sub-title 'An Outline of Political History.' This brilliant comment of a liberal Englishman on the history and institutions of this country is of the utmost value to Americans, who will not be repelled by its occasional injustice, but who will be materially helped to a juster conception of the results of American civilization, and who will be immensely entertained and interested by the vivacity and freshness with which the comment is made." — *The Outlook.*

" We know nothing on the subject at all approaching it in brevity, joined to clearness and completeness, as an essay, nothing where intellectual disinterestedness so dominates all things, none where a happy sentence or a striking phrase so effectually tells a story which many pages in other hands have in vain sought to tell." — *New York Times.*

THE MACMILLAN COMPANY,

66 FIFTH AVENUE, NEW YORK.